PENGUIN BOOKS
IN THE NAME OF DEMOCRACY

Bipan Chandra (1928–2014) was born in Kangra, Himachal Pradesh. He was educated at Forman Christian College, Lahore, and at Stanford University, California. He was professor of modern history at Jawaharlal Nehru University, New Delhi, member of the University Grants Commission and chairman of the National Book Trust. He was a prolific writer, who founded the journal *Enquiry*, and wrote several books on nationalism, colonialism and communalism in modern India.

IN THE NAME OF DEMOCRACY

JP Movement and the Emergency

BIPAN CHANDRA

PENGUIN BOOKS

An imprint of Penguin Random House

PENGUIN BOOKS

USA | Canada | UK | Ireland | Australia
New Zealand | India | South Africa | China | Singapore

Penguin Books is part of the Penguin Random House group of companies
whose addresses can be found at global.penguinrandomhouse.com

Published by Penguin Random House India Pvt. Ltd
4th Floor, Capital Tower 1, MG Road,
Gurugram 122 002, Haryana, India

Penguin
Random House
India

First published by Penguin Books India 2003

ISBN 9780143029670

Typeset in Times New Roman by SŪRYA, New Delhi

Printed at Manipal Technologies Limited, India

For the late S. Gopal

gentleman, friend and teacher who initiated
contemporary history in India

Contents

Acknowledgements

I am most grateful to the large number of friends who have helped me in this work. My friends Mohit Sen, V.P. Dutt, Gargi Dutt, G.K. Arora, Mridula and Aditya Mukherjee, Sucheta Mahajan and Rakesh Batbayal have gone through the manuscript and made valuable suggestions and even otherwise help form my hypotheses. Kewal Verma, Inder Malhotra, Girish Mathur, P.C. Joshi, C.P. Raghavan, Subir Roy, G.S. Bhalla, K.P. Jain, D.N. Gupta, Mohinder Singh, Salil Mishra, Visalakshi Menon, Anthony Thomas, Bikash Chandra, Madho Narain and Sarojini Dewan have helped in various ways, especially by acting as sounding boards for many of my ideas. I and my friends, students and colleagues, especially members of the Delhi University Socialist Group, spent hours discussing both the JP movement and the Emergency during 1974-77. Some of my ideas were formed at the time, though my friends are in no way responsible for the final shape of my thoughts in the present work.

I am indebted to the librarians and staff of Jawaharlal Nehru University, New Delhi, for going beyond the rules in helping me to procure books from the library. I am also thankful to the librarians and staff of the Nehru Memorial Museum and Library, India International Centre, Bhai Vir Singh Sadan, and *Hindustan Times*.

My many thanks are due to Om Prakash for deciphering my near illegible writing and putting it on computer.

I am also very thankful to Raj Kamini Mahadevan of Penguin Books India for encouraging me to write this book and then patiently editing it and making it more readable.

In the end I must thank Usha Chandra, my wife, for having given me invaluable help at every stage of this book's preparation. Every idea in it was discussed threadbare by us. She went through each page of the draft, made valuable suggestions, smoothened the language in places, gave me encouragement when I needed it, and helped me check the typescript and page-proofs. In fact, as I put it in my first book, if any errors of language or printing remain in this book, she shares the responsibility with me.

1 *Introduction*

Two crises of an unprecedented magnitude rocked India during the years 1974 to 1977. From January 1974 to June 1975 the country went through a turbulent period marked by a series of agitations—*bandhs* and *gheraos*, strikes and shutdowns, closures of colleges and universities, two massive popular movements in Gujarat and Bihar, that demanded resignations of the state governments and dissolution of the state assemblies. While the movement in Gujarat was successful in achieving these twin objectives, that in Bihar, popularly known as the JP movement (after its leader Jayaprakash Narayan, popularly known as JP) failed to do so. The latter, however, soon spread, especially in North India, and developed into a movement for the ouster of Prime Minister Indira Gandhi. This was followed by the second 'watershed' in India's recent history: the imposition of the Emergency by Mrs Gandhi on 26 June 1975. The step sent shock waves across the nation and the trauma continued for nearly nineteen months. Political observers, both at home and abroad, talked of a crisis of India's political system and its democracy, with many predicting that the dark night of a long-term dictatorship had descended on the country. This book attempts to make sense of these two connected happenings and their consequences for the people and the polity.

I

Many journalists and a few scholars have written about the JP movement and the Emergency separately, but very few have studied them in tandem with each other. While the functioning of the Emergency may be seen in isolation, any analysis of its causes, its historical significance, as well as consequences, has to be in the context of the JP movement. Likewise, the JP movement cannot be understood except with reference to the role of opposition parties and organizations such as the RSS (Rashtriya Swayamsevak Sangh) in it, besides JP's ideas and personality.

Such a study has not been attempted so far, except very briefly. The present work is an attempt to fill that void.

This is, however, not an examination and evaluation of the politics and intellectual development as a whole either of JP[1] or of Indira Gandhi.[2] Rather, I focus on their politics and thought, their pronouncements and deeds at a particular juncture when JP was the leader of the mass movement associated with his name during 1974-75 and Indira Gandhi was the prime minister against whom it was directed. A full account of the events between 1974-77 is avoided, though some degree of narration, as in Chapters 2, 3, and 4, has been found necessary.

My effort is primarily to understand what actually happened during those crucial years and why and with what consequences. After all, movements, parties, governments and individuals seldom stand for what they claim, and the JP movement and the Emergency regime were no exceptions. The personalities of JP and Indira Gandhi were quite complex and often displayed paradoxes. The issues that they raised, therefore, deserve critical attention. The main justification given by JP for his movement was that it aimed at ending corruption in day-to-day life and politics, whose fountainhead was Mrs Gandhi, and to defend democracy which was threatened by her authoritarian personality, policies and style of politics. Her continuation in office, he said, was 'incompatible with the survival of democracy in India'.[3] Mrs Gandhi's primary defence of the Emergency and her main criticism of the JP movement was that its disruptive character endangered India's stability, security, integrity and democracy. 'In the name of democracy it has been sought to negate the very functioning of democracy,'[4] she said on the morrow of the Emergency. Thus, both of them justified their actions by appealing to democracy. It is also significant that the people overthrew Mrs Gandhi and the Emergency regime decisively in March 1977, gave an opportunity to the participants in the JP movement to exercise power, and then, equally decisively, brought Mrs Gandhi back to power at the end of 1979. Why?

The effort here is to understand both the JP movement (JPM) and the Emergency and not merely to condemn their negative aspects. In my view, a critical look at the JPM does not exonerate Mrs Gandhi of what happened during the Emergency, nor do the excesses of the Emergency and the loss of the citizens' liberties scale down the major weaknesses of the JP movement and the inadequacies of JP as its leader. I do not agree that either of the two—the JPM and the Emergency— were fascist, but, as I would argue, both had the potential of being fascist or totalitarian. I deal with this aspect in the concluding chapter. A related but a more significant question is raised in the discussion on the limits in terms of both methods and objectives, that a mass movement against a democratically-elected government must observe in a political democracy.

The book also seeks to explore what did the two—the JPM and the Emergency—mean for the future of democracy in India. Has the ghost of authoritarianism been laid to rest for a long time to come? Or did the two generate forces and create some of the conditions for it to re-emerge? My unstated perspective throughout will be to understand both phenomena so that the same should not happen again.

II

My effort has been to study both events in their larger historical context—both local and global. Consequently, the experience of the fascist regimes in Italy and Germany and the authoritarian regimes in Tsarist and Communist Russia, inter-war Japan, Eastern Europe, Latin America and Kuomintang China, as also in our neighbourhood in recent years, has constantly informed my understanding of the developments during 1974-77. History shows that not all popular mass movements lead to or strengthen democracy, nor do they necessarily stand for what their leaders claim, or what their followers believe. Moreover, quite often not only participants but even observers manage to see the reality in a skewed manner. Often enough, regimes which claimed to be defending democracy have themselves ended up as dictatorships.

There is also the difficulty of writing about events which are close to us in time. But this problem of distance is a relative one. For example, India's national movement, given the constant striving struggle and contention around the values of its legacy, is for most of us quite contemporary. Similarly, the economic and cultural impact of colonialism— the colonialization of our minds—is very much a part of our day-to-day life, affecting deeply our socio-economic and cultural development. Even the ancient and medieval periods of our history take on a very contemporary hue in the context of the efforts to spread or oppose the communalization of our society.

On the other hand, after a detailed examination, I have come to the conclusion that in some respects the JPM and the Emergency can be considered as much closed chapters of our history as the end of colonial rule in 1947, and may perhaps appear to be even more remote. Neither has left an abiding legacy. The impact and even the memory of the years 1974 to 1977 have faded even in the minds of those who lived through those eventful years. For most Indians, independence and Partition in 1947, the India-China War of 1962 and the Bangladesh War of 1971 are more etched in their memory than the JP movement or even the Emergency. A researcher found in the sixties that a Punjab peasant remembered events by their proximity to World War I, or the Jallianwalla massacre, or Bhagat Singh's martyrdom, or the Great Depression, or World War II. It is my impression that today's peasant or even urban-educated person is likely to connect events more to 1947, or 1962, or 1971, or to Indira Gandhi's assassination than to the JP movement or even the Emergency. And this, despite the fact that newspapers and magazines routinely publish articles on the Emergency around 25 June every year. But for the JP movement even this doesn't happen. And, certainly, for us, Gandhiji is more contemporary than JP and Nehru more than Indira Gandhi. And yet the years 1974-77 are worth remembering and studying for their valuable lessons about our polity's development and future scenarios.

The problem of producing supporting documentation for statements made about a recent period is real. But, then, this is also true not only for the ancient and medieval periods of our history but also of the modern era, as for example, the national and other popular movements. For example, the private papers of most of the political leaders and other activists of the modern period are not available. Most of the leaders of the national movement from Dadabhai Naoroji, M.G. Ranade, Gopal Krishna Gokhale to Lokmanya Tilak, Gandhiji, Sardar Patel and Subhas Chandra Bose did not keep any private papers of consequence. The records of the Indian National Congress, trade unions, kisan sabhas and like organizations are scanty, for they were regularly subjected to police raids and their records had to be periodically destroyed. The records of the colonial government are much more useful. But they suffer from many lacunae. The records of the Central Intelligence Department are still highly classified and are not likely to be made available, at least in our life time. Also, the Home Department preserved and transferred to the National Archives only highly selective records, transferring primarily those records which were relevant from the point of view of its administrative needs. Consequently, these records are quite inadequate for the period up to 1918 so far as the study of national and other popular movements is concerned. Another example: the National Archives has hardly any meaningful files on Bhagat Singh and his comrades; the main one on them deals with the problem of forced-feeding Bhagat Singh and others when they were on hunger-strike in 1930!

For the period of this study the absence of certain primary sources is felt even more intensely. For example, Indira Gandhi's private papers, if they exist, are not open to scholars. JP's papers in the Nehru Memorial Museum and Library are private in name only as they consist almost entirely of his articles and speeches, even otherwise available, or of his non-political personal correspondence. The records of the home ministry and other government departments dealing with this period have not yet been released to the public. But, going by the quality of those which have been opened for the fifties, they are likely to be of little value to researchers.

In the absence of more direct historical material, much of what actually happened has to be reconstructed through careful reasoning. For example, JP's political calculations during 1974-75, or his and other leaders' plans or conception of the character, content and course of the movement that was to be launched after 29 June 1975 to force Mrs Gandhi to resign, or Mrs Gandhi's political calculations in imposing the Emergency, or in withdrawing it in January 1977 are still not fully known for lack of relevant information. Another interesting example is the complete confusion, then as now, regarding the role of the RAW (Research and Analysis Wing) during the Emergency. The opening up of the home ministry's files to public scrutiny and the release of the private papers of Indira Gandhi and other political leaders and bureaucrats is bound to lead to fresh research and analysis on many aspects of the present work. Apart from the issues raised above, fresh material would help shed light on such questions as Mrs Gandhi's claims of the growth of subterranean foreign influences in Indian politics and of the deep penetration of the country's institutions, bureaucracy, political leadership and so on by foreign intelligence agencies, or the RSS's influence over the JP movement or its penetration of the army, police and bureaucracy, or the extent of Sanjay Gandhi and his coterie's control over government policies and administrative apparatuses. Similarly, scholars would like to know whether there was any well thought-out plan to use the Emergency for any specific, long-term purposes and, if so, was it prepared much before June 1975? Or, for example, what was the role of the family planning and slum-clearance drives in the implementation of the design for the Emergency or were these just the whims of a young man who had suddenly gained political and administrative power? Even the nature and extent of the suppression of civil liberties or of the Emergency excesses are not adequately known despite the exertions of the Shah Commission. And, then, why were national elections suddenly announced on 18 January

1977? The answer to the last of these questions is critical to the understanding and evaluation of Indira Gandhi's role as a major leader of post-independence India. And, of course, most of these questions may never be completely answered even on the basis of direct evidence of private papers, memoirs and government files, for historical actors are seldom fully conscious of their own motives, actions and political calculations.

However, we cannot afford to wait for fresh historical source material to be available or unearthed. We have to try to understand these two 'watershed' developments with the aid of the available source material, however inadequate, and with the knowledge of the historical processes at work in Indian society. The existing studies are, in my view, inadequate in their hypotheses regarding both the JPM and the Emergency. At the time, or even later on they failed to provide citizens and political activists working propositions that were predictive or offered guidelines for political action. For example, in none of the writings of 1977-78 could I find anything that could foretell the re-emergence of Mrs Gandhi in 1979 as a decisive actor in politics and, therefore, suggesting the possible reasons for this. Nor did any of the studies of the JPM, with the possible exception of Ghanshyam Shah's, advance or provide an explanation for its failure to stand up to state repression after 25 June, unlike the 1942 movement or the Dandi March, with which JP was so fond of comparing his movement, or the subsequent disappearance of JPism, to coin a phrase, from the Indian political stage.

As against the problems of 'doing' contemporary history, there is the advantage of the historian having lived through and 'experienced' a part of the period. Consequently, whenever necessary and useful, I have relied on my personal experience and that of friends and colleagues. This has, of course, its own advantages but also its drawbacks. Living through a particular happening, one develops a certain specific understanding of and approach towards events. The possibility of the contemporary bias of the historian becomes obvious; but, then, personal hindsight and 'empathy' with the events can help impart a certain depth of understanding, beyond the study of historical documents. This is so provided the historian is aware of his bias and makes a conscious attempt to overcome it.

Despite my best efforts, like any historian writing about a past event, ancient, medieval or modern, my present intellectual and political positions also tend to impinge, for better or worse, on my understanding of the JP movement and the Emergency. Yet, I do believe that a certain detachment and a relatively, though not fully, objective view of events, even if contemporary, is possible; and I have tried my best to maintain this distance.

This is also the reason why I have relied upon and quoted at length from the writings, speeches and interviews of JP and Indira Gandhi, the main characters in my narrative, for an indication of their attitudes and approaches so that the reader can draw his own conclusions. I would also like to add that while my present understanding of the period under study is before the reader, during the years of the actual events I was highly critical of both the JP movement and the Emergency and did what I could to counter the impact of the latter in my university (JNU). My view of what would have been the desirable course of action both for JP and Mrs Gandhi is discussed in Chapter 5 as also to a certain extent in the concluding chapter. I may also point out that such a dispassionate view of an event is possible has been demonstrated by Bhola Chatterji, a 'JPite' in outlook and sympathies, who was on JP's side of the barricades during 1974-77, but who wrote what is arguably the best critical study of the movement.

Still, I am aware that the subjective element is far greater in the case of a historian of the contemporary period and because of this, as also because of the scantiness of primary sources, he has to be much more tentative in his findings and analysis than the historian of other periods—his answers have to be much more provisional. The element of conjecture and speculation is also far greater in his case. As Hobsbawm has put it, it is perhaps 'too early' for a historian of contemporary events 'to draw up a historical balance sheet.'[5] Accordingly, depending on the nature of evidence, some parts of this work are firmly rooted in facts, others are interpretative and still others speculative.

When faced with inadequacy or even absence of source material on some aspects of the political developments under study, I have taken recourse to what is perhaps the most difficult aspect of a historian's craft, namely, heuristic devices or counter-history, that is, looking at a possible alternative scenario or course of action, at what did not happen but might have happened, to throw light on the actual course of events. This I have done, above all, in Chapter 5 while discussing what alternative approaches could have been adopted by the two sides after 12 June 1975. I have, of course, assumed the open-ended character of the situation existing at the time, with both sides having several options. To a certain extent I have also adopted a heuristic approach in discussing the role of different social groups towards the Emergency, or the more interesting question as to why Mrs Gandhi called for elections in January 1977.

My critique of JP and his movement for relying upon the RSS and its cadres for popular mobilization outside Bihar and in the civil disobedience movement planned at the end of June and of the consequences thereof if Mrs Gandhi had given way or been swept aside, is also based on my understanding of the RSS and of what the result of depending upon it could have been for the polity and society. This approach relies upon comparative history—the historical record of countries that fell prey to fascism in the inter-war period (i.e. from 1918 to 1939)—to speculate and create an alternative scenario of what could have happened; that is, to create counter-history. The liberal historians of fascism have unanimously, whatever their other differences on the origins of fascism, condemned the Italian liberals and King Victor Emmanuel for not taking a stand against Mussolini and the March on Rome, and Marshall Hindenburg for letting Hitler tinker with the German Constitution. But what would have these historians written if Victor Emmanuel had helped suppress the March on Rome and thus prevented Mussolini from capturing power, or Hindenburg, as the President, had not let Hitler become or remain the Chancellor of Germany despite a near majority in the Reichstag? It may be suggested that if counter-history is not used where necessary, then to talk of employing history to predict events would be, to use a mild adjective, a non-starter.

I have tried to bring out the role of different classes, strata and groups in both the JP movement and the Emergency. But I have not taken recourse to a class analysis of either, though I have discussed the attitude adopted by different social classes, strata and groups towards both. And this for two reasons. First, politics is 'guided' by classes and is the 'consequence' of class interests. But when, where, how and by whom are questions to be analysed in a complex manner, with abundance of materials and the acumen of a Karl Marx—and even he was only rarely successful when dealing with specific events. Second, class analysis is possible only in the case of long-term social, economic and political trends, such as communalism, movements, structures, and revolutions such as the French, Russian, Chinese or Indian. For example, the generalization can be made, though it might be disputed by some, that despite Nehru's intentions India developed as a capitalist society. However, class analysis cannot be easily applied to specific, short-term movements and events, such as the JP movement which lasted only seventeen months and the Emergency which operated only for nineteen months.[6] Moreover, neither attempted or led to changes in the socio-economic organization or structure of Indian society or the country's political system or even the course of politics once the Emergency ended and the Janata government was formed. There was another paradox in the Indian situation. In Indian conditions, the popular social base of a long-term dictatorship could have been provided only by the rich peasantry, which enjoyed power in the countryside, and the petty bourgeoisie. But, as brought out in Chapters 2 and 8, in North India, both were opposed to the Congress and Mrs Gandhi both before and during the Emergency. On the other hand, both could have supported communalism, as was the case in Punjab and later, in the nineties, in most of the Hindi-speaking states; and communalism would have inevitably led to a dictatorship or fascism in a multi-religious society like India's.

I have also not dealt at length with the excesses of the sterilization drive and slum clearance and jhuggi-jhopri resettlement. For one, this required a detailed look into the hospital, Municipal and Delhi Development Authority records or the type of oral history research that Emma Tarlo has carried out in one of the resettlement colonies.[7] I was not in a position to do that. But a more important reason for devoting relatively little attention to these two issues is that, though they played an important role in Mrs Gandhi's defeat at the polls in March 1977, they were not basic to the Emergency. The case against the Emergency regime rested on its very character and not on the degree of its excesses. The excesses were important partly because they revealed the inherent bureaucratic, authoritarian and extra-constitutional character of the Emergency. But their extent and degree is, if I may say so, only marginal and even irrelevant for determining the character of the Emergency. This point can be made in a simple manner. I do not think that those who stress the degree of the excesses would suggest that minus those the Emergency was acceptable or unblemished. Therefore, a critique of the Emergency and an understanding of its character would have to be arrived at, even if there had been no family planning and slum clearance excesses.

III

I have extensively, but critically, drawn on contemporary accounts though many of them are quite superficial and simplistic in their understanding and analysis. Many of them were published immediately after the formation of the Janata government in March 1977 and were clearly 'rush jobs', more often based on gossip and rumours which were treated as facts, though some of them did contain certain insights. Unfortunately, there was little serious and penetrating reportage on both events; no great contemporary effort to critically assess what was happening in 1974-75 or 1975-77. An exception is Ghanshyam Shah's outstanding reportage on the Gujarat and Bihar movements. The report on Gujarat was published in *Economic and Political Weekly* in August 1974. The report on Bihar was prepared on the eve of the Emergency, but could be published in the *Economic and Political Weekly* only in April 1977. The two reports were published in June 1977 as a book entitle *Protest Movements in Two Indian States*. Shah's articles were based on detailed fieldwork and interviews with participants in the two movements and offered deep insights and meaningful generalizations. I have used his work extensively for Chapter 3 on the Gujarat and Bihar student movements. There are two other outstanding works on JP and the JP movement. The first, Bhola Chatterji's *Conflict in JP's Politics*, published in 1984, was informed by the author's close acquaintance with and admiration for JP and other socialist leaders, including Chandra Shekhar. The second, Balraj Puri's long essay, was first published in 1978 in *Revolution Counter-Revolution* edited by him, and then reprinted as 'A Fuller View of the Emergency' in the *Economic and Political Weekly* of 15 July 1995. The JP movement has been better covered by writers than the Emergency. Vasant Nargolkar's, Minoo Masani's and S.K. Ghose's accounts of the former have not been matched by any accounts of the latter, though Kuldip Nayar's two works came close to them. Geoffrey Ostergaard's work, *Nonviolent Revolution in India*, is indispensable for his treatment of Vinoba Bhave's and the Sarvodayites' relations with the JPM and the Emergency. Max Jean Zins' is one of the few analytical works on the Emergency which is informed by a well-grounded Marxist approach. Various writings of Ajit Roy, referred to in the text, also belong to the same genre. I would also like to recognize the contribution of the biographies of Indira Gandhi by Inder Malhotra, Zareer Masani and Mary C. Carras for a fuller understanding of her life and politics. The accounts of the Emergency written by Henry C. Hart and W.H. Morris-Jones, when it was still in operation, contained many insights and retain their relevance, as does the contemporary analysis of the JP movement by C.N. Chitta Ranjan. Works of Bimal Prasad and Ajit Bhattacharjea enable one to follow JP's intellectual journey. However, except for Bhola Chatterji, Balraj Puri and Geoffrey Ostergaard, authors dealing with the JP movement and the Emergency do not view the two sequentially. Interestingly, Balraj Puri, in his all-too-brief study, comes to the conclusion that both weakened the political system.[8] P.N. Dhar's recent book provides some fresh insights into the working of the minds of both JP and Indira Gandhi as also does the day-to-day diary kept by B.N. Tandon, joint secretary in the prime minister's secretariat. Unfortunately, only the first volume of the diary covering the period from 1 November 1974 to 15 August 1975 has been published so far. Apart from its other virtues, Granville Austin's study is definitive in its treatment of constitutional changes brought about during 1975-77.

I have kept references and, therefore, footnotes to the minimum and in general, with rare exceptions, used them only for quotations. Still, there are a large number of them. This is because it was necessary to authenticate the many statements made by JP and Indira Gandhi and major commentators, especially in Chapters 4 and 6. Their words would also enable the reader to come to his own conclusions.

2 *The Years of Disillusionment*

Indira Gandhi became the prime minister in 1967 with the substantially reduced majority of the Congress, following the severe drubbing it had received at the Centre and in the states in the general elections. There was also a crisis in the economy and planning as the rate of economic growth had been slowing down since 1962. With other discerning Congressmen she realized that substantial steps had to be taken to reverse these two processes, of the decline of the Congress and the deterioration in the socio-economic situation. Thereupon Mrs Gandhi precipitated the 1969 split in the Congress, adopting a left-of-the-centre position, and then went to the polls in February 1971.

As in her 1969 intra-party struggle against party bosses, this time too she decided to go into battle against her opponents with a radical reform ideology as her main weapon. She appealed to the poor, the landless, the scheduled castes and tribes, women and the unemployed youth, promising them elimination of mass poverty, economic betterment and abolition of glaring disparities in income and opportunity and social status. Rousing the hopes of the underprivileged and making them conscious of their rights, she promised to wage a bitter struggle for them against vested interests and the status quo. To the middle classes and the propertied she promised strong and stable governments at the Centre and in the states, besides full scope for the private sector to play an active role in the mixed economy.

Cutting across regional, linguistic, caste and communal lines, the Congress had swept the 1971 polls winning 352 of the 518 Lok Sabha seats, to once again assume the predominant position it had in the Nehru era of Indian politics. The elections also marked an overwhelming personal triumph for Indira Gandhi. She had become the unchallenged leader of Congress and the government and the dominant political figure in the country. Her enormous self-confidence was apparent when on a BBC programme she asserted: 'We are not dependent upon what other countries think or want us to do. We know what we want for ourselves and we are going to do it, whatever it costs ... we welcome help from any country; but if it doesn't come, well, it is all right by us.'[1] The Bangladesh war had further enhanced her prestige: India had not only defeated a troublesome neighbour but had asserted its independence in foreign affairs and in defence of her national interest. She had shown that on the world stage, India was not a weak political entity even if it was not as yet a world power. By the end of 1971, Indira Gandhi was 'at the pinnacle of her power and glory'. Many Indians referred to her as a modern-day Durga and 'incarnation of Shakti or female energy'. Hope and optimism were once again pervasive.

The year 1972, marking twenty-five years of Indian independence, saw the beginning of a period when conditions existed for the government to fulfill its electoral promises, and progress to be made in the tasks of nation-building and economic development accompanied by social justice, with economic betterment and removal of gross inequality in incomes and standards of living as necessary concomitants. There was political stability in the country; the government had a two-thirds majority in the Lok Sabha; and people seemed to have acquired fresh and heightened self-confidence in themselves as well as new faith in the political leadership.

But before this phase of development was inaugurated, the Congress leadership felt that it must acquire the levers of power in the states, which were, after all, the agencies for implementation of much of the needed reform and the developmental programmes and policies. Consequently, elections were held in March 1972 for the legislative assemblies in all states except UP, Tamil Nadu, Kerala and Orissa. Reiterating its commitment to socialism and land reforms as in 1971, the Congress won a massive victory and secured a majority of seats everywhere. The political command at both the Centre and the states was now unified. Indira Gandhi had now virtually complete control over the party, her cabinet, and the chief ministers. The dominance she now enjoyed across the political system surpassed even that of Nehru in his time.

II

This favourable situation, however, did not last long. The political euphoria that bank nationalization, the *Garibi Hatao* slogan, the massive electoral victories of 1971 and 1972, and the triumph in Bangladesh aroused soon began to subside. In fact, already by the end of 1972, the glow had started to fade and the popularity of the government had begun to decline in the urban areas, with people's unfulfilled expectations taking their toll. The 1971 and 1972 elections reflected the further politicization and radicalization of the masses and the deepening of the political process. Reposing their faith in Indira Gandhi, the poor and the middle classes had given her the mandate she had sought for rapid economic development and social transformation. She had now to deliver on her promises. There could be no alibis or excuses for failure to do so, for she had been given the political strength to pass any necessary laws, to take any needed administrative measures.

The government did undertake several measures to implement its left-of-centre agenda. In August 1972, general insurance was nationalized, as was the coal-mining industry soon after; banks had been nationalized earlier. The Foreign Exchange Regulation Act (FERA), passed in 1973, had placed numerous restrictions on foreign investment and the functioning of foreign companies. Ceilings were imposed on urban land ownership. An MRTP Commission was appointed in 1971 to implement the Monopoly and Restrictive Trade Practices (MRTP) Act of 1969 which aimed at checking concentration of industrial enterprises in a few hands. However, the government refused to go further in nationalizing industry, despite pressure from the leftists within or outside the Congress party, and remained fully committed to a mixed economy. The central government initiated several anti-poverty programmes. These included distribution of cheap foodgrains to the economically vulnerable sections of society, crash schemes for creating employment in rural areas, projects to provide subsidies and subsidized loans to small and marginal farmers and agricultural labourers for land improvement and adopting improved production practices, taking up subsidiary farm occupations like cattle raising, poultry farming and goat, pig and sheep rearing, and provision of subsidies on the cost of wage-labour works in construction of roads, irrigation and soil conservation. It became compulsory for nationalized banks to open branches in areas with few banking facilities such as small towns, rural clusters and the poorer parts of the cities and to make credit available to small industries, farmers, road transporters and self-employed persons. Indira Gandhi also tried to strengthen the Planning Commission and the planning mechanism and to resume the process of rapid industrialization. She announced a policy of support to small capital.

The government also got passed two important constitutional amendments. The Supreme Court had in two judgements in 1951 and 1965 upheld Parliament's right to amend the fundamental right to property so as to make any legislation regarding it non-justiciable. But in 1967 the Supreme Court had in the Golak Nath case reversed these decisions and later set aside bank nationalization as well as the abolition of privy purses. The twenty-fourth amendment to the Constitution, passed in 1971, restored Parliament's authority to amend fundamental rights. The twenty-fifth amendment passed in the same year gave Parliament the power to decide the amount to be paid as compensation, and also the mode of payment in case of any private property taken over for public purposes. Thus, the Supreme Court would no longer have the power to declare such compensation to be inadequate. These two constitutional amendments were intended to counter the courts' conservative stand on agrarian reform legislation, nationalization of industries and other business enterprises, measures to check concentration of wealth and economic power in private hands, and socio-economic transformation in general. They questioned the judiciary's assertion of supremacy over the Parliament, and assumption of powers over the constitutional amendment process which the makers of the Constitution did not perhaps intend. By a further, less significant, constitutional amendment the privileges as well as the privy purses of the former princes were abolished. In this way, the government succeeded in eliminating all constitutional and judicial impediments to bringing about a more equitable social order and a better distribution of national wealth. In 1973, the Planning Comission also completed the Draft Five Year Plan which charted a road map for a 5.5 per cent growth rate of national income along with self-reliance and significant dent on poverty.

Despite the government's plans and good intentions, in practice, all these steps, especially the anti-poverty programmes, had little impact on the vast majority of the poor. More and more people started feeling that *Garibi Hatao* was a mere slogan, that in fact hardly any dent was being made on rural and urban poverty or economic inequality. Neither the basic needs of the poor nor the rising expectations of the middle classes were close to being met. No headway was being made in the implementation of land reforms. Above all, the people felt that Congress legislators and ministers were far more interested in feathering their own nests than in fulfilling electoral promises. Indira Gandhi, increasingly on the defensive, argued, as in April 1973, that 'if anybody tries to say that poverty can go in my lifetime or during my tenure as Prime Minister, it just cannot. It has very deep roots.'[2] She was right but, then the populist rhetoric of 1971 (*Garibi Hatao*) had roused expectations that were radical and they were beginning to come home to roost. Moreover, her critics argued that adequate steps were not being taken to improve the existing situation.

In 1973, the economy and the polity started going downhill as also the credibility of Indira Gandhi's leadership and the Congress governments at the Centre and the states. The Congress was defeated in several by-elections across the country, and despair and frustration with the existing situation became widespread. Even the explosion of a nuclear device in 1974 and India's entry into the exclusive nuclear club only briefly boosted the national morale and the government's popularity. And, then, came two popular movements in Gujarat and Bihar, the latter culminating in the JP movement.

Responsible for the rising discontent and political unrest of the years 1973-75 were several factors. There was a marked deterioration in the economic situation due to medium-term economic trends. A combination of two-successive crop failures, economic recession, rising defence expenditure, growing unemployment, rampant inflation and scarcity of foodstuffs and other essential goods created a serious economic crisis.

The years 1964 to 1967 had been those of plan holiday and the economy had shown a negative rate of growth. After 1967 the economy had picked up but had failed to resume its previous rate of growth. While national income had grown at the annual rate of about 4.3 per cent during 1954-1964, despite recovery from the recession of 1964-1967, it went up only by 2.9 per cent per year from 1967 to 1973. Similarly, growth of per capita income had slowed down from an annual rate of 2.1 per cent in 1954-1964 to 0.6 per cent in 1967-1973.

There was virtual stagnation in industrial production which had grown at the annual rate of nearly 7 per cent during 1956-1961 and about 9 per cent during 1961-1965 but had declined to about 3.3 per cent during 1965-1970 and 2.8 per cent during 1970-1974. Moreover, there was a fall in the production of basic goods such as steel, cement, power, coal, mill-made cloth, jute, vanaspati and transport. The rate of industrial investment had also come down. The rigid regulation of the private sector and restrictions on the expansion of large business houses had limited private investment in the economy, while large budgetary deficits prevented the government from increasing public investment.

On the morrow of taking office, the government was faced with the 1971 Bangladesh crisis, and the economy was put under a heavy strain. The burden of aiding the Bangladesh liberation struggle and feeding, clothing and sheltering nearly ten million refugees from

Bangladesh on a generous scale during 1971 depleted the food reserves and, combined with the cost of the war against Pakistan, put a heavy strain on India's finances and economic resources, and led to a large budgetary deficit. The war had also led to the termination of US aid. The budgetary deficit, which had grown beyond Rs. 2,000 crores, also ballooned because of large-scale expenditure on poverty-alleviation programmes without a commensurate tax effort.

A major achievement had been an increase in foodgrain production by 35 per cent between 1967 and 1970. But the monsoons, and to a certain extent winter rains, failed for two years in succession in 1972 and 1973. Most parts of the country suffered a terrible drought, which persisted in some areas up to 1975. There was a sharp decline in agricultural production. Despite import of five million tons of foodgrains in 1974, there was a massive shortage—between April 1971 and April 1974 per capita availability of foodgrains fell by 11 per cent—which fuelled their prices. Imports of costly foodgrains further increased the fiscal deficit of the government. Water reservoirs dried up with the drought, leading to a drop in power generation and heavy power cuts which, combined with lack of demand for manufactured goods in the rural areas due to the fall in agricultural production, led to industrial recession and, the accompanying rise in unemployment.

It is said that misfortunes rarely come singly. The low-growth economy received another blow from the notorious oil-shock of October 1973 when the oil-producing countries cut back crude oil production and the world price of crude increased more than four-fold within a year, leading to massive increase in the price of petroleum and its products such as fertilizers. The shortage of and resultant high prices of fertilizers affected adversely the production and prices of foodgrains. Transport charges too went up. Because of India's dependence on imports of petroleum and petroleum products, its import bill suddenly went up by nearly a billion dollars. This produced a large gap between imports and exports and drained India's foreign exchange reserves and further increased the budgetary deficit and deepened the economic recession. India had to appeal to the World Bank and the International Monetary Fund for emergency aid and, consequently, accept the harsh conditions they imposed.

Given these adversities, the economy saw galloping inflation as prices rose continuously. In 1972-73 they rose by 22 per cent, escalating to 30 per cent by the middle of 1974; an average rise of 2.3 per cent per month. The price rise, the worst since independence, was most serious in the case of rice, wheat, pulses and other articles of daily consumption. It was accompanied by acute shortage of essential items of consumption such as cooking oil (Dalda, for example), kerosene, matches, wood, paper and cement, many of them disappearing from the shops. Ration shops witnessed long queues for rice, wheat and kerosene. Because of inflation and shortages, not only the poor but also the middle classes began to feel the pinch. Drought and shortages also gave an excellent opportunity to unscrupulous traders and manufacturers to indulge in speculation, hoarding and black marketing. People accused the ruling party politicians of colluding with hoarders and black-marketeers and thereby giving a boost to the flourishing black market and the parallel economy. There was massive erosion of support for Congress in urban areas. In many places foodgrain godowns and trucks carrying foodgrains were looted. There were food riots in Nagpur, Bombay and Mysore. Some critics accused the government of removing not Garibi (poverty) but the *Garibs* (the poor).

To contain inflation and lessen the budgetary deficit, the government imposed cuts in expenditure, thus further fuelling unemployment and discontent. Unemployment had been in any case growing since the plan holiday began in 1964. The total employment in the organized manufacturing sector (both public and private) had grown at the annual rate of 5.6 per cent between 1960 and 1965; during 1968-1974 the rate was only 2.8 per cent. The number of applicants registered for jobs in the employment exchanges increased from 2.6 millions in 1966 to 8.4 millions in 1974. Unemployment among the educated, middle-class youth, which had decreased after independence and during the first two Five Year Plans, from 1957 to 1962, became increasingly more acute as public investment and government expenditure shrank and industrial growth slowed down. For example, the service sector growth, where most of the educated and middle class youth found jobs, had also tapered off. It had grown by 7 per cent annually from 1954 to 1964 but only by 2.8 per cent in 1965, 3.2 per cent in 1966 and 4.5 per cent annually from 1967 to 1973.

Economic recession, unemployment and price rise, which eroded workers' real income, led to large-scale industrial unrest and a wave of strikes and sit-ins in different parts of the country during 1972-1974. In Bombay alone there were over 13,000 strikes between October 1973 and June 1974. In 1974 alone, 31 million work days were lost by industry as against 6.5 million in 1965. The railway strike in May 1974 was the high point of the industrial unrest. Fully supported by the opposition parties, it lasted twenty-two days but was in the end unsuccessful. Unable to meet the demands of the railway workers, and to thus appease them, because of financial stringency, the government decided to break the strike. The strike was declared illegal under the Defence of India Rules and the striking employees dealt with severely. The political price of this was that Mrs Gandhi's popularity among the workers was eroded further. The government's approach towards the railway strike also made it clear that it was no longer possible for the government to meet popular agitations by catering to or appeasing all the disgruntled social groups as it had done earlier.

One of the highly unpopular steps it took to reduce its expenditure, and thus its budget deficit, and also to curb consumption and thus check inflation, was to introduce a scheme of compulsory deposits amounting to a freeze of wages and salaries on 6 July 1974. In order to immobilize part of their wages, salaried employees were to deposit all wage increases and half of the additional dearness allowance received into compulsory deposits with the government. This measure meant particular hardship for those whose incomes were too low to meet their minimum consumption needs. Simultaneously, to placate the disgruntled salaried groups, the government imposed a ceiling on all dividends paid by private companies. Also all tax payers whose annual income exceeded Rs. 15,000 were asked to put an additional 4 to 8 per cent of their income into compulsory deposits.

III

The people, especially in the urban areas, and particularly during 1973 and 1974, began to express their discontent through strikes, student protests, demonstrations, anti-government rallies, *gheraos* and *bandhs*, which often turned violent. Many colleges and universities—and at one time most of them—were closed for prolonged periods, often preceded by gheraos of university and college administrators, bus burning, stone throwing and other forms of violence. There was deterioration in and breakdown of law and order in some areas, particularly during 1974-75. Increasingly, the opponents of the government took recourse to extra-constitutional means and acts of violence which became a near daily occurrence. The state governments, in nearly all cases headed by Mrs Gandhi's nominees, invariably failed to handle the turmoil politically. They increasingly took recourse to police and para-military forces to deal with popular protests, sometimes calling out the army to help. Demonstrators and the police clashed in many parts of the country.

In May 1973, India's largest state, UP, witnessed an unprecedented mutiny by an armed force of the state. Several units of the Provincial

Armed Constabulary (PAC) rebelled, seized several armouries, and clashed with the army sent to discipline them, leading to the death of over thirty-five constables and soldiers. The chief minister, Kamlapati Tripathi, was asked to resign and the state put under President's rule. Three batallions of the PAC were disbanded.

In early 1975, the country was again rocked by a wave of violence. On 2 January, the Railway Minister, L.N. Mishra, was assassinated in a bomb blast while addressing a public meeting at Samastipur in North Bihar.

IV

The failure on the economic front was compounded by the government's inability to effectively meet the major economic and administrative challenges. The firm leadership evident at the time of the Bangladesh crisis and in the handling of foreign affairs was now lacking. The ruling party was not able to use its massive majorities at the Centre and in the states to deliver effective administration or provide even political stability in the latter. Instead, even as more and more power got concentrated in even fewer hands at the Centre, the government tended to put all the blame for the increasingly dismal state of affairs on the Opposition, the Press, the judiciary, the civil services, big business houses and trade unions. The opposition parties too performed little better. While the left-wing opponents of the government preached that capitalism and the 'bourgeois democratic' parliamentary system was in any case incapable of ever delivering the goods, the right-wing opposition accused Indira Gandhi of 'lust for power' and 'dictatorial' tendencies and of playing the Soviet game. The latter increasingly pointed to the danger of Communist and Soviet takeover of India, using Indira Gandhi as a conscious or unconscious instrument. Faith in democratic political institutions tended to be eroded by both the Opposition, through its political stance, pronouncements and extra-constitutional tactics, and the government, through its political behaviour and administrative practices.

A major initiative taken by the government to control prices turned out to be an ill-thought experiment and a total fiasco. In early 1973, the wholesale trade in foodgrains was nationalized with the state taking over the entire purchase of wheat from the farmers, with rice purchase to follow later in winter. The government had hoped to reduce prices and prevent hoarding by removing the middlemen. Instead, foodgrains disappeared from the markets and their prices rose steeply, especially as drought in the previous two years had already reduced production of rice and coarse grains, and the wheat crop in 1973 was smaller than expected. The amount procured by government agencies fell from 8.4 million tonnes in 1972 to 5.6 million tonnes in 1973. The farmers were reluctant to sell their produce to the government agencies at fixed procurement prices when the black-market prices were much higher. The government was forced to reduce rations from fair-price shops. Apart from its inherent weaknesses, the trade nationalization scheme had been prepared in haste; nor had a proper machinery for its implementation been created, especially at the village level, where traders operated freely, though illegally.

The government found it neither had adequate food stocks nor was able to replenish them or prevent hoarding and illegal trade by traders, shopkeepers and rich farmers. The scheme was abandoned the following year but the government had earned the wrath of grain traders and *arhtiyas* (market middlemen), rich peasants and the political leaders and parties tied to these interests.

The government's drive against smugglers of gold, drugs and durable consumer goods not produced in India on a sufficient scale also came to nought. The government amended the MISA (Maintenance of Internal Security Act) on 17 September 1974 to enable smugglers and hoarders and evaders of foreign exchange controls to be booked under preventive detention. Over 130 smugglers were arrested under the amended MISA, and the government won immediate acclaim from the people and the media. But while big smugglers were in jail, where they enjoyed all manner of comforts and facilities, smuggling as business resumed quickly with the covert support of both politicians and customs, police and other officials.

The government was also not able to put into effect its declared policies of bringing about greater social and distributive justice. The administrative machinery had been run down for some years and the administration now faced a near crisis of efficiency and integrity. What was worse, it was becoming more and more alienated from the people and, in fact, oppressive towards them, especially the poor, the landless, the Harijans and tribals. The police, in particular, became notorious for its brutal approach towards the common people and atrocities perpetuated upon them. It tended to take the law into its hands and use high-handed, often violent, methods in dealing with individuals and crowds.

V

The political situation was worsened by the play of four other factors over the years. The Congress party had been declining as an organization and proved incapable of dealing with the political crisis of 1974-75 at the state and grassroots level. The new Congress (R), formed by Indira Gandhi in 1969 after the split, had acquired new middle and higher level leaders but little else had changed. Mrs Gandhi had failed to use her complete domination of the party to restructure and refurbish the party or to check groupism and factional rivalries. As Inder Malhotra, an acute observer of Indian politics, was to note, most of the Congress leaders 'had no interest in changing their mental outlook, working methods, lifestyle, factional functioning and addiction to self-advancement by hook or by crook'.[3] Nor were they interested in strengthening the party organizationally or in politically mobilizing the people behind it. Indira Gandhi did not improve the sad state of the party by her style of functioning. She concentrated and centralized authority and decision-making in the party in her hands. She virtually destroyed the federal structure of the party, developed during the freedom struggle and carefully nurtured after 1947 by Jawaharlal Nehru. Already weakened by the party bosses, democracy within the party virtually disappeared during the period of her domination. She regularly shifted and nominated party office-bearers. She replaced Congress chief ministers and state party leaders, who had an independent political base by men and women who had little, if any, popular support, and who were little help in political mobilization or in providing support for her policies or in providing stable administration in the states.

Factionalism in the party was not confined to the states. Even at the Centre, tension in organizational and ideological matters had been developing since 1972 between those who had come into the party from CPI and those from PSP and socialist parties. Traditional Congressmen increasingly either tended to align with one or the other faction or form a rightist group of their own. While the left accused the other two of undermining Indira Gandhi's socialistic and progressive programme, the ex-socialists accused the former of trying to bring about, with Soviet help, a Soviet-style dictatorship. The ex-socialists also attacked the Congress alliance with the CPI, accusing the latter of infiltrating the party. In 1974-75 the ex-socialist faction pressed for a compromise and entente with the JP-led opposition and openly worked for Indira Gandhi and JP to jointly lead the country. The increasingly open confrontation between the two factions contributed to the growing policy and organizational paralysis in the Congress party.

The government's capacity to redress the economic, political and administrative situation as also popular belief in the sincerity of its efforts to do so were seriously impaired by growing corruption in large areas of public life and the widespread belief that the higher levels of the ruling party and administration were involved in it. Common people experienced petty corruption in their day-to-day life. They had to grease palms to get anything done in a government department; and there was no authority to which they could complain. Besides, political corruption was seen as setting the pace for various kinds of petty corruption. The Press, which had overall turned hostile to the government and Mrs Gandhi, regularly regaled its readers with rumours and tales of bribery in high places, sale of licences, collection of black money by politicians, and other financial scandals.

The air of scandal touched even Indira Gandhi when her younger son, the twenty-three-year old Sanjay Gandhi, was given a licence by the ministry of industries out of eighteen applicants to annually produce 50,000 cars, to be named Maruti. Maruti was to be small and cheap and an entirely indigenous product. Bansi Lal, the chief minister of Haryana, obliged by acquiring 290 acres of prime farm land near Gurgaon at far below the market price for the Maruti factory. Its location violated the rule that no factory should be built within 1,000 metres of a defence installation—in this case a munition dump. Sanjay Gandhi raised a large sum of capial from individual businessmen. The enterprise was extended large, unsecured loans by nationalized banks. The Maruti affair was to become a major political problem for Mrs Gandhi. The Opposition repeatedly raked it up in Parliament; nor did the Press lag behind. She was accused of nepotism and corruption, of having used her position and power as prime minister to persuade the licence-granting authorities to decide in favour of her son even though he had no business experience or technical training—Sanjay had completed just one year of training as an apprentice at a Rolls Royce plant in Britain. Mrs Gandhi refuted the charge of nepotism and said that the licence for the Maruti factory was granted by an independent committee. Rising to her son's defence, she said that a young man should not be deprived of an opportunity simply because he was the prime minister's son. This did satisfy many but even those who did not go along with the charge of nepotism against her were unhappy with the position she took on the question and supported the demand for a White Paper on the subject.

The daily dose of scandals, often involving politicians and bureaucrats, and the widespread feeling that nothing was being done about the all-pervading corruption led to public anger and cynicism. What was much worse, public attention was increasingly rivetted not on economic and political problems and ideologies but on scandals and nebulous charges of corruption. The central and state governments' credibility and moral authority and belief in their integrity were eroded by mounting charges of corruption against ministers and administration. The political injury in the case of Mrs Gandhi was compounded by her refusal to see corruption as a serious social political malady, her ignoring the many scandals, and doing little about either taking action against the perpetrators or exposing the baselessness of stories of corruption in high places.

VI

A major new factor in the socio-political situation was the growing detachment from the Congress of three major social groups who were the main beneficiaries of the social system and economic development since 1947, i.e., the middle classes, the rich peasants and the capitalists, big and small. But before examining this aspect, note has to be taken of another significant feature of the political situation.

The poor, constituting the major political base of the Congress, especially since 1971, having been further politicized during 1969-1972, remained steadfast in their support to the Congress and Indira Gandhi. They felt that the right-wing opposition parties did not offer any real alternative solutions to their existential problems. Despite the incompleteness of the 1950s land reforms in many states, the failure to enforce land ceiling legislation, the continued social discrimination against and oppression of the Harijans and other lower castes, the inadequacy of the poverty alleviation schemes, and the failure to check shortages of essential commodities and the spiralling rise in prices, the rural poor still accepted Indira Gandhi as their champion and continued to support her, though more passively than before. The same was true of women and the minorities. No serious outbreak of rural discontent or rural response to the urban upheaval took place. This was in part because the rural poor—the small peasants and agricultural labourers—were not seriously affected by the price rise or the shortages of goods, which hurt the Congress's support in urban areas. They also felt that they had benefited or hoped to benefit from anti-poverty measures and other government policies. As Francine Frankel pointed out on the basis of her fieldwork in UP and her observation of the early 1974 UP assembly election, the Harijans and Backward Castes 'were impressed by the bounties that had come their way and others that had been promised. Some small and marginal farmers and landless labourers had personally received subsidized loans from cooperatives or nationalized banks, or jobs on government work projects under the central sector schemes. Others looked forward to the distribution of government-owned land for house sites, and even surplus agricultural land under new state legislation. Those who benefited or hoped to benefit from such new programmes attributed their good fortune directly to "Indiraji". They did not blame the prime minister for other government failures.'[4]

Certain long-term socio-economic changes and policies such as the land reforms of the 1950s also prevented the erosion of the rural poor's support to Congress. As P.C. Joshi, perhaps the most perceptive of the contemporary observers of the rural scene, has pointed out, 'Congress rule has been responsible for initiating a process of change in the erstwhile semi-feudal social order . . . The stability of peasant support to the Congress since independence is explained largely by this historical onslaught on the semi-feudal social order.'[5] The landlord-moneylender-trader combine was gradually getting weaker in rural society and economy while the landowning peasants and the rural poor were becoming increasingly assertive, even when they had not gained economically. We may also keep in view the fact that the peasants of the seventies were close enough to the colonial period to remember the difference between their lives previously and then. This became evident during the Gujarat student-led agitation discussed below, when the rural poor refused to join and even opposed this rich-peasant supported movement. The June 1975 election in Gujarat, in which Congress was reduced to a minority, also showed that it was still capable of mobilizing the rural poor vote. The Congress got 41 per cent of the vote, fully 7 per cent more than the votes of the opposition Janata Morcha which was able to win 87 out of the 182 seats, with Congress winning 75.

Similarly, despite the price rise and the virtual wage freeze of July 1974 and the heavy-handed suppression of the railway strike, the working class was not politically active during 1973-75. This was partially because it was organizationally fragmented and in any case a large part of it was unorganized. Furthermore, almost exclusive emphasis on economic demands and struggles had made even its organized segments politically passive. Nor was the working class attracted to the right-wing political parties. It was, therefore, not surprising that the working class and the rural poor did not participate to a significant extent in any of the popular movements of 1974-75. They kept out of even the Bihar movement, leading Jayaprakash Narayan to turn to students as the revolutionary vanguard of his movement.

On the other hand, the urban lower-middle and middle classes—teachers, lawyers and other professionals, government servants and other salaried employees, officers in the armed forces, shopkeepers and shop assistants, small and petty traders—whose living standards were being rapidly eroded because of soaring prices and shortage of goods, virtual freeze of salaries in July 1974 in a period of rampant inflation, and growing unemployment among the educated youth, were getting alienated from the ruling party. They were now sceptical about Mrs Gandhi's radical or even democratic credentials. The pervasive corruption further fuelled this feeling.

This hostility of the middle classes was a major political blow to the Congress and Mrs Gandhi; they had played a major role in the freedom struggle and had provided leaders and cadres to all political parties after independence. They had been mainly responsible for the Congress's ideological commitment to the socialistic pattern and its emphasis on public sector and planning and later, its policy of bank nationalization and the like. The middle classes were also the politically most active and articulate social strata. Any check to their upward social and economic mobility was fraught with serious but unseen political consequences, as the developments in the Europe of the 1920s and 1930s had shown.

In the 1960s, a segment of the middle-class youth had veered around to the radical politics of the Naxalites, CPM and CPI. But the growth of this tendency was stalled by 1972 in part because of state suppression, but also the adventurist politics of radical groups, and the radicalism of the Congress under Indira Gandhi. Large segments of the middle classes had supported the right-wing parties after 1962, taken up by their slogan of challenging of Congress's monopoly of power and following the debacle of the India-China War. But they, too, were disappointed with the performance of these parties in the conglomerate SVD (Samyukta Vidhayak Dal) state ministries after the 1967 elections. These parties, too, were as riven with corruption and factionalism as the Congress. Nor could these parties accommodate the still-prevailing radicalism of the lower-middle classes. After 1972, the middle classes were looking for fresh political pastures which would enable them to once again become an authentic political force. They were waiting for the JP movement to happen.

Mrs Gandhi's sharp turn to the left after 1969 was seen by two major social groups, the rich peasantry and the capitalist class, as a threat to their economic position and social status. The two had tended to oppose Congress in 1967 and had supported the 'grand alliance' of opposition parties in 1971 in large parts of the country. During 1973-75 they sought alternative political representation and gave active or passive support to the opposition parties and their agitations, but the weakness of their political position was that the opposition parties, singly or in alliance, were unable to become a sound alternative to the Congress.

As a result of the land reforms of the early fifties and the ushering in of the electoral process, land ownership and social and political power had gradually shifted to the rich peasants. They had also cornered a disproportionate share of the benefits resulting from the government's developmental policies and measures such as the heavy public investment in irrigation, rural electrification, road building, community development projects agricultural extension programmes and growth of co-operative societies. Nor were they asked to pay, through taxes, irrigation charges, betterment levy, and the like, their share of this public investment. They wielded immense influence over political parties and administrative organs of democratic government, from the village level to the state capitals, and over the power structure as a whole. Even before 1971 the rich peasants had been getting alienated from the Congress, which was no longer seen by them to be an effective instrument for satisfying their interests and aspirations. They wanted to play a far greater and direct, in fact hegemonic role, in the making of government policies. They wanted direct control over rural affairs, unencumbered by any radical-sounding official intervention. Not that the Congress was, in any sense, anti-rich-peasantry, but increasingly they felt threatened by the repeated official pronouncements about implementation of the existing land reform laws and the passing and implementation of fresh land ceiling legislation, besides schemes of the state take-over of wholesale trade in foodgrains and other essential commodities, such as edible oils, organization of farmers' service cooperatives for providing cheap credit and other services at subsidized rates to rural poor, and imposition of income-tax on agricultural incomes. In fact, legislation to reduce existing ceilings on agricultural holdings and distribute surplus land to the landless and marginal farmers was passed in several states in 1972 and 1973. The government also antagonized the rich peasants by its refusal to increase procurement prices of foodgrains in 1974. But more than any actual steps—the actual land ceiling legislation was quite liberal towards existing owners of land; its implementation was tardy; and actual land redistribution paltry—it was the radical rhetoric, for example of the *Garibi Hatao* slogan, and the deepening of the democratic process which made the rich peasants feel threatened.

There was also growing class cleavage in the countryside. The high percentage of the poor peasants, agricultural labourers and tribals in the rural population and their growing politicization had started to endanger rich peasant domination of the village. This was in particular true of northern India—Bihar, UP, Haryana, Punjab and Gujarat—where the rich peasants formed their own parties like the Bharatiya Kranti Dal (BKD), Bharatiya Lok Dal (BLD), Samyukta Socialist Party (SSP) and Akali Dal. The rich peasants had the advantage of carrying with them large segments of the middle and even small peasants, sharing with them a common ideology of peasant proprietorship and common aspirations to own and control land, besides common interests such as prices of agricultural products and adversial relationship with agricultural labourers. Often, they also belonged to the same intermediate or backward castes. In these northern states, the Congress came to be increasingly identified with the rural poor, especially the Harijans and tribals. In South India, on the other hand, the class and caste structure or configuration was different from that in the North and the Congress remained an umbrella party as before. In Kerala and Bengal, the large presence of communists among the rural poor kept the rich peasantry tied to the Congress.

In reality, of course, Congress was nowhere anti-rich peasant. But it could not satisfy rich peasant demands without alienating the rural poor or endangering the path of economic development and industrialization that had been adopted. The rich and middle peasants had gradually acquired hegemony over the rural social, economic and political scene. Politically, they either controlled rural vote-banks, and therefore the votes of marginal farmers and agricultural labourers, or when they were unable to do so, they used their muscle power to prevent the agricultural labourers, largely Harijans or dalits, from going to the polling booths. Under Indira Gandhi's leadership the Congress had tried to challenge this hegemony in 1971, though without attacking the interests of the rich peasants. The Congress had also enabled the dalits to exercise their vote in the 1971 and 1972 elections and the early 1974 election to the UP assembly.

The old rural elite, the semi-feudal landlords and zamindars, were a declining force in Indian society and politics. They were incapable of sustaining an anti-government movement or opposition. But they were ready to throw their limited weight behind any anti-Congress force or movement. In the 1950s itself they had withdrawn their support from the Congress and gone over to regional or all-India right-wing parties and groups. The Congress was also willing to ignore them, except when their support could be had without loss of support from other rural strata.

The capitalist class's approach towards the Congress and Indira Gandhi was much more nuanced. Since 1969, the Congress had made a significant shift to the left and adopted radical and egalitarian slogans. It had nationalized banks and coal mining and announced a policy of converting government loans to private limited companies into government-owned equity. As already indicated, an MRTP Commission was appointed in 1971 to ensure better implementation of the MRTP Act so as to check concentration of industrial enterprises and economic power in the hands of a few leading business families.

The capitalist class was troubled by these and other government policies and ideological stances of the ruling party even though Indira Gandhi had refused to yield to pressure from the CPI and left-Congressmen and go further in nationalizing industries or foreign trade and had repeatedly reiterated her commitment to a mixed economy and sought the Indian industrialists' support for her developmental policies. While most capitalists felt confined by the Licence-quota Raj and restrictions on foreign capital, their response was splintered.

A small section of the capitalist class felt that its economic expansion depended on overall socio-economic development, which the Congress alone could ensure, and that despite its radical slogans and restrictions on economic enterprises, the Congress rule posed no danger to it. Another large section of the class was at heart anti-Congress, but chose not to overtly express their reservations or directly politically challenge the government. The industrialists were dependent on government not only for industrial licences, quotas, import allocations, but also for investment funds from nationalized banks and other government-controlled industrial development and financial institutions. The hostility of this section to Congress took two forms. The big business houses went on an investment 'strike'. While the MRTP Act permitted them to enter areas of industry where they were not dominant or in economically backward areas or in certain 'core sectors', these houses followed a policy of withholding fresh investment and withdrew into their own shells. As one industrialist said at the time, 'I have enough capital to last my several coming generations. I can afford to sit out the present tough period.'[6] This investment strike was in part responsible for the economic downturn of 1973 and 1974. Other capitalists felt that 'it was time to abandon the overt campaigns which were evident in the mid-1960s and early 1970s, in favour of less conspicuous and more familiar approaches of boring from within the Congress and working at many levels behind the scenes.'[7]

Still there was a section of the capitalist class that continued its open hostility to the Congress, believing that bank nationalization, the MRTP Act, and other similar steps were measures 'on the road to their demise'. This became evident in its support to the opposition parties during the Gujarat movement in early 1974 and the election to Gujarat assembly in June 1974.

The detachment from the Congress of the three social groups—the middle classes, the rich peasantry in northern India, and a large section of the capitalist class—also contributed to the atmosphere of violence and their recourse to extra-legal and extra-constitutional means along with the disillusioned youth as they found no alternative party or grouping of parties which could electorally displace Congress or represent their interests through constitutional means. As Antonio Gramsci pointed out nearly seventy years back: 'At a certain point in their historical lives, social classes become detached from their traditional parties. In other words, the traditional parties in that particular organizational form, with the particular man who constitute, represent, and lead them, are no longer recognized by their class (or fraction of a class) as its expression. When such crises occur, the immediate situation becomes delicate and dangerous, because the field is open for violent solutions, for the activities of unknown forces, represented by charismatic "men of destiny".'[8]

A large number of academics and other intellectuals rallied behind Indira Gandhi after 1969. Believing that personality and power-oriented politics should be replaced by politics based on issues and ideology, they thought that Mrs Gandhi was going to bring about this change and that with a two-third majority in Parliament, Indira Gandhi would be able to put into practice her declared programme and policies. Iqbal Narain, a leading liberal political scientist, expressed the hope that the 1971 elections would 'usher in an era of politics of commitment in the country' and that the 'phase of sheer politicking' would pass into 'the initial stage of purposive politics of nation-building'.[9]

Apart from the small section of right-wing intellectuals who were opposed to Congress from the Nehru days, most of the intellectuals retained faith in Indira Gandhi throughout 1973-75, though with far less enthusiasm as they saw little progress being made towards the promised objective of growth with social justice. Another smaller section of the intelligentsia, repelled by the unchecked growth of corruption, became increasingly critical of the government and supportive of the JP movement. A large number of left-wing intellectuals were also alienated from the Congress and the government by the unlawful treatment meted out to the Naxalites and members and supporters of the CPM in Bengal, and the inhuman treatment of Naxalite detenus in prisons, with a large number of them being tortured and killed. They were, however, equally put off by the anti-communist and anti-Soviet stance adopted by the socialists and the right-wing parties. Though the bulk of Indian intellectuals still had a soft corner for Mrs Gandhi till the proclamation of the Emergency, the number of those who were willing to stand by her publicly was beginning to diminish rapidly.

VII

The desperation of the opposition parties in the seventies also contributed to the political turmoil. In 1974 and 1975, India witnessed the strange spectacle of conservative and right-wing political parties going in for massive, extra-legal agitational politics to remove duly constituted ministries and dissolve legislatures. While Indira Gandhi was facing a crisis of hegemony, the opposition parties, 'dejected', 'demoralized', 'emasculated' and unsettled by the massive Congress victories in 1971 and 1972, were in no position to fill the vacuum. Ideologically and programmatically, they were utterly disparate and their leadership suffered from ego clashes. The only factors uniting the leaders were anti-Congressism, persistent frustration and hunger for power. In 1971 they had formed an opportunistic and unprincipled electoral alliance without any ideological coherence or a minimum positive programme— in 1969 some of them had opposed bank nationalization and abolition of the privy purses; others had been enthusiastic supporters of these measures—and challenged Indira Gandhi on a personal plane with the *Indira Gandhi Hatao* slogan, but had suffered a crushing defeat. In the 1971 elections they had been considerably down-sized. The assembly elections of 1972 confirmed this verdict.

Since 1972, the right-wing opposition parties had felt that none of them on their own, or even in combination, could hope to gain political power in the foreseeable future and through normal electoral or constitutional processes. They were not at all sure of meeting the electoral challenge in 1976 when the next general elections to Lok Sabha were due. Their sense that despite popular anger against the runaway inflation, they might not prevail against the ruling party in the coming electoral combat was strengthened by Congress victories in the UP and Orissa assembly elections in February 1974. These parties were also not willing to wait to come to power for what appeared to be 'eternity'. Consequently, instead of giving the growing discontent of the people a political direction within the constitutional framework, they looked for short-cuts to gain power. Their one and only common resolve was to oust Indira Gandhi from power even if the legitimacy of the parliamentary process and the party system was put into jeopardy. Unhappy with the growing ties between the Congress and the CPI, these parties held up the spectre of the eventual communist takeover of the country. Along with a section of the Press, they were also responsible for creating an atmosphere of hatred and hostility against Indira Gandhi, personally.

One example of this 'campaign of calumny', was their innuendo that she had arranged the assassination of L.N. Mishra, one of her trusted cabinet ministers, to prevent him from divulging the details of her corruption, and in order to bring a bad name to Jayaprakash Narayan. Another was the Nagarwala episode, discussed at length by all of Indira Gandhi's biographers in which Indira Gandhi was accused of having arranged Nagarwala's death in jail.[10]

The opposition parties were egged on in their endeavours by a section of the intelligentsia, which was wary of Congress and Mrs Gandhi, 'hankered after almost anything' other than the Congress and was willing to back any party from the Marxist CPM to the communal Jan Sangh and the conservative Bharatiya Lok Dal (BLD), formed after the merger of Swatantra, SSP and BKD of Charan Singh. As Dom Moraes has put it, 'In this atmosphere of hysteria, the mistakes of Mrs Gandhi, magnified by rumour and the press, stood, defined in scarlet, as her sins.'[11] Nor is it surprising that in 1974 the opposition parties grasped at JP movement as an opportunity to destabilize the government and forge an alternative coalition which would bring them to power.

It may also be pointed out that the threat to the regime at the time did not come from the left, which was in disarray. Naxalite uprisings had been crushed and the Naxalites reduced to myriad petty sects. The CPM was rudderless, unable to choose between insurrection and parliamentary forms of government or between joining and opposing the JP movement. The CPI was dependent for its electoral growth or even survival on the Congress and was in any case the latter's political ally. It is because of the weakness of the left that, among other reasons, the right-wing parties, or even Jayaprakash, were willing to take recourse to extra-legal militant agitation or dare to fight the government in an open and ruthless manner. If the left had been waiting in the wings, the right-wing parties would not have dared to make a bid to destabilize the government, to wage a war to the knife against Indira Gandhi and the Congress, lest the communists pick up the pieces that resulted. It was, of course, equally true that Indira Gandhi and the Congress would also not have dared to attack the right-wing parties and JP movement the way they did, if there was any possibility of the CPM or CPI, together or separately, gaining politically from the weakening of the right.

3 Popular Movements and Political Crisis

The economic and political crisis facing the nation turned into a virtual crisis of the political system with the two popular movements in Gujarat and Bihar against the faction-ridden Congress governments, dominated by those who had little authority or influence over the people or enjoying scant credibility even among their own followers. The leadership provided to the movement in Bihar by Jayaprakash Narayan (popularly known as JP) further deepened the political crisis.

I

Severe drought and the failure of two crops in succession had caused a rise of more than 100 per cent in the prices of foodgrains and cooking oil in Gujarat during 1973. In addition, a 60 per cent reduction in the central allocation of foodgrains to this deficit state had resulted in a sharp cut in supplies to ration shops and ration-card holders in the latter half of 1973. Even the foodgrains supplied were of poor quality and full of dust and small stones. Simultaneously, essential commodities started disappearing from the market. The people, in general, and students, in particular, whose hostel bills for bad quality food had increased by nearly 40 per cent in the month of December alone, blamed the price rise and the scarcity of essential goods on the collusion between traders, blackmarketeers and the politicians in power. Chief Minister Chimanbhai Patel was in particular accused of having entered into a deal with traders in groundnut oil by which they were allowed to increase oil prices in return for 'donations' of lakhs of rupees to party funds. Consequently, an intense and spontaneous political upheaval occurred in Gujarat in January 1974 when popular anger, building up over months and fanned by a perception of an inept, unresponsive and corrupt administration, now exploded across cities and towns of the state, taking the form of a violent student movement.

On 20 December 1973, students of the L.D. Engineering College, protesting against a substantial increase in mess charges, set fire to the college canteen and attacked the Rector's house. A fortnight later, on 3 January 1974, they went on a strike and destroyed college and hostel furniture. The police was brought in, and a large number of students were arrested and others beaten up. Incensed students of the university, colleges and high schools of Ahmedabad went on a strike demanding release of all those arrested, a reduction in mess charges, resignation of the minister of education, and arrest of the hoarders and blackmarketeers responsible for the rise in prices of essential goods. Broader issues like corruption, or other social evils, or changes in the structure of education or in the educational system were absent at this stage. To appease the students, the government released all those arrested but still it could not stem the rising tide of protest.

When the students gave a call for an Ahmedabad bandh on 10 January to protest against police brutality and price rise, it was supported by the opposition parties, a large number of Sarvodaya workers, the powerful college and school teachers' associations, white-collar employees of banks, insurance companies, and the city and state governments, and middle classes in general. Large-scale rioting followed. Soon the protest and attendant rioting spread to Baroda, Surat and nearly all the other towns and cities of the state, when student leaders gave a call for an indefinite strike in all schools and colleges of the state. Bandhs and dharnas occurred on a large scale with burning, looting of shops and rioting by mobs on one hand and excessive use of force by the authorities on the other.

On 11 January the students formed the Navnirman Yuvak Samiti (Youth Organization for Regeneration) with the objective of waging a non-violent struggle for students' demands and for purifying and rebuilding society. The movement now took a new turn. Escalating its demand, it now sought the resignation of the government, which had the support of 140 members in a house of 168, and the dissolution of the state assembly. By now the movement had acquired a strong popular base in urban areas and the support not only of the opposition parties but also of a large number of Congress workers and a section of the anti-Chimanbhai Congress faction. Finally, on 9 February, the central government was forced to ask the state government to resign and suspend, not dissolve, the state assembly, and President's rule was imposed. The students, however, with the active support of the Cong (O) and Jan Sangh, continued their agitation for another five weeks demanding the dissolution of the state assembly and fresh elections. It was at this stage, on 11 February, that Jayaprakash visited Ahmedabad. Lauding the students, he said that he was inspired by their movement and it 'should be an example for the youth in other parts of the country.'[2] He wrote a few months later: 'For years I was groping to find a way out. In fact, while my objectives have not changed I have all along been searching for the right way to achive it (sic. them) . . . Then I saw students in Gujarat bring about a big political change with the backing of the people and the moral support of Ravishankar Maharaj (Sarvodaya leader) and I knew that this was the way out.'[3] He advised the students to give up studies for a year, devote themselves to the eradication of corruption and work for a 'Youth Revolution'—an advice that students quietly ignored. The movement now entered its most violent phase. To quote Ghanshyam Shah: 'The riots continued in many cities and towns. Attempts were made to loot banks and cooperative societies. Stone-throwing incidents and looting and burning of public and private property continued on a large scale. Attempts were made to close the borders of the state, so that products of the state did not go out. Violence became widespread. Terror prevailed in the state and nobody could oppose the agitators.'[4] In addition, one of the tactics adopted by the agitators was to persuade or compel members of the assembly and municipal corporations of the big cities to resign. Many of them were *gheraoed*, noisy demonstrations organized in front of their houses, their houses attacked, their cars and other properties set on fire, several beaten up, and in general, terrorized into submitting their resignations. One Congress leader was stripped naked and forced to walk from village to village. The agitators were successful in their attempts for, apart from nearly all the opposition MLAs, about forty Congress MLAs and a large number of corporators were persuaded or coerced into resigning. Interestingly, the former chief minister, Chimanbhai Patel, against whom the entire agitation had been initiated, left the Congress, formed a party of his own and joined the chorus for the dissolution of the assembly.

The penultimate act of the Gujarat drama was played on 16 March when, faced with a continuing agitation and a fast unto death by Morarji Desai started on 11 March for dissolution of the assembly and fresh elections, Mrs Gandhi finally surrendered. She dissolved the assembly and announced elections would be held six months later, in September, when they were due in any case.

This scene was replayed on 6 April when Morarji Desai again went on an indefinite hunger strike. Despite her tough stand at the time against the JP movement in Bihar, discussed later, Mrs Gandhi again gave in, and advanced the elections in Gujarat to June, in peak summer, as demanded by Morarji—she was not willing to countenance death by fasting of a veteran Congress leader, her father's colleague as well as hers, and the most popular leader of Gujarat at the time.

The students now went back to their studies and the Navnirman Yuvak Samiti soon disintegrated and broke up into warring groups.

There were several significant features of the Gujarat students' agitation. For more than ten weeks most of Gujarat was in a state of near anarchy despite the state government supplementing its police force by calling in contingents of the Border Security Force, the Central Reserve Police, and in the end, even the Army. The agitation often turned violent leading to strikes, gheraos, bandhs and looting. The state police, pressed into service indiscriminately, retorted with excessive force, large-scale arrests and frequent recourse to lathi-charges and firing. In all, over a hundred persons were killed, over 3,000 injured and over 8,000 arrested.

Another feature of the agitation was that in the main it was confined to the disaffected urban middle classes and students. It was only after Chimanbhai Patel's resignation as chief minister that the rich and middle peasants and businessmen and industrialists extended it their support. Urban workers and the rural landless and the poor kept out of the agitation and in some areas even came into conflict with the agitators. According to Ghanshyam Shah, 'The urban factory workers and landless labourers felt that the agitation was really not for curbing the price-rise but was politically motivated and directed against the Congress which was sympathetic to the poor.'[5] At the same time, the agitation won the support of a large section of Gujarat's intelligentsia.

The Navnirman movement did not turn out to be an idealistic, not to speak of an incorruptible, revolutionary movement. We may sum up its character and political meaning in the words of Ghanshyam Shah who made a first-hand study of the Gujarat and Bihar movments at the time:[6]

> It was essentially an urban middle class agitation. Being unorganized and diffused in its interests, the middle class could not direct the agitation . . . On the one hand, it followed the organized interest groups and political parties, and, on the other, it also sometimes initiated *ad hoc* and impulsive programmes to ventilate their (its members') grievances against hawkers, milkmen, bus drivers, bus conductors, traders,

industrialists and politicians ... Students, one of the more organized sections of the middle class, spearheaded the agitation ... During the agitation, they felt a sense of power and self-importance. But they lacked direction, commitment and sense of purpose ... there were a few radical students who were the brain behind the agitation. In the course of the agitation, they were, however, isolated by the political parties and the rebellious students ... But because of their *ad hoc* approach, lack of organization and direction they merely became instruments of organized groups; they lost track of their own objectives ... Later on, after Chiman Patel's resignation, the Congress (O), Jan Sangh, Sarvodaya Mandal, businessmen, and rich peasants undermined the economic programmes of the agitation such as lowering of prices, and directed the agitation to political ends—mainly the dissolution of the State Assembly.

The Navnirman movement was, however, to become a model for similar agitations in other parts of the country in which popular discontent was to be harnessed by political opponents to demand dismissal of ministries and dissolution of elected legislatures, irrespective of constitutional niceties. The political significance of the movement was to go even deeper. As Francine Frankel has put it, 'The Gujarat uprising can be considered a political watershed. It marked the collapse of shared consensus on legitimate methods of conflict resolution between the government and opposition groups ... Each side became convinced that the other would no longer abide by the rules of democratic politics. Each side justified its own excesses in the name of safeguarding democracy from the assaults mounted on it by the other.'[7]

II

On the heels of the Gujarat agitation, and inspired by its success, an agitation on the same lines and with similar objectives was started by students in Bihar in March 1974.

For years, conditions were ripe for a mass movement in Bihar. Bihar was economically more backward and politically far worse governed as compared to Gujarat. There was absence of law and order and security for common people. Even the pretence of combating crime and corruption had been given up by the administration. People were badly affected by galloping prices, shortages of essential commodities and high unemployment and the rampant casteism, corruption and nepotism in administration and politics. Intense factionalism and internal feuds pervaded the ruling Congress. Bihar had had eleven Congress and opposition governments and three spells of President's rule in the seven years between March 1967 and March 1974. The people, in general, and the students and youth, in particular, felt that there was no other way to get grievances redressed than demonstrations, strikes, gheraos, bandhs and street violence. The students also believed, no doubt with enough justification, that the state's educational structure, from appointment of teachers and selection of textbooks to admissions and examinations, was riven with corruption.

Ever since 1956 Bihar had had a tradition of student protests, often resulting in clashes with the administration and rioting, over the usual issues of reduction of fees, right to organize student unions and judicial enquiry into police excesses. A new wave of student agitation started in early December 1973 in Patna and then spread to other towns. Following an anti-price rise bandh all over Bihar on 21 January 1974 by the non-Congress parties, a conference of more than 300 student leaders from colleges all over the state, organized by the Patna University Students Union and presided over by Laloo Prasad Yadav, set up on 18 February the Bihar Chhatra Sangharsh Samiti (BCSS). The objective of the Samiti was to wage a struggle for student demands which included the lowering of prices of foodgrains and other essential commodities, reduction in tuition fees and prices of textbooks, exercise books and cinema tickets, better hostel accommodation and better food in hostels, students' participation in university management, jobs for the educated unemployed, Bharatiya education, and action against hoarders, profiteers and blackmarketeers. Though the BCSS included the Samajvadi Yuva Jana Sabha (SYS) of the Samyukta Socialist Party, Sarvodayite Tarun Shanti Sena (TSS) and some non-party students, it excluded the Communist-led student organizations, and was from the beginning dominated by the Akhil Bharatiya Vidyarthi Parishad (ABVP). The leftist students refused to join the BCSS and organized the Bihar Chhatra Naujawan Sangharsh Morcha (BCNSM) which, however, soon faded from the scene.

Widespread student agitations, led by BCSS and BCNSM, started in middle March, often turning violent and clashing with the police sometimes leading to lathi-charges and firing. The BCSS now put forward twelve demands, eight pertaining to university affairs, and four of wider scope, dealing with corruption, high prices, unemployment and fundamental changes in the educational system. The Bihar students' movement attracted all-India attention when on 18 March, the BCSS organized a gherao of the governor and the assembly on its opening day for the failure of the education minister to reply to its memorandum of demands. The gherao, resisted by the police, led to large-scale violence and riots and arson in Patna. The police behaved with extreme brutality, and five people died in police firing. The events of the day have been described by Ghanshyam Shah as follows: 'Different groups adopted different methods: one mob set fire to government buildings, another looted posh hotels and godowns of the Food Corporation, yet another broke open six railway wagons and looted mustard and vegetable oil. A mob attacked newspaper officers, and set fire to the offices of the English daily *Searchlight* and the Hindi daily *Pradeep*, both housed in the same building . . . The city was under almost complete control of the mobs.'[8]

The agitation immediately spread to other Bihar towns. By 20 March, curfew had been imposed in eleven towns, where administration had been paralysed. The army and central police forces were called out in Patna and many other towns to contain violence and restore order. In one week about two dozen persons died, several hundred injured and many more arrested. In fact processions and demonstrations, gheraos and bandhs, and looting and burning, on the one hand, and police brutality and government incompetence in dealing with the situation, on the other hand, were to become a hallmark of the student agitation during the rest of the year. Bihar increasingly seemed overrun by chaos and anarchy and gave the appearance of a vast armed camp. Moreover, as in Gujarat, the opposition parties quickly joined forces with the students agitation and, in fact, took it over. They also added the demand for the resignation or dismissal of the state government and the dissolution of the assembly, holding the government responsible for the failure to maintain law and order on 18 March and, in general, for all the current evils including price rise, hoarding and blackmarketeering. This demand was adopted by students and was soon to supersede all economic and other demands. The agitation also now attracted the support of lawyers, doctors, teachers, shopkeepers and other sections of the urban middle classes.

III

A new dimension was added to the Bihar movement by Jayaprakash Narayan agreeing to take over the leadership of the student movement in April and lend it credence.

A major socialist leader of the freedom struggle, JP had retired from politics and devoted himself to leading the Bhoodan and Sarvodaya movements in Bihar. But with the disappointing outcome of the movements in bringing about a non-violent social revolution, or even land reforms, and the persistent feeling that they had reached a dead end by 1972, JP started looking for alternatives, taking greater interest in politics and preparing to re-enter it by opposing the ruling Congress party. Perhaps it can even be said that he had never really kept off politics and had 'struggled all his life (before, during and after his specific commitment to Sarvodaya) not just to express and embody, guru-like, an abstractly moral aspiration, but to intervene practically in the political process.'[9] According to one of his friendly biographers, he had already by 1967 'unmistakably returned to active politics.' After the 1967 elections, he had expressed gratification 'at the opposition's electoral success' and had, at the same time, 'continued to cultivate the regime, particularly Indira Gandhi.'[10] In May 1967, he actively campaigned for Zakir Husain as President. He also pleaded for the formation of a national coalition government. He intervened in the Hindi-English controversy and praised Indira Gandhi's 'firmness' in withstanding 'the opposition's onslaught'.[11] In 1969, he advised the central government to dismiss the Opposition-led Bihar government and impose President's rule instead. In the same year, he opposed bank nationalization as 'wrong and unwarranted'.[12] He also expressed himself against the 1969-split in the Congress party. Before the 1971 elections to the Lok Sabha, he had tried to unite the opposition parties, irrespective of ideology, in an anti-Congress, anti-Indira Gandhi front, primarily because of her electoral alliance with CPI.

In July 1972, in a press interview, JP expressed the fear that the danger of authoritarianism in the country was growing as power was getting concentrated in the prime minister's hands at a time when the opposition parties were weak.[13] In the same year, in a statement, he again said: 'In the name of socialism, a totalitarian State has been erected, with all economic power in the hands of the centre, and all its decisions dependent on the personal command of the Prime Minister.'[14] He also emphasized the need for a fundamental change in the electoral system which had brought Congress sweeping victories in 1971 and 1972. At the end of 1972, he persuaded a conclave of Sarvodaya workers to launch a new journal devoted to political commentaries. The journal, with JP as the chairman of the editorial board, made its appearance in July 1973 as *Everyman's Weekly*. It was to become the chief vehicle for his political-ideological views during 1974-75. In May and June 1973, he vehemently criticized Mrs Gandhi for supercession of three Supreme Court judges while making the appointment of the Chief Justice and added that the government was putting the judiciary's independence in jeopardy and thus threatening democracy itself. In June 1973, JP supported the efforts of J.B. Kripalani and several opposition leaders for the consolidation of the opposition parties ranging from the Jan Sangh to the Socialists and Swatantra party. He also set up 'Citizens for Democracy' for protecting citizens' rights and democratic institutions. He also unsuccessfully tried to bring together the opposition parties so that Congress could be faced with a credible Opposition.

Influenced by the worldwide student movements of the sixties, JP came to believe that the youth were to be the historical agents of social change in the country. In early December 1973, he wrote an open letter to the youth of the country urging them 'to enter the national arena', to bring into action 'Youth Power' by launching a Youth for Democracy movement to act as the watchdogs of democracy and to 'play a decisive role in establishing the primacy of the people and securing their victory over the power of money, falsehood and brute force.' He would leave it to the youth to decide 'what form their action should take.'[15] A few days later, on 29 December 1973, in the inaugural address to the all-India conference of the Radical Humanist Association, he criticized 'party democracy, that is democracy based on and manipulated by political parties', for being a 'most unsatisfactory and defective system of democracy.' Arguing that the people were 'fed up with all political parties and the present form and practice of democracy', he issued a call 'to the people, particularly to the youth . . . to build an alternative type and structure of democracy.' He also asserted that the time was ripe 'for a leap forward to a real people's democracy.' He asked the country's youth 'to seize this favourable opportunity and play the revolutionary role that the present age demands of them.'[16]

JP was to stress the revolutionary role of students and youth throughout 1974 and 1975 during his political campaign. For example, inaugurating the All India Youth Conference at Allahabad on 23 June 1974, he compared the Bihar struggle with the Bardoli struggle led by Sardar Patel, called upon the youth to be prepared to dedicate their lives, make all sacrifices for playing 'their historic role of spear-heading the revolution.'[17]

One of his major points of advice to students, to give up studies for a year to 'save democracy', was, however, aired earlier in the third week of December 1973 while addressing an ABVP meeting, and was again repeated on 22 January 1974. Later, in June 1974, he also asked the students to boycott the coming examinations.

Inspired and enthused by the Gujarat and Bihar student movements, Jayaprakash came to believe that, with people's disillusionment with Mrs Gandhi and the government, a revolutionary situation had arisen in Bihar and was building up in India as a whole, that only a spark was needed to ignite it, and that the student movement in Bihar would provide this. Throughout 1974 and 1975, he repeatedly expressed the sentiment that the country was ripe for a revolution and the movement that he was leading had the potential of becoming one. For example, addressing students at Kanpur on 3 February 1974, he said: 'The country is fast heading towards a new revolution. There is another 1942 movement in sight to change the course of history.'[18] In June-August, he repeatedly asserted: 'This is a revolutionary movement. Let there be no mistake about it. Do not think for a moment that the aims of eradicating corruption and unemployment, of bringing down prices and radical change in the system of education can be achieved without a social, economic, political, moral and cultural revolution.'[19] Similarly, on 25 November 1974, he told a conclave of opposition leaders, presided over by Charan Singh: 'The struggle in Bihar is not just a flash in the pan of history but a continuing process of revolutionary struggle. That is why I have called it a struggle for total revolution.'[20]

For several years JP had been talking about Total Revolution. He now believed that its moment had come, and the instruments for it were at hand. He was ready to guide this revolution and its vanguard, the students and youth. As his co-fighter and biographer wrote in 1975: 'Revolutions took their own time to mature he (i.e. JP) believed; they could not be created, but could perhaps be guided when the moment was ripe. And his instinct told him that this was the moment. In fact, his life seemed a preparation for this time.'[21] JP himself told the Patna rally on 5 June: 'Ever since I first gave the call of Youth for Democracy, I have been telling the youth that they should be their own leaders. I will only advise. But friends insisted that I should accept the burden of leadership . . . I accepted the task in all humility.'[22] Certainly, JP and some of his followers genuinely believed that in Bihar they were initiating the process of Total Revolution that would sweep the entire country and change not only the political system but the social system as a whole.

On 6 April, the president of the Patna University Students' Union and some other student leaders of the ABVP met JP and requested him to guide and assume the leadership of the student movement. While accepting their pleas, JP made it clear that he would be in full command of the movement: 'I won't agree to be a leader only in name.

I will take the advice of all, of the students, the people, the Jana Sangharsh Samitis. But the decisions will be mine and you will have to accept them.'[23] He also declared his revolutionary intent. While announcing that he had no interest in changing the government for that would be 'like replacing Tweedledum with Tweedledee', he said, 'I have decided to fight corruption and misgovernment and blackmarketing, profiteering and hoarding, to fight for the overhaul of the educational system, and for a real people's democracy . . . This is not meant as a threat, but as a friendly warning. That shall be the beginning. The rest will follow.'[24] He advised the students to carry out their struggle in a peaceful manner, to function in a politically non-partisan manner and not to get involved in the game of toppling governments—this last piece of advice would be ignored by the students and even him almost immediately. From now on the students' movement in Bihar, as also its wider all-India extension, came to be generally known as the JP movement (JPM).

To start off the process of Total Revolution, on 8 April JP led a silent procession in Patna to protest against the police excesses of the previous three weeks. To demonstrate its non-violent character, those participating bound their mouths with strips of cloth. At a large public meeting at Patna the next day, JP declared that 'for 27 years I have watched events unfold, but I can stand on the sidelines no longer. I have vowed not to allow this state of things to continue' and call for a moral revolution in the country and a 'struggle against the very system which has compelled almost everybody to go corrupt.'[25] This was followed by a five-week long programme of dharnas, more silent processions, observation of black days and so on. Also the demands of the protest movements were widened to include the dissolution of the elected Bihar assembly. JP wholeheartedly endorsed these demands, the last one explicitly on 23 April, when he asked the students, youth and Sarvodaya workers to collect ten million voters' signatures supporting this demand. An important change in the movement occurred at this time when CPI and CPM and the trade unions under their influence withdrew from the movement.

The main objectives of the JP movement related at this time to all-round changes in the pattern of education, elimination of corruption in the government, checking the moral decline in public life, arousing public opinion against corrupt ministers and legislators, saving democracy from authoritarian trends, ushering in of basic electoral reforms to ensure fair, free and inexpensive elections and the elected legislators reflected the will of the people, and in general, building up of 'people's power'. Of course, the ultimate objective of the movement was to bring in Total Revolution. As JP was to put it on 5 June: 'Friends, this is a revolution, a total revolution. This is not a movement merely for the dissolution of the Assembly. We have to go far, very far.'[26] By now he was also convinced that the Bihar government and assembly were a major obstacle in the path of the success of the revolutionary movement. He had also no doubt that however long it might take the Bihar movement would result in a Total Revolution. He asked the students to put moral pressure on the existing legislators, through measures such as peaceful demonstrations, gheraos of their houses, to resign. Later, he gave a call to the students and the people to paralyse the government at every level, close the universities and colleges, including medical and engineering colleges, for a year, gherao the state assembly and government offices, and set up parallel governments all over the state. He appealed to the teachers to use the one year of forced leisure to draw up a new revolutionary programme of education. In order to paralyse the government, in July, JP asked the people not to pay land revenue and other taxes.

As organs of struggle, Chhatra Sangharsh Samitis (CSS) (Students Struggle Committees) were to be formed in every college and high school, and Jana Sangharsh Samitis (JSS) (People's Struggle Committees) in every village and town from the panchayat to the district level. They were in turn to set up Janata Sarkars (People's Governments) from village to the bloc and district level. The Janata Sarkars would be elected indirectly except at the primary village level. Their main functions would be to prevent crime and maintain peace, adjudicate disputes outside the framework of the police and the courts, check blackmarketing and hoarding and irregularities at ration shops, distribute essential commodities at fair prices, distribute *bhoodan* land among the landless and ensure implementation of land ceiling laws, fight against social evils such as dowry system and caste oppression, and ensure equal treatment to Harijans. In general, the Janata Sarkars were to be the 'permanent organs of people's power', through which people would 'develop their own power to become guardians of democracy.'[27] To strengthen democracy at the grassroots, the Samitis would also select the candidates for most of the seats in the assembly elections whenever they were held. For the remaining seats, the opposition parties would have to agree among themselves and set up only one candidate per constituency.

The programme of the Janata Sarkars never really took off. They remained 'embryonic or just conceptual.'[28] After one year, by May 1975, the Janata Sarkars were formed in only 20 out of 587 blocs. Even in the few places where they actually existed they tended to be dominated by the upper strata of rural society and became inoperative soon after their formation. Nor did the reformist, redistributive, anti-corruption and anti-blackmarketing parts of the JPM's programme take off or make much of a headway. Most of them remained non-starters, and the Total Revolution a distant goal. Very soon, the primary objective of the entire mass movement narrowed down to changing the Bihar government and the dissolution of Bihar assembly because of its 'anti-people and corrupt character'. By the end of September 1974, JP himself was to admit that 'the exigencies of the struggle have so dictated [the movement] that resignation of the Bihar Ministry and dissolution of the State Legislative Assembly have become its immediate goals. The offensive to begin from 2 October is meant to achieve these immediate goals after which it would be possible for the students and the people to concentrate on the long-term ends of the struggle.'[29]

Between March and November 1974, the JPM was characterized by almost continuous satyagraha campaigns, state and local bandhs, gheraos of government offices and ministers' and MLAs' houses, and massive meetings, processions and demonstrations in Patna and other towns and cities of Bihar, demanding dissolution of the assembly. Most of the campaigns paralysed the state administration, especially at the district and subdivisional level, and tended to become violent despite JP's repeated exhortations to adopt peaceful methods and eschew violence. Gheraos in particular often led to confrontation of the demonstrators with the police. At its different stages, the JPM also got the support of a large number of Bihar's intellectuals—poets, painters, academics and professionals. Two well-known Bihar writers, the poet Nagarjun and the novelist Phanishwar Nath Renu, returned the awards and pensions granted to them by the government.

On 8 April, JP led the silent peaceful procession, as mentioned earlier. On 12 April, there was a 'paralyse the government' demonstration in Gaya where police firing led to the death of eight people. On 5 June, there was a half-million-strong march on the Raj Bhawan (Governor's residence) in Patna under JP's leadership demanding resignation of the Ghafoor ministry and the dissolution of the assembly. The same evening, at a mammoth public meeting at Patna, JP called for a Total Revolution. There was a prolonged *dharna* or *satyagraha* campaign at the gates of the assembly from 7 June to 12 July, when batches of *satyagrahis* tried to prevent the MLAs from attending the assembly. On

13 July, there was a massive student demonstration in front of the Raj Bhawan demanding closure of all colleges and universities in Bihar for one year. JP led a satyagraha before the secretariat building on 3 and 4 October. To force the dissolution of the assembly, he also called a three-day Bihar bandh which was to paralyse life all over Bihar. To achieve this, the running of all trains was to be stopped during the three days of the bandh.

JP held another large rally in Patna on 10 October where he declared that if the assembly was not dissolved he would hold elections for a 'People's Assembly' and thus establish a parallel government. He also announced a 24-hour gherao of the secretariat and the residences of legislators and ministers on 4 November to compel the ministers and MLAs to resign, a no-tax campaign beginning on that day and the initiation of a programme to completely paralyse the functioning of the government throughout the state and at every level from the block to the district. For the first time he also called upon Mrs Gandhi to resign, though increasingly he had been sharpening his attack on her. Addressing the mass rally on 10 October, he said: 'The people have given their verdict. At least 95 per cent of the people of Bihar have unmistakably demanded that the present Ministry and Assembly in the State must go. If the Prime Minister refuses to see the reality, I say it with full responsibility that she should quit her post, she is unfit to be the Prime Minister of a great country.'[30] On 17 October, he specifically announced that his objective was the removal of Indira Gandhi from office. On 4 November, JP led a 20,000-strong procession to the secretariat to gherao the ministers and demand resignation from them. In a lathi-charge, JP received a lathi blow and would have been seriously hurt if others had not intervened and physically protected him. He now gave another call for Patna bandh on 6 November.

For the organization of the protest movements, JP relied on the Bihar Chhatra Sangharsh Samiti (BCSS) and the local, village, town and city level Chhatra Sangharsh Samitis (CSSs) which were to be directed by the BCSS. Both the BCSS and CSSs were beset with internal quarrels over leadership and direction, especially between RSS-ABVP and non-RSS-ABVP youth. JP also formed at the outset of his campaign the Bihar Jana Sangharsh Samiti (BJSS) as a non-student organization but it remained inactive. Jana Sangharsh Samitis (JSSs) were formed in most of the towns and some villages, 'but they were paper organizations.'[31] Moreover, as Bhola Chatterji, JP's friend, admirer, and critic, has remarked: 'As for the so-called student-youth struggle committees, they were just so many collections of adolescents who could hardly be relied upon to work his will.'[32]

We may end this part of the discussion with three sets of critical observations on the Bihar movement made by Ghanshyam Shah, who has made the only first-hand study of the movement.

Firstly,[33]

> between the issues that were taken up from time to time and the professed objective of the movement there was often no perceptible connection. Not all the programmes, lopsided as they were, were well received by the followers. Some programmes were announced for their publicity value, and there they remained; some did not get off the ground, and some fizzled out soon after they were launched; only mobilizing programmes of processions, demonstrations and meetings demanding the dissolution of the Assembly were taken up enthusiastically by the leading elements of the movement.

Secondly,[34]

> the movement was not broad-based; it was confined to certain areas of the state and certain sections of society. The urban middle class and students who were active in the pre-March 1974 agitations continued to remain active in the movement. Two groups entered the movement after 18 March: businessmen and rich and neo-rich farmers. Businessmen were against the agitation in February and March because students were engaged in bringing down prices and unearthing hoarded stocks. They started supporting the movement when it took a political turn. The farmers had already been agitating against the government, demanding more agricultural facilities and higher prices for their products; they were thus predisposed to make common cause with the movement directed against the government. Industrial workers, who had joined hands with the middle class in January 1974, kept aloof from the movement. The movement failed to draw in poor peasants, agricultural labourers and casual labourers.' It must, however, be noted that the movement evoked a degree of sympathy from the latter as it represented 'the common man's frustrations and silent anger.

Thirdly,[35]

> the non-communist political parties and Sarvodaya organizations became, officially or unofficially, the constituent

partners of the movement; the Jan Sangh and its student wing, the ABVP, came to occupy a dominant position in the movement, with the Sarvodaya workers trying to check them . . . The leaders of the ABVP made every attempt to dominate the CSSs (Chhatra Sangharsh Samitis) by giving key positions to the cadre of Rashtriya Swayam Sevak Sangh (RSS) . . . The TSS (Tarun Shanti Sena) and SYS (Samajwadi Yuvajan Sabha) worked as a counterforce to the ABVP, and tried to isolate the ABVP, RSS and Jan Sangh boys. At some places the rivalry went to such an extent that parallel CSSs came into existence.

ABVP also occupied a dominant position in the Bihar Chhatra Sangharsh Samiti, having eight out of its twenty-four members; eleven others belonged to other organized political parties, only five were non-party student leaders.

IV

An important feature of the situation was the firm refusal of Mrs Gandhi to give way to the JP movement and concede the demand for the dismissal of the state government and dissolution of the assembly in Bihar as she had done in the case of Gujarat. She had been taken by surprise by the sudden developments in Gujarat. Also she had assumed that the agitation there was a localized affair. But now that Gujarat had been followed by the Bihar agitation she realized that surrender in Bihar was likely to set off a chain reaction in other states and, in the end, threaten her position through a domino effect. In fact, she now came to believe that the real and ultimate target of the Bihar agitation was her government at the Centre. In an interview to the *Blitz* in December 1974 she said: 'From the very beginning we have known that this movement was aimed at the Central Government and at me.'[36]

There is also no doubt that, as Bhola Chatterji was to point out, 'the range and content of the movement was widened to the extent that the authority was left the only option of either capitulation to or total confrontation with Jayaprakash.'[37] Mrs Gandhi also believed that having secured political power through democratic and constitutional means she had every right to continue to be in power—and that this logic also applied to the Bihar government and legislature. She also held that, despite the many weaknesses and failures, the many electoral malpractices and the prevailing large-scale political and administrative corruption, the existing political system as it had evolved since 1950 on the basis of the Constitution could not be said to have failed. 'So far,

I see no better alternative', she told *Blitz*. Regarding the electoral system, she agreed that electoral malpractices and the massive use of money power in elections had led to distortions that should be curbed, but, at the same time, she argued that it was basically a sound system. In any case, whatever changes were needed—and some basic changes in educational, administrative and legal structures were due—had to come through discussion, not agitation. Negotiations were, therefore, possible on the content of the needed changes and the methods of bringing them about. Compromise and consensus were a normal way of dealing with political differences and confrontation, but not if political power as such was threatened, as by Jayaprakash especially after he joined forces with opposition parties first in Bihar and then at the all-India level.[38]

V

Having reached an impasse on the question of the dissolution of the Bihar assembly, Jayaprakash felt that to exert adequate pressure on the central government it was necessary to widen the base of the movement beyond Bihar's borders to the entire country, by uniting all political parties other than the Congress and CPI and persuading them to take up its programme. His first effort in this direction was unsuccessful. In April 1974, he formed the non-party 'Citizens for Democracy' in Delhi, with himself as its president, to work for free and fair elections and to defend democracy, in general, and the freedom of the Press and the judiciary, in particular. The Citizens for Democracy was, however, stillborn. More successful was JP's other approach, when from June 1974 onwards, he repeatedly toured the country, addressing large and receptive crowds, especially in Delhi and other parts of North India which were Jan Sangh or Socialist party strongholds. Drawing the attention of the people to the Bihar movement, its genesis and its revolutionary objectives, in his speeches he often compared it to the Bardoli Satyagraha of 1928, Mahatma Gandhi's Dandi March of 1930, and the Quit India movement of 1942 and predicted that a revolution was taking place in Bihar. In the *Everyman's* of 21 September, he declared: 'The Bihar struggle is no longer a State issue. It has acquired an all-India importance and the country's fate has come to be bound up with its success or failure.'[39] Everywhere, he asked the students to boycott colleges and universities for one year and to serve the people instead.

The movement acquired a certain sweep and strength and attracted wide support from students, the middle classes, traders, and a section of the intelligentsia. It also got the backing of nearly all the non-left political parties and groups, consisting of such disparate political formations as the RSS, Jan Sangh, Anand Marg, Congress (O), BLD (which later came to include Swatantra party), DMK, Akali Dal, SSP and Naxalites. The political fortunes and morale of these parties and groups were at a low ebb since their electoral rout in 1971. In early 1974, they had failed to capitalize on popular discontent in the UP assembly elections. Despite JP's non-party approach and his slogan of Total Revolution, these political formations saw in him, what they most needed, a popular leader or rather a popular and respectable figurehead who would enable them to acquire the much-needed credibility as an alternative to the Congress and provide them with a short cut to power, a task in which they had failed miserably in 1971 and 1972 as also in the UP elections. Moreover, as JP shunned political power, he would not stand in the way of these leaders acquiring and wielding it. JP could also act as a cementing force in keeping together the otherwise mutually incompatible national and regional parties. These parties therefore enthusiastically decided to climb onto his bandwagon.

As brought out at greater length in Chapter 6, JP in turn realized that without the organizational structures and cadres and workers of the opposition parties he could not hope to face Mrs Gandhi and Congress at the all-India level, in the streets or at the polls. Of course, JP did not just fail to keep the opposition parties away; he actively joined forces with them. He also overlooked the fact that a combination of such right-wing parties as the Jan Sangh and Congress (O), BLD and Akali Dal could hardly contain any potential of forming a revolutionary force working for Total Revolution. But more on this aspect in Chapter 6.

JP and the opposition parties made all-out efforts to initiate Gujarat—and Bihar-type agitations in other states of India. In UP, JP himself helped in the organization of student, youth and people's struggle committees with a comprehensive programme of agitation.

VI

A significant development for the Bihar movement was the emergence of a serious rift within the Sarvodaya movement, and between Vinoba Bhave and JP over the goals, methods and direction of the movement. A large number of Sarvodaya workers—in fact the majority of those in Bihar—took up active leadership of the movement in Bihar. On the other hand, Vinoba Bhave and some members of the Sarva Seva Sangh, supported by him, disapproved of JP's and other Sarvodaya workers' active involvement in politics (they saw any involvement in politics as opposed to Sarvodaya principles) and in the Bihar movement, their support for the demand for the resignation of the Bihar ministry and dissolution of the Bihar assembly, their participation in elections, their anti-Indira campaign and their association with the Jan Sangh and other political parties. They were also critical of the use of 'non-violent direct action' as manifested in the coercive methods of dharna and gherao, often leading to violence. Such satyagraha, as a political weapon, they said, was not suited to nor desirable in an independent and democratic India. In other words, they felt the Bihar movement and its outlook and methods were opposed to their philosophy, would bear no positive results and would harm the Sarvodaya movement. Vinoba Bhave also felt that problems such as corruption, price rise and electoral malpractices could not be effectively tackled through satyagraha or dissolution of assemblies.[40] Vinoba, in fact, for long had a soft corner for Mrs Gandhi, feeling that her views were close to his own. He wanted the Sarvodaya movement to follow, at least, a policy of neutrality towards the Congress. He also told JP 'that with America arming Pakistan again and China also helping . . . there was a possibility of a conflict with Pakistan and so a struggle against the government would weaken the country and therefore a struggle against the government was not advisable.'[41] He also felt uneasy about the JPM. He believed that the Sarvodaya workers and JP did not have the strength and capacity to control an agitation like that in Bihar. How did the agitation begin in Bihar, he asked in June 1974 and then answered. 'With looting and arson. Do you have the capacity to check that? You could perhaps check it if you took a small district and started action.'[42] He also predicted that nothing would come of the Bihar agitation. Bhave, therefore, tried to dissuade JP from continuing the movement or at least from extending its scope beyond Bihar.

JP, on the other hand, was not willing to accept any of this critique and a substantial majority of the Sarvodaya workers and members of the Sarva Seva Sangh supported him. Some even suggested that Vinoba Bhave was tied to the apron strings of the government and criticized him for having 'discarded Satyagraha as a means for effecting social change'.[43] In the end, the Sarvodaya workers agreed to disagree; individual Sarvodaya workers were given the freedom to act as their conscience dictated. In the long run, however, the Sarvodaya movement was a major victim of the conflict between the JP movement and the Congress and Mrs Gandhi. While all others involved in the conflict, including JP, Mrs Gandhi and the Jan Sangh-RSS survived, the Sarvodaya movement suffered a death blow; since then it faced near-extinction.

VII

Though Jayaprakash retained much of his popularity, the Bihar movement gradually lost its spontaneity as well as appeal by the end of 1974 and had begun to stagnate and even decline. Even the Press, almost unanimously favourable to the JPM, seemed to agree that by the end of 1974 it 'was a spent force'. It had also failed to establish itself outside Bihar. The 4 November gherao of the Bihar assembly can be seen as the last major attempt to give the movement in Bihar a renewed momentum. There were hardly any bandhs, gheraos or even demonstrations after November. Bihar reverted to normalcy. Even before November, Arvind Narain Das had reported in the *Economic and Political Weekly*, 'the youth of the towns of Bihar turned its mind away from the agitation and got down seriously to organizing Durga Puja.'[44]

Grassroots organizations such as Janata Sarkars and Chhatra and Yuva Sangharsh Samitis remained anaemic. The activists involved in these organizations and, in fact, in the movement as a whole, were losing their commitment and enthusiasm and their moral halo was getting dim. Student interest and involvement, never very intense except in demonstrations, bandhs and gheraos, proved to be ephemeral, as it was bound to, and waned as students lost their enthusiasm and even the activists among them tended to become politically passive. By the end of 1974, most of JP's student followers had gone back to their classes, ignoring his advice to devote a whole year to taking the movement to the villages and helping restructure rural society. In any case, even in their most enthusiastic phase, most of them had refused to go to the villages, and the few who had done so had returned very soon to take part in the more exhilarating urban activities. As Ghanshyam Shah has pointed out: 'In response to Jayaprakash's appeal to visit villages and educate the voters, some students from different parts of the state visited villages in July and August 1974. But after a week or so they returned home and resumed their studies. They complained that they did not have any concrete programme for sustained work.'[45] When the colleges reopened on 18 July, after a long recess of four months and examinations were held, students rejoined in large numbers. They also ignored JP's advice to boycott the examinations and less than 10 per cent of them abstained. Medical and engineering students had never joined the movement. According to Shah, even at the height of the movement during the famous 3-day Bihar bandh from 3 to 5 October, examinees at different examination centres had turned up as usual.[46] By

November Jayaprakash was forced to scale down his demands on the students. He now gave them the option of devoting an entire year to the movement or of continuing their studies even during the movement but devoting one day in a week to it. But these concessions did not improve matters. Only 300 of the 13,000 students of the Patna University opted for the first option and 2,500 for the second. As Minoo Masani pointed out, 'this was certainly a setback for the movement.'[47] Similarly, when JP called for 5,000 volunteers to become 'total revolutionaries', few responded.

Even more important was the fact that not only the students had lost their enthusiasm but their lustre and credibility in the public eye had also begun to fade. To quote Ghanshyam Shah again: 'Several respondents, including Sarvodaya workers, reported to me that students were irresponsible and corrupt.'[48]

Unlike in Gujarat, in Bihar the campaign to persuade or pressurise the MLAs to resign also turned out to be disappointing. Even the opposition MLAs were reluctant to oblige. Only 38 of the 88 opposition MLAs and in all 42 out of a total of 318 MLAs resigned. What was worse, some of the Harijan and tribal MLAs, who had resigned, took back their resignations, alleging that they had been forced to do so. All the opposition parties, including even the Jan Sangh, got split on the question.

The processions and demonstrations were also becoming fewer and smaller, and the bandhs and gheraos less in frequency as also intensity. Jayaprakash made efforts to give the movement a shot in the arm by raising it to higher levels, by giving calls for a no-tax campaign, boycott of liquor shops, setting up of Janata Sarkars and holding of elections for a 'people's assembly' in Bihar. But there was hardly any response to any of these calls or exhortations.

Of course, there was nothing surprising about the movement declining after a few months. This was inevitable, for a popular movement like the JPM could not be carried on for a long time at a fever pitch, especially when it was opposed resolutely by a duly-elected government with a solid majority in the state legislature and in the Lok Sabha at the Centre. What was surprising was Jayaprakash's belief that he could do so. Perhaps, this only showed up his inexperience as a leader of mass movements, despite his long innings in Indian politics.

The response to the JPM in other regions was also disappointing. The movement remained in essence a Bihar movement. It failed to consolidate itself as a strong national alternative to the Congress. Nowhere else in the country had it the same freshness and spontaneity as when it began in Bihar. Moreover, in the country as a whole, including Gujarat and even in Bihar, the movement had remained confined to the urban areas and the middle classes. It had failed to affect the rural areas or to attract the rural and urban poor, the working class, the Harijans and Muslim and Christian minorities. Also, few in the country believed the charge that Indira Gandhi was subverting political institutions and destroying democracy. Of course, few gave credence to a similar charge by Indira Gandhi against Jayaprakash. In any case, Indira Gandhi still remained popular especially among the poor, women and minorities, though her popularity was certainly dented.

In the meanwhile, the economic situation in the country had begun to improve appreciably, in part because of the anti-inflationary policies adopted by the government. By October prices had begun to fall and supplies of essential commodities had begun to improve. Also the government undertook stern and much publicized action against hoarders and smugglers. The political situation even in Bihar had been gradually defused and was no longer unmanageable, though it still called for corrective policies and administrative steps—as it does even today! Most people in the country also came to believe that Jayaprakash and the agglomerate of parties he was leading provided no alternative to the existing government.

The JP movement had also failed to garner enough support on the left. As pointed out earlier, the two major parties, the CPI and CPM, and their trade unions had already by the middle of April withdrawn support from the movement even in Bihar, and neither of the two joined it later. The CPI, which had a significant political base in Bihar, was firmly opposed to the JPM and was, in fact, leading regular campaigns against it both in Bihar and the rest of the country, portraying it as the representation of 'forces of reaction and counter-revolution and of being 'a typical fascist mass movement designed to destroy elected assemblies, subvert parliamentary democracy and create a constitutional crisis.'[49] On 3 June 1974, it organized a massive march of peasants, workers, students and government employees in Patna and presented a memorandum to the Governor opposing the demand for the dissolution of the state assembly. It put forth its own charter of demands against high prices, blackmarketing and hoarding and for government takeover of wholesale trade in essential commodities, increased wages for agricultural labourers, and measures for weeding out corruption in administration. On 11 November, it organized another 'anti-fascist' and 'defeat rightist plot', mammoth demonstration and mass meeting to expose the JPM. After 12 June, it asked Mrs Gandhi not to resign under the pressure of right-wing forces and offered its full support to her. It wanted the left parties and the 'left and democratic elements in Congress' 'to adopt a friendly approach towards one another, to open dialogue and to come together on platforms and in action'.[50] It believed that, by extending support to Mrs Gandhi, it could shift Indian politics to the left.

The CPM, divided in its understanding of the JPM, sat on the fence and adopted an ambiguous attitude towards it. Having faced repression in West Bengal since 1967 and large-scale rigging in the state elections of 1972, it agreed with JP's critique of the Congress and Mrs Gandhi and branded the latter as 'the fountain-head of reaction' and as semi-fascist. It supported the campaign for the dismissal of the Bihar ministry and the dissolution of the assembly. It condemned the repressive measures of the government against the Bihar movement and urged JP to place alternative, concrete economic and political policies and programme before the people, to mobilize and lead the masses into action around their immediate implementation and to break links with the Jan Sangh and right-wing parties. It vehemently criticized the CPI for supporting the Congress government and opposing the JPM. Initially, for some time, the central leadership of the party thought of forging links with the JPM with a view to radicalize it and of organizing joint actions and joint action committees with all the opposition parties, including the Jan Sangh. But, after some time, it decided not to associate with the JPM or its action-programmes such as those of 5 June, 3 to 5 October, 4 November 1974 and 6 March 1975 because of JP's alliance with communal parties such as the Jan Sangh and Anand Marg and other right-wing parties and reactionary forces, who were seen as diverting mass discontent in wrong directions and increasing their hold over the movement. The CPM was also critical of the movement for its failure to reach out to the working class, poor peasants and agricultural labourers. All the same, it did not believe that the JPM or the Jan Sangh were capable of implanting fascism in India. It agreed to keep in touch with JP and to support the JPM from outside on specific issues. For example, the General Secretary of the party, P. Sundarayya, and its Political Bureau member, Promode Dasgupta, signed a joint statement with JP and the socialist leader Madhu Dandavate, on 18 September 1974, agreeing to 'have frequent consultations among ourselves to radicalize and intensify the movement in Bihar while adhering to our respective ideological stances.'[51]

After 12 June, the CPM supported the demand for Mrs Gandhi's resignation but would not join the Opposition's campaign for the same. One of its parliamentary leaders, Jyotirmoy Bosu, attended the Janata Front meetings on 22 and 25 June though without making any commitment on behalf of the party. The party also announced that in case of elections it would fight them on its own without any all-India alliance with JP-led parties. In the long-run, however, because of differences in the leadership between those favouring an anti-Indira front, including parties like the Jan Sangh, and giving it a leftward turn and those opposing such a front, the CPM gradually reduced itself to a state of political indecisiveness and passivity.

Several Naxalite groups supported the JP movement but their association with it was not fully welcomed by JP and his associated parties because of their reliance on violence as the favoured mode of politics. The Naxalite groups too were unhappy with JP's alliance with the Jan Sangh and right-wing parties such as the Congress (O), and some of them later withdrew their support to the JPM.

VIII

Many of JP's friends and Indira Gandhi's advisers thought that the issues raised by the JP movement could be resolved through rapprochement between the two sides. By September-October 1974, JP's friends could see that the JPM had reached a dead-end. JP's hope that under the pressure of the movement the Congress party would split or, even better, force a change in its leadership was nowhere near realization. Instead, it was the JP movement that was flagging. The one way out, therefore, was an adjustment between JP and Indira Gandhi which, some believed, was still possible. For example, JP's close friend and confidant and Indira Gandhi's vehement critic, Minoo Masani, wrote as late as March 1975: 'Despite all the current talk of "fascism", the rule of law, by and large, still prevails and a dialogue is possible.' Masani added: 'In this context, it is a pity that terms like fascism should be bandied about. It is, of course, idiotic to describe Jayaprakash as a fascist . . . On the other hand, can one call the Prime Minister and her government fascist? If they really were, would Jayaprakash be alive and functioning, would the great march in Delhi of 6 March have passed off so peacefully and successfully, and would not a great deal in India be different from what it is?' In fact, he went so far as to hope: 'Would not then sharing power with Jayaprakash, a comrade in the struggle for independence and a friend of her father's, be a much more attractive alternative, whether from the national or personal point of view?'[52]

Indira Gandhi too was aware of the popularity of Jayaprakash and the people's anger at high prices, scarcity of essential commodities and the high level of corruption in politics and administration. She also knew that an important section of the Congress organization and parliamentary party favoured a dialogue and compromise with JP. For example, the Young Turk leader and ex-socialist Chandra Shekhar related later how he 'pleaded with Mrs Indira Gandhi time and again' that the two should meet, discuss and resolve their differences, so as to combine their energies. He had argued that 'with the political power Mrs Gandhi enjoyed and the moral power Jayaprakash possessed both should unite to lift the country out of the morass.'[53]

Mrs Gandhi made several informal contacts with JP through various channels including through her principal secretary, P.N. Dhar, and the old socialist leader and comrade of JP, Achyut Patwardhan, but with little result. She tried to find out what JP wanted the government to do concretely regarding corruption, high prices, economic policies, electoral reform, threats to democracy, and the like. JP, on the other hand, was keen on getting his main demand, that is, the dissolution of the Bihar assembly, accepted. He had no other concrete demand, nor did he know what the other terms of a compromise would or could be.

Indira Gandhi, on the other hand, was convinced that the JP movement would lead to anarchy and political instability and that JP was working under the influence of the forces of reaction and 'outside forces'. But above all, she believed that JP was personally hostile to her, had been jealous of Nehru, and resented the fact of not becoming the prime minister. She told Pupul Jayakar later in July 1975: 'Jayaprakash and Morarjibhai have always hated me . . . Jayaprakash has always resented my being Prime Minister.'[54] As an example of this hostility, she was later to point to JP and other JPM leaders judging people according to their proximity to her: 'When they know that somebody is with me, the attack is on that person and when the same person is not with me, he becomes perfectly good and honourable and independent-minded.'[55] Mrs Gandhi also accused JP of being a hypocrite, albeit an unconscious one: 'Why does he refuse to accept that he has never ceased to be a politician and desires to be the Prime Minister?'[56] She was also to write on similar lines to Fiori Nehru, B.K. Nehru's wife: 'It is nonsense to say that he did not want office. One part of him did, very much so . . .'[57]

It seems that apart from mutual distrust, their personality traits and ego clashes lay behind the failure of Indira Gandhi and JP to come together. For example, in 1971, despite taking a common stand on the

Bangladesh problem, the two drifted apart when dealing with it. In an outburst, JP told his socialist comrade Ganga Saran Sinha at the time: 'What does Indira think of herself? Does she think she can ignore me? I have seen her as a child in frocks';[58] while Indira Gandhi complained to Pupul Jayakar: 'Jayaprakash has never taken me seriously.'[59] Ganga Saran Sinha, who was a close friend of both, commented at the time: 'I have always felt that from that time Jayaprakash and Indiraji did not trust each other politically.'[60]

Similarly, referring to the failure of his attempt in 1974 at rapprochement between Jayaprakash and Indira Gandhi on policy matters, P.N. Dhar refers to 'the discovery of the real reason for JP's displeasure with her.' He quotes Sugata Dasgupta, Director of Gandhian Institute of Studies, Varanasi, one of the intermediaries he used, telling him: 'Frankly speaking, these policy questions are secondary matters. My advice to you is, *un ko kuch maan deejiye* (he should be shown some reverence).'[61] Continuing, Dhar writes: 'According to Dasgupta and Radhakrishnan (of the Gandhi Peace Foundation and the other intermediary, B.C.), JP expected that, after she became prime minister, Indira Gandhi would establish with him the same sort of relationship that her father had with Mahatma Gandhi.'[62] Similarly, Minoo Masani concludes his *Is JP the Answer*?, published before June 1975, with the wish: 'If [only] Indira Gandhi were to invite Jayaprakash's *guidance* and *advice* in solving the country's problems and join with him in a campaign for creating a more prosperous, healthier and happier India.'[63] (Emphasis added) Indira Gandhi, on the other hand, would not accept JP as a guide.

Certain personality traits of JP and Indira Gandhi too militated against a compromise between the two. Indira Gandhi was self-consciously decisive and ruthless; JP was indecisive to the extreme. Indira Gandhi told Pupul Jayakar in 1971: Jayaprakash 'does not understand that, for action to be potent, time is of the essence . . . One has to be really ruthless if the need arises. I am ruthless for what I think right. The difficulty is I move.'[64] JP was more often than not unable to make up his mind. He was vacillating and invariably hesitated to decide. Even in the thirties, he was jibed in the Congress Socialist Party circles as: '*Yeh bhi theek hai, woh bhi theek hai, main kya karoon*?'[65] (This is correct, that is also correct, what should I do?) And when he did take a decision, he adopted rigid positions. Achyut Patwardhan told the author in 1984 that JP's indecisiveness was responsible for the failure of his attempt to mediate between JP and Indira Gandhi, and that just when an agreement had been arrived at, JP vacillated and did not put the final seal of endorsement on it.[66]

As a final attempt to arrive at a mutual understanding, JP and Indira Gandhi decided to meet face to face. At this 1 November meeting it became apparent that there was really no common ground between them. Though willing to discuss such issues as electoral reform and corruption and also to agree to the dismissal of the Bihar ministry and the suspension of the Bihar assembly, if assured of no similar demand in other states, she was adamant about not dissolving it.[67] This was JP's main operational demand and he would not give it up, nor would he give the assurance that Indira Gandhi wanted. The meeting, therefore, proved to be a complete fiasco.

IX

Indira Gandhi now decided to take on the JP movement as a challenge which she had to meet politically, through a broader political strategy. To mobilize the party ideologically and organizationally, the All India Congress Committee organized in late November a three-day camp at Narora, a village in western UP, that was attended by Mrs Gandhi and other major Congress leaders. To those who still urged her to negotiate with JP, she countered: 'I do not understand what "negotiations" mean. What do you negotiate about? How to destroy democracy? Is this negotiable? . . . The other main point is to "remove Indira Gandhi". How can I negotiate about that? There is no other point.'[68]

Denouncing the JP movement for trying to change the government through unconstitutional means and declaring that she made a mistake in dissolving the Gujarat assembly, Indira Gandhi challenged JP to test her government's legitimacy and his popular support in Bihar, as also throughout the country, in the coming general elections, due in February-March 1976. Elections and not unconstitutional means were the best means of finding out the will of the people, she said.

JP readily accepted the challenge, especially because, as pointed out earlier, the movement he led in Bihar had reached an impasse, a dead end. He had earlier been criticizing the opposition parties for limiting their political vision to elections. He now agreed to let the fate of the Bihar movement be decided by elections even though these would be conducted under the existing electoral laws. The movement now took a critical turn and entered a new phase. On 18 November, at a mammoth meeting at the Gandhi Maidan in Patna, he virtually announced the end of the first phase of the struggle and the beginning of its next phase and declared: 'I have accepted the challenge. Neither I nor my boys are in a hurry. We shall wait till the next elections for the people's verdict. Since the Prime Minister has dragged the conflict into the election arena, I shall take my position in the battlefield, not as a candidate, but as a leader . . . the contest will be only between two parties—one of those who support the struggle and the other of those who oppose it. This will be a new type of election, part of the struggle.'[69]

On 20 November, he met a large group of Congress MPs and leaders and condemned both Mrs Gandhi and Congress president, D.K. Barooah, whom he described as a 'court jester.' On 25 November, he called a conference in Delhi of fifty leaders of non-communist parties and the Sarvodaya movement and prominent public figures from various walks of life to discuss various ways of putting pressure on the central government to change its policy on Bihar and to prepare for the forthcoming elections. JP told the conference that Total Revolution could not occur in Bihar alone and had to be extended to the entire country. In turn, the conference endorsed JP's long-term goals of 'basic social, economic, political, cultural and educational changes leading ultimately to a total revolution.'[70]

The conference also decided to set up a twenty-member National Coordination Committee with JP as chairman and to organize national cooperation and some form of coalition of the Jan Sangh, Congress (O), BLD, SSP and Akali Dal. The leaders of these parties decided that even while waiting for elections, they would organize Bihar-style movements all over the country to harness popular discontent whose harvest could then be reaped in the February-March elections. They also decided to organize a massive gherao of the Parliament on 6 March, the first day of the budget session, besides similar gheraos of all state assemblies and state secretariats. Later, in January, this plan changed to a people's march on the Parliament. Once the elections to Gujarat assembly were announced in March 1975, JP and the allied parties decided to come together to contest them.

The character of the JP movement changed significantly from now on as dislodging of the Congress and Indira Gandhi from power at the Centre increasingly became its goal. The JP movement's general campaign thus acquired an Indira Gandhi *hatao* edge, and the National Coordination Committee began to look like the Grand Alliance of 1971. Though as late as January 1975, JP had said in an interview to the *Blitz* that 'in spite of all that Mrs Gandhi has done, the Bihar movement has not reduced itself to just an "Indira Hatao" affair because it is not against any Individual but against a system', he had also announced: 'If Mrs Gandhi does not take any steps to change radically the system and persists in standing in the path of revolutionary struggle she cannot complain if, in its onward march, the movement pushes her aside with so much else.'[71]

To stir up and consolidate anti-Congress, anti-Indira Gandhi sentiment, JP continued to tour the country one state after another, addressing mammoth meetings, portraying the coming electoral battle as another arena of 'the ongoing revolutionary struggle'.[72] On 27 November, he told a Kurukshetra audience: 'I want you to see to it that this Haryana Chief Minister goes and the regime at the Centre headed by Shrimati Indira Gandhi is also dislodged . . . She had assumed the role of a solitary leader like a dictator and ignored the people.'[73] He asked the people to remain vigilant against the threat of one-party dictatorship, bureaucratic-military rule and fascism and asked them to organize and participate in peaceful dharnas, gheraos and demonstrations. He also asked the police not to 'obey orders that are illegal or go against their conscience'.[74] Regarding the Army he said: 'If the rulers do venture to use the army to suppress a peaceful revolution, the army should not allow itself to be so used. On such occasions the leaders of the revolution may call upon the army to come over to their side.'[75] (The latter aspect is discussed in greater detail below in Chapter 6.)

On 6 March, JP led an eight-kilometre-long procession of several hundred thousand people to the Parliament and presented a Charter of Demands to the speaker of the Lok Sabha and chairman of the Rajya Sabha demanding an end to the External Emergency declared in 1971 at the time of the Bangladesh war, dismissal of the Bihar ministry and dissolution of the Bihar assembly and the holding of fresh elections in Gujarat and Bihar, major electoral reforms including proportional representation, and an end to the power of money in elections. Later, at a largely attended meeting, JP compared the march to the Dandi March led by Gandhiji in 1930. However, despite his massive efforts, the JPM did not at any stage make much of a dent in South India and Maharashtra. In fact, it remained as a whole confined to the Hindi-speaking regions of North India.

JP placed a great deal of hope on a split in the Congress party. During February-March, he repeatedly appealed to Jagjivan Ram, Y.B. Chavan and other Congress leaders to oppose Mrs Gandhi and to save the Congress from destruction and join him in defeating her in elections.[76] His main effort was, however, to persuade the ex-socialists in the Congress led by Chandra Shekhar and Mohan Dharia to work for his movement or to split the Congress parliamentary party. These nearly forty-strong Young Turks, moved by motives ideological, political or factional, maintained contacts with JP and the opposition parties. They defended JP's motives and publicly argued for a dialogue and reconciliation with him and for an all-party effort to tackle the country's basic problems. The communists, they said, were the main beneficiaries of the confrontation between the Congress and JP and the opposition parties. They also tried to work up support for the JPM inside the Congress and to even undermine Mrs Gandhi's position within it.

On 1 March, five days before the Opposition's march to the Parliament, Mohan Dharia, union minister for works and housing, pleaded in a public lecture for immediate talks between Mrs Gandhi and the opposition leaders. Next day, he also strongly condemned as brutal the police treatment against the young demonstrators in Bihar and condemned the CPI for its 'sinister designs' in trying to weaken the Congress and make it dependent on the CPI.[77] Mrs Gandhi's reaction to Dharia's statement was to strip him of his ministerial position, asserting that his views were not in conformity with the thinking of the Congress party or compatible with his position as a member of the Council of Ministers.[78]

Still, by the middle of 1975, the situation had got defused and was not beyond repair and the capacity of the political leadership to manage it within the normal political process. Also, both sides having accepted the role of elections in determining the will of the people, it appeared at this stage that there would take place a democratic resolution of the political conflict that had occupied much of the political space during 1974 and 1975; and the issue as to who represented the Indian people would be resolved through the electoral process. But this was not to be, for a fortuitous event intervened.

4 *The Emergency Imposed*

Indian politics witnessed an unexpected turn when on 12 June 1975 Mrs Gandhi's moral and political authority received a hard blow at the hands of Justice Jagmohan Sinha of the Allahabad High Court. Giving a judgement on an election petition filed by Raj Narain, the candidate she had defeated in the 1971 election to the Lok Sabha, he convicted her of having indulged in corrupt campaign practices and declared her election invalid. The conviction also meant that she could not seek election to Parliament or hold an elective public office for a period of six years and, therefore, continue as prime minister. She was, however, allowed to appeal to the Supreme Court and granted a stay of the court's order for twenty days so that the Congress parliamentary party could choose a new leader and prime minister.

Most observers at the time noted that Justice Sinha had dismissed the more serious charges against Mrs Gandhi, including bribery, lavish election expenditure, illegal soliciting of votes, and use of religious symbols, but convicted her on two minor technical and trivial, even frivolous, offences under electoral law. The two offences were the illegal use, during the election campaign, of the services of Yashpal Kapoor, a gazetted government servant, who had resigned from the government service but his resignation had not yet been accepted by the President and gazetted, and the erection of a dais (platform) by police officials from which Mrs Gandhi spoke, and the supply of electricity for the relay of her election speeches. The latter two were long-standing practices for the sake of the prime minister's security. Moreover, UP was at the time of election in 1971 being ruled by an opposition party and the minister in-charge of police at the time was the election agent of her electoral opponent, Raj Narain. A gazetted government servant's leave or resignation becoming effective as soon as it was sanctioned by the higher officer, without waiting for the President's approval and formal gazetting was a normal practice in the government. Any rigid adherence to the formal rule would have in practice meant that the government servant could not in effect go on leave at all, for sometimes the notification was delayed by months and the leave-period would be over before the gazetting took place. Even a sharp critic of Mrs Gandhi, Kuldip Nayar, who was jailed during the Emergency, was to write that the two offences for which Mrs Gandhi was convicted 'were too thin to justify unseating a prime minister. It was almost like unseating the prime minister for a traffic offence.'[1] Justice Sinha's judgement was an example of an immature but egoistic judge who lacked an understanding of the world of politics, throwing the country into a perhaps unintended but certainly undesirable political turmoil.

Mrs Gandhi suffered another political setback when the results of Gujarat assembly elections, held on 10 June, also were declared on 12 June. Despite her vigorous campaign in Gujarat, the Janata Front, an alliance of the Congress (O), Jan Sangh and BLD, led by Morarji Desai and backed by Jayaprakash, won 87 seats as against 75 by the Congress in a house of 182. Even then, the Congress got 41 per cent of votes cast, more or less its normal strength, and the Janata Front 34 per cent. The election marked not so much a decline in the Congress votes as consolidation of the opposition votes. Having failed to win a majority, the Janata Front succeeded in forming a government only after forging an alliance with the same Chimanbhai Patel for whose dismissal the Gujarat's student movement had been initiated.

I

The Allahabad Judgement and the Gujarat assembly results revived the opposition movement. Its leadership felt that Mrs Gandhi's prestige had been given a severe blow, that she had exhausted her political capital, that in the eyes of the people her political legitimacy had been completely eroded and she had lost the moral right to continue as prime minister, and that, if pressed hard, she would be left with no choice but to resign.

The opposition movement's strategy now took another radical turn. The opposition parties were no longer willing to wait for the result of Mrs Gandhi's possible appeal to the Supreme Court and for the general elections due in eight months, especially as they were insecure about the electoral outcome. They decided to strike while the iron was hot and make a bid for power. They accused Mrs Gandhi of 'clinging to an office corruptly gained', of committing 'a constitutional impropriety in holding on to office', of behaving in a 'most shameful and cynical' manner; they demanded her immediate resignation, declared that they no longer recognized her as prime minister, and decided to initiate a countrywide campaign to force her to resign. To start with, they started a series of protest rallies in Delhi and a dharna outside the President's house. The CPM did not join the opposition's movement, though it supported the demand for Mrs Gandhi's resignation. Most of the newspapers too urged Mrs Gandhi to 'uphold democracy' and 'uplift and transform the political scene' by stepping down from her high office at least till the Supreme Court decided on her appeal.

The leadership of the five opposition parties—the Jan Sangh, Congress (O), BLD, SSP and Akali Dal—formed on 22 June a Janata Front or Jan Morcha and a ten-member National Programme Committee to organize a mass movement and draw up the plan of a campaign to secure Mrs Gandhi's resignation. The movement's programme was drafted by Nanaji Deshmukh, a top-ranking leader of the RSS and Jan Sangh. The programme included the organization of a Delhi bandh, an indefinite dharna outside the prime minister's house and a series of processions, demonstrations and gheraos in Delhi.

JP had announced at an all-India conference at Jabalpur on 15 June, that is, after 12 June, that he would go to Bihar and concentrate on the movement for Total Revolution by building Janata Sarkars in Bihar villages. He had also announced that he would not come to Delhi to lead the opposition parties' demonstration outside the President's house. But the opposition leaders felt that they could not do without JP's participation and leadership and sent a delegation to persuade him to reverse his decision of 15 June, postpone the development of revolutionary forces in Bihar and lead the movement in Delhi to oust Mrs Gandhi. JP agreed to do so and returned to Delhi, going against his own warning that the JPM should not concentrate on the objective of 'Indira Hatao'.

There is a little ambiguity about Mrs Gandhi's initial response to the Allahabad verdict. According to Pupul Jayakar, her intimate friend, her instinctive response was 'I must resign immediately'.[2] At the same time, she appealed to the Supreme Court against Justice Sinha's judgement. According to several other writers and her private secretary, N.K. Seshan, Mrs Gandhi did, on the advice of some of her senior partymen, seriously think of temporarily giving up prime minister's office in favour of a senior but trusted party leader and then resuming office after winning her appeal in the Supreme Court. But, finally, she decided not to follow this course but to accept the advice of those who asked her to stay in power. There were several probable reasons for this.

She and her close advisers came to the conclusion that Justice Sinha had tried to do what the Opposition had failed to achieve at the polls in 1971, and that the minor or technical irregularities on which she had been convicted were not sufficient cause for invalidating her election to the Parliament.[3] She was also told by several legal luminaries, such as Nani A. Palkhivala and Fali Nariman, that evidence against her being flimsy, there was hardly any chance of Sinha's judgement being upheld by the Supreme Court. Her decision was influenced by several national, political and personal factors. For one, she was not sure that her resignation would put an end to the opposition agitation and would not, instead, act as a spark to set off political conflagration leading to her successor, whether Jagjivan Ram or D.K. Barooah, and the Congress being swept aside and replaced by an ineffective opposition government, with no electoral mandate to rule. Above all, she believed that her leadership was indispensable to the country at this point of time. According to her principal secretary, P.N. Dhar, as a prime minister she was also worried 'about the consequences of her exit on the governance of the country', and 'the opposition coming to power . . . was a spectre that haunted her because she believed it would be a disaster for the country.'[4] Mrs Gandhi told Dom Moraes in 1978: 'After my judgement in 1975, what could I have done except stay? You know the state the country was in. What would have happened if there had been nobody to lead it? I was the only person who could, you know. It was my duty to the country to stay, though I didn't want to.'[5] Similarly, she told Mary Carras in 1978, that in her absence at the helm, 'There would have been utter political and economic chaos and nobody to fill the vacuum. I wanted to remain because I did not see who would handle it at the moment.' And she added: 'I felt—and some Chief Ministers also said—that if the opposition sensed a victory over me, they will not allow any other Congress person to remain.'[6]

At a personal level, there was a concern that the temporary successor she chose might try to consolidate his own power in the party and the government, rather than let her come back. Sanjay Gandhi, her younger son, who was already a major influence on her life, forcefully urged her not to resign.

From the beginning Mrs Gandhi got the support of her Cabinet colleagues, chief ministers and party leaders who publicly asked her not to resign and pledged their loyalty to her. The Congress parliamentary party also met on 18 June and reiterated 'fullest faith and confidence' in her leadership. The resolution was moved by Jagjivan Ram and seconded by Y.B. Chavan. It was at this meeting that D.K. Barooah, the Congress president, coined the notorious phrase: 'India is Indira, Indira is India.' Daily demonstrations of support, mostly by peasants and workers from outlying villages and towns, began to be organized by her party in front of her house. There is some evidence that the bureaucracy in Delhi and the governments of Haryana and UP, guided by Sanjay Gandhi, played a major role in mobilizing popular support for the government, especially by requisitioning trucks and private and government buses to bring the demonstrators to her house. Many post-Emergency writers have described these rallies and demonstrations as stage-managed with the help of ample funds and misuse of government power. But there is also no doubt that Mrs Gandhi still enjoyed wide popular support in the country 'even without her son's rent-a-crowd operation.'[7] This became evident from the huge rally she addressed near the Boat Club in Delhi on 20 June. But dissidence in the Congress party also was beginning to grow.

Many of the ex-socialists in the Congress parliamentary party known as Young Turks had been for some time urging Mrs Gandhi to open negotiations with JP but without success. Many of them secretly welcomed the judgement and wanted to settle old scores with Mrs Gandhi, now that she was beleagured. Others believed that she had become a political liability and that, therefore, this was a fine opportunity to oust her. Mohan Dharia now publicly demanded that for considerations of propriety she should step down in favour of some other senior Congress leader, such as Jagjivan Ram or Swaran Singh. Dharia was privately supported by many of the other Young Turks. According to political rumours, Jagjivan Ram and Y.B. Chavan were quite receptive to this idea though publicly they fully supported Mrs Gandhi's staying in power. In any case, one of the factors that strengthened the opposition parties' intransigency was the hope of taking advantage of a possible split in the Congress, with the rebels making a common cause with them. The political strength of the rebellious Congress MPs was, however, not significant. Though the potential rebels claimed the support of thirty or more party MPs, in effect, in the words of Kuldip Nayar, 'they could count their supporters on the tips of their fingers.'[8] On 24 June, when Chandra Shekhar, the leader of the rebels, hosted a dinner for JP only twenty Congress MPs turned up.

II

While the Supreme Court was to hear Mrs Gandhi's appeal against the Allahabad Judgement on 14 July, Justice V.R. Krishna Iyer, the vacation judge of the Supreme Court, created further confusion by a ruling delivered on 24 June. While Mrs Gandhi had asked for an absolute stay of Sinha's order, Krishna Iyer, while holding that Mrs Gandhi had not been convicted of 'any of the graver electoral vices', gave her only a conditional stay of the High Court order on the ground that the High Court ruling, until upset, holds good, however ultimately weak it may prove. He decided that till the final disposal of her appeal by the full bench of the Supreme Court her electoral disqualification 'stands eclipsed' and she could continue as prime minister and participate in Parliament's proceedings but she could not vote or draw salary as an MP. Both the opposition parties and the Congress claimed Iyer's decision as a victory. The Opposition argued that the conditional stay was a snub to Mrs Gandhi, that the 'stigma of corruption continues' and 'her credibility stands destroyed' and that she could no longer function as a prime minister. The Congress, on the other hand, pointed to the court's permission to let her stay and function fully as Prime Minister and said that the judgement as a whole had virtually exonerated her and fully vindicated her stand.

Few judges on record have managed to create a national crisis. Justices Sinha and Iyer had succeeded in doing so: one by a basically frivolous judgement, and the other by his non-committal approach. Justice Iyer could have silenced the Opposition by giving an absolute stay of Sinha's order to Mrs Gandhi or virtually assured her resignation by refusing to give any stay at all. But now both sides decided to throw all their forces into battle. The Opposition's call for Mrs Gandhi's resignation was renewed even more vociferously after Justice Iyer's ruling. The opposition leaders had tasted blood and by now 'consumed by one single passion, namely, to bring down Indira Gandhi from power,'[9] would not let the law take its course; they would not wait for the final judgement of the full bench of the Supreme Court.

In a mammoth rally held in Delhi on 25 June, under the auspices of Jan Morcha, the opposition leaders declared that Mrs Gandhi having lost the moral right to rule, they would not let her function as prime minister, and that to dislodge her from office and to force her to resign they would organize a nation-wide one week-long campaign of mass mobilization, demonstrations and civil disobedience throughout the country. The campaign was to be organized by a new body, the Lok Sangharsh Samiti (People's Struggle Committee), set up on 25 June by the five-party Morcha and JP, and headed by Morarji Desai with Nanaji Deshmukh as its general secretary. The week-long campaign of civil disobedience and defiance of laws would be initiated on 29 June in the 356 district headquarters and state capitals. Batches of volunteers would also go daily to the prime minister's residence and hold demonstrations. The campaign would be intensified after one week and end with the gherao or an encirclement of the prime minister's house by lakhs of volunteers who would permit no one to enter or leave the house. According to Kuldip Nayar, the intelligence bureau reported that the opposition volunteers 'would squat on railway tracks and see that the trains did not move. The courts would not be allowed to function, government offices would not be able to work;' the movement would 'bring everything to a stand-still.'[10] Moreover, the volunteers who would surround Mrs Gandhi's house were already getting ready to do so.

In his speech at the rally, JP denounced Mrs Gandhi's continuation in office as illegal and unconstitutional. Mrs Gandhi and her government had, he declared, 'no moral, legal or constitutional right to govern'. He gave an ultimatum to Mrs Gandhi to resign within four days. He said a time might come when he would ask the people to 'derecognize the government', withdraw cooperation from it, refuse to pay it taxes and in general make it impossible for it to function. He asked the students 'to walk out of classrooms and walk into jails'. He once again appealed to the military, police and government servants not to take orders from 'a disqualified head of a discredited government' and to refuse to obey the government's orders that they considered wrong or 'illegal' or that were 'repugnant to their conscience'. He also dared the government to try him 'for commiting treason' for making the appeal. He said that the people should not allow the All-India Radio to function as it was broadcasting 'lies'. He called upon them to gherao I.K. Gujaral, the minister for information and broadcasting, for using the All-India Radio to 'do personal propaganda' for Mrs Gandhi. He also urged Jagjivan Ram and Y.B. Chavan 'to come out in the open and say that Mrs Gandhi should step down.' JP and Morarji Desai also accused Mrs Gandhi of moving towards dictatorship and fascism.[11]

In an interview that very evening with the Italian journalist Oriana Fallaci, Morarji Desai described Mrs Gandhi as a 'second-rate' leader who 'boasts no capacities except for intrigue, maneuvering, craft . . . has a genius for blackmail and favouritism, . . . lacks culture, learning', and who 'is a fascist who acts only on behalf of her own interest and suppresses freedom'. He also said that 'there are few countries in the world where fear holds such sway as in Indira Gandhi's India,' and that 'I, thanks to Mrs Gandhi, have discovered that a woman is unsuited to head a government or rule a country'. He explained the Opposition's strategic plan as follows:[12]

We intend to overthrow her, to force her to resign. For good. The lady won't survive this movement of ours. She won't be able to because it is on a national scale and includes all possible political trends, and even some members of her own party ... We are strong, at last, and we've proclaimed a *Satyagra* (sic.). *Satyagra* means civil disobedience. It consists in ignoring every prohibition, every law, every arrest, every police attack ... Thousands of us will surround her house to prevent her going out or receiving visitors. We'll camp there night and day shouting to her to resign. Even if the police arrest us, beat us up, slaughter us. How many can they slaughter? And what will they do with all the corpses? To prevent such action, Mrs Gandhi has but one course open: to eliminate us all this very night.'

Interestingly, Morarji Desai and others were not expecting a sudden attack from Mrs Gandhi. When Fallaci asked Morarji what if Mrs Gandhi should launch such an attack on them, he replied:[13]

I don't believe she will. I exclude the possibility. To arrest the opposition would lead to too great a national and international scandal. She would reveal her true Mussolinian nature and she cares too much to appear formally democratic at least. Oh, no! It isn't possible. It would spell the end of democracy in India. She'd have to lose her mind to do something like that ... To arrest us all, she'd have to involve the army and that would feed the discontent prevailing among the young officers. The army is too divided. She can trust only the chief of staff she has lately appointed. May be, in the early stages, the army would lend itself to playing the game, but it would soon rebel and establish a military dictatorship. Even an incomplete intelligence such as Mrs Gandhi's should understand this fact. I prefer to believe that before committing such a monstrosity Mrs Gandhi would commit suicide.

Morarji was half wrong and half right. Mrs Gandhi did precisely what he thought she would never do, but she did it without involving the Army. In fact, as we shall see, one reason for her actions was the desire to avoid involving the Army.

Indira Gandhi took serious note of the agitational and civil disobedience plan of the Opposition and of the plan to gherao her house as well as of the call to the armed forces, the police and government servants to disobey government orders, regarding it as a call to them to mutiny. A gherao of her house and office by a crowd of lakhs of people or a nation-wide militant movement which would aim at paralyzing the state governments could not be contained by the police and could be countered, especially if they took a violent form, as they were likely to, only by the large-scale use of the military and para-military forces. Mrs Gandhi was not willing to adopt this course as she did not want to rely on the military. Ruling with the help of the armed forces was distasteful to her, both personally and ideologically, and against the entire tradition of the national movement and the Nehru era. Moreover, when faced with a determined crowd of several lakhs or even thousands, the armed forces would have to shed a great deal of blood and, in fact, to enact another Jallianwala massacre. She could not countenance that either.

Given the nature, character and structure of the Congress as a party, Mrs Gandhi was also not in a position to effectively face the projected opposition campaign politically through her party, even when supported by the CPI. She was also not willing to let Delhi or a few other large cities decide the political fate of the government, since she felt that her rural political base, especially in the southern and western parts of the country, was as a whole still intact and that the JPM was confined to Bihar, UP, Delhi and Haryana. She was, however, not in a position to mobilize her basically passive rural and urban voters and supporters and bring them to Delhi. On the other hand, the RSS-Jan Sangh cadres had a strong and politically dominant base in Delhi and possessed the capacity to mobilize active crowds of thousands and lakhs there. Mrs Gandhi was also not willing to concede the demand for her resignation, convinced as she was that it was unjsutified and that the Opposition was planning to seize power or instal a puppet Congressman—for example, Jagjivan Ram—in her place. And if she had to use the state apparatus to meet the threatened agitation, it had better be done before the agitation had taken off.

Consequently, in a lightening response to the projected campaign that was anticipated neither by her opponents nor by her supporters she declared a state of Internal Emergency under Article 352 of the Constitution on 26 June (External Emergency, declared in 1971, was already in operation), arrested a large number of opposition leaders, such as JP, Morarji Desai, Asoka Mehta and Charan Singh, and several Congress dissidents, such as Chandra Shekhar and Ram Dhun, imposed a strict censorship on the Press, and suspended all other fundamental rights, thus stifling all opposition to the government. She promised to return to normalcy as soon as the conditions warranted it. In the bargain, she put an end to JP's movement for Total Revolution.

III

How and why did the Emergency come about? What was its legitimacy? What did it mean in practice? And why was it lifted in the end and with what consequences? We may take a critical look at both the JP movement and the Emergency, starting with the justfications that JP and Mrs Gandhi offered for their respective positions.

As brought out, at length, in Chapter 6, Jayaprakash believed and argued that the JP movement was basically a harbinger of Total Revolution and the initiator as well as the motive force of a continuous process of 'revolution in every sphere of social life and organization.'[14]

Apart from commitment to Total Revolution, JP throughout emphasized eradication of corruption from public life and preservation and deepening of democracy. For example, he declared in early April 1974: 'I cannot remain a silent spectator to misgovernment, corruption and the rest . . . It is not for this that I at least had fought for freedom.'[15] And in his major speech on 5 June 1974, he repeated: 'The problem of corruption has become intolerable to me personally and I have come out to openly wage a fight against it.'[16] Rooting out of corruption, of which he saw the central government headed by Mrs Gandhi as the fountainhead, was to be a primary justification for the rise and development of the JPM in Bihar. Raising the question, 'why am I taking up corruption in the political and administrative spheres first?' he said: 'Because the roots lie there. All aspects of the lives of the people have been corrupted by this source.'[17] Later, in jail, he was to write in his *Diary*: 'Corruption has been the central point of the movement, particularly corruption in the government and the administration.'[18]

The second and, in the end, the most important justification for the movement offered by JP was that it was necessary to defend democracy which was corrupted by the Congress and threatened by the electoral system and above all by Mrs Gandhi's authoritarian personality, dictatorial tendencies and style of politics and administration.

So far as the threat to democracy from the distortions of the electoral process was concerned, he summed up his oft-repeated critique as follows in May 1974: 'The unlimited use of money, large-scale impersonation, use of force to prevent the weakest sections from exercising their franchise, abuse of electoral machinery, hoodwinking of the people, particularly the poor and unsophisticated, by attractive but false promises, etc., have robbed the elections of much of their value and eroded the people's faith in them. And if this loss of faith persists and deepens, we would soon have a dictatorship in this country.'[19]

But it was the danger of authoritarianism and the threat to democracy from Indira Gandhi that was a constant theme of JP's public pronouncements during the JPM and even earlier. In his December 1973 appeal to the youth, he said that the main issue—one of 'deeper and fundamental significance'—to which he wanted to draw their attention was 'the issue of democracy'. The youth could not afford to 'look on idly at this strangulation of the democratic process.' Stressing the urgency for action on this issue, he said: 'Time for action is here and now.'[20] During 1974 and 1975, JP repeatedly accused Mrs Gandhi of abandoning democratic practices, conventions and weakening and destroying democratic institutions and trying to establish a dictatorship in her hunger for power.[21]

JP's overall justification of the JPM, especially in its later phases, was its objective of removing Mrs Gandhi from power for he held that she was the source of all ills from which the polity was suffering, leading to a threat to the democratic structure itself.

It should, however, also be noted that JP believed that through his movement he was widening democracy's horizons, making it real by involving the people in it and laying the foundations of true democracy based on people's power. But more on this aspect in Chapter 6.

Why, according to JP, was the Emergency imposed? Not because of any reason provided by the JPM, for the movement was entirely peaceful and there was no plan 'to paralyze the government' or organize 'any struggle involving civil disobedience'.[22] But he did provide two concentric explanations in his *Prison Diary*.

One simple explanation was that because of 'the looming certainty of Opposition unity and the mass awakening as a result of the movement, she was mortally afraid of a possible electoral reverse.' Thus the objective of the Emergency and the accompanying arrests and the suppression of the freedom of the Press and other fundamental rights was 'to keep Mrs Gandhi safe and warm', and to enable her 'to cling to power'.[23] Also Mrs Gandhi felt threatened by the revolutionary character of the JPM: 'When the Congress found that the movement was not going to be satisfied with superficial remedies but that it was also aiming to bring about basic fundamental changes in society, including basic political changes—in short, a total revolution—it was too much for it to stomach . . . frightened by the revolutionary prospect, Mrs Gandhi has tried to bar the way.'[24]

But there was, believed JP, also a more deep-seated and devious plan behind the policy that led to the declaration of the Emergency. This declaration was no mere response to the Opposition's threat of a civil disobedience movement. That threat, delivered through the Opposition resolution of 25 June, determined only 'the timing of the blow that came down on the head of Indian democracy in one fell swoop.' The Emergency plan 'had been thought out and planned in some detail much earlier'. The objective of the plan was that 'Mrs Gandhi and those who supported her in the Congress and the CPI should never, never be dislodged from power, no matter what the people or the voters felt and wanted'. But, in fact, the plan was even more diabolical and dangerous. For one, it was not planned in the Congress Working Committee or the Home Ministry or the Political Affairs Committee of the Cabinet or even 'in the so-called Inner Cabinet'. Mrs Gandhi's fears of loss of power were used by others to plan a more hidden strategy, whose full import was hidden even from her. Who were these planners? The Emergency was 'planned in a secret cell of the PM's confidants, comprising almost certainly pro-Soviet members, one or more of whom must be in close touch and regular communication with some India cell in Soviet embassy', and, then, unfolded on 26 June 1975. And what was the plan prepared by 'Indiraji, the disguised communists in her party, the CPI and, behind the scene, Soviet agents'? It was 'for substituting a totalitarian system for the democratic one that we had until 25 June. To all three of them—the PM, the communist stooges in the Congress and the CPI—democracy was anathema and they were planning for long years the steps by which their goal could be reached: first "social democracy" and then naked communist party rule under carefully disguised Russian tutelage.' But the secret strategy, wrote JP, went even further: 'There must be two plans instead of one. One, to which Indiraji is privy and is made to believe that it is her plan. In this plan Indiraji is always at the top till death intervenes. The other plan is a Soviet plan which the CPI has been made to believe has emerged from their own brilliant heads.' This second plan was 'not known to Indiraji though she might have some private suspicions.' It was not known even to the 'communist stooges in the Congress'. Only a few 'whom the Soviets trust' were privy to this plan, and these were persons who were not even known as communist or pro-communist. They had 'by their outward actions . . . never shown any sympathy for the CPI or even the Soviets'. In fact they might 'even have appeared at times to be critical, if not hostile, to the fatherland of socialism.' This second plan 'was to take effect at the point of transition from social democracy to undisguised communist dictatorship. Many heads were then to roll.' Thus, predicted JP: 'A time may come ('will come', he wrote a few lines later) when, having squeezed the juice out of Mrs Gandhi, the Russians through the CPI and their Trojan horses within the Congress will dump her on the garbage heap of history and instal in her place their own men.' All this, of course, was not inevitable, wrote JP: 'May be the people would rise, the army may oppose and take over itself. There may be other possibilities.'[25]

IV

Indira Gandhi justified her action in imposing the Emergency in two consecutive broadcasts on 26 and 27 June, in several speeches including two during the discussion on the parliamentary approval of the Emergency proclamation in Lok Sabha and Rajya Sabha on 22 July 1975, and in innumerable interviews to Indian and foreign press persons during 1975 and 1976. Consistently maintaining before June 1975 that whatever the current problems and disturbances, the Indian political system had not failed, she repeatedly asserted after 25 June that the stability, security, unity, the 'fabric' and the very survival of the nation were in danger due to national and international threats. According to the government's White Paper entitled 'Why Emergency', laid in both Houses of Parliament on 21 July 1975, the Emergency was imposed 'to withstand the calculated onslaught on the country's political institutions and economic progress.' Furthermore, 'Some political parties with fascist leanings had combined with a set of frustrated politicians to challenge the very basis of democratic functioning and to destroy the country's self-confidence. They campaigned in the name of democracy to paralyze the national economy, to subvert democratic institutions and create anarchy and chaos in order to overthrow the duly elected government . . . the damage that might have resulted was such that hard decisions had to be taken . . . No Government worth the name could stand by and allow the country's security, stability and economy to be imperilled. The nation's interests demanded firm and decisive action to put democracy on the rails again.'[26]

Mrs Gandhi's justification of the Emergency, sketched briefly above, may be discussed primarily on three grounds.

The first ground was that India's stability, security, integrity and unity—'its very freedom'—were in danger from the disruptive character of the JPM. Mrs Gandhi summed up this aspect in an interview to Norman Cousins, editor of the *Saturday Review* of New York, on 1 August 1975 as follows:[27]

> The state of Emergency was proclaimed because the threat of disruption was clear and imminent. When an organized attempt is made to exhort workers and farmers to withhold work and produce, when government offices are not allowed to function, when students are advised to boycott schools, when duly elected legislators are called upon to resign, when open statements are made that the Prime Minister will not be 'recognized' and Parliament will not be allowed to function, in spite of the clear verdict of the highest court of the land that legally I am entitled to function as Prime Minister, and when, finally, a call is given by a combination of five parties for countrywide civil disobedience and, over and above all, the armed forces and police are publicly asked to disobey orders, is the situation not grave? These were not the actions of a lunatic fringe to be ignored. There has been sabotage in Bihar and disruption of the administration this last year. Now it was to be a nationwide programme proclaimed by leaders supposedly responsible. They were ready to adopt extra-constitutional methods and deliberately cross those limits and self-restraints which are basic to democracy. To permit them to go ahead would have meant conniving at the beginning of the disintegration of the bonds that hold the country together.

Reversing JP's main critique, she said that the Emergency was imposed to save, preserve and safeguard democracy: 'This action is totally within our constitutional framework and it was undertaken in order not to destroy the Constitution but to preserve the Constitution, to preserve and safeguard our democracy.'[28] It was the Opposition and JPM which were disrupting democratic functioning and undermining democratic institutions and posed a threat to democracy. Even before 26 June, she had accused JP of 'undermining the roots of democracy while simultaneously masquerading as its saviour.'[29] In July 1974, she said: 'The Bihar agitation was primarily aimed at weakening the government and killing democracy.'[30]

The threat to democracy posed by the JPM became a regular theme in Mrs Gandhi's comments after 26 June 1975. The threat to democracy was posed primarily because the Opposition and the JPM were not democratic or were rather anti-democratic and were not willing to abide by democratic norms. In her first broadcast on 26 June after declaration of the Emergency, she said that the Opposition had, in the name of democracy, 'sought to negate the very functioning of democracy.'[31] In her speech in the Lok Sabha on 22 July 1975, she said: 'Democracy has not been endangered by what Government has done, but democracy was being weakened, was being endangered and would have been destroyed had the Opposition Front been allowed to launch the direct action and its plan of sabotage under RSS guidance and to go ahead with its campaign to create dissatisfaction in the army, the police and amongst our industrial workers.'[32]

Mrs Gandhi repeatedly accused the minority opposition of 'attempting to submerge the voice of the majority', of not being 'ready to abide by constitutional and legal considerations', and of trying to 'force' the issue of the Allahabad High Court and Supreme Court judgements 'through extra-constitutional direct action' and 'paralyze the functioning of democracy'.[33] She also suggested a close connection between violence and the threat to democracy. In particular, she repeatedly cited the examples of the violent and therefore undemocratic and unconstitutional character of the Gujarat and Bihar movements.[34]

Interestingly, Mrs Gandhi did not accuse JP of being anti-democratic or a votary of violence, either before or after the Emergency. She often said that JP and some of the other leaders of JPM, especially those belonging to Cong (O) and BLD, wanted to have a non-violent movement and did not favour violence or the end of democracy. They had, however, because of their lack of mass support and organization, started to lean towards, align themselves with and organizationally depend on organizations and parties which opposed non-violence and favoured both violence and dictatorship.[35] This last was true of the Naxalites and Anand Margis, and in particular of the RSS.[36] The JPM included parties like the RSS which were communal, anti-minority, had a secret constitution and believed in violence.[37] On another occasion, she had earlier declared in the Lok Sabha on 22 July: 'I deplore the type of training that they give to younger people in their *shakhas*, the violence they preach. But their real weapon is something else—it is the whispering campaign they indulge in. Yesterday another member of the Opposition wanted to know what fascism was. Fascism does not mean merely repression; it does not mean merely that the police use excessive force or that people are imprisoned. Fascism is the use of falsehood. Over and above everything, it is the propagation of the big lie. It is the use of whispering campaigns, the search for scapegoats.

This has been the major weapon of the Jan Sangh and the RSS.'[38] To a German interviewer she said in September 1975: 'I should like to say that I have not called all the political opponents "fascists" at anytime. I have called one group so, which does not consider itself a political group, which is the RSS. They follow what is almost, I would say, the text-book techniques of Fascism, that is, believing in the superiority of one race, having a sort of a private army; even propagating the big lie day in and day out so that people start thinking well there must be some truth if it is said so many times, and then a minority group trying to force its opinion on the majority.'[39] She also accused the RSS of trying 'to infiltrate into our services—in the administration and everywhere.'[40]

Even otherwise, Mrs Gandhi declared, communal parties, which were an important part of the opposition alliance, were undemocratic because they were communal, for democracy in the Indian context had to be secular democracy.[41] Consequently, 'if a political alliance, which depends upon the muscle power of the sinister Rashtriya Swayamsevak Sangh, should come to power at the Centre, then not only Indian democracy but India's very integrity will be threatened.'[42]

Mrs Gandhi also charged the Opposition with unwillingness to 'abide by constitutional and legal obligations' and 'challenging law and order throughout the country with a view to disrupt normal functioning', 'to obstruct and subvert government' and 'to paralyze the system'. 'Our very survival as a nation' was threatened. 'The aim of the Opposition parties was obvious: to paralyze the Government and indeed all national activity and walk to power over the body of the nation.' Mrs Gandhi linked this threat above all to the 25 June programme of the JPM.[43] This threat, she argued, could not be met without the imposition of the Emergency.[44] The strong negative forces could not 'have been contained by the (due) processes of law'.[45] 'Some rights have to suffer a little,' she told the Rajya Sabha, 'if it is in the cause of strengthening and survival of our country. It is only when we have a country that we can have a democracy.'[46] She also linked the threat to country's stability with the adverse effect on its 'production and prospects of economic improvement.'[47]

In the context of the threat to nation's governance, unity and stability, Mrs Gandhi brought in four other themes. Communalism was another force which threatened national unity and which was given comfort and support even by the secular opposition parties. The government, she declared, would not permit the spread of communal poison or allow communal organizations such as RSS, Jamaat-i-Islami, and Anand Marg to function.[48]

Similarly, referring to JP's speeches, she accused the Opposition of attempting to 'undermine the loyalty of the police and military' and of 'inciting our armed forces to mutiny and our police to rebel.'[49] She took very serious note of these attempts though she expressed public confidence that they would not materialize because 'our defence forces and the police are disciplined and deeply patriotic' and 'would stand firm'.[50] But, we may note that, in fact, she was quite cautious in this respect. She did not involve the armed forces in the Emergency at any stage. And perhaps, as we have suggested earlier in section II of this chapter, one reason she imposed the Emergency was because she did not want to rely on the Army for dealing with the projected civil disobedience movement, which she probably would have had to do.

Though perhaps as an afterthought, the Emergency was also portrayed by Mrs Gandhi as an opportunity for promoting and implementing her 'progressive economic agenda' of rapid economic development, social justice and social change. In an interview in August 1975, she said: 'The economic programme now announced was not the reason for Emergency but Emergency has created the right climate for its implementation.'[51]

Mrs Gandhi also linked the Emergency to what she regarded as her radical politics. She often referred to the 'forces of reaction'—the big capitalists, the rich farmers, and other reactionary sections of Indian society—who were opposing her 'progressive measures of benefit to the common man and woman of India' and her policies of social change and changes in the status quo.[52] 'The emergency had to come', she told the Rajya Sabha on 8 January 1976, 'if we want to change the country and bring about a transformation in the society.'[53]

Third, though not directly offering intervention and subversion from abroad as the causes of the Emergency, Mrs Gandhi did strongly imply this was also responsible when she constantly warned the people against them. Reiterating after June 1975 what she had believed since 1968, and had been saying repeatedly since early 1973 in many of her speeches and interviews, she pointed to the danger of penetration by foreign powers—of the 'hand of foreign government',[54] of 'outside influence'.[55] She accused the latter of wanting 'to change the sort of India that we want to build' of trying to weaken and destabilize India by all sorts of means, including 'financing disruptive activities' because they saw its emergence as a great power as a potential threat to their world hegemony.[56] She did not concretize the foreign threat or specify 'the foreign hand' in precise terms and, in fact, put it quite cautiously. She also drew a parallel with Chile, as she had done in 1973, citing the example of the overthrow and murder of Allende. For example, she said in January 1976: 'The country has never been in such grave danger before. Some powers which had tasted success in their destabilization game in Chile nurtured similar designs against India.'[57] Later she drew comparisons with the killing of President Mujibur Rahman and his family in Bangladesh.[58] In her interview with Mary Carras in 1978, she stated the accusation much more strongly: 'There was a conspiracy by foreign agencies, not just during the emergency but from way back' since the days of Nehru and 'the movement against us was engineered by outside forces.'[59]

We may, in the end, take another important aspect of the imposition of the Emergency emphasized by Mrs Gandhi. She vehemently denied that she resorted to the Emergency to keep herself in office.[60] There is, however, little doubt that a personal factor was involved so far as control of the Press during the Emergency was involved. She repeatedly referred to a campaign of calumny and hatred against her by the Opposition, which was abetted by a large section of the Press. Though at no stage did she offer this as a cause or reason for the Emergency, she did refer to it as a justification for the rigid censorship of the Press, which was such an important element of the Emergency. The opposition parties, she said, had unleashed a campaign of 'hate and calumny' and 'virulent character assassination' against her.[61]

V

In fact, at that particular historical conjuncture, both the JPM and Mrs Gandhi were at fault; there was in the stand of both some elements of truth as well as many half-truths. To a certain extent both masked the real reasons for the positions they adopted and the actions they undertook.

JP's and others' critique of the Bihar government and of the central government headed by Mrs Gandhi, the working of the political and administrative system and the political parties, and the decline in public political morality was justified in part. They did not, however, have a ghost of an idea as to what to do to cleanse the system of its evils except the jejune one of somehow removing Mrs Gandhi from power.

Undoubtedly, serious flaws had developed in Mrs Gandhi's policies and administration. Despite the Congress party's overwhelming majority in Parliament and in most of the state assemblies, it had failed to bring about far-reaching socio-economic changes or combine economic growth with social justice or move the country towards greater social and economic equality. During her nine-year-long political reign, Mrs Gandhi had not only failed to develop the political system and democratize the administrative structure, but had even been unable to prevent their further downslide. Despite her undoubted political dominance she was unable to make the institutional changes in the political or governmental apparatus—Parliament, Cabinet, police, bureaucracy, the Congress party or the educational system—necessary for the implementation of her own social, economic and political agenda. Little or no effort was made to reform old institutions, such as the police, erosion in most of them went unchecked, and, in fact, contributed to their decay.

Too much power and authority in the party and the government was concentrated in her hands, and she developed a personalized style of decision-making. She weakened the cabinet system and reduced the role of the party in making decisions. She failed to check the almost continuous factionalism in the party at the local and state levels and the weakening of the position of her party's chief ministers. She successfully managed and controlled the Congress party but failed to build it up as an organization and reshape it as an instrument of popular political education and mobilization, with the result that the Congress failed to come to her aid when she was under seige from the JPM. Instead, the composition and structure of the party became worse with the induction of black money and morally dubious elements into it. Consequently, though she, personally, remained popular, she could not prevent the rise of general discontent against the Congress, state governments and the central administration. She also began to lose some of the high political ground she had occupied during 1969-1972.

In fact, Mrs Gandhi's crucial weakness as a political leader lay in the absence of any strategic design and long-term perspective around which her economic, political and administrative policies were framed. Even the declaration of the Emergency was an *ad hoc* response to a specific situation of political crisis and not part of an alternative strategic design for better management of the political system. As a result, its timing cast doubts on any wider significance, such as checking the rise of fascism or defence of the country's unity and stability. On the contrary, it appeared that it was imposed only for the preservation and strengthening of her own position and power.

Nevertheless, despite concentration of power in her hands, it would be incorrect to say that Indira Gandhi was undemocratic by nature or tried or even wanted to impose an authoritarian regime. Till June 1975, she functioned within the parliamentary framework. She accepted, even when she did not like it, the authority of the judiciary. She did not tinker with the Press, even when it subjected her to calumnies, or with academic freedom, even when a large number of academicians had become her severe critics. Moreover, she functioned as prime minister under difficult conditions: lack of a majority in Parliament from 1969 to 1971, Bangladesh crisis during 1971, and severe economic conditions because of causes that were beyond her control during 1972-74. During 1974-75 she was constantly troubled and harassed by popular movements and agitations. It may also be pointed out that she did accommodate the Nav Nirman Movement in Gujarat and was willing to do so in Bihar, though without dissolving the assembly. It was, on the other hand, not possible to accept the demand for her own removal from office, especially as she was likely to be replaced by an unmanageable and unnatural coalition of left-right and secular-communal parties, some claiming to represent the rural poor and some being open spokesmen of the rich peasants and even semi-feudal landlords. Moreover, the leader of the popular movement against her was not willing to shoulder the burden of office. There is no doubt that her removal from office through an extra-constitutional movement and procedure would have weakened the structure and the constitutional fabric of the Indian state.

In Chapters 6, 7 and 8, I will take a critical look at both positions, those of the JPM and the Emergency—in the case of the JPM of its potential, and in the case of the Emergency of its actuality. 'Each side became convinced that the other would no longer abide by the rules of democratic politics.'[62] Both accused each other of leaning towards dictatorship—the JPM was accused of being fascist, and Indira Gandhi of taking the country towards Soviet-style and Soviet-backed dictatorship. In my perspective, it is not true that the JPM was a fascist movement or that JP was planning a fascist takeover. It is also not true that Indira Gandhi was authoritarian by nature or intent, or that she and her government were fascistically inclined, or that she deliberately created the crisis of 1974-75 so that she could establish an authoritarian regime, or that she imposed the Emergency to consolidate her personal position and power. But, at the same time, I believe that both the JPM and the Emergency had the potential of becoming very different from, even the opposite of, what they were believed to be or desired to be by their proponents. As Sudipta Kaviraj has put it, what was wrong was the remarkable 'similarity between the two sides in the great confrontation: the same resort to populism, the same reluctance to go by institutional norms, the same tendency to substitute a programme by a personality, the same shortsighted eagerness to ride a popular wave of negative indignation, the same confusion between what was a defeat of its opponent and a victory of its own.'[63]

But before I analyse the JP movement and the Emergency, I would like to bring out an interesting feature of the situation in the next chapter.

5 *The Democratic Option*

Democracy was the key word that both JP and Mrs Gandhi used to appeal to the people. Each accused the other of endangering it, held the other responsible for the 'rising menace of fascism', and justified their own political actions in the name of safeguarding democracy 'from the assault mounted on it by the other.' Ironically, neither of them chose the democratic way out or advocated the adoption of the basic constitutional remedy of appealing afresh to the electorate, and, therefore, of holding fresh elections to the Lok Sabha. These elections were in any case due in February-March 1976 (i.e., eight months later) and could have been preponed to October-November 1975. By adopting this course, JP and Indira Gandhi could have provided in June 1975 a practical, democratic alternative to both a civil disobedience campaign for Mrs Gandhi's ouster and declaration of the Emergency.

I

In the case of JP and the Opposition, instead of trying to force Mrs Gandhi's resignation through a coercive mass movement, there were democratic and constitutional options open to it. The first option was to let the law take its course and to wait for the judgement of the full Bench of the Supreme Court on Mrs Gandhi's appeal and, if the judgement went against her, to demand its implementation. The second course was to wait for the verdict of the people in the general elections to the Lok Sabha due eight months later, and in the meanwhile to use peaceful agitation and propaganda to undermine Mrs Gandhi politically erode her popularity and standing among the people, to make Mrs Gandhi's refusal to resign as a result of the Allahabad judgement an electoral issue, and reap the rich harvest of popular discontent in the form of electoral victory. After all, this was the course JP had agreed to follow in November 1974, when he had accepted elections as the means to resolve the political conflict. The third option was to assert that the people had a right to demand resignation of a duly-elected government in an extreme situation of the sort that was then prevailing, and that because of the Allahabad judgement Mrs Gandhi's electoral mandate to rule had become null and void and she must immediately seek—say in October-November—a fresh mandate from the electorate, if the Supreme Court upset the Allahabad judgement.

Only if elections were denied or rigged could it be claimed that the parliamentary democratic system was no longer functioning or was incapable of bringing about a democratic resolution of the conflict between the ruling party under seige and a resurgent Opposition. A popular movement could then be launched to force Mrs Gandhi to either hold free and fair elections or to resign. But, then, not only the main demand but also the character and organization of such a movement as also its forms of mobilization and political struggle would have to be very different from those projected before and on 25 June.

In fact, the conglomerate of the opposition parties constituting the movement had from the beginning, in November 1974, also vacillated on the approach to be adopted on this point. The Congress (O) and other right-wing parties and one wing of the Jan Sangh wanted to defeat Mrs Gandhi at the hustings while another wing of the Jan Sangh and RSS felt that it was not easy, or even possible, to fight the Congress and Mrs Gandhi in the electoral field. They, therefore, favoured the seizure of power by other means whenever the moment seemed right. The electoral-route school won out in October-November 1974 when JP threw his weight behind it and announced that he was accepting Mrs Gandhi's challenge to let the next general elections, due in February-March 1976, decide the fate of his movement's demands, as also test the Congress's and her strength and popularity. JP now began to tramp the whole country, his entire activity being geared to delegitimize Mrs Gandhi and defeat her in the coming elections.

But a year or even six months is a long interlude in politics. A popular movement could both gain or lose momentum in that period. People could tire of it, for no popular movement can be carried on for a long time merely on the strength of the leaders' or cadres' enthusiasm. In Mrs Gandhi's case, there was also the distinct possibility that the Supreme Court might overturn the Allahabad court judgement because of the trivial and technical character of the grounds on which Justice Sinha had disqualified her. There was also no guarantee of success in the coming parliamentary elections. The economic situation was beginning to improve. The JP movement's position itself was precarious.

By most contemporary accounts, it was losing momentum and was even on the wane. It had failed to develop outside the Hindi-speaking states. In an article in the *Everyman's* of 20 April 1975, Anand Patwardhan, an ardent supporter, had answered in affirmative the question he had raised in the title, 'Is JP's Movement at the Crossroads?'

There was also no sign that the poor had deserted Mrs Gandhi. The Congress's base in South India, and also, in other parts of the country, among agricultural labourers, tribals, women and minorities seemed to be intact. As Romesh Thapar, a major critic of Mrs Gandhi, wrote it in his column in the *Economic and Political Weekly* of 22 March 1975: 'Indira Gandhi remains dominant despite the black eyes, the bruises and the smears.' In the North, by-election results pointed both ways. Even the result of the Gujarat election held in June 1975 in which the Opposition had secured more seats than Congress had not been entirely reassuring since it had failed to get a majority. But equally important, Congress had received 41 per cent of votes as against 34 per cent by the Janata Front, and this despite the massive student movement, the united front of all the major opposition parties, no lack of money, and campaigning by Morarji Desai and JP. Consequently, as Rajni Kothari, another critic of Congress and Mrs Gandhi, put it: 'Gujarat was by no means representative of the country and there was more than a fair chance that the Congress would once again emerge triumphant in the national election which was barely eight months ahead.'[1]

And then came the Allahabad judgement on 12 June 1975 which marked a turning point. According to Balraj Madhok, at that time a BLD leader, some of the opposition leaders did not want to adopt a confrontationist approach and suggested instead that 'the leaders should fan out in the country and educate the people about the constitutional and moral impropriety of Mrs Gandhi's refusal to resign. A discredited Mrs Gandhi would have proved the biggest liability for her party and the greatest asset to the opposition in the elections to the Lok Sabha which were due in February 1976.'[2] Initially, JP too seemed to agree with this view. After asking Mrs Gandhi to resign immediately after the Allahabad judgement, he decided to go back to Bihar and build up the movement from below. But other leaders, some of whom were even earlier not in favour of the electoral option, sensed the possibility of the immediate ouster of Mrs Gandhi and a short cut to capture of power. They believed that Mrs Gandhi was at the end of her tether and needed just one last push. They persuaded JP to return from Bihar on 23 June, join the 'coup d'etat' school of thought and lead the movement for Mrs Gandhi's overthrow.

The entire rationale of the 'hawks' was indicated with his usual candour by Morarji Desai in his interview with Oriana Fallaci on 25 June 1975. Fallaci had put the question to him: 'But if yours is a democratic opposition, why didn't you wait till Mrs Gandhi's electoral mandate expired? Why didn't you attack her in the course of the normal election campaign due six months from now?' And Morarji had replied: 'One must strike the iron while it is hot, and it's becoming increasingly difficult to defeat her in a general election.' Referring to Mrs Gandhi's superior financial and administrative resources, he had added: 'We couldn't afford to wait. People would have gotten tired. We had to attack at once.' He had also expressed the apprehension: 'If, during the appeal trial, the Supreme Court should reverse the Allahabad verdict, that shouldn't surprise us.' Replying to the question, 'So what do you intend to do now?', he had asserted: 'We intend to overthrow her, to force her to resign. For good.'[3]

II

The imposition of the Emergency by Mrs Gandhi was also flawed. As already mentioned, she was to assert later that, faced with an extra-constitutional challenge, the Emergency was the only way out and that resignation was not an option. That would have meant strengthening communal fascist forces, which, aided and abetted from abroad, were threatening the democratic process and trying to take the country to the edge of anarchy, chaos and dictatorship. She also felt, on being advised by the eminent constitutional lawyers N.A. Palkhivala and Fali Nariman, that there were no legal or moral reasons for her to step down during the hearing of her appeal to the Supreme Court.

A full critique of the Emergency in Chapters 7 and 8 follows. But I am of the view that no compromise or concessions were possible at the time from Mrs Gandhi's side when the only opposition demand was for her removal from office. Nor could she have at that stage, in June, agreed to yield to a movement of which RSS was such an important, if not the dominant, component. The two options of politically facing the movement, including the gherao of her residence, or of stepping down from office temporarily, and then returning if she was cleared by the Supreme Court were also not really open to her.

A political fight was not possible, especially in the capital, which was a stronghold of the Jan Sangh. Mrs Gandhi was not capable of facing the type of campaign planned by the opposition with a counter-mass campaign because of what the Congress party had become. With few active cadres or committed members and a creaky institutional apparatus, the Congress had become little more than an electoral machine. During the Nehru era the party structure had been run down; Mrs Gandhi weakened it further. The CPI, its ally, did work towards organizing public opinion, but was too weak to perform the task. The CPM was sitting on the fence, but tilted towards the Opposition. Sanjay Gandhi's efforts to oppose the Mrs Gandhi-*hatao* movement with hired crowds were counterproductive in the long run. The bureaucracy, on which Congress governments had been relying since 1947 for implementing their policies, was obviously incapable of countering a mass movement.

As pointed out earlier, any efforts to counter a civil disobedience movement, of which Mrs Gandhi's gherao by hundreds of thousands of men and women was a part, would have resulted in a Jallianwala-style bloodbath and the use of massive force, including the use of armed forces. Mrs Gandhi was not willing to countenance either. The Opposition had rightly assumed that if she used existing laws and the police and bureaucratic machinery to deal with its movement, it would be on a winning wicket.[4]

The other option of resigning temporarily and then coming back after a favourable Supreme Court judgement was also not really feasible, or perhaps even desirable. Resignation in favour of loyalist political lightweights, such as D.K. Barooah, Swaran Singh or Siddhartha Shankar Ray, would not have been acceptable to the Opposition and would, therefore, not meet the political situation. Nor would resignation and having Jagjivan Ram or Y.B. Chavan in place as a stop-gap arrangement avert the threat of a "coup" by right-wing civilian neo-fascist forces. That the Opposition would let her Congress successors survive was only a possibility and not a certainty—they would carry far less weight than her; as tainted men, they would have had even less political strength to stand up to the Opposition movement for their resignation. The bureaucracy, the police and the army would know which way the wind was blowing and would shift their loyalties—and knowledge of which 'legal' orders to obey—accordingly. The leaders of the opposition movement would know that those who had yielded once to the pressure of a movement would do so again. Take, for example, the case of Jagjivan Ram. Pressed in Parliament, he had accepted on its floor that he had 'forgotten' to file income-tax returns for ten years! Stories of his corruption were widely current and believed. He could have been dislodged and swept aside with far greater ease than Mrs Indira Gandhi. Her overthrow could thus have a domino effect.[5]

True, this last scenario was only a possibility, but, then, after the historical experience of Mussolini's rise to power and his March on Rome (see appendix), could any democratic government or society take a chance with even a slight possibility of a fascist coup? No democracy can operate on a percentage basis. Moreover, if Mrs Gandhi had not stopped the non-democratic take-over of power, however little the possibility or potential of it becoming fascist, she would have been condemned by historians, political scientists and liberal analysts the way Italian liberals and conservatives, and King Victor Emmanuel were for their inaction in the face Mussolini's coup. As Mary C. Carras has put it: 'Indira Gandhi, for all her flaws, failures, hesitations, and retreats, recognized the explosive dimensions of the problem and sought to deal with it, plunging fearlessly into the Indian political labyrinth, with its awesome and enticing traps. In the end she may have yielded to them her better-judgement and her people's laurels.'[6] Unfortunately, Mrs Gandhi put forward all sorts of red herrings to justify the imposition of the Emergency instead of arguing in a straight forward manner that it was the only way to counter a potentially fascist movement.[7]

But apart from the negative record of the Emergency, it is my view that the Emergency was not the only way of countering the extra-constitutional movement for her removal; not the only way out of the blind alley. Mrs Gandhi, too, had another real democratic option which she could have pursued. Apart from appealing to the Supreme Court against the Allahabad judgement, or asking the Opposition to wait and test its support among the people till early 1976 elections (which also she did), she could have declared that the Lok Sabha would be dissolved and fresh elections to it held in October-November, with her fighting elections subject to the Supreme Court or the Parliament, through fresh legislation with retrospective effect, lifting the ban placed on her by the Allahabad High Court.

If JP and the Opposition accepted this offer, the door to a democratic resolution of the political impasse through an appeal to the electorate would have been opened. If they did not, and stuck to their demand for her resignation and to their declared methods to bring it about, she could legitimately declare that in view of the Opposition's rejection of the democratic option she was imposing an Internal Emergency or prime ministerial dictatorship till elections as the only viable and available option of meeting their extra-constitutional challenge. She could at the same time announce that the Emergency would be lifted as soon as the Opposition gave up its demand for her resignation, agreed to adhere to the Supreme Court's judgement, and accepted the test of elections. There was a good possibility that JP and the majority of the Opposition would have had to respond positively to her offer; but if they had not, they would have committed political *harakiri*, for then the charge against them of being at least undemocratic if not also neo-fascist would have been credible to the people.

Interestingly, it may be pointed out that this is exactly what General de Gaulle did in France when faced with the much more pervasive and radical upsurge of students and workers in May 1968. And, of course, the protesting students and workers and most of their leaders accepted the challenge to face de Gaulle in elections.

The probable reason why Mrs Gandhi did not exercise this electoral option was that, like JP and the Opposition, she also was not confident any more about her mass appeal and, therefore, the outcome of elections. She had also cause to be worried about the dissidence in her party.

After the Emergency was imposed, both JP and Mrs Gandhi were to suggest that going in for elections would have been the best solution, and would raise the question why did the other side not demand or wait for elections instead of going ahead with their respective moves, the movement of 22-25 June in one case and the imposition of the Emergency in the other. For example, according to P.N. Dhar, during Mrs Gandhi's negotiations with JP through the mediation of Dhar and Sugata Dasgupta, JP told Dasgupta that he would withdraw the movement if the pre-26 June situation was restored and the government announced the dates for a general election.[8] Similarly, JP noted in his diary on 10 October: 'I was quite clear in my mind that if parliamentary elections are announced to be held at the scheduled time, I would advocate stoppage of the confrontation with government and call for an all-out effort to win the elections. But for that the Emergency should be revoked . . .' On the other hand, he rightly added, if these things did not happen and if he was released, he would 'try to reorganize the revolutionary forces and refashion, if necessary, the concrete programmes of action.'[9] The entire case for relying on elections as the democratic answer to political problems was put by JP in his letter of 17 September 1975 to Mrs Gandhi in a manner that cannot be surpassed: 'You should announce in unambiguous terms that elections to the Lok Sabha would be held early in 1976 and that the Election Commission would fix the dates in due course. You will find, Madam, that that single announcement by you would work a miraculous change in the political climate of the country. *In a democracy, a General Election (provided it is fair and free) acts like a powerful catharsis, cleansing the political atmosphere, easing tensions and bringing health and vigour to the body politic.*'[10] (Emphasis added)

Even after his release on 12 November 1975, JP worked hard to get the government to hold the postponed general elections and to undermine Mrs Gandhi's political standing for refusing to do so. For example, when Vinoba Bhave asked him to retire from politics, his reply was that Mrs Gandhi should announce elections and end the Emergency and he would withdraw the movement. On 30 October 1976, he had announced: 'I can say that no question of any demonstration, mass movement, or civil disobedience, or any kind of trouble will arise if the decision for elections is announced.'[11]

Mrs Gandhi, too, later stressed the importance of elections in a democracy and chided the Opposition for not letting elections decide the contest between them. For example, she told an interviewer on 20 August 1975: 'Elections were only a few months away, and if they had waited they would have the verdict of the people.'[12] And in another interview on 22 September 1975: 'Elections were not too far off. So far we have never avoided elections. All they had to do was to work for the defeat of my party during the elections.'[13] And in January 1976, she taunted the Opposition in the Rajya Sabha: 'If you are so sure as you today say, 'Go to the elections and see', why don't (didn't) you wait for the elections? Why do (did) you want to destroy the Government just a few months before the elections?'[14] And in the broadcast to the nation on 18 January 1977 announcing elections, she once again asserted that in June 'the democratic way would have been to work towards the next elections, which were not far off.'[15]

In summary, it may be suggested that both JP and the Opposition as well as Indira Gandhi were responsible for initiating one of the darkest chapters of post-independence India; the former to a greater extent than the latter, because they tried to remove her from the seat of power through unconstitutional means. Both shunned the option of elections which in a democracy are the vehicles for the legitimization of a political regime and for expression of the voters' will. This happened partly because of the manner in which the political conflict during 1974-75 had developed. The tragic consequence of this was a political atmosphere in which dialogue and accommodation between the two opposing forces was not possible. If JP did not recognize that there have to be limits to any agitation, however popular, in a democratic polity and that the movement he was leading had a fascist potential, Mrs Gandhi, too, was unable to understand that the Emergency should not serve as an excuse for the suppression of all liberties and that it was bound to become authoritarian, especially as a hide-bound bureaucracy and a handful of decision-makers at the top rather than the Congress party were responsible for its implementation. In any case in any society the temptation to misuse emergency provisions when implemented was likely to prove to be very strong. Moreover, there was no justification for extending the Emergency or for its draconian measures once the perceived threat to law and order was over.

It is hard to be definitive about which way the JP movement would have ended had it been successful, though some speculations have been made here. It is, however, possible to discuss what happened during the Emergency. As we shall see, the authoritarian potential of the Emergency regime nearly came to be realized, especially with the rise of Sanjay Gandhi's unofficial 'leadership'.

6   *JP as a Leader and Thinker*

The JP movement (JPM) gathered force on its claim, following JP, of fighting corruption and distortions in the political system, especially in the electoral system, and to make democracy more effective. It had, however, many facets that were contradictory; in many respects, in its composition, actions, and potential consequences or the personality traits, outlook and thought of its leader, the movement was marked by weaknesses.

I

The JPM acquired a large part of its political strength and popularity from the moral authority and political appeal of Jayaprakash Narayan. JP, as he was popularly known, was born in Bihar in 1902. During the Non-Cooperation movement he left college in 1921 and then went to the US for higher education. Completing his Master's in sociology from Wisconsin University he returned to India in 1929, firmly committed to Marxism. In 1934, along with a number of other brilliant young political workers, he founded the Congress Socialist Party (CSP) which was a part of the Congress. In 1936 he was nominated by Nehru to the Congress Working Committee. Actively involved in the Quit India movement, he made a dramatic breakout from the Hazaribagh jail in 1942. The CSP broke away from the Congress in 1948, but, failing to grow, put up a poor performance in the 1952 general elections. A disillusioned JP enthusiastically joined Acharya Vinoba Bhave's Bhoodan movement in 1952 itself and took virtual charge of it as also of the Sarvodaya movement in Bihar later on. He renounced politics in 1957, declaring that party politics was not suited to India and advocating, instead, 'partyless democracy'. However, he continued to comment on politics. And, as we have seen in Chapter III, from 1973 he once again got involved in active politics, guiding and leading the JP movement in Bihar and later on in the whole of India.

JP was widely respected by people and the intelligentsia for his integrity, idealism, indomitable spirit and high moral stature, and disinterest in political office, having turned his back on several opportunities that came his way. Many saw him as 'an idealist and visionary' and as the embodiment of fearlessness, sincerity, sacrifice and selflessness. He was known for a simple lifestyle, personal incorruptibility, love for the country and its people, and a life-long commitment as a socialist and Sarvodaya leader to the establishment of a just, egalitarian and more humane society. He had also never shied away from taking up sensitive and unpopular issues of the day. Many considered him, as the Magsaysay Award citation put it, as 'the conscience of a people'.

JP was among the last of the stalwarts of the freedom struggle. A great deal of his political strength was an outcome of his reputation of being above party politics. Also, since he had given up active politics in the fifties and devoted himself to the Bhoodan and Sarvodaya movements, he was unsullied by the political dirt of the intervening twenty years, since 1947. He became a symbol of protest because of people's widespread disillusionment with politicians. As Vasant Nargolkar, a Sarvodaya worker and one of his admirers, put it in 1975: 'He is the embodiment of selflessness in an atmosphere which is murky with corruption and selfishness.'[1] Similarly, another of his friends and biographers, Ajit Bhattacharjea, correctly pointed out at the height of the JP movement: 'People flock to him today because of his patent sincerity; he has captured the credibility that the politicians have lost.'[2]

Undoubtedly, JP took up certain very important issues for agitation during 1974-75 and adopted some significant political positions. His refusal to tolerate what was going on in the country was justified. He rightly highlighted several serious ailments from which India was then suffering. Among these was the issue of corruption, especially political corruption, which was eating into the very vitals of the country and its political system and also affecting the daily life of the common people.[3] And he warned: 'If there is dishonesty, corruption, manipulation of the masses, naked struggle for personal power and personal gain, there can be no socialism, no welfarism, no government, no public order, no justice, no freedom, no national unity—in short, no nation.'[4]

Throughout his campaign, JP repeatedly highlighted electoral malpractices, which affected the conduct and result of elections, and emphasized the urgent need for reforms to ensure a free and fair exercise of the vote. In particular, he condemned the increasing and excessive use of money, especially black money, in elections; the questionable and corrupt means adopted by political parties, especially the ruling party, for raising funds, the use of caste power and physical force—'lathi and muscle power'—to prevent Harijans and other weaker sections from voting, especially in rural areas, ballot stuffing, impersonation and booth capturing, and the intimidation and buying up of the polling officers. All these electoral evils were vitiating democracy and posed the most serious danger to it.[5]

Throughout his agitation, JP emphasized the need to defend our existing democracy and to deepen it, even as he highlighted the repressive and anti-democratic tendencies of the Indian state. Pointing to some of the weaknesses of parliamentary democracy, he urged that people should be involved 'more intimately and continuously in the processes of democracy'.[6] This involvement should not be confined to their going to the polls every five years and thereby changing a government they did not like.[7] People should also be able to intervene in political and administrative processes in between elections. Moreover, those elected should remain responsible and accountable to the electors. Proper peoples' organizations should be created for this purpose.[8] Moreover people should acquire 'the capacity to stand up to injustice, oppression and corruption.'[9] They should be able, as part of democratic politics, to take to peaceful protest against government action and policies and even take recourse to direct political action and popular political movements including 'civil disobedience, peaceful resistance, non-cooperation—in short, satyagraha in its widest sense' in case of extreme discontent.[10] According to him, people also had the right to demand resignation of an unpopular government and to start a popular campaign to enforce the demand.[11] JP recognized that people were increasingly resorting to violent and extra-constitutional agitations. But for this, he pointed out, part of the responsibility lay with those in power, who tended to ignore peaceful protest and paid heed only when people resorted to violent means.[12] Besides, violence was fuelled by the police reacting to popular protest through undue and unprovoked recourse to lathi-charges, teargassing and firing.[13]

Most of the positions JP held on this aspect of democracy were widely accepted. The real question was about the mechanisms to be used to put these ideas into practice and enforce the popular will. For example, how were the elected to be made responsible to the electors and how were the people to exercise effective control over the former? Popular movements could be and had been used to put pressure on the governments to change their policies, but could they be utilized to change governments and reverse the verdict of the elections? What were to be the limits of satyagraha and other forms of popular protest? How was democracy to be deepened? JP had only confused answers, if any, to such questions. This aspect of JP's thought and activities is discussed in a later section.

He rightly raised the issue of the defence and development of democratic state institutions, for there is no doubt that the years since 1962 had witnessed a certain disarray, a deterioration in political institutions. Consequently, many of them had also been losing their moral authority and governance had become difficult. JP agitated for the independence of the judiciary. He emphasized the need for the healthy development of local self-government institutions at the village, bloc and district levels, for the parliament to put constraints on its own unbridled power, and for a healthy balance between the Centre and the states, between the judiciary, executive and the legislature, and between a state government and the organs of local self-government. In general, he repeatedly raised his voice in defence of fundamental rights, except that he accepted the need for reasonable restrictions on the right to property.

Drawing attention to the moral decline in public life, he said, 'The most frightening thing, that is happening is the complete breakdown of public political morality, especially at higher levels.'[14] Moreover, 'there is no branch of public life—politics, government, business, education, trade unions, social work and the rest—that is left untouched. The difference is only one of degree, or one of opportunity. Not only the ruling Congress but also the opposition parties are stricken with disease, as the interregnum between 1967 and 1972 had sadly witnessed.'[15] One of the major objectives of the JPM, he said, was to cleanse politics of the accumulated moral grime and bring about 'a moral regeneration of our politics.'[16] And in this respect he emphasized the role of non-party movements and organizations.

At a more specific current level, he critiqued the Bihar government's incompetence in checking the price rise and scarcity of essential commodities, its corruption, its apathy towards people's demands, and its efforts to stifle popular agitations, particularly of students, with heavy-handed suppression. His criticism of Indira Gandhi for not bringing about sufficient socio-economic improvements during her nine years in office and for her tendency to concentrate power in her own hands was also justified to a certain extent.

JP focussed on the deterioration in the educational system and agitated for its reconstruction so 'as to relate education to the problems of the country and fit the educated to deal with them.' He also urged 'that a modicum of education should be made universal and illiteracy and ignorance banished from the land.'[17]

JP was also committed to a certain conception of a more humane society and the transformation of the people's social condition, based at present on 'unjust human and social relations'. This led him to criticize and condemn the all-pervading social and economic inequality, 'rotten customs and manners' and superstitions, the caste system and caste oppression, especially of the Harijans, the dowry system, specially among the upper castes, and the skewed system of land ownership and land control in Bihar.[18] But, surprisingly, this critique and the necessary redressal of these 'evils' never became a part of the agenda of the movement which he led, which concentrated almost entirely on the twin issues of corruption and removal of the governments of Bihar and later at the Centre or on the generality of Total Revolution.

II

Several significant questions need to be raised before we proceed further. How were these good wishes and intentions to be translated into practice? Did JP at any stage make a serious concrete analysis of the overall socio-political structure and situation in the country? Did he have a grasp of what caused the ills from which the Indian polity was suffering and against which he was agitating and building up a movement, or of the remedies and alternatives he was prescribing for them, or of the forces, organizations and institutions necessary to wage the struggle against them?

In the absence of positive answers to these questions, JP's socio-political critique and his heavy, though on the whole correct, political agenda remained mere truisms. For example, that elections should be free and fair, that corruption in all its forms should be eradicated from all walks of life, that politics should be morality based, that democracy should be deepened, that periodic elections were not sufficient to make the government fully democratic, that those 'elected should command the confidence and respect of the people of their constituencies' and should 'serve them honestly and selflessly', that the educational system should be overhauled, that the dowry system and caste discrimination were highly undesirable, that land reforms and land ceiling laws should be implemented, that a law against defections should be enacted, that the institution of Lok Pal was needed to check political and administrative corruption and the like, were commonplace in the political discourse of the time and issues with which hardly anyone disagreed. JP, however, certainly deserved credit for highlighting these shortcomings. Congress and Indira Gandhi, for example, had no difficulty in accepting nearly all of these truisms as major tasks to be undertaken. And, in fact, she and her Congress successors did enact some legislation for the purpose.

What becomes apparent from JP's writings and speeches of the period or the jottings in his *Prison Diary* is that he was unable either to diagnose the ills of the Indian polity (except to put the blame on Congress and Indira Gandhi) or suggest effective remedies for them. It was because of this basic weakness, and not because of any particular error of thought or judgement on a particular aspect of the movement, that it was possible for communalists and other tainted political leaders and parties, who had little in common with him, to appropriate his ideas and movement and popular appeal for their own purposes.

Frankly, an objective look at JP would suggest that, though having several marks of greatness, JP was not the man to play the role he had assigned himself, that is, as a leader of a mass movement for the rejuvenation of Indian politics and of a revolution, total or partial, for bringing about basic socio-economic and political changes in the country. Despite his own desire, and the conviction of many of his followers, he was not up to the task, as a thinker or political leader, to play the role of a Gandhi or a Lenin or a Mao. In fact, all his life he had groped for a role as a political leader far beyond his capacities and much larger than the one he was playing at the moment. A major problem was that what he wanted to achieve could only be gained by struggle for and assumption of political power; but he was not willing to take up that burden or even to openly struggle for it. It might be said that Gandhiji, too, did not take up political power in 1947, but then he had trained political lieutenants who could. JP relied in the end on the old war horses, the honest but conservative, veering to reactionary, Morarji Desai and the RSS leader and organizer, Nanaji Deshmukh.

In view of the stature that JP occupies in both the pre- and post-independence India, I have thought it necessary to deal at length with this difficult aspect of JP and the JPM; to understand JP's traits, the key shortcomings in his thought and character, and the inadequacies and contradictions in his leadership. The purpose of this critical look is not to reduce his stature but to explain the failure of the JPM and the manner in which it was hijacked by others who had little in common with him. This was amply brought out not only during 1974-75 but also later after April 1977 by the record of the Janata government. I am, of course, writing with hindsight, but a perceptive contemporary observer, C.N. Chitta Ranjan, already wrote in October 1974 that JP was 'aware of his inability effectively to guide and direct the movement he has launched with the backing of elements that never had faith in Gandhiji's ideas or methods. The battle against not only corruption but other evils in our society, including the gross inequalities . . . must be conducted as a national movement . . . Such a movement surely must have a leader with greater vision and comprehension than JP has shown himself to be capable of over long years.'[19] Similarly, in 1979, in his obituary of JP, the 'Analyst' wrote: 'If the yardstick of political greatness is to be intention and desire, then certainly JP had it in abundance. But if political statesmanship has to take into account the working out of a political line, with its strategy and tactics, with the creation of the leverage of change through an organization, then JP would have been the first to confess that he did not possess them.'[20]

III

An evaluation of JP demands that we focus on his role as the sole leader of a movement that set out to usher in a total revolution or transformation of Indian society and polity. Based on a study of his speeches and writings of the period 1973-78 and of the political leadership he provided to the movement named after him, this analysis would be revealing for what it shows about his thought and leadership.

As pointed out earlier, there is no doubt that throughout 1973-77, by highlighting the corrupt, repressive and anti-democratic tendencies and features of contemporary Indian polity and the general social, economic and political malaise from which the country was suffering, JP was raising some highly significant issues. Yet, much of his thinking and leadership of the movement he led from March 1974 to June 1975, however well-intentioned, was characterized by naivete, confusion, ambiguity, contradictions, inconsistencies and grand illusions. On close examination, JP emerges as a confused political leader lacking originality and clarity of thought. Despite his talk of Total Revolution, systemic change, youth-power and the like, his response to the problems and issues he took up was often either utopian and bereft of realism, lending a Don-Quixote like quality or character to many of his words or deeds, or commonplace and with which nobody could disagree and which did not require a revolution to be implemented. In his case, quite often rhetoric took the place of thought in the discussion of the causes and remedies of the social malaise or the conduct of the movement— a fatal flaw in the sole leader of a mass movement.

It is possible to cite many examples of JP's political positions that reflect this naivete and lack of realism. In fact, sometimes it becomes difficult to distinguish between his naivete and political opportunism. This is evident, above all, in the varied positions he adopted towards political parties. Before 1973, JP had argued vigorously for partyless democracy. He had been critical of both the ruling and the opposition parties and their immoral politics. During 1973-74, he characterized all of them as equally corrupt on a number of occasions. In July 1973, in his famous article 'First things First', he had declared: 'As I diagnose the root cause of the country's critical state of health, I identify it unhesitatingly as the precipitous fall in the moral standards of our public life.'[21] Referring to the defections from one party to another, he wrote on 8 September: 'The country witnessed the most shameful spectacle of political immorality and degradation . . . a brisk market flourished in which legislators were sold and bought as cattle . . . During the coalition government days in the States between 1967 and 1972, the opposition parties, which were the ruling parties then, played the game with as much gusto as the Congress had ever displayed.'[22] That there was no difference between the opposition parties and the Congress in regard to corruption and nepotism was asserted by JP on a number of occasions—e.g. on 23 September, at the end of December 1973 and again at the beginning of the Bihar movement.[23]

As late as April 1974, he had declared at the Conference of Citizens for Democracy: 'Let no one think that the ruling party alone has been guilty of distortion of the electoral processes and the electoral laws. Whichever party, irrespective of its ideology, that has found (it) possible to indulge in any of the corrupt or illegal methods has not hesitated from resorting to it on the ground that they are fighting elections to win and not to lose.'[24] In June 1974, when most of the opposition MLAs had refused to heed his appeal to resign their seats, he had exclaimed: 'All parties have come out in their true colours.'[25] He expressed distrust of all political parties even at the height of the JPM. Sometime in 1975 he told Minoo Masani: 'If the movement in the rest of the States (outside Bihar) is started by political parties, it is bound to fail.'[26]

Yet, despite this strong critique of the opposition parties, very soon, by November 1974, he accepted their support, irrespective of their character and composition, invited them to join and fight along with his movement, and worked hard for their consolidation. In November 1974, he convened a conference of the non-Communist opposition parties and helped them set up the National Coordination Committee with himself as the chairman. He asked the student revolutionaries to operate in close cooperation with this Committee. In fact, the opposition parties became the mainstay of the JPM and, increasingly, it became an instrument of their quest for power. In fact, in the entire movement, except for a few intellectuals and Sarvodaya workers, JP was the only one not attached to a party. Even most of the prominent student revolutionaries were activists of political parties. In Bihar, for example, all but five members of the Chhatra Sangharsh Samiti were attached to political parties or their student wings. In August 1974, a Chhatra Sangharsh Samiti was formed in Lucknow by the youth wings of Jan Sangh, Congress (O), BLD, Socialist Party, the Tarun Shanti Sena and the UP Sarvodaya Mandal. In October, same political parties along with some Sarvodaya workers formed a Coordination Committee for organizing the movement in Rajasthan. At the end of November 1974, JP convened an all-India Students and Youth Conference which formed a forty-member National Coordination Committee of Students and Youth. One of the two convenors was Arun Jaitley, leader of the ABVP. To avoid the accusation that the Committee was dominated by the ABVP, Anand Kumar, who at the time was a Free Thinker and had no student base outside JNU, was made the other convenor, as a sort of dummy.

We may cite yet another instance. In February 1974, speaking in Gujarat and asking the MLAs to resign, JP had said that if the Congress (O), the Jan Sangh and Swatantra staged a comeback after fresh elections, it would be a backward step.[27] Yet, in the Gujarat elections of June 1975, he completely surrendered before political parties and actively aided the organization of the Janata Morcha, a coalition of the opposition parties, primarily of the above-named parties, and campaigned for it.

During 1974-75 and in his *Prison Diary*, JP offered several simplistic justifications for his changed stance towards political parties. One was that 'it is not political parties with which we are identifying ourselves but with the people struggling against a corrupt, oppressive and incompetent regime and an iniquitous social order.' The JPM was, moreover, he said, 'a vast upsurge of the people in which the parties merge and lose their identity like rivers in the sea.'[28] He repeatedly denied that the JPM was dependent on political parties. He also solved the problem of ensuring that the movement remained a non-party one by asking the participating parties not to use it for their own partisan purposes. Thus, in April 1974, he wrote that he was appealing 'to the political parties and their student wings that their participation in the movement should be in a non-partisan spirit, and no one should try to "capture" the movement or use it for party political ends.' And, he was naïve enough to add: 'I am happy to say that the concerned party leaders have assured me that it will be so.'[29] He claimed shortly thereafter that both in Gujarat and Bihar the movements 'have been largely non-partisan in nature. Neither of them has been anti-Congres as such.'[30]

JP also hoped that the participation in the movement would transform the character of the opposition parties cooperating with him. In August 1974, he told the *Hindustan Times* that 'personally I am trying to put in as much of socio-economic content into the movement as possible. So far they are accepting it. I have said, for instance, that as we go down to the rural areas, it should not be merely a struggle against blackmarketeers and hoarders and administrative corruption, but against socio-economic injustices. I have also told them that they must take up the question of share-croppers, and of agricultural labourers ... So, as time goes on, in cooperation with these parties I hope to deepen the socio-economic content of the movement.' He admitted that two of the opposition parties, the Jan Sangh and Congress (O), were conservative, but argued: 'As time goes on and as the movement gets more and more radicalized, as it goes nearer and nearer to the people, these questions will be raised and may be these parties themselves will be radicalized in the process.'[31] On 20 April 1975, he told an interviewer that the major opposition parties had already undergone a change of heart. 'The BLD and Jan Sangh in Bihar have assured me,' he said, 'that they fully accept the goal of the total revolution.' He added that the Jan Sangh and Congress (O) 'had assured me that they would be with me till the end.'[32] He also justified his changed stance and abandonment of partyless democracy by saying that 'partyless democracy cannot be established before we succeed in achieving a classless society.'[33]

Similarly, ruminating in jail on the question of the participation of political parties in the JPM, he said that when he took over the leadership of the student movement, its leaders already 'undoubtedly were guided by the party leadership outside', these parties being Jan Sangh, Socialist Party, BLD and Congress (O). Thus, he continued, 'the political parties were there already'. What his influence had done was to keep 'the party influences low, helped to evolve a consensus, and give the movement—at the start the students' movement and then the people's movement—a non-party political character'. Accordingly, he said, 'the parties that entered the movement in Bihar did not enter as parties, and their leaders, workers and sympathizers came in as individuals.' The participation of the opposition parties, he argued, 'lends strength to the movement'. And, most importantly, 'the parties undergo a sea-change in the process' because of the 'strong non-party leadership in the movement.' In Bihar, in particular, he added, 'all the parties involved are committed to the aims of total revolution and to the dynamics of change: struggle'.[34]

Having virtually reduced the movement to the level of a campaign for the removal of Mrs Gandhi from office, he made this itself a justification for uniting with the opposition parties. In April 1975, asking the rightist and leftist parties to 'patch up' and unite in order to 'face the elections', he said: 'The Right and Left must realize that their enemy is the same.'[35]

JP's failure to see through the motives and character of his allied parties also revealed a certain naivete in his understanding of parties and their dynamics. After all, it should have been clear to him that the opposition parties joined him in order to use him as a charismatic leader and a unifying symbol against Congress in their search for power. And they did effectively discard him after March 1977 once they had achieved their objectives.[36]

On the other hand, perhaps it was not possible for JP to take a holier-than-thou attitude towards the opposition parties, for his joining forces with them was not entirely free of opportunism. He, too, united with them primarily to acquire political muscle and political workers for his crusade. As pointed out in Chapter 3, he had no organizational structure or political cadres of his own; and he was too old and in too much of a hurry to build a structure of his own and to recruit and train cadres loyal to him and believing in his political values and principles.[37] The only political workers he could rely upon were from the Sarvodaya; but outside Bihar they were negligible in number. Once he was convinced that the JPM should be extended to an all-India movement, he realized this would only be possible with the help of existing political parties. As pointed out earlier, even in Bihar he had developed the movement with their cooperation, especially of their student wings. That he was aware of the situation and his dilemma at the ground level is brought out by his note of 6 September 1975 in his *Prison Diary*. Expressing some doubts about his alliance with the opposition parties, he wrote:[38]

The question of the Bihar movement and other similar movements getting involved with Opposition political parties has worried a number of friendly intellectuals and many well-wishers. I have been no less worried myself about it. As I look back I ask myself, did I make a mistake, and if so, what was it? I have asked myself this question again and again during the movement also. What were, and are, the answers? There is no doubt that if the movement had not got mixed up with the Opposition parties, its character, its experimental utility, its educative value, its ability to enable the people to see their problems with their own eyes (not the eyes of the parties) and to think of their responsibility to do whatever lay in their power to solve their problems, to change themselves and change their material and social environment, and if they must offer peaceful resistance or non-cooperation in this process, to do so singly, in groups or in 'mass' (i.e., through a mass movement) would not have been compromised.

But he added with a touch of realism, or as some would say, opportunism: 'If the movement had been confined to the Sarvodaya workers alone and its principle was to keep away all political parties (including the ruling party), it would have been possible to keep them away. But, then, there would have been no *people's* movement.'

JP, thus, depended on the Jan Sangh, BLD and Akali Dal for political mobilization in northern India. The relative weakness or absence of these three parties in southern, western and most of eastern India was responsible for the limited inroad of the movement there. In fact, the opposition parties became the mainstay of the JPM, and the movement increasingly became an instrument of their quest for power.

Moreover, the consolidation of opposition parties and groups was carried on irrespective of their political and ideological character. The JPM came to include the communal Jan Sangh, Akali party and Jamaat-i-Islami, the neo-fascist RSS, the conservative though secular Congress (O), the right-wing casteist representative of the northern Indian rich peasants, the BLD, the socialists, who had given up socialism in favour of casteism, the extreme left Naxalite groups, and the Sarvodayists, votaries of non-violence. JP also tried to attract the CPM into the movement but with little success. In terms of programmes and policies these parties and groups had nothing in common and were ideologically incompatible and poles apart. Their only uniting force was the towering personality of JP and the fear and hatred of Mrs Gandhi. As Morris-Jones has put it, 'It all began to look too much like the discredited "grand alliance" of 1971'.[39] One also wonders how JP hoped to lead his revolt against statism and centralization of power in the company of Morarji Desai and RSS-Jan Sangh.

Several other examples of JP's naivete or the contradictory stances in his thought and politics are touched on briefly here. No eyebrows would be raised because of them if JP were an ordinary political leader, especially one participating in electoral politics. But coming from the sole leader of what he believed to be a revolutionary movement, these anomalies cannot be overlooked. JP repeatedly asserted that he was not interested in changing governments.[40] He advised his followers not to indulge in the politics of toppling governments and to relate their actions to the fulfilment of their concrete demands, to evolve a positive kind of politics rather than merely that of 'Indira Hatao'. Yet, the movement he led gradually, in a short span of time, made the resignation of the Bihar government and the dissolution of the Bihar assembly its only effective demand, and in the end its mainstay became Indira Gandhi's removal from office. He participated actively in the Gujarat state elections in May-June 1975 and did not object to the formation of a non-Congress government in cooperation with Chimanbhai Patel, the main target of the anti-corruption movement of Gujarat students. And in his message to the nation on 13 April 1977, he urged the dissolution of the legislatures of Congress-ruled states much before the expiry of their terms, in the bargain, setting a bad precedent.

It is also interesting that while for over a year he had been campaigning for high standards being observed and new ways of chosing candidates, he did not even try to have these imposed in the Gujarat elections which came at the fag end of this campaign in May-June 1975. Similarly, while the March 1977 elections were fought on the sole issue of ending the Emergency, he made no attempt to promote the electoral values he stood for in the choice of the candidates for the June 1977 assembly elections.

He repeatedly condemned booth-capturing and use of physical force in elections and yet came to ally with Charan Singh's BLD which was notorious for physically preventing Harijans or dalits from voting in western UP. Similarly, while the JPM stood for checking and finally eliminating the casteist and communalist tendencies in elections and politics in general, JP proceeded to join hands with a casteist party like BLD and communal parties like Jan Sangh and Akali Dal and diehard communal organizations like the RSS and Jamaat-i-Islami.

In early 1973, he laid down four conditions that an effective opposition party must fulfil: It should stand for forces of radical change even while relying upon peaceful and democratic means; it should unite opposition forces on a 'principled and not opportunistic' basis; it must not repeat the sad experience of the coalition governments in the states from 1967 to 1969; and it must not rely or negative aims such as 'Indira Hatao' but should put forward positive policies and programmes.[40a] Yet, within a short span of time, JP himself had violated all these four conditions.

His approach towards forms of mass action was also problematic. In September 1973, he had said that demonstrations, noisy processions, strikes and bandhs had been found to be ineffective and therefore 'we must break new ground' as far as the lines of action possible for citizens were concerned.[41] Yet, later in the movement, he relied primarily on strikes, bandhs, and such measures. What is more important he added gherao, especially of the residences of legislators and ministers, to these lines of action, though, as a votary of non-violence, he told his followers that the movement 'should not assume coercive character',[42] ignoring the fact that non-coercive gherao was an oxymoron, a contradiction in terms.

In many instances JP comes across as confused or given to woolly thinking. An important example is that of the reforms he suggested in the political system. Having rightly raised the question of making the existing political institutions more democratic, he spoke in general terms of government by participation and of 'grass-roots democracy', 'true' or 'real' or 'people's' democracy, of politics and government based on people's power', of the 'consolidation of the organized power of the masses', even establishing 'alternative type and structure of democracy', of making the legislatures 'as representative of the people's will as possible', of seeing to it that 'the will of the great majority must prevail over that of a small majority', and of making the elected representatives responsible and accountable to the people, so that they would be 'under the control of the people.'[43] Democracy, he said, had 'to be built up from below' and had to be based on '*gram raj* (village self-government)' or 'people's committees' embodying the will of the people at the village level.[44]

However, the several steps or reforms he suggested to implement his ideas in this respect were either commonplace or too general or not workable, though some of them were highly desirable. For example, during 1974, he suggested a plan for the selection of candidates, after the dissolution of the Bihar assembly, so that the people, and not party leaders, would have a dominant role in their selection. The representatives of the Chhatra and Jan Sangharsh Samitis (Students' and People's Struggle Committees) of a constituency, who should not belong to any political party, were to nominate a candidate on behalf of the people of the constituency by following the rule of unanimity or consensus and choosing the best available candidate. Thus, even if a party member was chosen, the chosen candidate would be a people's and not a party's candidate.[45] JP put forward several other versions of this plan. For example, sometimes people's committees of a constituency or the representatives of the gram sabhas were expected to choose the candidate, preferring the candidates who were honest, had sympathy for the poor and would serve their cause.[46] As pointed out earlier, JP made no effort to implement his suggestion in this regard in the Gujarat elections of May-June 1974 or the state assembly elections in Bihar or other states in June 1977.

Furthermore, JP laid down that the people should have effective control on their elected representatives. To exercise this, local people's committees and other permanent organs of people's power were to be formed. These people's committees should consist of 'non-party members with non-caste and non-class attitudes of mind.'[47] The woolliness of this conception was expressed in the concluding sentence of JP's dictum: 'These people's committees should not be *for* or *against* any party, whether ruling or opposition. They should only be pro-people.'[48] The elected representatives were to be further controlled by the people through the 'un-written' right to demand their resignation, that is, the right to recall a representative if he was to 'fail in his duty' or become 'corrupt and oppressive and inefficient.' People could exercise their right 'if and when necessary.'[49] JP did not, however, work out—or perhaps had little conception of what the right to recall involved—how this right was to be exercised in constituencies involving one lakh to over ten lakh voters. He did, however, lay down that 'any small number of disgruntled persons' could not exercise this right at their will,[50] that is, only a vast majority of the people could do so. But he was quiet on the mechanism for determining what the vast majority wanted. The only answer he gave during the movement was that the Sangharsh Samitis would keep an eye on those elected and could ask an MLA to resign 'if he goes wrong.' The Samitis could give the MLA instructions and tell him, for example, how to vote on a bill irrespective of the stand of the party to which he belonged; and if he did not obey they could compel him to resign. The Samitis would thus act as the 'instrument of people's control over legislators.'[51]

Reconstruction of education was a major plank of the movement, but JP's ideas on the subject were another example of his woolly thinking. His main critique of the current educational system, described by him as 'defective and outdated', was that it did not train the students for a job, was intended to produce babus and was, therefore, in part responsible for the unemployment problem. It did not 'teach them anything, it does not train them for any work. It does not help them to understand the world they live in. Look at the number of unemployed engineers and graduates . . . If the students go out into the countryside they will learn more in that one year than through all the courses they can read put together.'[52] Another problem with the educational system was its alien character which had led to 'defective' planners, economists and political leaders being produced.[53]

JP had, however, no creative ideas on how to remove these defects in the educational system. The remedies he suggested were commonplace and mutually contradictory, often based on hoary stereotypes and hardly deserving a place in the programme of a revolutionary movement designed to totally overhaul the education system. He was unhappy that students studied to get jobs and not out of a 'sincere desire for knowledge and skills.' 'I have been appalled to find', he wrote in September 1974, 'that only a small percentage of our students today are charged with such a desire. The rest want nothing more than a degree, which is prized not for its educational but commercial value. A degree for most students is a mere passport to employment.' Consequently, he argued that 'no educational reform of a basic nature is possible unless either (1) degrees are abolished or (2) degrees are delinked from employment.'[54]

Simultaneously, he demanded vocationalization of education. Academic education, he said, should be combined 'with manual work and training in different skills in farms, factories and offices'; he stressed 'the need to dovetail educational planning with economic planning so that the jobs for which the students have been trained are actually available.'[55]

In the main, JP relied on well-known and hackneyed generalities for educational reform. For example, laying down a programme for 'Direct Action of Youth and People' in December 1974, he placed emphasis on 'drastic educational reform to destroy its elitist character and relate it to the problems of socio-economic development and of the lives of the students themselves.'[56] In the end, he came to rely on committees of experts to find solutions to the educational problems. In his broadcast to the nation on 13 April 1977 he urged: 'It is time that the radical recommendations of the several education commissions, the Kothari Commission not being the least of them, are implemented.'[57] He was not wrong; but was this really revolutionary?

While one is reluctant to make connections between a movement and the consequent developments for which it might not be responsible, it cannot be ignored that the JPM did contribute to the drastic fall in the standards of college and university education in Bihar and to a certain extent in UP, leading to a large-scale exodus of students from Bihar to universities in Delhi and other parts of the country.

IV

The hazy, naïve, and unrealistic thinking of JP was most evident in his concept of Total Revolution. He viewed the JPM as a movement for total revolution. As brought out before (Chapter 3, Section II), he was convinced that a revolutionary situation was developing in the country and that the people were ready for a revolution that would determine India's fate for decades to come. He was to repeat this reading of the situation in June 1976 in an interview. Pointing out that even the greatest of revolutionary leaders did not create 'revolution at will' and that 'the secret of their leadership lay in the fact that they were able to recognize the signs of the times and skillfully exploited the historical opportunities', he asserted: 'There was undoubtedly a revolutionary climate in the country last year (1974) . . . the ferment has nearly died down by now . . . But the seeds of discontent are still there, and unless there is some miracle, the mass movement will again come to the boiling point in the near future.'[58]

Moreover, the problems faced by the people could only be solved by bringing about a total revolution, albeit a peaceful one. According to him, the country had, under his leadership, already entered 'the arena of the ongoing revolutionary struggle.'[59] He repeatedly asserted that in the Bihar movement he had created a revolutionary force and a revolutionary movement. He told the mammoth gathering at Patna on 5 June 1974, that though the immediate objectives of the movement were resignation of the Congress ministry and the dissolution of the state assembly, the movement would go far beyond these demands and was aimed at bringing about Total Revolution. 'Friends!', he declared at the meeting, 'This is a revolution, a total revolution!'[60] In April 1975, explaining the difference between Bertrand Russell and himself, quoting Marx, he told an interviewer that 'in my humble way I am trying to alter the world, while Russell merely interpreted it.'[61]

What was JP's conception of Total Revolution? Often describing it in the broadest of terms, this was, as indicated above, 'a continuous process of revolutionary changes.'[62] It implied the total transformation of the system.[63] In August 1974, asking the guardians and parents of the students not to look upon the movement as 'an ordinary kind of movement', he said that 'it is in fact the beginning of a revolution whose gains might transform the entire society.'[64] The revolution would change the society in a fundamental manner; it would cleanse society and politics and the political system. 'The struggle', he said, 'is not for the capture of power . . . but for purification of government and politics, including those of the Opposition and for fashioning instruments and conditions for taming and controlling power, irrespective of which party or parties happen to be in power for the time being.'[65] The people's struggle was, moreover, directed against an 'iniquitous social order'.[66] The revolution would do away with 'the continuing injustice of the present structure of property, polity and bureaucracy.'[67]

The Total Revolution would be total also in the sense that it would encompass all areas and aspects of life. In nearly all his major public speeches and writings JP made it a point to stress this aspect. Thus, in August 1974: 'There is no reason why this movement should not continue until some basic social, economic, political and cultural changes have been brought about.'[68] In December 1974: 'The struggle began with four objectives, namely, eradication of corruption, high prices unemployment and radical changes in education.' But even these objectives which might appear to be limited in character required, 'an all-round revolution—political, economic, social, educational, moral and cultural.'[69] Total Revolution also involved the transformation of individuals and the birth of a new value structure for human affairs.[70] 'For example', he said in August 1974, 'in the course of the struggle I think the boys are undergoing a change. Boys, who in the past, would have gone to beat up a principal, are now offering satyagraha and going to jail.'[71]

JP was to reiterate all this in his *Prison Diary* and the interviews he gave after his release in 1976 and 1977. For example, his entry on 18 August 1975 in his *Prison Diary* said: 'The struggle, the movement was for total revolution, i.e., revolution in every sphere of social life and organization . . . The basic systemic changes would happen first and the individual and group adaptations, mostly psychological, later. It seems to me that in such an atmosphere psychological forces are created that attract men and drive them to accept challenges and to change themselves and change others.'[72] And again on 7 October: 'I have been saying that total revolution is a combination of seven revolutions—social, economic, political, cultural, ideological or intellectual, educational and spiritual.'[73] And he clarified further in an interview in December 1977: 'One has noticed in history, that if there is a revolutionary upsurge, whatever be its mainsprings—political, economic, class struggle or anything else, once the revolutionary fire and fervour spreads, it affects everything and if it succeeds, nothing is left in its old form. There is a generalized change brought about; in some spheres more, some spheres less. This is what I had in mind.'[74] After coming out of jail in November 1975, he added another element to Total Revolution—it was to be a 'permanent revolution. It will always go on and keep on changing both our personal and social lives. This revolution knows no respite, no halt, certainly not a complete halt. Of course, according to the needs of the situation its form will change, its programme will change, its processes will change.'[75]

Perhaps the most important aspect of the Total Revolution was a change in the political system and political institutions. As JP put it in his *Prison Diary*, 'a revolutionary change of the political system was an integral and inescapable part of the total revolution and therefore of the struggle.'[76] He did not, however, spell out the new, more desirable political system and political institutions. All he would say was that the changed political system must be based on the 'continuous power of the people' or 'the organized power of the masses', or 'the people's will', that power must belong to the people, that the people must act 'for themselves', and that, as we have seen in an earlier section, the political system must be based on grassroots democracy and people's self government and rely on 'permanent organs of people's power from the village to the constituency and to the state level,' and on 'permanent institutions of people's power.'[77] JP also argued for greater and real devolution of power, authority and decision-making to the villages and blocks.

Throughout 1974-77, especially in the article 'A Manifesto for Bihar' in May 1975, JP made a radical socio-economic critique of Indian and Bihar society and asked the JPM and his followers to adopt radical remedies for social ills and introduce radical changes in society. In general, he spoke and wrote in favour of ending all forms of exploitation and social and economic inequality, and 'break-up of the power structure in the rural and urban society so that the domination of a few over many may end.'[78] In particular, he argued for peasant ownership of land and, therefore, land reforms for a reasonable ceiling on land holdings, strict enforcement of land ceiling legislation, and the distribution of surplus land among poor peasants and the landless. He asked the youth to struggle for the problems of sub-tenants, share-croppers, marginal and small cultivators, agricultural labourers and the urban poor and to unionize the latter.[79]

He also emphasized the need for radical transformation of social customs and institutions and for a casteless and classless society. In particular, he urged the abolition of communalism and the caste system, the uplift of Harijans and the tribals, and the eradication of social evils like the practice of dowry.[80] For example, in May 1975, in his 'A Manifesto for Bihar', he asked the young people to tackle in 'their own lives and the life of the society' such issues as those of 'high and low castes, of *dwijas* and shudras, of untouchability, of dowry and tilak, of the status and treatment of women, of inter-caste and inter-religious marriages, and a host of other social evils or social reforms whatever they may be.' These changes, he said, 'are the most difficult to effect. Yet, they are an important part of the total revolution that the Bihar movement is aiming at.'[81] And, as repeatedly pointed out earlier (Chapter 3 and Section II of this chapter), he urged radical transformation of the educational system.

JP kept up his radical stance after being released from jail. In August 1976, he urged 'redistribution of income and property' and the turning of 'the people's and the youth's minds against such evils as the dowry system, caste distinctions, untouchability, communalism, etc.'[82] In December 1977, he reiterated: 'A total revolution in the social sphere, particularly Hindu social sphere, would mean eradication of caste.'[83]

How was the Total Revolution to be ushered in and who were to be its agents or instruments? JP had no faith in elections or the Parliament. Instead, he talked of the revolution being made by the people and of relying upon people's power.[84] Even earlier still, in May 1974, referring to the upsurge of the people in Bihar, he wrote: 'Their upsurge might appear to some, especially those in power, to be unconstitutional and anti-democratic. Unconstitutional it certainly is, but not anti-democratic.' Warning against the danger of a dictatorship in view of the erosion of people's faith in elections, he added: 'Therefore, it is a healthy and welcome symptom of our democracy that the people—the real masters—should rise and take recourse to unconstitutional, but peaceful, means to assert themselves and bend the powers—that-be to their will.'[85]

Above all it was the youth who were to act as the vanguard of the revolution. Coming to the conclusion that in India, at least, the industrial workers were not a revolutionary force, JP told Minoo Masani: 'From what has happened generally in the USA, in Japan and recently in Indonesia and Thailand, I worked it out in my mind that it is the youth who must take the lead in this, and history proves me to be correct.'[86] He consistently referred to Jana Shakti (Peope's Power) and Yuva Shakti (Youth Power) as the two new forces in the country.[87]

The vanguard revolutionary youth would 'have no attachment to any political party, no attachment to any student or youth organization which has political affiliations.'[88] Moreover, they would change themselves and revolutionize their own lives; they would learn to lead a new way of life.[89] As pointed out earlier, he even believed that the youth—'the boys'—were already 'in the course of the struggle . . . undergoing a change.'[90]

The Chhatra (Student) and Jan (People's) Struggle Committees or samitis formed in every college and higher secondary school and in every panchayat and taluka were to be the organizational forms that the youth power and people's power would assume. These committees would implement the programmes of the Total Revolution. They were also to take over the functions of political parties such as selection of candidates and getting them elected. They would be responsible for the formulation of policies and programmes during elections. After elections they would act as watchdogs to ensure that the elected representatives followed the programmes and policies laid down by the samitis, did not misuse their position and, if they did, would be forced to resign. The samitis would also gradually function as Janata Sarkars at the village level. They would be the other agencies to implement the policies and programme of Total Revolution at the village and the block levels.[91]

In this broad elaboration of Total Revolution striking is the absence of a broad profile or outline of an alternative social order or an alternative society and political structure. Given this, the concept remained at best a romantic notion or a matter of mere rhetoric. When JP did try to define the objectives of Total Revolution, it was in such general and vague terms as 'a change in the structure of society,' 'a fight against the system', 'a new way of life', 'a classless and casteless society', 'welfare of the people', 'fulfilment of the people's desires and needs', 'an all-round revolution, political, economic, social, educational, moral and cultural'. As these terms or slogans were not assigned precise meanings, or were defined in broad strokes, or their meaning relativised, they could be interpreted in such diverse ways that the right-wing and communal parties and groups, such as the RSS, Congress (O), and BLD, had no difficulty in joining JP's crusade for Total Revolution. Formless, the concept of Total Revolution became over time nothing more than a slogan devoid of any content or meaning.

Nor was JP's crusade for Total Revolution based on a concrete critique of the existing social order or even of Indira Gandhi's regime except in terms of her evil personality. His critique of the existing social order was clothed in such general and sweeping terms as exploitation, oppression, inequality and corruption, but there was no theoretical framework or underpinning. As pointed out later in this chapter, JP's became a revolution without ideology. His crusade ignored the elementary propositions that not all expressions of discontent are meaningful and that solutions to problems must not lose sight of their underlying causes.

Also, though the JPM raised several important issues, it had hardly any concrete programme and well-formulated policies, any well-defined socio-economic objectives or even a substitute political structure or a practical alternative to the existing policies or programmes to be implemented after Mrs Gandhi was ousted from power. There was only recourse to generalities such as 'fight against corruption, high prices, blackmarketing, hoarding, artificial scarcities, etc., and fight against unemployment and against the present educational system.'[92] Similarly, defining the objectives of his movement as a People's Movement, he said: 'Obviously, they could only be fulfilment of the people's desires and needs, their freedom from exploitation, oppression, poverty and a host of similar injustices.'[93]

The political reforms or changes in the political structure JP advocated were also vague and indicative only of good intentions. Apart from reorganization of local government institutions through people's committees at the village, block and in the towns at ward level, no specific changes in political institutions or forms of government at the level of the Centre and states were suggested. He talked in general terms of 'government by participation', 'developing people's power', 'structural transformation of our polity', 'a new legal and constitutional frame', 'purification of government and politics', overthrow of 'bankrupt political system', establishment of 'permanent institution of people's power', 'true people's democracy' and 'participatory democracy', introduction of 'people's power to uphold democratic values', and 'fashioning instruments and conditions for taming and controlling power'. For implementing these ideas he even visualized the convening of a new Constituent Assembly. However, all these notions of embodying people's power were formless and without any political, constitutional or theoretical content. And at the heart of his political thinking and approach lay an ambivalence regarding understanding of, and attitude to be adopted towards, the existing democratic structure in India. As pointed out by David Selbourne, an admirer of his, 'There is a contradiction in JP's views on democracy in

India, which comes near to wrecking the whole structure of his thought. It is a contradiction which reflects his own ambivalence on the subject ... Is India a democratic country or is it not? If it is, but imperfectly so, is it necessary to replace it or to amend the particular forms which its "democracy" takes? And if it is sufficient merely to amend what is essentially democratic, what need then of a "total revolution".'[94] JP himself became aware of this ambivalence or confusion, though again in a rather vague manner, when he told Brahmanand, his secretary, in December 1977: 'At different times a total revolution might take different forms, even different meanings in the sense that its contents might also be different.'[95]

In any case, none of his radical ideas and proclamations—on land reforms and distribution of surplus land from land ceiling to the landless, abolition of the caste system, ending of social customs such as dowry, unionization of agricultural labourers and city poor, ceilings on income and wealth, notion of people's or partyless candidates, became at any stage a part of, or got associated with, the JPM's or student movement's agenda. They just remained JP's personal pronouncements, though undoubtedly many of them were relevant to the lives of the people.

JP's economic ideas, based on a village-based, small-machine and labour-intensive economy, were equally utopian or 'out of this world'. He claimed they were Gandhian and said that he was trying 'to return to Gandhi' in his model of socio-economic development.[96] But he ignored the fact that Gandhi did not make his economic ideas part of his programme for the nationalist movement; nor did he, in fact, claim to be leading any other than the nationalist revolution.

This lack of a coherent and concrete programme was noted by many contemporary observers. Zareer Masani, the critical biographer of Mrs Gandhi, for example, noted in early 1975: 'In the long run the movement's (JPM's) lack of any coherent social and economic programme, other than ousting corrupt Congress ministries, is likely to prevent it from developing into a serious national alternative.'[97] Similarly, JP's friend, Minoo Masani, was to write in early 1975: 'I have been among those who have drawn JP's attention to the danger that comes from the lack of an articulate and concrete socio-economic programme.'[98] Another of his admirers, S.K. Ghose, also wrote on similar lines: 'Though JP's own passion and motives are not in question, all these exhortations and expectation do not add up to a homogeneous programme. There is much that is inchoate about these ideas.'[99]

Mrs Gandhi also took note of this weakness of JP and the JPM. Agreeing with the need for anti-corruption measures, electoral reforms, and changes in educational, administrative and legal structures, she demanded from JP concrete policies on all such basic issues around which negotiations with him could be carried on.[100] It may also be suggested that a major reason for the failure of negotiations between the two, which their mutual well-wishers worked hard for till November 1974, was the absence of concrete demands and measures around which fruitful dialogue between the two could take place.

Being conscious that this particular critique of the JPM was widespread, JP adopted several approaches to meet it. One was to assert that a detailed or specific programme was not possible or desirable in a revolutionary movement. 'I have been often asked to define the socio-economic aims of the struggle, or, as some call it, "its frame",' he wrote in December 1974; but, he added: 'I do not think a detailed socio-economic programme such as that of a political party, particularly of the left, is advisable for the movement.'[101] Similarly, answering the question: 'Cannot your movement be programme-based rather than leader-based?', he told an interviewer in April 1975: 'I object to your formulations. I am aiming at a people's movement embracing the entire nation. A movement cannot have a clear-cut programme. The main purpose of a movement is to articulate the people's wishes ... If the movement is strong, it will see that the people's will is carried out.'[102] And he appealed to the example of Gandhiji who 'avoided defining Swaraj (Independence), even though such distinguished persons as Deshbandhu C.R. Das and Dr Bhagwandas had repeatedly urged him to do so.'[103] Maintaining that objectives of a mass movement did not have to be spelled out, JP was again to write in May 1975: 'The continued interest of the masses in the movement belies the view held among some elite circles that unless the objectives of the movement are clearly spelled out, it will gradually lose the support of the people ... But the history of the past years has shown that mass support does not depend upon detailed policies and programmes of political parties, but entirely on other factors.' It was then that he laid down that the objectives of 'a People's Movement' 'could only be fulfilment of the people's desires and needs, their freedom from exploitation, oppression, poverty and a host of similar injustices. What could the people want except fulfilment of their needs, aspirations, and a drastic change in the condition of their life?'[104]

Simultaneously, JP asserted that he and his colleagues in Bihar had 'a fair idea of the broad social, economic, political and cultural frame for the movement.'[105] However, this frame, too, was general, as was evident from his definition and description of it.[106] Clearly the demand for elimination of corruption, curbing high prices, checking growing unemployment, reform of electoral process, better government, linking education to employment, policies for the welfare of the people, and the like, did not amount to concrete policies.

JP also asserted that he was 'trying to put in as much of socio-economic content into the movement as possible' and that the political parties with which he had raised such issues were tending to accept his suggestions: 'I have said, for instance that as we go down to the rural areas it should not be merely a struggle against blackmarketeers and hoarders and administrative corruption, but against socio-economic injustices. There is, for example, evasion of the Ceiling Act . . . at the panchayat level the Samitis know the truth and should take up the question. He also promised to deepen the socio-economic content of the movement 'as time goes on, in cooperation with these parties.'[107]

In December 1974, in a long interview with R.K. Karanjia, JP dealt at length with the problem of a programme and policies for the movement. He promised that 'the first instalment' of these total changes, that is, 'the short-range socio-economic policy and programme of the movement, will more precisely be defined and published' in the next few weeks. Karanjia's next question was what alternate policies on such issues as industry, public sector, foreign policy and the like, would the regime that would replace Congress follow at the Centre. JP replied that while the socio-economic programme of the Bihar movement would be published soon, the need for a National Policy Statement regarding industry, trade, and so on, would arise only when a similar movement arose in the rest of the country. But, he said, such a movement would not develop before an all-India snap poll. Then it was for political parties participating in elections to frame their programme. 'In that case', he added sarcastically, 'I do not think I am called upon to act as a draftsman for the Opposition parties.' Moreover, 'It is only in the context of a nationwide people's and youth movement that I have any responsibility in such matters.'[108]

He also argued that once the goals and the broad values and objectives of the movement had been decided upon by its leadership, the concrete policies for their realization in practice were to be laid down by experts. He often appealed to the intellectuals and experts to do so. For example, he wrote in May 1975:[109]

I consider that given certain value commitments and certain goals, problem-solving and social reconstruction are serious party.' Instead, he added, 'I am encouraging them to restore democracy within the Congress, which is only possible by challenging the absolute leadership of Mrs Indira Gandhi.'[123]

Earlier, in early November 1974, he had declared that the Bihar movement was no longer 'between the people of Bihar and the Ghafoor ministry but between the people of India and the Prime Minister and it will continue.'[124] On 27 November, he had told a larger crowd at Kurukshetra in Haryana: 'There is no difference between Prime Minister and Haryana Chief Minister; both are bent on strengthening democracy in the country.' He asked the people in Haryana 'to ensure that the Haryana Chief Minister goes, and . . . that the regime at the centre, headed by Shrimati Indira Gandhi, is dislodged.'[125]

JP also did not come to grips with these problems: how to bring about revolution, on which social and political forces to rely on, and what type of political machinery should be used to go about the task. JP's notion of relying upon people's power and youth power was abstract and without political substance. There was something seriously wrong with the idea that students and youth as such had no vested interest in the existing social order and were, therefore, fit agents to make revolution and act as its vanguard. He completely ignored the social class background and the concrete demands and socio-political outlook and behaviour of the student agitators and their leaders. JP also seriously misunderstood the character of the New Left youth movements in Europe and the USA during the 1960s. Despite their revolutionary nomenclature they invariably took up a specific issue for agitation and struggle. They dealt with Civil Rights and the Vietnam War in the USA, nuclear disarmament in Britain and Europe, specific student demands in various countries, and restoration of democracy and civil rights in countries under authoritarian regimes; and they ebbed away when their specific issues were redressed or otherwise dealt with. Nowhere did they lead to revolution—social, economic or political. In any case, as repeatedly pointed out in this chapter, JP had no organization of his own, except a handful of Sarvodayites, and had to rely upon the organization and cadres of other parties and groups. What sort of revolution could be made in the company, and relying upon the cadres, of the RSS-Jan Sangh, BLD of Charan Singh, and the Congress (O) of Morarji Desai or even the motley crowd of socialists?

Undoubtedly, JP was genuine in wanting to lead a revolution—he had been trying to do so since his early youth. He sincerely believed that he was making and directing a revolution that would eradicate corruption, reform the electoral system, check high prices and the

scientific tasks. True, scientists also have their differences but their objectivity is a guarantee that they will not be limited by the blinkers of ideology. Some scientists too have ideological commitments, but in that case they have forfeited their right to be considered scientists . . . The fault of an ideology is that it insists that certain values, such as social and economic equality, can be achieved only within its own framework and no other. Whereas my contention is that once the goal is fixed and the values defined, it is a question for science to determine how the goal can be reached within the given value framework.

Similarly, again in May 1975, responding to the question, 'How would you ensure the minimum basic necessities of life for the majority of the people,' he said: 'Well, this is really a very very difficult question and I think this question goes beyond ideology—it is a practical question. Once the basic necessities are defined, then it is for engineers, social scientists, economic scientists, agricultural experts, industrial experts to get together and produce a plan which can do it.' The only condition he laid down was that the experts should be Indian and not foreign—'it should be a practical plan, a country-made plan, not from Russian, American or Polish experts.'[110] He was obviously demarcating his notion of a plan from that of Nehru's, for in the preparation of the Second Five Year plan many foreign economists and scientists had been involved. Similarly, for devising electoral reforms, he recommended the constitution of commissions of experts.[111] As late as 1977, he was appealing to intellectuals to 'provide a systematic and comprehensive content to the concept of Total Revolution.'[112]

When pressed to define the new social order, JP took two positions. First, he often suggested that it would be along the lines conceived by Gandhiji. Thus, he told R.K. Karanjia that 'broadly speaking,' the programmes and policies of the movement 'would be cast in the Gandhian mould.'[113] He wrote again in December 1974 that the broad social, economic, political and cultural frame for the movement would be 'a Gandhian frame.'[114] And in 1977, he asked the intellectuals 'to provide Gandhian substance to Total Revolution.'[115] Second, he harked back to honesty as being more important than a radical programme. As he put it in May 1975: 'From their sad experience of the last 27 years, the people have come to regard honesty to be a much greater virtue than radical programmes.'[116] The overriding role assigned to honesty also meant that removal of corruption became the main popular or publicly-known component of the JPM and the concept of Total Revolution.

The few concrete policies that JP did put forward were, rhetoric apart, either commonplace, with which hardly anyone would disagree—several of them were in course of time, both during and after the Emergency, adopted by Mrs Gandhi and her successor regime—or were such that a revolution was not needed to implement them. They could be implemented within the existing socio-economic and political structure. Hardly the stuff of which revolutions are made, they were, in fact, quite acceptable to the right wing.

Eradication of corruption, for example, did not require a revolution. Such concrete remedies to check and uproot corruption as the institution of Lok Pal at the centre and Lok Ayukts in the states and a Central Vigilance Commission empowered to take action against corrupt officials and ministers could have been agitated for and negotiated without a revolution. Similarly, checking coercion and rigging in elections, ensuring free and fair elections, reducing drastically election expenses, changes in electoral laws, and, in general, reform of the electoral process did not require a revolution. JP's campaign for decentralization of political power and for taking government to the lower levels in villages and towns and cities was quite significant but it, too, could be accommodated within the existing constitutional structure, as could be many of his other demands on the government. Among them were his demands that the government must 'learn to restrain its own violence', or take 'notice of peaceful and democratic action of the people', or 'set its house in order, remove corrupt ministers and officers, improve the administration, deal firmly with blackmarketeers, hoarders and profiteers, take immediate steps to give relief to the hungry, listen sympathetically to the students' demands',[117] take the help of economists, scientists and other intellectuals in drawing up plans and other measures for popular welfare and socio-economic development and electoral and other political reforms, distribute house sites to the landless and adopt better system of payment of wages to agricultural labourers.

On 6 March 1975, the million-strong opposition march on the Parliament, led by JP, presented the famous charter of demands.[118] Except for the right of recall, there was nothing revolutionary about these demands. Many were vague, others were capable of being discussed and adopted without revolution.

One reason why JP avoided advancing specific programmes and policies was the heterogeneous character of the multi-party coalition that the JPM had become. No attempt was made to build a fresh political consensus around aims, objectives and policies of the JPM and for an alternative social and political order among the constituents of

the JPM, as is necessary in any revolutionary or radical mo This was, it may be suggested, because of the right-wing cha most of his allies and effective cadres, whose only objective i the movement was to remove Congress and Mrs Gandhi fror As Ajit Bhattacharjea has put it, JP 'cultivated the support of C political parties, though this meant minimizing social and objectives on which they could disagree.'[119] The right-wing parties could easily accommodate vague and non-specif demands and rhetoric. On the other hand, hardly any concrete social and economic reforms suggested by JP got into JPM's agitational agenda.[120] They remained merely JP pronouncements.

Consequently, though the inchoate concept of Total remained JPM's goal, its only concrete and effective deman October 1974, the resignation of the Bihar ministry and th of the state assembly and later the dislodging of Mrs power, on the grounds that these three were the chief ob path of the revolution. In the absence of concrete p Revolution became, despite JP's disclaimers to the contra hatao" movement once it tried to embrace the entire co

JP and the JPM thus provided an umbrella to parties, which had supplied him organizational muscle political platform but were hardly interested in him or his Revolution. The only objective of these parties was Gandhi from power, which they had been unable to d In any case, the opposition parties did not agree with JP themselves on any other political objective.[122]

But, in fact, even for JP, well before June 1975, being in power was a part of the chief contradiction o His entire all-India campaign, especially after the between him and Mrs Gandhi, had acquired an anti-In and the immediate, as also the main, goal of the J 'breaking the Congress monopoly of power' and the r Congress as the ruling party by some other party bo the Centre. Thus, on 6 April 1975, he told an interv as the election dates were announced, his 'role w Opposition parties to offer a credible alternative to primary task is to fight the Congress . . . Mrs Gandhi of all authoritarianism of the ruling Congress . . . to democracy personified in her.' He also said th 'encouraging sympathetic elements within the Co scientific tasks. True, scientists also have their differences but their objectivity is a guarantee that they will not be limited by the blinkers of ideology. Some scientists too have ideological commitments, but in that case they have forfeited their right to be considered scientists . . . The fault of an ideology is that it insists that certain values, such as social and economic equality, can be achieved only within its own framework and no other. Whereas my contention is that once the goal is fixed and the values defined, it is a question for science to determine how the goal can be reached within the given value framework.

Similarly, again in May 1975, responding to the question, 'How would you ensure the minimum basic necessities of life for the majority of the people,' he said: 'Well, this is really a very very difficult question and I think this question goes beyond ideology—it is a practical question. Once the basic necessities are defined, then it is for engineers, social scientists, economic scientists, agricultural experts, industrial experts to get together and produce a plan which can do it.' The only condition he laid down was that the experts should be Indian and not foreign—'it should be a practical plan, a country-made plan, not from Russian, American or Polish experts.'[110] He was obviously demarcating his notion of a plan from that of Nehru's, for in the preparation of the Second Five Year plan many foreign economists and scientists had been involved. Similarly, for devising electoral reforms, he recommended the constitution of commissions of experts.[111] As late as 1977, he was appealing to intellectuals to 'provide a systematic and comprehensive content to the concept of Total Revolution.'[112]

When pressed to define the new social order, JP took two positions. First, he often suggested that it would be along the lines conceived by Gandhiji. Thus, he told R.K. Karanjia that 'broadly speaking,' the programmes and policies of the movement 'would be cast in the Gandhian mould.'[113] He wrote again in December 1974 that the broad social, economic, political and cultural frame for the movement would be 'a Gandhian frame.'[114] And in 1977, he asked the intellectuals 'to provide Gandhian substance to Total Revolution.'[115] Second, he harked back to honesty as being more important than a radical programme. As he put it in May 1975: 'From their sad experience of the last 27 years, the people have come to regard honesty to be a much greater virtue than radical programmes.'[116] The overriding role assigned to honesty also meant that removal of corruption became the main popular or publicly-known component of the JPM and the concept of Total Revolution.

The few concrete policies that JP did put forward were, rhetoric apart, either commonplace, with which hardly anyone would disagree—several of them were in course of time, both during and after the Emergency, adopted by Mrs Gandhi and her successor regime—or were such that a revolution was not needed to implement them. They could be implemented within the existing socio-economic and political structure. Hardly the stuff of which revolutions are made, they were, in fact, quite acceptable to the right wing.

Eradication of corruption, for example, did not require a revolution. Such concrete remedies to check and uproot corruption as the institution of Lok Pal at the centre and Lok Ayukts in the states and a Central Vigilance Commission empowered to take action against corrupt officials and ministers could have been agitated for and negotiated without a revolution. Similarly, checking coercion and rigging in elections, ensuring free and fair elections, reducing drastically election expenses, changes in electoral laws, and, in general, reform of the electoral process did not require a revolution. JP's campaign for decentralization of political power and for taking government to the lower levels in villages and towns and cities was quite significant but it, too, could be accommodated within the existing constitutional structure, as could be many of his other demands on the government. Among them were his demands that the government must 'learn to restrain its own violence', or take 'notice of peaceful and democratic action of the people', or 'set its house in order, remove corrupt ministers and officers, improve the administration, deal firmly with blackmarketeers, hoarders and profiteers, take immediate steps to give relief to the hungry, listen sympathetically to the students' demands',[117] take the help of economists, scientists and other intellectuals in drawing up plans and other measures for popular welfare and socio-economic development and electoral and other political reforms, distribute house sites to the landless and adopt better system of payment of wages to agricultural labourers.

On 6 March 1975, the million-strong opposition march on the Parliament, led by JP, presented the famous charter of demands.[118] Except for the right of recall, there was nothing revolutionary about these demands. Many were vague, others were capable of being discussed and adopted without revolution.

One reason why JP avoided advancing specific programmes and policies was the heterogeneous character of the multi-party coalition that the JPM had become. No attempt was made to build a fresh political consensus around aims, objectives and policies of the JPM and for an alternative social and political order among the constituents of the JPM, as is necessary in any revolutionary or radical movement. This was, it may be suggested, because of the right-wing character of most of his allies and effective cadres, whose only objective in joining the movement was to remove Congress and Mrs Gandhi from power. As Ajit Bhattacharjea has put it, JP 'cultivated the support of Opposition political parties, though this meant minimizing social and economic objectives on which they could disagree.'[119] The right-wing opposition parties could easily accommodate vague and non-specific radical demands and rhetoric. On the other hand, hardly any one of the concrete social and economic reforms suggested by JP got assimilated into JPM's agitational agenda.[120] They remained merely JP's personal pronouncements.

Consequently, though the inchoate concept of Total Revolution remained JPM's goal, its only concrete and effective demands were, till October 1974, the resignation of the Bihar ministry and the dissolution of the state assembly and later the dislodging of Mrs Gandhi from power, on the grounds that these three were the chief obstacles in the path of the revolution. In the absence of concrete policies, Total Revolution became, despite JP's disclaimers to the contrary, an "Indira hatao" movement once it tried to embrace the entire country.[121]

JP and the JPM thus provided an umbrella to the opposition parties, which had supplied him organizational muscle and a wider political platform but were hardly interested in him or his ideas or Total Revolution. The only objective of these parties was to remove Mrs Gandhi from power, which they had been unable to do on their own. In any case, the opposition parties did not agree with JP or even among themselves on any other political objective.[122]

But, in fact, even for JP, well before June 1975, Indira Gandhi's being in power was a part of the chief contradiction of Indian politics. His entire all-India campaign, especially after the failure of talks between him and Mrs Gandhi, had acquired an anti-Indira Gandhi edge and the immediate, as also the main, goal of the JPM had become 'breaking the Congress monopoly of power' and the replacement of the Congress as the ruling party by some other party both in Bihar and at the Centre. Thus, on 6 April 1975, he told an interviewer that as soon as the election dates were announced, his 'role will be to help the Opposition parties to offer a credible alternative to the Congress. The primary task is to fight the Congress . . . Mrs Gandhi is the fountainhead of all authoritarianism of the ruling Congress . . . I can see the threat to democracy personified in her.' He also said that he had not been 'encouraging sympathetic elements within the Congress to leave the party.' Instead, he added, 'I am encouraging them to restore democracy within the Congress, which is only possible by challenging the absolute leadership of Mrs Indira Gandhi.'[123]

Earlier, in early November 1974, he had declared that the Bihar movement was no longer 'between the people of Bihar and the Ghafoor ministry but between the people of India and the Prime Minister and it will continue.'[124] On 27 November, he had told a larger crowd at Kurukshetra in Haryana: 'There is no difference between Prime Minister and Haryana Chief Minister; both are bent on strengthening democracy in the country.' He asked the people in Haryana 'to ensure that the Haryana Chief Minister goes, and . . . that the regime at the centre, headed by Shrimati Indira Gandhi, is dislodged.'[125]

JP also did not come to grips with these problems: how to bring about revolution, on which social and political forces to rely on, and what type of political machinery should be used to go about the task. JP's notion of relying upon people's power and youth power was abstract and without political substance. There was something seriously wrong with the idea that students and youth as such had no vested interest in the existing social order and were, therefore, fit agents to make revolution and act as its vanguard. He completely ignored the social class background and the concrete demands and socio-political outlook and behaviour of the student agitators and their leaders. JP also seriously misunderstood the character of the New Left youth movements in Europe and the USA during the 1960s. Despite their revolutionary nomenclature they invariably took up a specific issue for agitation and struggle. They dealt with Civil Rights and the Vietnam War in the USA, nuclear disarmament in Britain and Europe, specific student demands in various countries, and restoration of democracy and civil rights in countries under authoritarian regimes; and they ebbed away when their specific issues were redressed or otherwise dealt with. Nowhere did they lead to revolution—social, economic or political. In any case, as repeatedly pointed out in this chapter, JP had no organization of his own, except a handful of Sarvodayites, and had to rely upon the organization and cadres of other parties and groups. What sort of revolution could be made in the company, and relying upon the cadres, of the RSS-Jan Sangh, BLD of Charan Singh, and the Congress (O) of Morarji Desai or even the motley crowd of socialists?

Undoubtedly, JP was genuine in wanting to lead a revolution—he had been trying to do so since his early youth. He sincerely believed that he was making and directing a revolution that would eradicate corruption, reform the electoral system, check high prices and the menace of unemployment, abolish the system of dowry, give land to the tiller and, more importantly, create an egalitarian social and economic system based on direct and participatory democracy. But his understanding of revolution and a revolutionary movment and programme left much to be desired, to say the least. A revolutionary leader had to have more than mere sincere belief and good intentions.

To lead and make a revolution—total or otherwise—an understanding of the nature of revolutionary objectives, process, forces and the resultant outcome was imperative. JP, unfortunately, had little conception of the systemic changes he wanted to bring about or how to bring about revolution and with what forces to do so, or with whom to ally for completing the task. His revolution was to proceed without revolutionary organization and ideology. He did not address the difficult task of organizing a mass movement for the purpose, or the forms of struggle it should assume. He talked of 'continuous mass action' without an understanding of its forms or its limits, although in jail he did take note of some of the problems when he wrote in his *Diary* that the question of 'how to bring about a systemic change in society ... becomes harder to answer when it is added that the total revolution has to be peacefully brought about without impairing the democratic structure of society and affecting the democratic way of life of the people.'[126]

JP also misjudged the political situation. He repeatedly asked the students and the people to make revolution and to repeat the Revolt of 1942. But in reality hardly any of the pre-requisites for a revolution existed in the India of 1973-75. His reading of the political situation, his view of the student upsurge in Gujarat and Bihar as precursors of a popular revolution were the sort of exaggeration and hyperbole that an agitator would adopt, but the sole leader of a revolution was expected to show greater restraint and understanding. He also mistook an economic crisis for a political and social crisis, for a systemic crisis—perhaps a heritage of his leftist past—and a situation of popular discontent wrought by paucity of goods and high prices as a revolutionary situation. In fact, there was no potential rebellion which the state could not control, as became obvious on the morrow of the imposition of the Emergency. Equally important was his failure to create even those conditions for a massive mass movement which as a leader he could have. Had he tried to make such efforts, he would perhaps have realized the lack of a revolutionary situation in the country.

Thus, at best we may say that JP was a sincere romantic, a Don

Quixote, who like Cervantes' hero, was constrained by his illusions, had an inadequate comprehension of the reality but was unwilling to look critically at himself or the world beyond. Consequently, he blamed Indian intellectuals for failing to understand him because they were 'cast in the mould of Western thought and modes of action'. Moreover, a major problem with the myth of revolution he created was that it could be put to diverse uses—it could be misused by others whose intentions were not as benign as his.

IV

Corruption was one the key political concerns of JP. Yet the manner in which he understood or dealt with the subject provides a prime example of his confused and impractical thinking and inconsistent or anomalous behaviour. As pointed out in Chapter 4, throughout 1973 and up to 1975, he propagated the view that the growing corruption, which had pervaded all areas and sections of society, was the most important issue facing the Indian people. He repeatedly said that 'this terrible evil' was 'eating into the very vitals of our nation',[127] and made its eradication 'the central point of the movement.'[128]

There is no doubt that corruption was the issue which had made JPM quite popular, especially in the urban areas and among the middle classes. Nevertheless, JP showed little understanding of the nature of corruption and its causes and remedies. He either indulged in such vague and inane generalities as corruption being the result of the 'system which has compelled almost everybody to go corrupt',[129] without telling his followers what was the nature of this corruption causing system. Or, he saw corruption as very largely the product of politics, especially because of the manner and extent of the fund collection by political parties for electoral and other purposes. To quote him: 'The way these funds are collected carry the corruption virus from the political into several other fields, such as business . . . and the bureaucracy.'[130] Raising the question why he was 'taking up corruption in the political and administrative field first', he said he was doing so 'because the roots lie there. All aspects of the lives of the people have been corrupted by this source.'[131] Similarly: 'I believe that the present all-pervading corruption has its roots in politics and power.'[132]

Even in this respect, however, instead of analyzing the 'roots' of corruption in politics in some depth and complexity, he made it into a partisan issue by holding the Congress, in general, and Mrs Gandhi, in particular, as almost entirely responsible for—as being the source of— the prevailing corruption. He agreed that the opposition parties, too, accepted black money for party funds, but he virtually exonerated them by holding that they did so 'more by compulsion of circumstances than by choice.' On the other hand, he said, 'the ruling party alone is in the position to take the lion's share.'[133] Consequently, there were other, rather strange, corollaries to this argument. Since the opposition parties were unable 'to match the unlimited funds of the Congress', they were 'driven to the conclusion' that Congress 'cannot be displaced through elections' and 'therefore they turn to protests, gheraos, bandhs and violence.'[134] Moreover, the reason why Congress governments in the states refused to meet popular demands half-way was because of 'the corruption among Congress Ministers.' Further, he asserted, 'Mrs Gandhi's own conduct in collecting crores of rupees from rich businessmen for party and election management is a piece of political corruption that has completely destroyed the moral susceptibilities of most power-seeking Congressmen.'[135] The role of party fund collection, the large-scale use of money in elections, and so on, was conveniently confused with holding Indira Gandhi primarily, if not wholly, responsible for their prevalence.

JP also made quite a simplistic linkage between corruption and the government's economic policies: 'It is also the insatiable appetite of the ruling party for vast funds, which can come only out of black money, that is responsible, on the one hand, for the plethora of controls and other similar impediments to production, distribution and price regulation and, on the other, for their failures.'[136]

On the issue of political corruption also JP's approach was highly arbitrary, even opportunistic. Ignoring his own widely publicized views, brought out in Section III above, that all parties, including those in the Opposition, were equally corrupt, and instead of keeping his distance from them, he very early joined forces with them and made them part of his movement and even its main thrust in several areas. Nor did he in his crusade against corruption hesitate to take the support of, or even make common cause with, many political leaders who had the reputation of being corrupt or who had been pronounced as corrupt by various judicial commissions; for example, Biju Patnaik, Mahamaya Prasad, K. Hanumanthaiya and Hare Krushna Mahtab. Several times he invited Jagjivan Ram to come over to his side. He refused to condemn the highly corrupt DMK government or to call for struggle against it simply because it was anti-Congress and friendly to JP movement. He let Ramnath Goenka, the owner of the *Indian Express*, finance his chief organ, *Everyman's Weekly*. Instances of corruption in his own movement's ranks were overlooked or underplayed, the worst case being that of Chimanbhai Patel, Gujarat's chief minister, who was at the outset the chief political target of Gujarat's anti-corruption movement. Mrs Gandhi was actually forced to make him resign. Yet, JP supported the government that was formed after the June 1975 elections with Chimanbhai's support, and after 1977 he was even admitted to the Janata party. Mrs Gandhi had a point when she wrote to JP in June 1974: 'The irony is that corruption charges are used by some people as a political weapon for partisan purposes. There are instances—I shall not name names—when people who were called corrupt while in the Congress seem to have (be)come clean the moment they are out of the Congress.'[137] In fact, at no stage did JP pause to ask how he could wage war against corruption with the help of and in the company of corrupt people. His only comment was that either the corrupt people in the movement are 'going to be weeded out' or they are 'going to be cured of their corruption by the rigorous demands of the movement.'[138]

What steps did JP suggest to eliminate corruption? As he put it in an interview to the *Hindustan Times* in August 1974, 'I have no specific steps to suggest myself.' Instead he referred to the suggestions in various reports dealing with corruption such as the Santhanam Committee, the Wanchoo Commission, the Administrative Reforms Commission, the Anti-defection Committee and so on. He also strongly supported the institution of the office of a Lok Pal at the Centre and a Lok Ayukta in the states with wide statutory powers.[139] Also, he supported the suggestion that members of legislatures should be asked to publicly declare their assets. For evolving further remedies based on fresh data, JP suggested reliance on experts who were to be asked to frame more concrete and effective steps. We may note that most of the recommendations of these commissions and committees favoured by JP have been given legislative shape by successive governments since 1975, but without producing the desired results—political and administrative, as also other types of corruption, are even more rampant today.

In any case, these were all long-term steps. What should the people do immediately? They should, he said, demonstrate against known hoarders and corrupt officials and rouse public opinion against corrupt ministers and other politicians. They should organize satyagraha and picketing against and social boycott of corrupt officials and traders. Descending to an inane level, he laid down that 'sons and daughters of corrupt persons including ministers, officers, businessmen and big farmer hoarders will observe a 12-hour fast in their homes to impress upon their elders that they must end corrupt and anti-social practices.'

Furthermore, students should pledge 'themselves not to indulge in corrupt practices.'[140]

The steps JP suggested for removing corruption, though laudable, were certainly inadequate, coming from a person who made removal of corruption the raison d'etre of his movement. Moreover, none of these steps constituted the bricks and mortar of a revolution. Most of them were either quixotic or could have been negotiated and implemented without a revolution. JP was, it seems, aware of this position. That is why he talked of a change of the system in order to end corruption, poverty and unemployment, though again leaving ambiguous what that system was. In fact, in the 1974-75 context all that the anti-corruption rhetoric boiled down to was anti-Congressism. And that was slippery ground on which to build a revolution. Historical experience has shown that if the slogan of anti-corruption becomes the central issue of politics rather than being one of the many issues of socio-economic reform, it, at best, diverts attention from reformist or radical politics and, at worst, brings in reaction and authoritarianism, as is evident from the experience of fascism in Italy in the twenties and in Germany and Japan in the thirties, dictatorships in Latin America throughout the twentieth century and military rule in Pakistan under Ayub Khan and after.

V

JP's ideological and political confusion was further expressed in his public pronouncements and activities during 1974-75. Many a time his speeches were marked by rhetoric and bordered on the inflammatory. He also paid little heed to the consequences of his exhortations. Convinced that the country had entered a period of revolution, he tried to transform the growing anti-Congress and anti-Mrs Gandhi sentiments into revulsion against the political system. JP was the first major Indian political leader to raise doubts about the Indian political system. In the atmosphere created by the JPM, many started to question the capacity of the parliamentary political system and the democratic process to 'deliver the goods' or meet the needs and wishes of the masses. The logic of the movement was to discredit and erode the legitimacy of the existing political system and parliamentary democratic institutions.

For years, ever since he withdrew from party politics in the early 1950s, JP critiqued parliamentary politics and party-based democracy as being inherently corrupt and incapable of reflecting and implementing the wishes of the people. Inherent in the party system, he wrote in 1957, at the height of the Nehru era, was 'the corroding and corrupting struggle for power', with democracy being 'reduced to the mere casting of votes' and party rule to 'the rule of a caucus or coterie.'[141]

In 1958, addressing members of the Parliament, he said that the system they represented 'is not suited to our country; this democratic system which we are running is a game of a very small class of people ... The real guarantee of democracy is the faith of the people in democracy, the capacity of the people to run democracy ... This is not happening in our country ... and this is a great danger. Out of this anything may emerge, even a dictatorship of the left or the right.'[142] Consistently, he sowed distrust of political parties. For example, in a well-thought out article "A Plea for Reconstruction of Indian Polity", he wrote in 1959: 'Party rivalries ... give birth to demagoguery, depress political ethics, put a premium on unscrupulousness and aptitude for manipulation and intrigue. Parties create dissensions where unity is called for. Parties often put party interests over the national interests ... the parties, that is to say, small caucuses of politicians, rule in the name of the people and create the illusion of democracy and self-government.' He went on to say that 'For my part, it is not the party system that is the main culprit, but parliamentary democracy itself, which gives it rise.' And two of the basic weaknesses of parliamentary democracy were that it was 'based on the vote of the individuals' and it had 'an inherent tendency toward centralism'. 'It is not only in the totalitarian countries', he added, 'that the "rape of the masses" happens. The basic difference is that in a democracy there is a competition between the violators while there is no competition in totalitarianism.' To parliamentary democracy, he counterposed communitarian democracy which would be partyless and based on 'organic integration' and 'a natural decentralization and a multi-central pluralistic state.'[143]

JP's hostility to parliamentary democracy and the party system found fuller expression in 1973-75 when he consistently denigrated them and promoted distrust of political parties, though he said that partyless democracy was his ultimate and not immediate goal. He repeatedly talked not only of the need for a change of the political system but of breaking the system itself, at least in Bihar. He demanded that 'the whole system must go lock, stock and barrel.'[144] Instead, he called for 'an alternative type and structure of democracy ... a real people's democracy.' He also argued that the people were tired of 'all political parties and the present form and practice of democracy.'[145]

We must point out at this stage that highlighting the shortcomings, weaknesses and defects of the parliamentary political system, criticizing its existing functioning and distortions, trying to cleanse it of the dross it had acquired, or making it more meaningful, particularly through decentralization of political power and decision-making and implementation, was acceptable and quite distinct from what JP was proposing here. His exhortation to do away with the parliamentary system, his attempt to discredit it, to create aversion to it, or shake people's faith in it was quite another matter.

JP also ignored his own earlier advice that political democracy had to be based on political consensus among political parties and compromise with and by popular movements. He failed to see that by dismissing the Congress government in Gujarat, Mrs Gandhi had compromised and retreated in a big way. And she was willing to do the same in Bihar, short of the dissolution of the assembly there. To him, the dismissal of the Gujarat government represented an act of surrender on Mrs Gandhi's part and which had to be repeated in Bihar.[146]

Moreover, while questioning the viability of the existing democratic political system and trying to demolish it, JP was unable to offer any concrete, well-defined alternative as a replacement. All he could propose were generalities such as: the struggle was 'for purification of government and politics . . . for removal of corruption,' or that the time was ripe 'for a leap forward to a real people's democracy'; or what were needed were 'permanent institutions of people's power.'[147] The sole concrete suggestion he made of partyless or non-party democracy was a nebulous and formless idea. At no stage was he able to delineate or explain what a political system without political parties would involve or how the popular will would get expressed or implemented.[148] Quite often, he suggested, equally vaguely, that Sarvodaya and decentralization of political power were to constitute the alternative political system.

Inevitably, JP's anti-parliamentary democracy discourse was picked up by others less devoted to the cause of democracy. Denigration of parliamentary system tended to become fashionable. As pointed out earlier (Chapter III), the Jan Sangh parliamentary leader, Atal Behari Vajpayee, announced his resignation from the Lok Sabha on 8 December 1974 on the grounds that 'parliamentary democracy is no longer an effective instrument to serve the people in our country. In fact, it has become a means to get power and prestige.'[149] Similarly, in early 1975, Minoo Masani supported what he believed to be JP's 'belief that hope for India lay neither through elections nor Parliament.'[150] Discussing the impact of the electoral victory of Congress in UP elections in December 1974, the resident editor of the *Statesman* wrote on 12 December 1974 that the opposition parties 'became painfully aware that the Congress knows how to win elections and that it is an almost hopeless struggle to fight the party on its own ground. Plainly, they were frustrated and were looking for a way out. A measure of disillusionment with the system of parliamentary democracy as it has been practised was inevitable.'[151] In fact, many among the middle class began to openly hope for replacement of parliamentary democracy by military dictatorship.[152] Though JP was not responsible for the spread of this sentiment, his campaign speeches certainly contributed to it.[153]

One of the most negative features of JP's critique of India's parliamentary democracy was his branding it as a Western, non-indigenous concept and structure.[154] It was one thing to make a political and ideological critique of parliamentary democracy as theory or as practised and another branding it as Western or un-Indian. By doing so he was playing into the hands of communal, obscurantist and anti-democratic elements, not unlike the case of China by Chiang Kai-shek and Kuomintang, and Japan in the 1930s, by the militarists and fascists, and in Pakistan since the early 1950s by the military dictators.

In fact, JP came close to obscurantism when he attacked those intellectuals who failed to understand and support what he was doing in Bihar for being 'cast in the mould of Western thought.'[155] Or when in 1978 he asked Indian social scientists to 'test their theories or models on truly Indian, that is, Gandhian value premises.'[156] (By the way, it may be noted that Gandhiji never claimed 'true' Indianness for his 'value premises' but claimed universality for non-violence, Truth, and like values.) Also, one of JP's major objections to the Nehruvian model of development was that it was 'largely un-Indian.'[157]

There are numerous other examples of JP's irresponsible rhetoric and provocative statements, even while asserting that his movement was peaceful and non-violent. For one, even his attitude towards violence was ambivalent. Very early in 1974, according to a newspaper report, he announced that 'though he would not take part in any armed insurrection or rebellion, he could not restrain revolutionaries from taking to the gun.'[158] According to another newspaper report, he said that though he believed in non-violence, 'he would follow the violent method if any opposition party was capable of toppling the Government.'[159] According to Minoo Masani he told a Patna audience in April: 'A stage has now come when a flare-up is a must.'[160]

During 1974-75, JP repeatedly asked the people to make the government dysfunctional. He gave several calls asking the people not to pay taxes. At a time when the country was suffering from drought and famine and there was severe shortage of foodgrains and their prices were rising, he advised the farmers to withhold the state levy on foodgrains meant for public distribution system. He urged the people to make the functioning of the All India Radio 'impossible'. In November 1974, JP and the allied political parties decided to gherao the Parliament, though later this decision was changed to a demonstration before it. He asked the people to set up Janata Sarkars and other forms of the people's parallel system in place of the official one, to manage their everyday affairs and to settle their disputes instead of taking them to thanas and courts. Drawing a fine line between the concepts of democracy and constitutionalism, he declared that his movement was unconstitutional though still democratic and peaceful.[161]

Even more serious was JP's repeated incitement to the army, police and civil services to rebel. Several times during the course of the movement, he called upon them not to obey superiors' orders that were 'unjust and beyond the call of duty', or 'illegal and unjust', or 'wrong, immoral or partisan', or 'unconstitutional, illegal or which went against their conscience'. Implicit was that the decision regarding illegality, unconstitutionality, immorality, etc., of the orders was to be made by the individual members of the army, the police, or the bureaucracy themselves. A few examples are in order here. Addressing a large crowd at Jamshedpur on 28 July 1974, JP 'urged policemen, even the senior officials in Bihar to disobey orders that their conscience told them were improper.' He further declared: 'For the present the call is on Gandhian lines and should not be mistaken for a call for rebellion. But a stage will come, when I will give a call for a total rebellion'; and he added, 'For the present, the policemen should restrict themselves to disobeying orders, if these means using force against peaceful agitators or doing such other injustices.'[162]

In the *Everyman's* of 3 August 1974, in an article headed 'Important Changes', he wrote: 'The day will come when I will ask policemen and others not to obey their officers but to obey the leaders of the movement. I am not saying so now. Today I say to them what Gandhiji said: Do your duty but do not act against your conscience. Do not obey illegal orders. Do not use your lathis and guns against peaceful citizens and boys.'[163] According to the *Hindustan Times* of 16 February, addressing government employees on 15 February, he said: 'If an order appears to your conscience as something against the popular will and the national interests, then it is your duty not to obey such an order.'[164] Similarly, the *Hindustan Times* of 1 April 1975 reported that he told the students at Bhubaneshwar that 'at an "appropriate hour", he will give a call for the army and the police establishment in the country to "revolt" against the present Congress rulers. That hour has not yet come but when it comes he "will give that call unless he was in prison or out of the world" . . . And the time may come when the Army and police will revolt against their present rulers whom they are "fast coming to know and analyze",' he said.

Clarifying his stand in an interview published in *Everyman's* on 20 April, 1975 under the heading 'The Army' he asserted, 'I categorically deny that I have ever asked the army or the police forces to join the movement or to rebel', that 'on March 6, I had said at the mass rally at the Boat Club, New Delhi, in the context of the possibility of some sort of authoritarianism scuttling our democracy that the loyalty of the army was to the country, its flag and to the Constitution'. At the same time, he observed that it was 'the duty of the army to defend the Constitution of the country from authoritarian threats'. 'If any party government or party leader intends to use the army as a means to further their party and power interests', he argued, 'it is the clear duty, to my mind, of the army not to be so used.' But he also added: 'In that connection I often point out, which is a fact of history, that a violent revolution does not succeed unless the existing state of the ruling class begins to disintegrate and the bulk of the armed forces, particularly of the army, either remains neutral or goes over to the side of the revolution. I point out further that in a peaceful revolution there is no need for any army to do that. But if the rulers do venture to use the army to suppress a peaceful revolution, the army should not allow itself to be so used. On such occasions the leaders of the revolution may call upon the army to come over to their side. But I have always made it clear that it was certainly not such an occasion.' Furthermore, 'I consider it my duty to explain to the police that I am not asking them to rebel. They must do their duty. But they must not obey orders that are illegal or go against their conscience. I do not think it is dangerous. But if it is, it is a part of the peaceful total revolution.'[165]

The one exonerating aspect of JP's various exhortations possibly was that he did not actually mean what his words implied and that these pronouncements were more expressions of his hazy and confused thinking than actual calls for rebellion by the people or by the army, police and the civil services. For this reason, we may accept his later denial, in his letter from prison to the Prime Minister on 21 July 1975, that he had any plans to paralyze the government or that he had tried to 'sow disaffection in the armed and police forces.'[166] He may also not have realized that disorganization and unreliability of the armed forces has created conditions for fascist or other authoritarian forces to succeed in overthrowing civilian democratic regimes. Similarly, he seems to have backtracked when in his letter to the Prime Minister he said that the proposed parallel Janata Sarkars would be harmless and their programme was 'for the most part constructive.'[167]

JP was, of course, quite right in arguing that the people have a right to intervene in policy-making and administration in between elections, and to even demand resignation of the elected government if it was misruling or was utterly unresponsive to popular grievances. In such a situation the people would be justified in taking to mass action and starting protest movements and even a civil disobedience campaign for the purpose.[168] But, the problem was that JP did not face the question as to what were the limits to such protest and to the methods that could be employed in it.

JP's failure to grasp the intricacies of the problem of the role of Gandhian non-violent mass action in an independent country governed under a democratic constitution is revealed by his constant comparison of the JPM with India's freedom struggle, seeing it as a replica of the latter,[169] without taking note of the basic difference between a movement against an authoritarian foreign regime and a government formed under the mandate of the democratic constitution of independent India. His constant appeals to the examples of Lenin, Mao and Gandhi, completely ignored the different circumstances in which they functioned and the different character of the forces with which they made revolutions.

It is also significant that when ruminating in 1976 on the lack of a popular upsurge against the imposition of the Emergency in June-July 1975, JP would not make any self-criticism of his assessment of the political situation and the popular mood as revolutionary before 26 June, or of his leadership of the JPM. Instead, he blamed the people for not acting. 'There was undoubtedly a revolutionary climate in the country last year (1974),' he said; but nothing happened after 26 June because the people had become 'supine'. To quote him at length:[170]

> The past year has shown that the people are still ignorant of and unconcerned about their rights and duties as citizens of an independent and democratic country . . . Had the people been conscious of their rights, in spite of the emergency there would have been country-wide protests and demonstrations . . . Perhaps there is something in our character, the character of the Indian people, that makes it easy for our rulers, even when they are democratically elected, to frighten us into

submission. The supine manner in which the people, with few exceptions, reacted to Mrs Gandhi's draconian measures of the 26th June, 1975 and thereafter is a proof of this weakness in our character.

Noteworthy is that when the euphoria of 1974 and 1975 was over, JP himself came down to earth and talked in a language different from the one he had used earlier. This is how he now described the role of the Opposition in a democracy in his *Prison Diary*:[171]

> As I look at it, the primary role of an Opposition in a parliamentary democracy is to endeavour to replace the ruling party through the electoral process. Between elections the Opposition works as an Opposition to the Government in parliament and through propaganda, constructive work, peaceful demonstrations and other usual democratic means of winning public support, on the one hand; and by putting public pressure on the Government, on the other, the Opposition tries to enlarge its sphere of influence over the electorate as well as bring relief to sections of the public who may have been adversely affected by administrative or legislative action.

He would still allow recourse to civil disobedience in 'exceptional circumstances', but not as 'the general method' for removing elected governments and legislatures. But even in the former contingency, he wrote, 'the new government and legislature must be established only through a general election according to law.' In fact, in 1978, as the patron-saint of the Janata Party, he talked very much like Mrs Gandhi of 1974-75. On the occasion of the anniversary of Gandhi's martyrdom, he drew the attention of the Patna audience on 29 January 1978 to the 'twin dangers to the freedom we so recently regained.' 'The first danger', he said,[172]

> Is that having regained freedom, we will take it for granted. Today many sections—some employers, some trade unionists, some students—are again pressing their sectional demands without heeding the national interest. They must remember that in doing so they are assaulting the open society ... I would hope ... all would act with the self-restraint and maturity with which they conducted themselves during the election campaign ... It is that self-restraint, that awareness of the larger issues at stake which must guide our actions today.

The forces that would take advantage of disorder, of a
breakdown of the system, are far from gone. Indeed they are
regrouping, and they represent the second danger.

It has to be admitted that, above all, JP lacked some of the qualities
essential for a leader of a mass movement. A life-long weakness of his
as a leader was his indecisiveness and the consequent tendency to be
pushed by others around him into taking political positions which were
not necessarily his own. Also, a poor judge of people and situations,
this often led to his inability to distinguish between genuine followers
and co-workers and opportunists and careerists out to exploit their
closeness to him.

While throughout his life he was able to inspire or head a party,
a radical group or a mass movement, he was unable to provide them
effective ideological or political leadership. This often led to others
determining the ideological or programmatic content of the movements
he inspired or developed or formally led. Thus, he was incapable of
withstanding the RSS-Jan Sangh penetration and even control of the
JPM.

More important, JP should have been able to see that the basic
prerequisites of a revolution did not exist in the India of 1974-75. He
should also have realized that the right-wing parties he was relying
upon to mobilize the people could possibly not be allies in and active
agents of the struggle for the radical transformation of society.

JP also did not reveal an understanding of or control over the
forces he was unleashing. He relied on 'student power' to bring about
a non-violent revolution, but, unlike Gandhiji, did not realize that
students were a volatile force that tended to take recourse to violence
and could not, therefore, form the main task force of a non-violent
revolution. Consequently, he often ignored the repeated manhandling
and coercion of political leaders and other acts of violence by students
in Gujarat, Bihar and elsewhere. Instead, he tried to find excuses for
them.

Moreover, not willing to take up the burden of political office and
power, he would not assume the reponsibility of leading a political
party with a view to form an alternative government in Bihar or in
India and follow alternative policies. This refusal to take over political
power might be regarded by some as a personal virtue, but was a major
shortcoming in a political leader in a democracy. Apart from the fact
that this trait of his led to the debacle of the Janata experiment in
1977,[173] it was another factor which made him an ideal candidate for

being politically used by others. True, as pointed out earlier, Gandhiji, in whose footsteps JP often suggested he was walking in this respect, too shunned political office, but then Gandhiji had throughout attracted and trained brilliant co-workers such as Jawaharlal Nehru, Sardar Patel, Rajendra Prasad and C. Rajagopalachari, who could carry the burden of office with great competence and integrity. JP never raised the question whether any of the leaders of his allied parties were capable of ensuring, at least minimally, the ideals he was fighting for: grassroots democracy, secularism, anti-casteism, reform of education and police, a non-corrupt administration. Perhaps, as suggested by some, if JP did not want to wield political power he should not have come back into politics after he had retired from it in the fifties.

We are thus constrained to conclude that, as pointed out earlier, JP's basic problem as a leader was that during 1974-75 he wanted to play a role far beyond his capacities.[174] This was, for example, in contrast to Jawaharlal Nehru who knew his limitations as a leader and who therefore refused to be an Indian Lenin at the height of his Marxist phase and who at crucial stages of the national movement bowed before Gandhiji's leadership.

VI

JP's ambivalent relationship with political parties, discussed in Section II above, illustrates the woolly and inconsistent character of his political thinking and the nebulous and perhaps opportunist character of his politics. His failure to see through the motives and ideological character of his allied parties also reveals a certain naivete in his understanding of politics and its dynamics.

However, mixing up with and relying upon political parties was not the most negative feature of his politics. What we need to explore is the alignments JP made with parties and groups that were unsuitable even from the point of view of his own politics. Most of his allies were right-wing parties, groups and individuals who could 'hardly be regarded by political literates as ardent votaries of any brand of popular democracy.'[175] How could any kind of revolution be ushered in with the help of communal Jan Sangh, Jamaat-i-Islami, Anand Marg and Akali Dal, the neo-fascist RSS, casteist BLD, conservative Congress (O), maverick socialists and sundry individuals such as Minoo Masani. With such a political conglomeration little scope existed for basic systemic changes or the social transformation that JP advocated. Any changes could only be right-wing, as the Janata experiment from 1977 to 1979 revealed.

As he increasingly leaned on right-wing political forces, JP came to be more and more identified with them, and the JPM appeared to be an alternative right-wing coalition under anti-Congress garb. JP's role increasingly became that of providing the much-needed, and hitherto elusive, legitimacy to the right-wing forces which hoped to capture political power, which they had failed to do so far through the electoral process. Increasingly, JP's radical rhetoric masked right-wing domination of the movement. Moreover, as will be discussed in the next section, even within right-wing parties, it was the growing dominance of RSS-Jan Sangh which was significant. JP's political naiveté was leading the movement in a dangerous direction.

Because of this reliance on the right wing, the left parties and their student and trade union wings withdrew quite early from the movement even in Bihar. Besides, the JPM neither had the support of, nor made an appeal to, the working class, poor peasants, agricultural labourers, tribals and the urban poor. The CPM was favourably inclined towards the movement but would not join it because of the preponderant role of Jan Sangh, Congress (O) and BLD. The only left party to join the JPM was the SSP, which did talk of social transformation but defined it in terms of the interests of the middle and rich peasant castes.

It needs to be asked what made JP acceptable as a leader, and as a rallying point, to the right-wing parties, groups and individuals, apart from his mass appeal on which they could ride to power. In other words, what else had he in common with them?

For one, JP did not put forward any comprehensive definition of Total Revolution or any clearcut programme or any concrete alternate policies for his movement. Apart from confusion of thought, this was to a certain extent due to the effort to placate his conservative allies. A high moral tone and an ambiguous radicalism, based on such vague notions and concepts as eradication of corruption, morality-based politics, and fight against high prices, black-marketing, hoarding, artificial scarcities, unemployment and the existing educational system or undefined concepts of 'social change, economic change, political change, administrative change, cultural change, and so on' were quite acceptable to the right-wing forces. Such amorphous and inchoate radicalism did not bother them, as it has not bothered extreme right and populist parties and movements the world over—for example, the Bonapartists in nineteenth century France, the fascists in Italy and Germany, the extreme right in the thirties in Japan, and Peronistas in Argentina.

A common factor between JP and the right wing was his strong anti-Congress sentiment since the mid-fifties and his strong antipathy to Mrs Gandhi, based on the belief that she was responsible for all the ills of the country since 1969. The two also shared a dislike for Nehru's political and economic policies and 'the general framework of Nehru's political economy' which Mrs Gandhi was perceived to be following since 1969. In the Foreword to J.D. Sethi's book *Gandhi Today* (1978), JP claimed that his critique of 'the mixed liberal and Marxian model' of economic and political development that 'Nehru put forward before the country' was based on a Gandhian approach and the need he felt 'for a more indigenous approach'. He added: 'I could see the germs of its (Nehruvian model's, B.C.) destruction and that is why I parted company with him.' He went on to say:[176]

> the model itself was largely un-Indian and elitist and thus
> ultimately was bound to fail. It is no coincidence that the
> Nehruvian model produced the greatest disparities of income
> and wealth. It pushed more people below the poverty line than
> ever before. It created the most cynical elite class. And above
> all it caused the deepest permeation of corruption and
> immorality in our public life. What Mrs Indira Gandhi did
> during the eleven years of her rule was in many ways the
> accelerated projection of the Nehru model, except that Nehru
> worked through a democratic system.

JP's strong ideological attack on parliamentary democracy and search for 'an indigenous model', discussed earlier, also suited the ideological proclivities of the RSS-Jan Sangh component of the opposition parties.

JP's long-time and outspoken anti-communism and anti-Sovietism also led to rightist forces being comfortable with him. On the other hand, his anti-communist stance was in part responsible for his joining hands with anyone who was anti-communist and anti-Soviet, irrespective of the political and ideological orientation. In the fifties, for example, he had joined the Council for Cultural Freedom, the notorious anti-communist organization.

JP's anti-communism was the result of certain earlier events which had left a deep impact on him. One was his unhappy experience with the CPI in the late thirties during the period of joint front between the Congress Socialist Party (CSP), whose General Secretary he was, and the CPI. He had, somewhat justifiably, felt betrayed by CPI's efforts to capture or undermine CSP in different parts of the country. He had also reacted strongly to Stalin's terror after 1936 and the Russo-German Pact of 1939. These experiences had led him at the height of the Cold

War in the fifties not only to join the Council for Cultural Freedom but to play an active part in it.

It is likely that some of his dissatisfaction with and growing dislike for Mrs Gandhi arose from her decision to develop a working relationship with CPI after 1969, have an electoral alliance with it in 1971 and 1972 and establish close political and military relations with Soviet Union He started believing that Mrs Gandhi had come under the Soviet influence, especially as a result of the Indo-Soviet Treaty of 1971, and even made India a part of the Soviet orbit. He feared there was a grave danger that Mrs Gandhi would establish a totalitarian system in India at the behest of CPI and in the interests of the Soviet Union. Moreover, he felt that the logic of Mrs Gandhi's economic policies was totalitarian. Consequently, as early as 1971, he had tried to put together an alliance of non-communist parties to oppose the Congress in the elections.

We have already seen an example of his virulent anti-communism (at the end of Chapter 4 above) in his viewing the Emergency as the result of a hidden communist plot. Even earlier, in 1949, he had argued that communists 'have no honesty, no integrity. They are out-Goebbelising Goebbels.'[177] Similarly, commenting on the behaviour of the Youth Congress in West Bengal, he said in an interview in April 1975: 'They have lost the power to question the orders that are passed down to them from the Moscow-Delhi syndicate.' The communists, he added, 'are made to think alike and act alike. And how they will think or act will be decided by the Communist Party of the Soviet Union.' In the same interview he defended his action in appealing to Y.B. Chavan and Jagjivan Ram to rebel against Mrs Gandhi on the ground that it would help restore internal democracy in Congress and 'stop infiltration into it by those whose loyalties are elsewhere.'[178]

Another aspect of JP's deep-seated anti-communism was his frequent use of derogatory words of the MacCarthy era to describe communists as 'commies' and 'stooges' of the Soviet Union and Congressmen friendly to the communists as 'cryptos' and 'dupes'.[179]

VII

An important, perhaps critical, question in any movement, apart from its ideological orientation, is that of its organization. A fatal flaw of the JPM, especially in its later, all-India phase, was its organizational dependence on RSS-Jan Sangh, which, along with their front or constituent organizations, had a strong well-knit structure, trained cadre and branches all over the country, especially in northern and central India, and were in a position to provide muscle to the movement.

JP had no grassroots organization of his own to organize and carry on the movement in a disciplined manner, no political party he could count upon. In fact, he had never been much of an organization man, nor perhaps had he the capacity to act as one.[180] But he soon realized that without a strong organizational structure and trained cadre, it was not possible to lead or sustain a mass movement against an entrenched party and government; that students, however enthusiastic, could not be expected to perform the task on their own even under his leadership. Though he hoped that his youthful followers would one day cohere into such a cadre, as matters stood the disciplined cadres of RSS-Jan Sangh would have to be harnessed, especially after the movement had expanded from Bihar into the rest of Hindi-speaking northern India and in particular Delhi, which was to be its epicentre, as the march on Parliament on 6 March 1975 and the gherao of the Prime Minister's house projected on 25 June were to show. Though he had some of his Sarvodaya cadre in Bihar, these were not enough and he had hardly any cadre of his own outside Bihar. But, in fact, JP had found that even at the initial stage of organizing the Chhatra and Yuva Sangharsh Samitis, he had needed the cadre of Akhil Bharatiya Vidyarthi Parishad (ABVP), one of the RSS front organizations. Consequently, after November 1974, JP depended more and more on RSS-Jan Sangh to keep the movement going. In fact, the cadres of the RSS-Jan Sangh were from now on to become the nucleus, the organizational mainstay of the JPM. Even in states like Karnataka whatever little success the movement enjoyed was because of the RSS-Jan Sangh presence there.

The RSS-Jan Sangh in turn also realized that they could become a political force only by using JP and cashing in on his mass appeal, though they had little in common with him in respect of democracy, liberalism, secularism, Gandhism or any kind of revolution, and were in fact antagonistic to them. The RSS, for example, did not believe in democracy, nor practised it within its own organization. Nevertheless, the RSS-Jan Sangh enthusiastically joined JP's crusade for democracy and revolution, despite his earlier denunciation of them and his affirmation of commitment to socialism, because that gave them an opportunity to ride to power via a coup d'etat, using JP as a *mukhota* (mask). Consequently, the leadership of the RSS-Jan Sangh threw the entire weight of their organizations and cadres behind the JPM, idolized JP and proclaimed him to be a near *avatar* or Messiah—'That in her ruthless pursuit of power the PM should come into clash with JP was almost inevitable. Every Ravan ultimately met Ram, every Kansa, a Krishna'[181]—and loudly acclaimed the coming Total Revolution and its objectives. In December 1974, the Working Committee of Jan Sangh passed a resolution in favour of full participation in JPM because 'it seems to establish the primacy of the people over the government.'[182] Many Jan Sangh leaders also tried to echo JP, especially his distrust of democratic institutions. For example, Atal Behari Vajpayee announced on 8 December 1974 his decision to resign from the membership of the Lok Sabha on the ground that 'Parliament had been reduced to a mere rubber stamp to serve the ends of the majority party.'[183] Earlier, in September 1974, Vajpayee had written of a 'confrontation between the government and the people' and declared: 'The established leadership has been using the parliamentary method only as a cover for protecting their evil designs. The response cannot be confined to the parliamentary level. This war has to be fought in the streets, in the chambers and legislatures, in the corridors of power, in all sensitive power centres of the establishment.'[184]

Thus began 'the marriage of convenience between JP and RSS-Jan Sangh': JP remained the movement's chief mobilizer and public face, but it came to be increasingly organizationally dominated by RSS-Jan Sangh as his dependence on them grew with time. This caused consternation among many of his followers. For example, his staunch follower, Anand Patwardhan, expressing his concern at JP's 'strange myopia' in this respect, wrote in an article 'Is JP's Movement at the crossroads' in the *Everyman's* of 20 April 1975: 'When old political enemies like the RSS, or old individual politicians of dubious virtue have come out in his support, JP has almost invariably welcomed them as prodigal sons who have undergone a change of heart.' He asked JP to overcome 'naivete or otherwise', this 'strange myopia', if his 'credibility as a champion of a clean social order is to be maintained.'[185]

The dependence of the JPM on the RSS-Jan Sangh became clearly visible when later on 25 June 1975 Nanaji Deshmukh, the organizing secretary of Jan Sangh and one of the top RSS leaders, was made the movement's chief organizer, as the secretary of the Lok Sangharsh Samiti (People's Struggle Committee) formed to force Indira Gandhi to resign. It is important to note in this respect that there is a basic difference between cadres and leadership thrown up from within democratic parties and in the course of a democratic movement and cadres and leadership trained in an authoritarian organization.

Disciplined and trained on paramilitary lines, the RSS cadres were brought up from their adolescent years on a communal and basically authoritarian ideology. RSS was clearly neo-fascist in its origins.[186] Its organizational structure was centralized, non-democratic and authority-based. Its head and supreme leader functioned on the Fuhrer principle, a lá Mussolini and Hitler. As is the case with fascist organizations the world over, it had no detailed ideological, programmatic or policy documents. Elements of its ideology and its policies were conveyed to its members only orally in the *shakhas* or branches in which they met daily or periodically. The only written and published guidelines to its thought and politics were the 100-page pamphlet, *We, Our Nationhood Defined*, written by M.S. Golwalkar, its supreme leader, and published in 1939, and *Bunch of Thoughts*, a collection of Golwalkar's speeches after 1945. As examples of the thinking of the founders of the RSS can be cited in the following extracts from these two books. In *We*, after pointing out that the fascist Italy and Nazi Germany were two countries where 'the ancient Race spirit' had 're-risen' and that 'Even so with us: our Race spirit has once again roused itself', thus conferring on Hindus 'the indisputable right of excommunicating from its Nationality all those, (i.e. Muslims) who having been of the Nation, for ends of their own, turned traitors and entertained aspirations contravening or differing from those of the National Race as a whole', Golwalkar went on to add: 'German race pride has now become the topic of the day. To keep up the purity of the Race and its culture, Germany shocked the world by her purging the country of the semitic Races—the Jews. Race pride at its highest has been manifested her. Germany has also shown how well-nigh impossible it is for Races and cultures, having differences going to the root, to be assimilated into one united whole, a good lesson for us in Hindusthan to learn and profit by.'[187]

RSS' communalism was open and unabashed. Taking a cue from Germany's 'purging the country of the semitic Races—the Jews', Golwalkar excluded the followers of other religions in India from the Indian nation and expressed extreme hostility towards them. V.D. Savarkar had earlier in the twenties used the concept of common blood or race to define a nation. But Golwalkar realized that Muslims and Christians in India were converts to Islam and Christianity and had therefore the same 'blood' as Hindus. He therefore used the concept of 'Race Spirit' to define a nation. This 'Race Spirit' was, according to him, lost with the change of religion.[188] Declaring Muslims to be the old enemies of Hindus, Golwalkar condemned the nationalist leaders for spreading the view by which Hindus 'began to class ourselves with our old invaders and foes under the outlandish name—Indian—and tried to win them over to join hands with us in our struggle.' He, then, went on to add: 'The result of this poison is too well-known. We have allowed ourselves to be duped into believing our foes to be our friends and with our own hands are undermining true Nationality. That is the real danger of the day, our self-forgetfulness, our believing our old and bitter enemies to be our friends . . . We, Hindus, are at war at once with the Moslems on the one hand and British on the other.'[189]

Giving expression to rabid and vicious communalism, Golwalkar added:[190]

The non-Hindu peoples in Hindusthan must either adopt the Hindu culture and language, must learn to respect and hold in reverence Hindu religion, must entertain no idea(s) but those of glorification of the Hindu race and culture, i.e., they must not only give up their attitude of intolerance and ungratefulness towards this land and its agelong traditions but must also cultivate the positive attitude of love and devotion instead— in one word they must cease to be foreigners, or may stay in the country, wholly subordinated to the Hindu nation, claiming nothing, deserving no privileges, far less any preferential treatment—not even citizen's rights.

RSS's dislike of Gandhiji and other leaders of the national movement was also quite well-known. Operating on the principle of the bigger the lie the better, Golwalkar denounced them as virtual traitors to and enemies of the 'Hindu nation'.[191] Referring to them in *Bunch of Thoughts*, Golwalkar said: 'Those who declared "No *swaraj* without Hindu-Muslim unity" have thus perpetrated the greatest treason on our society. They have committed the most heinous sin of killing the life-spirit of a great and ancient people.'[192] Another example of Golwalkar's anti-Congress venom expressed in 1947 was his accusation that its leaders were asking the 'Hindu'.[193]

To ignore, even to submit meekly to the vandalism and atrocities of the Muslims. In effect, he was told: 'Forget all that the Muslims have done in the past and all that they are now doing to you. If your worshipping in the temple, or your taking out gods in procession in the streets irritates the Muslims, then don't do it. If they carry away your wives and daughters, let them. Do not obstruct them. That would be violence.

During 1974-75, as from its very inception, in true fascist style, the RSS-Jan Sangh relied heavily on the 'big lie' propagated through rumours, whispering campaigns, innuendoes, insinuations and character assassination. For example, a rumour widely circulated through word of mouth was that Indira Gandhi had got the Soviet government to kill Lal Bahadur Shastri in order to clear the way to power for herself.[194]

JP did not oppose the RSS-Jan Sangh penetration and domination of the JPM and, instead, gladly accepted their active participation, even though he had been all his life a staunch opponent of communalism and communal organizations as also a sharp critic of RSS-Jan Sangh. He was fully aware of the RSS's fascist ideology, its record of spreading communal hatred and fomenting communal riots, and the threat it posed to the Indian people. In his presidential address to the Second National Convention Against Communalism on 28-29 December 1968, he had said:[195]

> India being a country of many religions, almost every religious community has its own brand of communalism. They are all pernicious, but Hindu communalism is more pernicious than the others. One reason is that because Hindus constitute a great majority of the population of India. Hindu communalism can easily masquerade as Indian nationalism and denounce all opposition to it as being anti-national. Some like the Rashtriya Swayamsevak Sangh (RSS) might do it openly by identifying the Indian nation with *Hindu Rashtra*, others might do it more subtly . . . Those who attempt to equate India with Hindus and Indian history with Hindu history . . . are in reality the enemies of Hinduism itself and of the Hindus.

He went on to add:

> When the Sangh was under a shadow after Gandhiji's murder there were many protestation(s) about its being entirely a cultural organization. But apparently emboldened by the timidity of the secular forces it has thrown its veil away and has emerged as the real power behind, and controller of the Bharatiya Jana Sangh. The secular protestations of the Jana Sangh will never be taken seriously unless it cuts the bonds which tie it so firmly to the RSS machine. Nor can the RSS be treated as a cultural organization so long as it remains the mentor and effective manipulator of a political party . . . If they (RSS) persist in their present politics and happen to make headway they will most certainly kill the soul of *Hindu dharma* and sap the foundations of the nation.

Similarly, after the horrendous riots of 1968 and 1969, JP told a press correspondent in an interview in October 1969:[196]

> There are well-organized Hindu bodies like RSS—there may be several others—who are extreme and militant communalists, who believe in a Hindu nation, who think that Hindus alone are the sons of the soil and that Muslims are aggressors and enemies. Some of them may be leaders and members of the Jana Sangh. Certainly there is anti-Muslim, anti-Pakistan propaganda going on all the time in the Hindu community, the shakhas (morning rallies) of RSS are held every day. The RSS organization is like an iceberg, a part of it is visible, the greater part invisible. It is a secret or semi-secret organization, certainly not a cultural organization.

When asked what was his remedy, JP said that those 'who have the interest of their country at heart and who understand the danger of communalism (should) undertake an intensive campaign of mass education.' Reiterating that the real remedy was 'political education, national education, healthy education of people's minds', he added: 'This is something on which all nationalist, secular, democratic parties should get together forgetting their ideologies and personal differences, their power struggle and so on. They could join hands at least on this one programme and meet the challenge of Hindu, Muslim or any other communalism because communalism of any kind is anti-national and a danger to the country.'

Earlier, at a meeting of the National Integration Council in 1962, he was reported to have demanded a ban on RSS and when Deen Dayal Upadhayay went to JP and asked him to reconsider his views about RSS, JP 'was so brusque that Upadhayay left in a huff', refusing to wait even for a cup of coffee.[197]

However, during 1974–75, JP not only ignored the anti-secular, communal and anti-democratic character of RSS-Jan Sangh and sought their active support in his movement but also gave them good chits and lent them an aura of respectability. On 5 March 1975, he attended the all-India session of the Jan Sangh at New Delhi and thanked the party and its members for active support to his movement. In turn, he promised to reciprocate their support. Replying to those who criticized him for relying upon RSS-Jan Sangh cadres, he said: 'The Jan Sangh and RSS are neither reactionary nor fascist. How can any party which had lent its support to total revolution be called reactionary or fascist?' And, then, he went to the extent of saying: 'If the Jan Sangh is fascist, then I too am a fascist.'[198]

Later, in April, he reasserted the statement quoted above in an interview: 'I do not think I have anywhere described the RSS as fascist or non-fascist. Though I do not know much about it, I feel that it has also been changing like so many other things in the country. What I did say at the All-India session of the Jan Sangh was that if Jan Sangh was fascist I too was a fascist. I do not see any reason to change my view.'[199]

The question naturally arises as to why did JP give respectability to RSS-Jan Sangh when he had earlier shown full awareness of their divisive communal ideology. JP's naïve answer was that they had changed and accepted Total Revolution.[200] Similar sentiments were expressed by JP in his discussions with P.N. Dhar, principal secretary to Indira Gandhi, in July 1976. Reporting on his discussions, P.N. Dhar writes, 'I intervened and told him that the prime minister felt that the opposition were taking advantage of him. The Jan Sangh and the RSS had trained cadres and a well-defined ideology from which they were not going to be swayed, I said. JP replied that he knew some people thought they had made a fool of him, but the fact was "they have met me, including the Poona group (he meant the RSS leadership, B.C.) and surrendered to me."[201] Further, he was convinced that struggle would purify these forces. In any case he said that he did not depend on Jan Sangh and other parties. 'Whatever success I have achieved is due to the fact that the Bihar movement is not dependent upon them,' he said and added: 'It draws its strength from the power of the youth and the people, on Yuva Shakti and Jan Shakti and not *Dal* (party) Shakti.'[202] Also, denying that RSS-Jan Sangh were playing a dominant role in the JPM, he referred to the active participation of the RSP, the Forward Bloc, the Naxalite Marxist Coordination Committee, the socialists and the Congress (O) and the support of the CPM. The majority of participants and supporters of the movement, he said, 'are radical'.[203] He also denied that RSS as an organization, as distinct from its members, was a 'constituent part of the movement in Bihar or elsewhere.'[204] It can also be surmised that one reason he was willing to work with some of the most disreputable leaders in the states was an effort to counterbalance the strong role of RSS-Jan Sangh in the movement.

Finally, we are constrained to agree with Bhola Chatterji, one of his disillusioned admirers, that he gave the RSS-Jan Sangh a clean chit basically out of opportunism. Because of his organizational dependence on them, he felt it necessary to placate them. To quote Chatterji:[205]

One cannot however avoid drawing the conclusion that the compulsion of events prevailed upon him to put a premium on expediency. Circumstances alter cases and Jayaprakash, who had all along apparently insisted on sticking to the straight path of principled politics and whose major pre-occupation had been the question of ends and means, seemed to have caved in when he should have stood most firmly for his principles.

Interestingly, once the JPM wound up and JP's euphoria subsided, he again became critical of the RSS though not to the extent prior to 1973. In a September 1977 newspaper interview he asked the RSS to disband itself for he saw no justification for its separate existence 'in the changed circumstances.' If the RSS could not do so, it should at least open its doors to Muslims and Christians and let them 'hold the highest office in the organization.' Feeling that 'in their heart of hearts' the RSS leaders 'still believe in the concept of *Hindu Rashtra*', he expressed the hope that 'they will give up the concept of *Hindu Rashtra* and adopt in its place that of Indian nationhood, which is a secular concept and embraces all communities living in India.'[206]

With the effective leadership of the JPM passing into the hands of RSS-Jan Sangh and leaders such as Morarji Desai and Charan Singh, the political character of the movement and the political conjuncture also underwent a major shift. After November 1974, its chief goal was not to change the policies of the central government or to change the Bihar state government but the removal of Mrs Gandhi from office.

Even earlier to June 1975, the JPM had potentially undemocratic features, in terms both of its demands and the methods adopted or planned. Unlike any popular movement in a democratic polity, at no stage did it aim at blocking of or bringing about changes in particular government policies or behaviour of certain state functionaries, including ministers, or causing their resignation, but it harped on bringing down the governments first in Bihar and then at the Centre. Moreover, neither RSS-Jan Sangh nor JP showed commitment to a democratic electoral structure or accepting a constitutional 'system of elections as the sole means of achieving state power'. Both believed that means other than parliamentary democratic ones—non-violent in the case of JP and violent in the case of RSS—could be used to achieve state power.

Thus, the democratically elected legislatures and governments were to be dissolved and replaced not through elections but through extra-constitutional mass agitations, mainly confined to urban areas and relying on middle class youth. This amounted to a covert demand for a change in the country's political system. In fact, sometimes, JP realizing the logic of his movement, made explicit his stand: 'A revolution will not come either through elections or from Parliament or Assembly but a revolution, peaceful or bloody, will always be of the people and by the people.'[207] We may point out that Gandhi-led mass movements in India and the Gandhi-inspired Solidarity-led mass movement in Poland had openly aimed at bringing about a basic change in the political system because they opposed authoritarian regimes, which did not permit a change in government by electoral means. On the other hand, Martin Luther King's Gandhi-inspired, mass movement in the USA worked for changes in state policy and civil society. Even the New Left movements of the sixties were goal-specific: for Civil Rights and end of the Vietnam war in USA, for nuclear disarmament in Britain and other countries in Europe, and for radicalization of universities in Western Europe and USA.

Moreover, a distinction had to be made between the nature of the demands for a change of government under popular pressure at the state level and the Centre. In the case of a state too, the demand for the dissolution of its legislature at the behest of a popular movement was non-democratic, but the central government could, in an extreme case, constitutionally dismiss a totally inefficient or unpopular government. There was, however, no such provision in the Constitution for the dismissal of the central government which could fall, as has happened several times since 1979, only when it lost its majority in the Lok Sabha or when the government itself willingly dissolved the Lok Sabha and went in for fresh elections. A change in the central government in any other manner would amount to a coup d'etat or capture of state power by undemocratic, unconstitutional means.

As has been pointed out at various places in earlier chapters, the agitational methods adopted or propagated by the JPM, for example, dharnas, bandhs, gheraos of ministers, MLAs' houses, state assemblies, etc., were also undemocratic and extra-constitutional. Though in many cases JP did not initiate such tactics, he did come to justify and even encourage them. For example, he was to justify a gherao if it was peaceful and non-violent.[208] But a gherao by its very nature was extremely coercive and, therefore, violent in character; a gherao meant the encirclement of individuals and groups and not letting them go out of, or letting others come into, the encircled space until the protestors' demands were met. Gherao, confinement to one's residence, and other tactics of intimidation and mishandling and coercion, including threats of personal injury, were also used on a large scale, first in Gujarat and then in Bihar to compel elected legislators to resign from assemblies and thus secure their dissolution. Bandh or the complete shutting down of shops and offices and all public activities, usually enforced through coercion, was also a favourite weapon of the JPM, and had the tacit approval of JP.[209] In general, gherao and intimidation of individuals—legislators, teachers, students and educational administrators and bureaucrats, and so on—and use of private coercive power against those opposing the movement became a common tactic during 1974-75.

JP also failed to lead or control his followers, especially students, and direct their energies in peaceful directions. He was right in criticizing the police and administrators for their repressive outlook and behaviour and the tendency to take immediate and undue recourse to lathi-charge and firing. But, at the same time, he tended to ignore the rowdyism, hooliganism, violence and coercion of individuals by his followers, often looking the other way, or to pass off their misdemeanors as minor, or to find excuses for them, or, in some cases, condemn them without taking any concrete action, partially because he really had no control over them. Invariably, he refused to accept any responsibility for his followers' behaviour and actions or when things got out of hand. And whenever students and others took perceptible recourse to violence, he blamed it on provocation by the police, agent provocateurs and conspiracies by the opponents of the movement, CPI being a favourite in this respect.[210]

VIII

As detailed earlier in Chapter 4, Section II, the climax of the JP movement came on 25 June 1975, a day after the judgement delivered by the Supreme Court vacation judge. At a huge rally at Delhi's Ramlila grounds, JP and the JP-led non-communist parties gave an ultimatum to Mrs Gandhi to resign within four days. They also threatened that if she did not do so, they would launch a nation-wide, mass civil disobedience movement and a no-tax campaign from 29 June and bring the government all over the country to a halt until Mrs Gandhi resigned. At the meeting JP repeated his call to the Army, police and government employees to 'refuse to obey' Mrs Gandhi's 'illegal orders' and to 'abide by the Constitution instead', to the students to leave their classes and to the people to refuse to pay taxes. The opposition movement, after being initiated on 29 June, was to be rapidly accelerated and brought to completion on 5 July. The plan was to organize daily demonstrations at all the state capitals and tehsil and taluka, block and district headquarters in the country for a week. The finale of the movement would come on Sunday, 5 July in Delhi, the stronghold of RSS-Jan Sangh, where they could command thousands of volunteers and activists, with a huge rally at the prime minister's house, in defiance of a ban. The prime minister was then to be gheraoed, her house surrounded by a mass of humanity, making it impossible for her to function. She would be either forced to resign or call the army to enact another Jallianwalla Bagh type massacre of hundreds if not thousands of people—a massacre she could not survive or ever live down. Alternatively, the army might disobey her and thus overthrow her, assume power itself or hand it over to the opposition. The entire opposition game plan was made explicit by Morarji Desai in an interview to Oriana Fallaci later in the evening, quoted at length earlier in Chapter 4. To repeat, Morarji said: 'We intend to overthrow her, to force her to resign. For good. The lady won't survive this movement of ours ... Thousands of us will surround her house to prevent her from going out or receiving visitors. We'll camp there night and day shouting to her to resign.'[211] In other words, the opposition plan had all the hallmarks of a non-military coup d'etat.

The JPM thus created a situation where people were being aroused for an insurrection. The tactics it evolved and employed over time—gheraos, bandhs, coercion of individuals, especially legislators, civil disobedience, no-tax campaign, calls for virtual rebellion and paralysis of the government leading to its overthrow, appeals to the armed forces, police and bureaucracy to refuse to obey government's orders and virtually rebel against it—were all aimed at leading to a revolution. But this was to be a revolution without a political instrument, in the form of a revolutionary party organization to give it direction, or even a leader or leaders who would take over power after its success. JP, the only person projected as a leader of the movement, was opposed to assuming administrative power himself. The proposed revolution was without any semblance of an ideology or a carefully crafted or well-articulated, however broad, socio-economic and political programme that could provide alternatives to the existing policies and structure. Nor did the intended revolutionary struggle have a basic and long-term strategy.

In fact, the revolution was to rely on a mix of ideology-less cadres of Chhatra Vahinis, the rag-bag conservative cadre of the Congress (O), BLD (BKD) and Swatantra Party and the highly ideological, trained, and committed communal and neo-fascist cadres of the RSS-Jan Sangh. The fragmented and rapidly dwindling socialists were the only component of the JPM that had some acquaintance with radical thinking. The other active agents of the revolution were to be the mass of students bereft of ideology and over which JP had no effective control.

JP's neglect of ideology was not accidental. He was conscious of the need for a programme qualitatively different from Indira Gandhi's, but he could not evolve one because of the mixed bag of parties he was carrying. Consequently, when questioned by critics, he referred in general terms to 'the Gandhian way'. He also consciously eschewed an ideological commitment. Already, in 1973, presenting the policy of the journal *Everyman's* that he had launched, JP announced that it was not wedded to any ism—'whether left, right or centre.'[212] On 15 June 1974, the *Statesman* reported JP as telling an interviewer that 'ideology was a very deceptive word, what was wanted was the end of all ideologies.' He added: 'I do not think ideology helps clarity. I think all ideologies have become old. It is not ideology but science that can answer the question. Let scientists and economists sit and chalk out a programme.' He claimed that 'common sense and intelligence can solve all social evils.' Referring to the necessary conditions in a party or leader, he said: 'The first condition is honesty and sincerity and the second is the attitude towards exploitation, which has nothing to do with ideology.'[213] Similarly, in August 1974, when asked by the deputy editor of *Hindustan Times* 'what would be the criteria governing the setting up or endorsing of candidates? Will they have a specific political or economic orientation?', JP replied: 'In the present juncture, politically speaking, and from the social, economic and cultural points of view also, the most important ideology is honesty. I tell them to select a person or endorse a person who is honest . . . Now, if there are two honest people to choose from, choose the one who is nearer to you, whose life and career have shown that he has sympathy for the poor, that he will serve the cause of the poor. These are the two criteria to be kept in mind.'[214]

The essential weakness of the JP movement was captured at the time by Sham Lal, certainly the most well-read and perceptive of the contemporary journalists. In an editorial in the *Times of India* of 29 May 1975, he wrote that JP's 'Total Revolution', far from being a revolution, was merely 'a ploy to beat the Congress at its own game.' Total revolution was, he said, 'a phrase so empty of content that it brings at least the sceptics among us face to face with the void at the heart of our real life.' He went on to add: 'What kind of revolution can it be which can dispense with a strategy, a vanguard and even cadres? . . . What are the new weapons with which he intends to fight entrenched communal and caste interests? And what are the new sanctions he plans to forge against all the elite classes which have come to acquire a stake in corruption of one kind or another? . . . The talk of a "total revolution" doesn't even permit a search for an honest answer.' The opposition's movement would 'only replace what is in fact a comparatively well-knit coalition of interests with a loose federation of interests.' The danger was that the movement would 'only create a political climate propitious not for a revolution but for anarchy.' Sham Lal's critique was echoed by several friends of JP who had otherwise actively supported the JPM. J.B. Kripalani, for example, said as early as February 1974 that it was idle to talk of revolution at the time. In his view, 'it is not revolution round the corner, but it is chaos.' 'The three conditions for a revolution', he wrote, 'were an ideology, an intellectual community vigorously and uncompromisingly expounding it, and thirdly, a constructive programme of social change.' None of these were present in India of the time. 'Where', he asked, 'is the ideology. Where is the Gandhi for that.'[215]

Similarly, J.D. Sethi, a great admirer of JP and one of the few intellectuals of any substance supporting the movement, warned in early June 1975 that unless JP removed three 'glaring weaknesses' besetting the movement he would 'run the risk of losing his movement both in Bihar and the rest of the country.' The three weaknesses were: the 'very weak' organizational structure; JP's failure 'to create well defined second rank leadership' and lack of clearly defined 'socio-economic objectives'.[216] We may add one more long comment by Bhola Chatterji in 1984: 'Imagine a total revolution to rebuild a complex subcontinental society being started without any ideology, policy, programme or organization . . . The truth is that the term total revolution was a slogan that could be put to a variety of uses, depending on what exactly one intended to achieve at a given point.'[217]

In his more thoughtful moments, JP himself could recognize the need for leadership and organization and the harm their absence could do. Writing in jail on 18 August 1975, he said that, whether a revolution was violent or peaceful, 'in either case, leadership and organization would be necessary to bring out of the revolutionary situation, a revolutionary movement. In the absence of leadership and organization, the revolutionary situation might end in chaos or imposition of a dictatorship.'[218]

The adoption by a popular movement of the rhetoric of revolution, even if it is based on revolutionary ideology and programme and revolutionary leadership and organization, and of extra-legal and extra-constitutional and often violent agitational methods is not compatible with the functioning of a democratic political system in which political and socio-economic changes can be brought about peacefully. But, what is even more important, when such rhetoric and methods are not part of a revolutionary design to change the socio-economic structure in a fundamental manner in line with the objectives and ideology of the revolution, when masses enter into a chaotic and disorganized movement without the leadership of a properly constituted and led revolutionary party, when faith in a political system is destroyed without creating faith in an alternative system, when the leader at the head of the movement is confused and politically and ideologically irresponsible, the result could be utterly opportunist politics or, more likely, a recipe for an authoritarian, often fascist, regime or for political chaos, anarchy and violence, which could endanger the political system and could lead even to the disintegration of the political entity. Historically, such a mix, accompanied by vague talk of ending corruption, cleansing politics, youth power, permanent institutions of people's power, has been the hallmark not of a revolution but of a counter-revolution, as the rise of fascism in Europe, militarism in Japan and authoritarian regimes in Latin America and, nearer home, in Pakistan and Bangladesh indicates.

Let me add a caveat. JP himself was not the stuff of which dictators are made. The danger of authoritarianism did not come from him. He was basically a democrat and had functioned as such in the Congress as well as in the Socialist party, both before and after independence. Far from being a fascist, he was not even, by intention or otherwise, hungry for and working for personal political power. It wasn't that he was planning or giving direction to an authoritarian coup d'etat. It would be wrong even to see him as an 'agent of fascist forces'. His advocacy of partyless democracy, however hazy and impractical, could also not be described as fascist.

However, there were, as pointed out earlier, others around him who were so inclined, and who were increasingly coming to dominate the movement organizationally, and only too willing to capitalize on JP's ideological woolliness, political confusion and other political and personal weaknesses. They could use his popular appeal for their own, very different purposes. He could become their instrument, for he was not aware of the risks involved in the character of his movement and of his bed-fellows. At the end of June 1975, he might not have had "the faintest plans for what to do if they brought Mrs Gandhi down", but there were others who probably had. A confused leader can be used by other, more clear-headed persons, unwittingly for purposes that may be contrary to his ideas or intentions. In any case, JP would have been a weak reed to rely upon by those committed to democracy.

So long as it lasted, the JPM did not become authoritarian or fascist. Nor can it be said that it would necessarily have ended up as such. It was, however, capable of creating a space for those of its constituents that were authoritarian or fascist; it carried the possibility of being transformed in that direction. That possibility, of course, might not have actually materialized for many aspects of India's history, polity and geographical and cultural diversity militated against it.

In JP's case, the talk of partyless democracy, Total Revolution, youth power, people's revolution, parallel administration and need for character in place of ideologies, the critique of parliamentary democracy and 'demonization' of politicians and political parties, and the emphasis on forms of extra-constitutional struggles was just nebulous and unclear and not part of a conscious authoritarian discourse. However, in the hands of less lofty persons and parties such ideas could be dangerous, for they undermined faith in democracy, encouraged cynicism towards politics, bred social despair and created other political and psychological conditions which could have led to a climate favourable for the emergence of authoritarian trends which could lead to dictatorship. This had happened in many countries including Italy in 1919, Germany and Japan in the 1930s, and Pakistan and Indonesia in the 1960s. Moreover, the fascists, the Nazis and other authoritarian regimes invariably appeared on the stage not as agents of the old order but as agents or proponents of new, often 'revolutionary' regimes with ostensibly radical programmes. They also claimed to stand above and against 'corrupt' parties and politicians. They also claimed to find their most effective agents or force in the 'youth'.

Moreover, in the absence of proper direction, collapse of the political system (and paralysis of the state) without putting an alternative in its place (and village-level self-government, even if realized, could not take this place) was likely to lead to power falling into the hands of a political formation such as the RSS, which could provide effective ideological and organizational leadership to rudderless youth. The other possibility would be the splintering of the polity into state-level power groups. Both possibilities could occur simultaneously as in

China after 1927. The authoritarian or fascist possibility also lay in the fact that, by mid-1975, the core of the JPM, especially in Delhi and the Hindi heartland, was provided by the RSS-Jan Sangh.

Contemporary fear of the possibility of the JPM leading to fascism was expressed at the end of 1974 by Zareer Masani who was a bitter critic of Mrs Gandhi during the Emergency: 'Given the middle class background of the youth involved and their lack of ideological clarity, a revolt of this kind, if it assumes national proportions, might well prove fascist rather than socialist.'[219] Another perceptive political observer, who too was a critic of Mrs Gandhi and an admirer of JP, Balraj Puri, also warned as early as May-June 1974 that 'if besides Congress, the system also collapsed, we are not sure what would replace it' and that 'in the ensuing confusion and instability, the danger of an authoritarian backlash cannot be ruled out.' In fact, Puri even foresaw a version of the Emergency when he observed that authoritarianism could result 'if the movement gets exhausted on account of organizational and ideological inadequacies or superior strength and tactics of the establishment.'[220]

Why many contemporaries and later writers such as Granville Austin have not seen the authoritarian potential of the JPM has been in part because it was snuffed out before this could develop, in part because it is and was difficult to visualize this potential when a person of JP's antecedents was heading it, and also because most of the writers were, and are, unfamiliar with the real ideology and organization of the RSS. The ultimate results of a movement are in any case difficult to gauge till its final denouement. After all how many could foresee the potential consequences of Mussolini's fascist and Hitler's Nazi movements before they captured power or even a few years after?

7   The Emergency: The Initial Years

At midnight of 25 June 1975, President Fakhruddin Ali Ahmed, pliant and acting on the advice of the prime minister, signed a proclamation that would come into effect the next morning, declaring a state of Internal Emergency[1] on the grounds that 'a grave emergency exists whereby the security of India is threatened by internal disturbances.' The Cabinet had no inkling of the deed; its members were woken up and gathered at a dawn meeting and asked to meekly endorse the decision retrospectively.[2] As a result of the declaration, the normal political processes were suspended, immense powers were conferred on the central executive, seeking to alter the basic, democratic character of the Indian state for the duration of the Emergency. The basic federal provisions of the Constitution and fundamental rights and civil liberties, such as freedoms of speech, the Press, and assembly, including the holding of meetings, processions and demonstrations, guaranteed under Article 19 were suspended. From then on the rule of law was severely curtailed; protest from any quarter was declared illegal and suppressed— political dissent was no longer permitted. Later, in January, the government suspended the right of citizens to appeal to the courts for defence of their fundamental rights.

I

In the early hours of 26 June, hundreds of prominent leaders and activists of the Opposition were arrested, mostly in northern states, where the JP movement was strong, under the Maintenance of Internal Security Act (MISA). Among those taken into custody were Jayaprakash Narayan, Morarji Desai, Charan Singh, Asoka Mehta, Atal Behari Vajpayee, and nearly thirty MPs, including dissident Congressmen such as Chandra Shekhar and Mohan Dharia. However, several prominent opposition leaders such as Nanaji Deshmukh, George Fernandes and Balraj Madhok evaded arrest. Several teachers, newspapermen, trade unionists and student leaders were also jailed. None of the top leaders of the CPM or DMK were arrested.

The news of the confinement of national leaders was withheld from the public by the expedient of cutting off power supply to all newspaper presses in Old Delhi. But the *Hindustan Times* and the *Statesman* managed to bring out their editions, and carried the news because their presses were in New Delhi!

A few days later, extreme communal organizations such as the RSS, Jamaat-i-Islami and Anand Marg and the groups affiliated with them were banned. Several far-left Naxalite groups were also banned. The leading cadres of the banned organizations were arrested.

Arrests continued throughout the period of the Emergency which lasted for nineteen months. People were arrested on the slightest suspicion or on the basis of rumours. However, most of those arrested were set free after a few days or months. JP was released on 12 November 1975 on grounds of health (he was suffering from a serious kidney ailment). Others including Asoka Mehta, Atal Behari Vajpayee, Charan Singh and Piloo Mody were set free during 1976.

In all nearly 110,000 persons were detained under MISA and Defence of India Rules (DIR) all over the country during the period of the Emergency. The Emergency provisions were also used by the government to take strong action against "anti-social elements" and arrest a large number of smugglers, foreign currency or *hawala* operators, hoarders, blackmarketeers and known goondas, who had used loopholes in the legal system and their links with the police, bureaucrats and politicians to escape arrest and punishment. Notable was the fact that the whereabouts of those detained and the reasons for their arrest were kept secret even from their relatives. Nor were the names of those arrested made public. Newspapers were forbidden to carry them. Besides, no allowance was given for maintenance of the detained persons families. Some of the detained were also ill-treated in the overcrowded jails, where even normally unhealthy conditions prevailed.

II

Through a series of presidential ordinances, strict censorship, and in many cases pre-censorship, was imposed on newspapers, magazines and other publication in order to control the news and views which reached the people.[3] Editors were instructed by the censoring authority as to what they could print. Any news, cartoons, photographs or advertisements which were seen to be even slightly critical of the government were censored, thus silencing independent journalists and reducing others to docility. The government also imposed censorship over the reporting of all parliamentary and court proceedings. In February 1976, the Prohibition of Publication of Objectionable Matter Act, which was being enforced as an ordinance since December 1975, was passed. It prohibited the publication of 'words, signs or visible representations' which might 'bring into hatred or contempt or excite disaffection towards the government established by law in India or in any state thereof and thereby cause or tend to cause public disorder,' or 'defame' the President, the vice-president, the prime minister, the speaker of the Lok Sabha, and the governors. This act made any criticism of the policies or actions of the government, ministers and officials virtually impossible. Nor could this act be challenged in a court.

Censorship sometimes descended to ridiculous levels. For example, quotations from Gandhiji, Tagore and Nehru or even Mrs Gandhi's own earlier speeches pertaining to civil liberties and freedom of expression were not to be reproduced. The *National Herald*, the paper founded by Jawaharlal Nehru, which throughout supported the Emergency, removed his famous quotation; 'Freedom is in peril, defend it with all your might,' from its masthead. The censor also objected to the well-known picture of Gandhiji walking away with his back to the audience on the grounds that it might be interpreted as his walking away from the Emergency.

While some, mostly communal dailies and periodicals, had been banned at the outset, given the environment, several others decided at different points of time to close down rather than bow before the censoring authorities. These included JP's *Everyman's*, *Shankar's Weekly*—a cartoon weekly edited by Shankar, the famous cartoonist whose caricatures had been appreciated by Gandhiji, Nehru, Linlithgow and Mrs Gandhi herself—*Seminar*, edited by Romesh Thapar, a significant organ of the Indian intelligentsia and *Mainstream*, edited by the pro-Communist Nikhil Chakravartty, who had stood by Mrs Gandhi throughout the period of the JP movement. Some periodicals, for example, the *Janata* of the Socialist party and the *People's Democracy* of the CPM, suspended their publication for varying periods.

The government tightened its control over the Press and other publications through several other steps. In December 1975, by an ordinance it abolished the Press Council, an independent body set up in July 1966 'for the purpose of preserving freedom of the press and maintaining and improving the standards of newspapers and news agencies in India' and to evolve a code of conduct for the Press. In February 1976, the government forced a merger of the four independent news agencies, Press Trust of India, United Press of India, Samachar Bharati and Hindustan Samachar, into a single news agency, Samachar, which functioned under effective government control. The government already owned the All India Radio and Doordarshan, the sole TV channel, which were now used to disseminate a one-sided version of the news.

Efforts were also made to manipulate newspaper coverage by regulating official advertisements favouring 'friendly' newspapers and denying them to 'unfriendly' and 'hostile' newspapers. Even the pro-government *Patriot*, controlled by Aruna Asaf Ali and friendly to Mrs Gandhi, was at one stage denied government advertisements for its refusal to praise and report the activities of Sanjay Gandhi.

Some of the newspapers which were critical of the government both before and during the Emergency, such as the *Statesman* and the *Indian Express*, were harassed and intimidated in multiple ways: some of their correspondents were denied accreditation; they were refused government advertisements, electricity to their presses was occasionally disconnected, their owners were threatened in various ways. In the end, the owners of the *Indian Express* were forced to agree to the appointment of the majority of its directors, including its chairman, by the government. Often private presses were persuaded to refuse to print smaller dissident magazines.

Individual journalists too came under pressure. The accreditation of some of them, even senior ones, was withdrawn or they or were refused permission to go abroad, or were even dismissed at the government's behest. Several foreign correspondents were expelled from the country for not accepting censorship or for violating the censorship rules. Others were denied entry visas. Only those who gave a written undertaking to abide by such rules could continue to report from India. The curbs on foreign correspondents were, however, lifted in July 1976. But total government control of the media had an unforeseen result. More and more people turned to BBC for finding out what was actually happening in the country.

The government could, of course, offer one justification for Press censorship: control of the Press was a key feature, the very essence of the Emergency, without which it could have little practical meaning. If the people's protests and the news and opinion critical of the government could be freely reported, then the situation would not be very different from that before 26 June. The constraints on bandhs, gheraos, demonstrations and satyagrahas and other forms of protest or on anti-government political activity would be easily violated by those keen on creating discontent against the government if their actions could garner enough publicity. As Mrs Gandhi put it in her speech to Rajya Sabha on 8 January 1976. 'It is obvious that the opposition movement was not merely getting publicity, but was actually built up by our Press; and it is because we denied the opposition the benefit of this, their special type of publicity, that the Emergency has succeeded. In a battle, the antagonists' lines of supply have to be cutt off, and this is what censorship has done.'[4]

As pointed out earlier, many student and teacher political activists, mostly belonging to the banned organizations or involved in the JP movement in Bihar and UP, were arrested in the initial days of the Emergency, though most of them were soon released. Intelligence agents also kept tabs on teachers and students in most university campuses.

Later, efforts were made to tamper with academic freedom by imposing so-called codes of conduct and by trying to frighten some of the dissident academics through telephone-tapping, harassment by income-tax and foreign-exchange control authorities and restrictions on their travel abroad.

The Emergency saw the Parliament being emasculated, made utterly ineffective and reduced to a body of yes-persons. It was used to rubberstamp government decrees, ordinances and constitutional amendments. On 21 July 1975, it was convened to deliberate on the proclamation of the Emergency. At the very outset the Question Hour was abolished so that the government could not be asked to give information regarding those arrested, their number, antecedents and affiliations, or the reasons for their detention. Members were also no longer permitted to submit motions on important public matters or move private member's bills. The proceedings of the Parliament were also to be censored; the speeches of the MPs, who spoke against the Emergency proclamation, were not allowed to be reported in the Press while those of its supporters were given full coverage. Later, in 1976, the Parliamentary Proceedings (Protection) Act was passed, putting a total ban on the publication of parliamentary proceedings.

Angry with these steps and with the arrest of thirty of their fellow members, all the non-CPI opposition members of the Lok Sabha and Rajya Sabha voted against the resolution approving of the Emergency and, then, most of them walked out and announced their decision to boycott the remainder of the Parliament's proceedings. The Opposition again boycotted the opening session of the Parliament on 5 January 1976.

In January 1976, the Parliament passed a resolution postponing elections to the Lok Sabha scheduled in February-March 1976. Elections to the Lok Sabha were again postponed for a year in November 1976.

To eliminate the existence or emergence of rival centres of power, the state governments, all but two of which were run by the Congress, were rigidly controlled throughout the period of the Emergency.

Of the two non-Congress state governments, the M. Karunanidhi-led DMK government in Tamil Nadu was dismissed on 31 January 1976 on grounds of corruption and the misuse of the Emergency powers.[5] In Gujarat, the other non-Congress state, defections were engineered in the ruling Janata Front and the government fell on 11 February 1976 when it was defeated on the budgetary demands. Thereafter, the state was brought under President's rule in March and its erstwhile chief minister, Babubhai Patel, was arrested in August. Even the Congress chief ministers of UP (H.N. Bahuguna) and Orissa (Nandini Satpathy) were forced to resign on 29 November 1975 and 16 December 1976 respectively and replaced for not being reliable enough, though they had been Mrs Gandhi's loyal supporters since 1969. They had, however, fallen foul of Mrs Gandhi's younger son, Sanjay Gandhi. For the same reason, Siddhartha Shankar Ray, chief minister of West Bengal, was throughout kept on tenterhooks, but escaped the chopping block.

The Congress party also came to be even more strictly disciplined and controlled by Mrs Gandhi. Dissent and internal democracy within the party were more or less completely suppressed. Its members and leaders were afraid to express disagreement with official policies even in private. Even those loyal to Mrs Gandhi since 1969 were humiliated and discarded or forced to keep quiet, especially after the rise of Sanjay Gandhi, when the Youth Congress led by him became more important than Congress, the parent organization. Existing party leaders were further marginalized. For example, the party president from 1974 to 1977, D.K. Barooah hardly carried any weight in the party or the government. Senior leaders like Rajni Patel and Siddhartha Shankar Ray, who had some political base of their own, were sidelined, while upstarts, like Bansi Lal, gained influence relying only on the personal popularity of Mrs Gandhi. The party structure was thus so completely weakened that it was incapable of even being used as the agency for popularizing and implementing the 20-Point Programme of the government. A silent rebellion now began to brew among disgruntled Congressmen.

While the Emergency proclamation had suspended all fundamental rights guaranteed under Article 19 of the Constitution, the President by an ordinance issued on 27 June suspended the right of a citizen to move any court for the enforcement of the fundamental rights guaranteed under Articles 14, 21 and 22. Later, the Supreme Court decided that the powers of a court to issue a writ of *habeas corpus*—a basic characteristic of the rule of law in a democracy—was also suspended for the period of the Emergency. Consequently, no specific charges were levelled against the persons imprisoned on 26 June or after, nor were they tried before a court. In fact, a series of ordinances, laws and constitutional amendments drastically reduced, in fact virtually nullified, the power of the judiciary to check the functioning of the executive.

As already indicated earlier, most of the people were arrested during the Emergency under the DIR and the MISA. The DIR were amended in June 1975 so that they could now be applied not only in cases of "defence of India" and "external aggression" but also of "internal security" and "internal disturbance".

The MISA was amended four times through ordinances and then, in January 1976, through an act of Parliament. According to the original MISA, passed in 1971, a detenu had to be supplied the grounds of his confinement within five days of his arrest and the duration of the detention was up to six months. According to the amended MISA, the duration of the detention was first increased to a year in the first instance and than to two years. Moreover, the grounds of detention were to be treated as confidential and not to be supplied to those arrested. The MISA was also made non-justiciable; that is, the right of a detenu to appeal to the courts for protection against undue arrest or the misuse of the act was taken away. Nor could a court enquire into the grounds of detention, which, in any case, were supplied neither to the detenues or to the courts.

The citizen was thus left completely defenceless against the harassment by or malice of officials, high or low.[6] India was on the way to becoming a police state.

II

Very soon the government went on a constitutional amendment spree that could have changed the basic structure of the Indian Constitution. As Inder Malhotra has remarked, 'all through those 19 months, she (Mrs Gandhi) was very particular that everything she did was seen to be within the Constitution. At the same time, she recklessly amended the Constitution itself to suit her purpose of building protective walls around herself and her office.'[7]

In July 1975, the government introduced the thirty-eighth amendment to the Constitution which decreed that the Emergency proclamation could not be challenged in the courts. Next, on 5 August, Parliament passed the amendment to the Representation of Peoples Act of 1956. The amendment was to have a retrospective effect and thus apply to any election held before the amendment. All of its many clauses were basically designed to invalidate Justice Sinha's judgement of June and validate Mrs Gandhi's election. One of its clauses also took away from the courts the right to decide whether a person should be disqualified and, if so, for what period, and vested it in the President.

Still, Mrs Gandhi and her advisers did not want to take the risk of an adverse judgement by the Supreme Court on her appeal against the Allahabad judgement. Consequently, the thirty-ninth amendment to the Constitution was taken up on 8 August 1975 and, after going through all the procedures, it was enacted in record haste on 10 August, a day before the hearing of Mrs Gandhi's appeal before the Supreme Court. Clause 4 of the amendment laid down that the election to the Parliament of the prime minister and election of a person as speaker, or President or vice-president could not be challenged before the courts and could be decided only by 'a body to be appointed by Parliament.' It also stipulated that no law about election petitions passed prior to the amendment was valid, and any judicial decision voiding an election under such law would become invalid. According to one of its clauses, the amended MISA and election law and several other legislative acts were added to the Ninth Schedule of the Constitution, and thus put beyond judicial review.

The fortieth amendment, passed in May 1976, placed in the Ninth Schedule the Prevention of Publication of Objectionable Matter Act and a large number of other laws dealing with property. The Supreme Court, in a 5 to 4 majority judgement delivered on 7 November, accepted the changes in the election law of 1951 as constitutionally valid and in the light of the changed law upheld Mrs Gandhi's election to the Parliament in 1971. But it struck down clause 4 of the thirty-ninth amendment, which had placed the prime minister's election beyond the scrutiny of the courts.

The Forty-first Amendment Bill, introduced in the Rajya Sabha on 9 August 1975, gave complete immunity from possible criminal proceedings to anyone who was or had been President or prime minister or governor, in respect of any act done by him before or during the term of office in his personal or official capacity. Even though the Rajya Sabha had passed the Amendment Bill, Mrs Gandhi allowed it to lapse because of its clearly ignoble character.

Pressure gradually built up in the ranks of the supporters of the Emergency for more far-reaching changes in the Constitution, ending up with the forty-second amendment in November 1976, which became an important landmark of the Emergency. This amendment will be discussed at length later in this section.

Many prominent jurists, including the ex-Chief Justice of India, P.B. Gajendragadkar, and the Supreme Court judge, P.N. Bhagwati, were unhappy with the Kesavananda Bharati doctrine of the immutability of the basic structure of the Constitution and the consequent limitation on the power of Parliament to amend the Constitution. They, therefore, argued for changing some of its features. Many others, disturbed by the political instability and breakdown of administration in many parts of the country before the Emergency, wanted constitutional changes to assure stability and law and order. Many were dismayed by the fact that a single judge had been able to upset a prime minister's election on inconsequential grounds.

The real impetus to the forces for constitutional change was provided by a political resolution adopted at the Chandigarh session of the All India Congress Committee in December 1975. The resolution urged a re-examination of the Constitution in the interests 'of the poor and vulnerable sections of our society' and to make, if necessary, 'adequate alterations to it so that it may continue as a living document.'[8] Consequently, a committee, under the chairmanship of Swaran Singh, the minister for foreign affairs, was set up in February 1976 for this purpose.

Certain important figures such as the bureaucrat, B.K. Nehru, Mrs Gandhi's principal secretary, P.N. Dhar, the jurist, N.A. Palkhivala, prominent Congress leader, Vasant Sathe, and many other eminent Congress and non-Congress leaders favoured a shift from the parliamentary to the presidential form of democracy. This, they hoped, would weaken Parliament's power to obstruct the executive, put an end to political instability and fragmentation and corruption, by strengthening the political executive at the centre and in the states.

Others supported the presidential system in the hope that it would lead to absolute power being exercised by the rulers of the day. For example, the Bombay Congress leader, A.R. Antulay, with the backing of Rajni Patel, president of the Bombay Congress Committee, presented to Indira Gandhi in January 1976 a very badly drafted note, in which he emphasized the weak position of the prime minister under the parliamentary system, argued for 'the unobstructed working of the executive' and said that 'the time of the Chief Executive should not be allowed to be frittered away in fruitless debate and discussion,' and suggested as alternative the presidential system in which the electoral President who being 'elected by a popular direct mandate . . . should, in the scheme of things, enjoy more authority and powers than even the US President.'[9] In another paper, this time circulated in his own name, Rajni Patel, arguing that 'Western democracy is not the last word on the subject', and that there was 'nothing sacrosant' about 'the Westminster model', suggested that the prime minister should be directly elected by popular vote which would enable 'him or her to exercise authority without the vexation of pulls and pressures that a Prime Minister elected indirectly is subjected to.' He also suggested measures to enhance the powers of the executive and weaken those of the judiciary.[10] A few advocates of the presidential system went to the extent of describing parliamentary system as a foreign implant which was acting as an obstacle in the path of national development and socialism.

Both CPM and CPI, the Congress ally, consistently opposed the presidential system as being less democratic and more authoritarian under Indian conditions and fought for the retention of parliamentary democracy. Their approach was partially conditioned by the support being given to the attacks on the parliamentary system by the emerging coterie around Sanjay Gandhi.

Along the CPI and a large number of Congressmen, Mrs Gandhi favoured some constitutional reform, but was not in favour of a changeover to the presidential system. She made this clear to B.K. Nehru when he broached the subject with her.[11] Instead, according to P.N. Dhar, she 'laid emphasis on improving the existing procedures.'[12]. Also, she told the PTI on 22 August 1975 that 'neither the spirit of our Constitution nor its essential characteristics can change.'[13] Later, in February 1976, she publicly rejected the idea and said, 'Power should not be concentrated but be with the people.'[14]

The Swaran Singh Committee's report, approved by the AICC in May 1976, rejected the proposal for a presidential form of government and asserted that the parliamentary system was 'best suited to our country.' Instead, it suggested that Article 368 of the Constitution should be amended so that courts would have no powers to question 'the constitutionality of any constitutional amendments.' This change would do away with Kesavananda Bharati judgement's doctrine of the immutability of the basic structure of the Constitution. The Committee also suggested that the Constitution should clearly specify that the

President was bound by the advice of the council of ministers. The Committee favoured the retention of the right by the courts to issue writs, such as the writ for habeas corpus, for the protection of a citizen's fundamental rights. However, it made the drastic recommendation that courts should not have the authority to question any legislation to implement any of the Directive Principles of State Policy on the ground that it violated the fundamental rights.[15] The Committee made several other proposals which were incorporated in the forty-second amendment, though the latter went far beyond the Committee's recommendations. But before I come to this amendment, another significant development has to be discussed, though briefly.

Sanjay Gandhi and his cronies like Bansi Lal, minister of defence at the time, were keen on postponing elections and prolonging the Emergency by several years. Taking advantage of the current talk of constitutional reform they came up with the proposal for convening a fresh constituent assembly to 'radically transform the Constitution'. To avoid fresh elections for the purpose, their proposal involved the conversion of the existing parliament, with its large Congress majority, into a constituent assembly. Whatever else this constituent assembly might or might not achieve, it was hoped that it would lead to the Emergency being extended for a long time. The main purpose of the new constituent assembly, Bansi Lal told P.N. Dhar, would be to make Mrs Gandhi President for life.[16]

To put pressure on Mrs Gandhi and to give the impression that the demand was popular, Sanjay Gandhi and Bansi Lal got the Congress committees and the Congress legislative parties of Punjab, Haryana and UP to pass resolutions demanding the convening of a constituent assembly to recast the Constitution.

The CPI and most of the newspapers and other organs of public opinion opposed the move. Some of the opposition parties did not object to it but demanded fresh elections for the purpose. However, alarmed by the proposal, Mrs Gandhi proceeded to scuttle it by asking the cabinet to submit the Swaran Singh Committee's proposals to Parliament.

In October-November 1976, an effort was made to change the basic civil libertarian structure of the Constitution through the forty-second amendment to the Constitution.[17] The 59-clause bill for the purpose was placed before the Lok Sabha on 1 September, taken up for discussion on 25 October and was approved both by the Lok Sabha and the Rajya Sabha and by thirteen states. The President gave his consent on 18 December 1976.

While the new description of India in the Preamble to the Constitution as 'a Sovereign Socialist Secular Democratic Republic'[18] and some of the changes suggested by the amendment were unexceptional, this was not the case for most of the amendments. The most important changes were designed to strengthen the executive at the cost of the judiciary, and thus disturb the carefully crafted system of constitutional checks and balance between the three organs of the government. Several amendments put an end to the judicial review of constitutional amendments because, it was said—perhaps with some justification—that the judiciary, given its class prejudices, had been obstructing pro-poor, socio-economic legislation, such as that on land reforms, in the name of defending fundamental rights and the basic structure of the Constitution. The forty-second amendment laid down that there would be no limitation whatever on the power of Parliament to amend the Constitution in any of its aspects, and that on no grounds would any amendment of the Constitution be called in question in the courts.

Several clauses of the amendment were designed to whittle down the power of the judiciary to review Parliament's legislation. For example, high courts could no longer review the constitutional validity of a law passed by the Parliament. Only the Supreme Court could do so, but even it could declare a central law to be unconstitutional only by two-thirds majority in a Bench consisting of at least seven judges. This meant that even a minority of three out of seven judges could block the adverse decision of the majority. On the other hand, the Supreme Court could not deal with the constitutionality of state laws unless the validity of a central law was also involved. One of its most regressive and dangerous clauses enabled Parliament to pass legislation banning 'anti-national activities and associations' without giving reasons for doing so. This legislation could also be put beyond judicial review. Moreover, anti-national activities were defined in a strange way. These included not only advocacy of secession from the Union and questioning the sovereignty and integrity of India but also 'creating internal disturbances' and threatening and questioning 'the security of the state, or disrupting, or intending to disrupt, public services' and 'harmony'. Fundamental rights could thus be easily dispensed with.

Fundamental rights were further emasculated indirectly by being made subordinate to an expanded version of Directive Principles of State Policy which were, according to the Constitution, to guide the working and policies of the Centre and the states. No law could be declared unconstitutional because it violated fundamental rights specified in Article 19 and other articles of the Constitution if it was meant to implement any of the objectives listed in the Directive Principles. This was allegedly done to protect legislation to better the lot of the poorer or weaker sections of society. One positive step in this direction was that under Article 31A, laws relating to land reforms were included in the Ninth Schedule of the Constitution and could not, therefore, be challenged in the courts.

The forty-second amendment transferred the final power to decide cases of the disqualification of Members of Parliament from the Election Commission to the President and of members of state assemblies to the governor. But, at the same time, amendment of Article 74 of the Constitution laid down that the President was bound to act in accordance with the advice of the council of ministers. This further augmented the power of the central executive.

The forty-second amendment also abridged the powers of the states in favour of the central government. It authorized the central government to send the Army, para-military and police forces to any state, without taking the latter's consent, for dealing with any grave situation of law and order there. It also extended the maximum period of President's rule from six month to one year. The list of concurrent subjects on which both the Centre and the states could legislate was expanded to include education, forests, family planning, protection of wildlife and certain other subjects which earlier lay exclusively in the state domain.

The amendment also raised the terms of the Lok Sabha and the state assemblies from five to six years.

Mrs Gandhi's defence of the Forty-second Amendment Bill was presented in her speeches to the Lok Sabha on 27 October and to the Rajya Sabha on 8 November 1976. She claimed that the bill was 'a vital step in curing our political system of some of the ills to which it is subject.' After all, she said, India had been changing since the fifties when the Constitution was framed, and no one generation had the right 'to tie down future generations.' Consequently, it was necessary for all organs of the government—the legislature, the executive and the judiciary to 'respond to the changing needs and aspirations of our people'. A Constitution 'has to be capable of meeting the challenge of historical forces.' More specifically, 'the purpose of the Bill is to remedy the anomalies that have been long noticed and to overcome the obstacles put up by economic and political vested interests.' She denied that the proposed amendments were 'intended to legitimize the emergency, emasculate the judiciary and Parliament, weaken the federal structure and take away the safeguards for individuals and minorities.' But she also asserted: 'We have always maintained Parliament has an unfettered, unqualified and unabridgeable right to amend the Constitution. We do not accept the dogma of the basic structure.' She recalled that JP and his friends had also earlier set up a committee to revise the Constitution. She denied that the amendment bill would abridge the powers of the judiciary or encroach on personal rights or curtail judicial power to protect them. The bill was only designed to curb 'some recent attempts of the judiciary to encroach into political and legislative spheres.' 'The objective of the Bill', she concluded, 'is the rejuvenation of the nation and the Constitution.'[19]

The bill aroused a great deal of opposition among intellectuals. There was a major campaign against it led by dissident Congressmen, opposition parties and a large number of intellectuals. A seminar organized by opposition parties in Delhi on 16 and 17 October was largely attended by journalists, academics, lawyers, jurists, writers and other intellectuals, and it passed a strong resolution opposing the bill. On 25 October, a well-argued memorandum, under the title 'Nation-Wide Demand', opposing the bill was presented to the President. Among its several hundred signatories were some of India's leading intellectuals such as the former cabinet minister M.C. Chagla, jurists V.M. Tarkunde, C.K. Daphtary and Soli J. Sorabjee, professor of law Lotika Sarkar, historians Susobhan Sarkar, S. Gopal and Romila Thapar, economists Raj Krishna, Mrinal Datta-Chaudhuri, V.M. Dandekar and Krishna Bharadwaj, sociologists Andre Beteille and T.N. Madan, artist J. Swaminathan, film director Mrinal Sen, writers P.L. Deshpande, Vijay Tendulkar, Jainendra Kumar and Mulk Raj Anand and journalists Nikhil Chakravartty, Romesh Thapar, and B.G. Verghese. The critics of the bill argued that such a significant constitutional amendment should be passed only after a wide public debate and fresh elections, the present Parliament, having outlived its five-year term, had 'neither the political nor the moral authority to effect such fundamental changes in the Constitution.' The Supreme Court Bar Association, too, protested against the bill. To accommodate the view that the fundamental right to property stood in the way of radical, pro-poor legislation, the critics of the amendment were quite willing to remove this as a fundamental right.[20]

Apart from the impropriety of a lame-duck Parliament amending the Constitution, the passage of this bill was on the whole a highly unsavoury political development, since most of the changes it brought about were very regressive and capable of being grossly misused. It is true that some of its clauses, despite being controversial, were perhaps worthwhile—for example, expansion of the concurrent list, setting up of special tribunals to deal with subjects wherein the adage 'justice delayed is justice denied' applied, and to some extent prevention of fundamental rights being used to block pro-poor and developmental legislation. But the latter purpose did not require tinkering with fundamental rights or abridgement of the judiciary's powers to block parliamentary authoritarianism. Legislation on such subjects could have been easily placed in the Ninth Schedule of the Constitution and made non-justiciable, as was done with land reform legislation. In fact, for any social objectives no changes in the civil libertarian structure of the Constitution were mandatory. Most of the changes wrought by the forty-second amendment had precisely this effect.

P.G. Mavlankar, an independent member of Parliament, brought out another very negative feature of the exercise at amending the Constitution. He warned Congress MPs that by doing so they were 'opening the floodgate to regimentation and dictatorship.'[21] There was great truth in this observation. Those who were weakening the judiciary and strengthening Parliament's powers in the genuine belief that they were working for socio-economic justice were not able to foresee that one day they could be on the receiving end of a communal-authoritarian regime. A strong and independent judiciary would then be needed to defend civil liberties and secularism from encroachment by this demagogic parliamentary majority.

The forty-second amendment was passed by the Parliament in November, but the opposition parties boycotted these sessions of it. Though the Indian Constitution had not lost its democratic and civil libertarian edge and had not become authoritarian, a dent had been made in this respect.[22]

Immediately after, on 5 November 1976, both the Emergency as well as the term of the Lok Sabha were extended by a year more on the grounds that there was still need for discipline. Automatically, the elections which were due in March 1977 were postponed to March 1978.

In conclusion, it can be said that the Emergency centralized and concentrated unlimited state and party power in the hands of the prime minister, Mrs Gandhi, to be exercised in an authoritarian manner through a small coterie of politicians and bureaucrats around her. Moreover, the institutions of the political system, as evolved since 1950, were, according to a political scientist, 'partly dismantled and greatly weakened. These include the Constitution, the federal structure, the Cabinet, the Parliament, the judiciary and the legal profession, the party system, the opposition parties and even the Congress Party, the electoral process, the planning process, the Press, labour unions and other organizations, traditional and modern.'[23]

IV

A very important aspect of the imposition of the Emergency was the reaction of the people.

While a section of the intelligentsia were markedly hostile to it, the large majority of Indians did not immediately understand what this unprecedented step meant. They responded to it with apathy and passivity, acquiescence and obedience; in some cases they even welcomed and supported it but were not overenthusiastic.[24] There were no spontaneous protests, or strikes and demonstrations against the arrest of the opposition leaders as had been the case in August 1942. Only some sporadic, though sometimes heroic, instances of protest by word or deed were registered; a few printed or cyclostyled leaflets appeared in a few places. There was some organized resistance by groups in Bihar; a few members of Jan Sangh in Delhi and of Akali Dal in Punjab courted arrest. CPM organized a few demonstrations in Kerala; however, it soon gave up when its leaders were arrested but soon released.

Most of the votaries of Total Revolution went quiet and the JP movement just 'melted away'. This was reflected in JP's despair at the lack of public protest and the manner in which the people had meekly accepted the Emergency.[25]

Of course, the passive acceptance of the Emergency and even its slight popularity among some lasted through only its early phase. With the passage of time, the Emergency regime became increasingly unpopular and opposition to it began to take root in large parts of the country. Nevertheless, the acceptance of the Emergency in the initial stages has to be explained.

Why were the people reconciled to and even welcomed the Emergency and the hard steps that went with it so readily? Why did democracy collapse so easily? Why were Mrs Gandhi's orders obeyed so completely? Why was the faith of Morarji Desai and JP belied, that the people would not let Mrs Gandhi do what she did? Why did the instruments of administration, including the Army, fall in line 'with a dictatorship without demur', as one commentator was to ask later.[26] And why was there no significant resistance to the government for a considerable period of time? To these may be added another significant question. Why was the Emergency experience forgotten so easily so that Mrs Gandhi, who got a drubbing in March 1977 elections, could come back to power at the end of 1979?

There are no simple answers to these questions. A few easy explanations suggest themselves. For one, the situation was unprecedented. Most of the people had no experience in recent memory, since independence, of authoritarian rule, especially of strict press censorship. Moreover, the very strength of the Emergency lay in its suddenness and broad sweep. People were taken by surprise and were stunned and bewildered, as they did not expect that a national, constitutionally-elected government would or could impose an undemocratic regime. The news blackout added to their confusion.

The JPM was also less popular and Mrs Gandhi not that unpopular outside or even in Bihar than JP and many of his followers believed, or as some of the newspapers portrayed.[27] That JP was leading a 1942-type movement or that the Indian people were in a revolutionary mood was simply untrue. JP was, in fact, living in a world of his own creation. Furthermore, the lightning arrests of 26 June had paralysed the leadership of the JPM.

Many intellectuals, many among the politicized, and many on the left, who were used to organizing popular protest movements, had, despite their misgivings, another reason for at least their lukewarm response to the Emergency regime or being neutral towards it. It was the communal right which was the chief target of massive government repression.[28] Apart from the arrest of JP and some other opposition leaders, the main edge of the Emergency's repressive measures seemed to be almost entirely directed against anti-social elements or against the extreme communal right and the far-left Naxalites, who enjoyed little popular support before the Emergency and who were in any case known to be averse to democracy. All the twenty-six organizations banned, for example, were communal or left extremists. Most of those arrested, except for JP and some opposition leaders and Sarvodayites, were the militants and active sympathizers of the banned organizations. No action as such was taken against the major secular or left opposition parties. Their top leaders and cadres were by and large left untouched, and the few lower level leaders who were arrested were soon released. Moreover, Mrs Gandhi and the government media consistently, from the beginning, played upon the theme that the communalists, in general, and the fascist and undemocratic RSS in particular were the main targets of the Emergency. They also emphasized the active role the RSS played in the JP movement.[29] But, more than these, a large number of people were impressed by the immediate positive outcome of some of the well-publicized measures of the Emergency. It was another matter that most of these measures could have been taken in the normal course of governance, without an Emergency. Some of these 'gains of Emergency' were appreciated by the poor, who believed that Mrs Gandhi was working for their welfare; others were appreciated by the middle and upper classes. Most of the 'improvements', however, as we shall see, proved to be short-lived and were overshadowed by the 'excesses' of the Emergency.

Also the situation in the country before June 1975 was not normal and most people were not averse to hard steps being taken. A large number of people were disgusted with the breakdown of law and order and administration. People were tired of 'apparently pointless confrontations' perpetual agitations, campaigns of mass civil disobedience, bandhs, gheraos, demonstrations, strikes and street violence, and students' and teachers' strikes and agitations, which had brought normal work in the universities and colleges to a standstill and created a disorderly atmosphere on the campuses. Many used the words 'chaos' and 'anarchy' to describe the pre-Emergency situation.

Suddenly, with the imposition of the Emergency, peace and public order were restored. Crime and hooliganism in the cities came down. Strikes, bandhs, sit-ins and gheraos, and mass demonstrations and rallies ended. There was perceptible lessening of tension in the air. Calm was restored on the campuses as students and teachers went back to classrooms, and examinations were held on time. After the turmoil of previous years industrial peace prevailed. There was a noticeable improvement in social discipline, for example, people stood in queues at bus stops and ration-shops, cities bore a cleaner look, traffic in the cities moved in an orderly fashion. The popular acceptance of the Emergency and relief at the improvement in discipline were reflected in Vinoba Bhave's description of the Emergency as '*Anusashan Parva*' or the Era of Discipline.

Many felt relieved that the country had been saved from the spectre of 'disorder', 'chaos', 'instability', 'anarchy' and destabilization. The short-term authoritarian measures were regarded as a necessary and 'strong though bitter medicine' to meet a dangerous situation.[30] At another level, some felt that Mrs Gandhi had saved the Indian state from instability and disintegration. Representing this view, H.Y. Sharda Prasad, information adviser to Mrs Gandhi at the time, has written recently that though he agreed with P.N. Dhar that the Emergency was 'an evil' and a painful interlude, he was convinced then as now that 'If

Indira Gandhi had thrown in the towel at that point of time, it would have greatly weakened the Indian state. Yes, the Emergency did damage our democratic roots badly, but the state had been saved from a very grave challenge.'[31] Similarly, Mohit Sen has argued that 'the Emergency was inevitable if the Indian state was to be preserved.'[32] Ultimately, as we have shown in Chapter 4, this was also the main justification Mrs Gandhi offered for the Emergency in her pronouncements after 26 June 1975.[33]

There was also an immediate and general improvement in administration—in government departments and public services. Government servants came to office on time and stayed in office till closing time, took fewer tea-breaks, attended to their work, and were more considerate to the general public. However, their work output did not necessarily improve, for the government institutions remained as rigid, bureaucratic and unproductive as before. Trains and aeroplanes arrived and left on schedule and the travellers were treated with courtesy by the employees. Many corrupt and inefficient government officials were dismissed or forced to take premature retirement. Efforts were also made to discipline governmental institutions to perform their allotted tasks and to show greater efficiency in implementing radical steps, though these met with little success.

Quick, well-publicized and stern action, stalled earlier by the courts, was taken on a large scale and in a determined fashion against smugglers, hoarders, blackmarketeers, illegal traders in foreign exchange and tax evaders. Several thousand of them were put behind bars under the MISA and their illegally acquired property was confiscated. Especially popular was the anti-smuggling drive under which nearly two thousand smugglers, including smuggling-kings like Haji Mastan and Yusuf Patel, were put behind bars, seriously disorganizing smuggling activities. Many well-reported income-tax raids led to the unearthing of large amounts of black money, while nearly Rs. 1,600 crore of concealed income was voluntarily disclosed. To check tax evasion, several luxury flats in Bombay and Delhi were raided. Upper ceilings was placed on ownership of vacant urban land to discourage concentration of land and speculation in real estate. Investment in luxury housing was checked by placing a limit on the plinth area of new houses.

The economy registered a major, dramatic improvement, though only partially due to steps taken under the Emergency for streamlining and accelerating the pace of economic development and improving production. Other factors responsible for the improvement in the economic field were excellent rains—the monsoon of 1975 was the best in five years—and some of the policies initiated much before the Emergency such as anti-inflationary measures initiated in 1974, leading to control of the fiscal deficit. No real restructuring of the economy, however, occurred.

Most welcome was the dramatic improvement in the prices, though breakthrough in this respect too had already been made by April 1975. Prices of essential goods, including foodgrains and fertilizers, came down as a result of vigorous control and were stabilized; blackmarketing in many commodities diminished and their availability in shops improved. Shopkeepers had to display prices and lists of stocks of essential goods and to attach price tags to them. Public distribution system also showed improvement. The rate of inflation, which was running as high as 30 per cent in September 1974, turned negative, with wholesale prices declining by 11.6 per cent by March 1976 and food prices by 20 per cent. The decline in prices gave enormous relief to urban consumers, agricultural labourers and small and marginal farmers.

Certain other major economic gains also followed. There was record output of foodgrains and edible oils during 1975-76, their production rising by nearly 21 per cent. Industrial production recovered from recession and rose by over 6 per cent, though mainly in the public sector. Gross domestic product (GDP) increased by an impressive 8.5 per cent. There was a spurt in exports which went up by over 21 per cent. Balance of payments and foreign currency reserves too improved sharply. The number of work-days lost in strikes or lockouts registered a dramatic reduction.

Popular expectations having been raised, the Emergency was sought to be legitimized and made further palatable by the announcement of specific steps to speed up the process of social and economic change and to implement the promise to eradicate poverty made in 1971. On 1 July, Mrs Gandhi announced the omnibus 20-Point Programme, which was designed to appeal to various sections of the people. Its edge was, however, the socio-economic uplift of the vast mass of the rural poor, the landless and the marginal farmers. A massive propaganda drive was organized behind the Programme.

The Programme, which in a way was 'the economic rationale' of the Emergency, promised to liquidate rural indebtedness and put a moratorium on the recovery of the existing debt of landless labourers, small farmers and rural artisans and provide for the extension of alternate credit to them; abolish bonded labour; strictly enforce agricultural land-ceiling laws passed earlier and speed up distribution of surplus land to the landless, even while completing compilation of land records; provide house sites to landless labourers and weaker sections on a scale much larger than hereto; revise minimum wages of agricultural labourers upwards; provide increased irrigation facilities and drinking water, especially in drought-prone areas, introduce workers' participation in the management of enterprises, provide special help to handloom industry; bring down prices; prevent tax evasion and smuggling; generate more power; streamline production, procurement and distribution of essential commodities; supply better quality cloth to the people at controlled prices; raise the income-tax exemption level from an annual income of Rs. 6,000 to Rs. 8,000; simplify and liberalize procedures for issuing industrial licences; provide cheap textbooks and stationery to students and supply essential commodities at controlled prices to students in hostels; and initiate a new apprenticeship scheme to enlarge employment opportunities for educated young people.

We may note, in parenthesis, that the 20-Point Programme bore an uncanny resemblance to the slogans of Gujarat and Bihar student movements and JP's exhortations, though the debt to JP went unacknowledged.

There is no doubt that though the 20-Point Programme was not part of a well-thought out scheme of structural reform of the economy, if implemented, especially its agrarian component, it would have brought real relief and benefit to the rural poor and the urban middle classes as also promoted economic growth. In fact, it would have increased the social and economic power of the landless labourers and poor peasants and led to a virtual rural revolution.

Mrs Gandhi had been complaining that the Opposition and its disruptive politics had been obstructing her efforts to move the country forward economically. She had, as she acknowledged, now got the power and the opportunity to implement her left-of-centre developmental agenda.[34]

Serious efforts were made to implement the 20-Point Programme. Non-official popular watch-dog committees, comprising Congressmen and Communists, were also set up in some places in the first few months of the Emergency for careful monitoring of the programme and involving the people in its implementation. As we have seen above, there were some quick results in terms of an increase in production, reduction of prices, freer availability of essential commodities, and check on hoarding, smuggling and tax evasion.

But at the heart of the 20-Point Programme was its agenda for the uplift of the rural poor and social change in the villages. Some immediate progress was made even in these respects, though nowhere near as much as the exaggerated claims of the government. Three million house sites were provided to the landless and the Scheduled Castes in the first year of the Emergency. However, two states—Gujarat and UP—accounted for the bulk of the house sites allotted.

Some progress in unearthing land above the legal ceiling was also made—nearly 1.7 million acres were recovered during 1975 and 1976 out of which about 1.1 million acres were distributed to the landless as against 62,000 acres distributed between 1972 and 1975. But the land so distributed was less than 10 per cent of such estimated surplus land that was needed. Moreover, simultaneously tenants and share-croppers continued to be illegally evicted by landowners in large parts of the country. A law was passed abolishing the practice of bonded labour, but little dent was actually made in this regard and only about 60,000 bonded labourers were freed during the nineteen months of the Emergency. This figure was a small fraction—less than 10 per cent of the actual number of bonded labourers in the country. Laws were passed in different states placing a moratorium on the recovery of the debts from landless labourers and small farmers and in some cases to scale down and liquidate this debt. But the scale of alternate credit provided by nationalized banks and rural cooperative institutions was small and dependence on the usurious moneylenders, who were also simultaneously the big landowners in a village, continued. In fact, the latter source also tended to dry up out of fear of the law. Minimum wages for agricultural labourers were enhanced but implementation in this respect too was tardy and the increased rates were seldom enforced.

On the whole, the rural part of the 20-Point Programme soon ran out of steam as its progress was stymied by the resistance of the rural rich—the large landowners and the rich peasants—and the apathy, if not opposition, of the unsympathetic bureaucracy, which had been hitherto responsible for thwarting all attempts to reform the agrarian structure. Because of the continued domination of the party and the administration at the lower levels by the rural upper strata, and the absence of any grassroots organizations through which the poor could be mobilized, the achievements in the rural sector remained insignificant and far short of the promises made. Nor were any durable structures created to implement the reforms after the initial push given to them.Though the limited implementation of the Programme brought some relief to the rural poor, there was little improvement in their basic conditions.

There was, however, one positive fallout of the Programme in the long run. It marked the initiation of many of the anti-poverty programmes which have had, over the years, a significant impact on the poverty levels in the rural sector. It also led to the beginnings of certain other significant and more successful measures subsequently, such as provision of agricultural credit through nationalized books and other cooperative and government institutions that led to curtailment of the moneylenders' hold in rural areas, abolition of bonded labour and initiation of popular campaigns around the issue, provision of house sites to the landless, women and the Scheduled Castes and the tribals, and increase in and better enforcement of minimum wages both in the villages and cities. However, the relatively successful execution of these measures later—after 1977—showed that the Emergency was not needed on their account.

V

A major reason why the Indian people accepted the Emergency and did not immediately protest against it, and why the instruments of administration, including the armed forces, obeyed the government's orders without hesitation, was its constitutional and legal character. The Emergency was proclaimed under Article 352[35] of the Constitution and was assented to by the President and legitimized by the Supreme Court. It had, moreover, several legal precedents: External Emergency had been imposed at the time of the India-China War in 1962 and the Bangladesh War in 1971. Many of the Emergency measures, including use of preventive detention or detention without trial had precedents since 1950 when the Constitution came into force. Even for the nation-wide arrest of political opponents there was the 1962 example of CPI leaders being detained without trial all over the country. In 1974, over 15,000 political detenus, mostly Naxalites, were in jail. Moreover, both MISA and the DIR were already in place before June 1975.

Mrs Gandhi grasped from the beginning the significance of functioning fully within the constitutional framework and had, therefore, carefully followed all the constitutional and legal procedures when imposing the Emergency. From the beginning, she emphasized this feature, proclaimed her full commitment to the Constitution and assured the people that she had no intention of changing India's political system. For example, defending the proclamation of the Emergency, she said in her speech to Lok Sabha on 22 July 1975: 'This action is totally within our constitutional framework and it was undertaken in order not to destroy the Constitution but to preserve the Constitution, to preserve and safeguard our democracy. Our Constitution-makers had foreseen that a situation might be created, not only external aggression but internal disturbances, when the fabric of national life might be threatened, and that is why they provided an entire part entitled "Emergency Provisions".'[36]

Similarly, she declared in an interview on 21 August 1975: 'Emergency has been proclaimed within the framework of our Constitution. It does not make any change to our system. On the contrary, it is intended to safeguard the system.'[37]

Also, throughout the period of the Emergency, Mrs Gandhi continued to govern within the forms of constitutional legality and, as we have seen earlier, nearly all her actions were provided legal sanction by the courts and thus had legal and constitutional legitimacy.

The people also expected that the Emergency was going to be of short duration. To them, it represented an interim measure, a temporary suspension of normal rules and institutions of democracy. They did not see it as a substitute for democracy, or as a new form of government, or as a long-term answer to their political and economic problems, or as an attempt to 'smother democracy' or to impose a dictatorship. The Emergency was considered, as W.H. Morris-Jones put it at the time, as 'something essentially temporary. It was a way out of an impossible deadlock, a short, sharp shock to the system, a drastic cure for certain diseases of the preceding period. Once the nasty medicine had been administered, the body politic would emerge restored to its earlier healthy state.'[38] Many expected the Emergency to be lifted before February 1976 and elections to be held on the due dates. Many persons close to her advised her to do so.

Mrs Gandhi consistently and publicly emphasized this temporary nature of the Emergency throughout its duration, starting with her two radio addresses to the nation on 26 and 27 June. She asserted time and again that she had no intention of prolonging it indefinitely, that the Emergency was not a desirable step and that she was unhappy to take it, but was forced to do so as an abnormal measure to deal with an abnormal situation. Further, she said that the Emergency would be revoked and democratic conditions restored as soon as the situation returned to normal.[39]

When attacked in Parliament and outside for taking to the path of dictatorship, Mrs Gandhi repeatedly asserted in nearly all her speeches and press interviews that democracy was not threatened in India, and that she was fully committed to multi-party democracy and a free Press. For example, she said on 13 July, 'Democracy has not been disowned. The foundations of our democracy have been well laid and we cherish its values.' On 6 August: 'Because we have Emergency, it does not mean that we have given up democracy or that we consider democracy unsuitable to India . . . In a country of India's size and vast diversity, I don't think that any other system can work.' On 14 August: 'We have done things which we would not normally do and, quite frankly, which I didn't like doing. But it was a question of that or of allowing this anarchy.' Also in August, she declared that she had 'no intention of enforcing one-party rule.' On 29 September she said: '. . . For a country which is as individualistic as India, which is as large and as diversified as India, it is essential to have democracy. Democracy is a slower form of progress. We have realized that from the beginning. But it is a surer way, we feel.'[40] As pointed out in Chapter 4, Mrs Gandhi also repeatedly stressed that the Emergency had been imposed to save democracy from being destroyed by the Opposition and to save the country from 'anarchy and chaos' and protect its 'unity, its integrity, and its very freedom.'[41]

Mrs Gandhi also reiterated her commitment to the existing federal structure of the polity and the scheme of Centre-State relations, though on the basis of a strong Centre.[42] She also, therefore, promised that the non-Congress governments (of Jammu and Kashmir, Goa, Tamil Nadu and Gujarat) would continue and she would work 'with understanding' with them.[43]

The people took Mrs Gandhi at her word and were willing to go along with her. The poor, in particular, still trusted her, though the intellectuals were losing faith in her. For the poor, she was not only Jawaharlal Nehru's daughter, but also their champion with regard to land reforms, removal of poverty and struggle against caste oppression. Likewise, women and minorities also looked up to her. The belief that she had already lost all her popularity among the common people before 25 June and that all public support for her was drummed up was just not true, for those who joined her rallies belonged to both categories of supporters, the genuine and the hired. Consequently, a large section of people believed her assurances that the Emergency was temporary and that she was still committed to democracy and its existing forms and institutions. They also accepted her explanation of how and why the Emergency had come about, and went along with her position that to yield to opposition would have been disastrous. Many reposed faith in her theory of the lesser evil.[44]

The people were willing to give Mrs Gandhi time to sort out a messy and difficult situation and to bring order and discipline into a turbulent society and recalcitrant administrative institutions. The mass of people also believed that the strident features of the Emergency would not affect them or their rights and these would be directed only against the agitators and their parties.

On the other hand, people did not fully accept the democratic credentials of the Opposition, which was seen to be not fully committed to liberal democracy. For example, for years JP had decried the usefulness and viability of a multi-party parliamentary democracy without offering a practical alternative. The communists had for long been deriding the Constitution and scoffing at democracy as practised in India as 'bourgeois' in contrast with 'proletarian' democracy as practised in the Soviet Union and China. The RSS's own consitution was entirely authoritarian; moreover, it had no faith in democracy which it decried as a Western implant. From the beginning, Mrs Gandhi played upon this theme. For example, in an interview to the *Times of India* on 3 July 1975, she said: 'There are parties like the RSS, strongly anti-Muslim and anti-Christian, which function in the twilight and have a secret constitution ... Those whose ideology is violence and disruption cannot be democratic. For them to take the name of democracy is like the teenager who killed his parents but pleaded for mercy on the ground that he was an orphan.'[45] She repeatedly criticized the socialists and others for going along with parties that 'are so deeply rooted in violence, in hatred'. She also said that 'communal parties are *ipso facto* undemocratic.'[46]

People also tended to believe Mrs Gandhi's references, often vague but sometimes explicit, to the interests of foreign powers in destabilizing her government and the country.[47] Many of them were aware of the CIA's role in the overthrow of Mossadaq in Iran, the overthrow and killing of Allende in Chile and the US Senate's revelations in 1967 of the CIA's role in the funding of the Council for Cultural Freedom and other anti-communist organizations the world over in the fifties and sixties. The brutal overthrow and massacre of President Sheikh Mujibur Rahman and his family in Bangladesh on 14 August 1975 in a military coup, possibly with CIA's help, further strengthened this belief. Later, when Western powers and the Western press criticized Mrs Gandhi for the Emergency, their criticism did not cut much ice with many because of the US and other Western powers' earlier hostility to Jawaharlal Nehru and India's policy of non-alignment and support to anti-colonial struggles in Asia and Africa. Moreover, these Western powers had tolerated and supported authoritarian regimes the world over.[48] People also had the recent memory of the hostile role of the United States during the Bangladesh War in 1971.

Two other factors, though of lesser importance, played a role in determining people's response to the promulgation of the Emergency. One was the support it was given by the socialist and non-aligned countries.[49] Second, the urban middle classes, the main support base of the JP movement, were exhausted by the time, and many of their concerns were addressed by the measures adopted in the early phase of the Emergency.

Another feature of the Emergency also led to resistance to it being weak. Immediately after the Emergency was declared a fear that was paralyzing especially gripped political workers, journalists, academics, businessmen and bureaucrats. It was fear of the unknown. Due to complete news blackout, rumours reigned supreme. Nobody knew what the Emergency meant or what was happening in the country, or what would happen to those who protested or spoke against it. As a contemporary journalist, Sachchidanand Sinha, put it, 'As people groped in the dark, fearful phantoms of all kinds assailed them. Lack of information and the resulting insecurity made terror an inner force deriving nourishment from men's own imagination.'[50] There was the fear of perfunctory arrest, or various kinds of harassment, of the omnipresent CBI spies noting down what one said or did, of widespread telephone tapping. Also there were rumours, often figments of popular imagination fed by fragments of reality, of people being arrested or at least interrogated for what they said in a bus or even during the morning walk. People were afraid to discuss the Emergency in public, and even in private they talked about it in hushed voices and with great care. In fact, not only in the beginning but throughout the Emergency people were ruled not so much through large-scale repression, torture, and such measures, as fear. After all, the number of the arrested in the first few days of the Emergency was rather small—only around 10,000—and many of these were released within weeks. As pointed out earlier, the total number of those imprisoned at various points during the entire period of the Emergency was about 110,000.

The other side of the paradox, as to why there was not much opposition to the Emergency in its initial months, was its comparatively mild character, as repressive regimes go, despite the fear aroused. Though India under the Emergency was certainly authoritarian, it was not totalitarian in the sense of Hannah Arendt's or any other such definition of the term. Nor was it as oppressive as the regimes of Nazi Germany or Mussolini's Italy or Japan or China of the thirties or Iraq under Saddam Hussein and Uganda under Idi Amin or even those in the Soviet Union, China or the post-war people's democracies of Eastern Europe, as Arun Shourie put it in 1977, 'We collapsed without struggle in the face of the mildest possible dictatorship . . . compared to what a Djilas or a Solzhenitsyn had to put up with.'[51] Mrs Gandhi and Congress had neither the machinery nor a coherent ideology behind the Emergency regime. The Congress party could not, by its very nature, provide these. The regime had also no stormtroopers or Gestapo or well-trained and well-disciplined party cadres to enforce its actions. It had only an incompetent, corrupt and run-down bureaucracy to ensure the implementation of its orders. Consequently, as Sachchidanand Sinha has remarked, 'the dictatorship . . . (was) a very flabby affair.'[52]

There was also no deployment either of the Army or on a significant scale even of the police, or violation of the letter of the Constitution, or disobedience of the courts. There was little effort to interfere with research or teaching in the universities. With the exception of Kuldip Nayar, no prominent journalist or intellectual was arrested or even lost his or her job. Such leading dissident intellectuals as Romesh Thapar, Nikhil Chakravartty, Rajni Kothari, J.D. Sethi, Mrinal Datta-Chaudhuri, K.N. Raj, Raj Krishna, V.M. Tarkunde, Ashok Mitra, Uma Shankar Joshi, Ajit Bhattacharjea and Irfan Habib and most of the opposition MPs and CPM leaders did not have to go to jail. Moreover, most of the prominent opposition leaders, including JP, were released during the period of the Emergency itself.

To make this point is not to ignore or condone the excesses and some of the crimes committed during the Emergency, including in its earlier phase, but to retain an analytical balance. Notorious were the cases of torture of Lawrence Fernandes and many others, the torture and deaths of Snehlata Reddy and Rajan in detention, Primila Lewis's arrest for organizing farm workers to fight for the officially decreed minimum wage, the undeserved imprisonment of hundreds, even by the government's own criteria, the solitary confinement of Morarji Desai for several months, the horrible conditions in most jails where the detenus were lodged, and the death of nearly twenty political prisoners in jail. Still, compared to other authoritarian regimes, little force was used and very few were killed or suffered long-term damage, physical or psychological. The Shah Commission was to mention only a few cases of torture.[53] In fact, the suppression of the railway strike in 1974 had been far more brutal; thousands of railway workers had paid a heavy economic and psychological price. That is why the Emergency was easily forgotten and Mrs Gandhi could be voted back to power within three years, at the end of 1979.

It is of some significance that most contemporary observers, both friendly and unfriendly, have suggested that if Mrs Gandhi had stuck to the mandated election schedule and held elections in February 1976, she would have scored an easy victory.[54] According to some, she was even inclined to accept the advice and was even planning to lift the Emergency or at least the press censorship on 15 August 1975. But in the end she did not do so, because, it has been suggested, of three reasons: the first was the assassination of Sheikh Mujibur Rahman and family on 14 August; the second was Sanjay's desire to prolong the Emergency in order to consolidate his growing power; and the third, Mrs Gandhi's sneaking suspicion that she might not be able to come back with a two-third majority and, therefore, undertake the planned constitutional changes. The public reason she gave was that she wanted to consolidate the 'gains' of the Emergency. To quote her: 'I don't want to go in for elections because that will put the 20-Point Programme in jeopardy. After it is implemented and the people benefited we would certainly hold elections.'[55]

VI

A year into the Emergency and the mood of the people began to change. By mid-1976, 'the glow had begun to fade' and there was considerable discontent at the level both of the masses and the intellectuals. Many, including the Congress's ally the CPI, had begun pressing to call off the Emergency. Despite the official easing of the Emergency regime—easing of press control, release of most political leaders and a large number of the detenus, public discussion of the constitutional amendments, permission to opposition leaders to meet, negotiations with JP, even subdued criticism of the government and its policies—people were unwilling to go along with it any more. Many, including some of its supporters, were starting to question the motives behind its imposition. Mrs Gandhi's claim, that its aim was to provide an opportunity for going ahead with a new social purpose and a new social order and implementing a fresh egalitarian developmental agenda, appeared dubious. By January 1977, the unpopularity of the regime had reached its nadir; the people in the North were preparing to reject it whenever the elections were held.

There were many reasons for this turnaround of public opinion. For one, relief provided by the Emergency to the people did not last long and most of 'the gains' turned out to be very short-term. Many of Mrs Gandhi's claims to radicalism began to sound hollow. Her policies continued in the old vein. Earlier she held that egalitarian and developmental policies could not be followed or implemented because she lacked the power to do so and the Opposition-led agitations came in the way. Now she had the authority but still nothing had really changed. For, as pointed out earlier, though a brilliant tactician, she lacked any strategic design to utilize this power for distinct economic and political policies. Even the imposition of the Emergency was hardly a part of an alternative framework for managing the political system, or overcoming the instability of the state or strengthening its administrative and institutional structure, or at least preventing its downslide or bringing about basic or radical socio-economic changes. It was merely an *ad hoc* response to a political crisis.

Also, economic growth in the first year of the Emergency was not sustained. In 1976-77, agriculture as well as foodgrains output fell by nearly 6 per cent; Gross Domestic Product (GDP) declined by nearly 2 per cent; inflation was back—after March 1976, there was a sharp, over 10 per cent, increase in prices by the year end—particularly significant was the rise in the prices of foodgrains, textiles, cotton, groundnut, sugar, coal, cement and steel. Only industrial growth retained its momentum, the increase during the year being 10 per cent.

Administration soon slackened as discipline arising out of sheer fear could not last and wore out within a few months. Addressing a conference of the chief secretaries on 7 May 1976, Mrs Gandhi complained: 'The Emergency has brought in some discipline, but I have a feeling, confirmed by many visitors, that the initial alertness has slackened.'[56]

Nor was there a significant check on corruption, the main issue taken up by the JP movement. The corrupt, the blackmarketeers and smugglers resumed their activities as the initial shock wore off. In fact, in the absence of any public accountability and the increase in bureaucratic power, there was a steep increase in corruption. Only, in view of the higher risks faced by the corrupt officials, the rates of bribery went up! Moreover, the police, sales-tax and income-tax inspectors and other officials had now greater opportunities, for they were now in a position to extort money even from honest businessmen and shopkeepers to a host of hawkers and rickshaw-pullers by threatening them with false cases, imprisonment and worse. They were to be soon joined by Sanjay Gandhi and his cohorts who operated at a much higher level. B.K. Nehru, in his autobiography, quotes Rajiv Gandhi as saying that Sanjay at his death had crores of unaccounted rupees.[57]

People also began to realize that even otherwise the tall promises of social change made at the beginning of the Emergency were not being kept. If the people were going to lose their liberty, their fundamental rights for some time, then at least as compensation, there had to be significant economic development, check on corruption and growth in public welfare. Above all, a major dent into poverty had to be made. The poor in particular were disenchanted with the progress in their welfare. Very little progress was made towards the advancement of the social and economic goals that Mrs Gandhi had herself set forth in the 20-Point Programme designed primarily to appeal to the rural poor. Instead, as we shall see later, the poor were hit hard by the sterilization and slum-clearance drives in northern India; they were also the main victims of police and bureaucratic harassment.

There were also other discontents. The middle classes and intellectuals were unhappy with the loss of liberty and lack of faster economic development, and workers because of limits on wages, bonus and dearness allowance and restrictions on the right to strike. The lower-level government employees and school teachers, too, felt the loss of civil liberties. But they were also unhappy on account of discipline being enforced in the work-place and because, in northern India, they were forced to fulfil sterilization quotas. Their dissatisfaction was important for they exercised a great deal of political influence in rural areas—they also acted as polling oficials during elections.

Shopkeepers were unhappy both with the restrictions imposed on the way they conducted their business and extortion by the lower bureaucracy and police. Also, the 20-Point Programme, however poorly implemented, frightened and antagonized the rich peasants, who were already estranged from the Congress in northern India. In fact, all the groups which were sought to be disciplined in the interests of development and sound administration became alienated from the government.

In any case, no progress along the proclaimed lines was possible because Mrs Gandhi failed to create any new agencies of social change or organs for popular mobilization. The Congress party was not a well-functioning organization and had little to no presence at the grassroots level, and was, in any case, based in the rich and middle peasantry. Furthermore, after 1947, the Congress straggled behind as a party of popular mobilization, except at election time. Its cadres were incapable of providing even correct information as to what was happening on the ground—nor was the higher leadership tuned to listen to them even if they did. In any case, the Congress party organization was more or less completely paralyzed during the Emergency.

As a result, reliance for the implementation of the 20-Point Programme and other developmental and welfarist policies was placed exclusively on the same old bureaucracy, manipulative and discredited politicians and the rural elite. Popular committees, comprising Congressmen and sometimes Communists, were set up for overseeing the effective implementation of the 20-Point Programme in the rural areas, but they worked only in a few places and that too only in the initial months of the Emergency. Very soon things were back to 'business as usual' as the old drags on development, the corrupt and inefficient bureaucrats, corrupt and inept politicians, on-the-make businessmen, and the rural rich and vote bank operators, adjusted to the new situation.

Minimally, social change in the agrarian sector required organized agricultural labour and poor peasant participation. Similarly, many of the programmes in the urban sector, such as dehoarding and inculcation of work discipline, needed the mobilization of the middle classes, workers and the urban poor. Mrs Gandhi had at the outset shown awareness of all this. When Norman Cousins, a sympathetic US journalist, had asked her on 1 August 1975, 'How can the measures you have instituted be kept from getting out of hand at lower levels?', she had replied, 'By associating the people in larger numbers with the administration of the regulations, which is what we are trying to do.'[58] Similarly, on 16 August 1975, R.K. Karanjia of *Blitz* asked her: 'The agrarian part of the 20-Point Programme ... implies a veritable rural revolution; but a revolution requires an effective agency. What is the agency which will implement this project?' Mrs Gandhi answered, though with greater caution: 'This programme involves the entire Central Government, the State Governments, the bureaucracy as well as every agency which the Government has. I don't think that there can be any new *official* agency. We do want, however, and are trying, to have far greater people's involvement, popular participation.'[59] But no steps were taken by the government in the direction of popular mobilization around the Programme.

In fact, one reason why the CPI had welcomed the 20-Point Programme so enthusiastically was the expectation that its implementation would, apart from bringing about revolution in the agrarian structure, give the party an opportunity to mobilize the people and thus extend its influence. But when the CPI tried to do so, its cadres too faced repression.

So far as the common people were concerned, matters soon took a turn for the worse. All protest or resistance was suppressed and there were no avenues of protest open, or any other mechanism for redressal left for getting some relief from the oppressive situation and the arbitrary acts of the police and the bureaucracy. The Press was gagged and could not ventilate people's discontent; the Congress party had become dysfunctional, opposition parties were not permitted to agitate; the CPI was virtually sidelined and was hamstrung and thwarted in its efforts to take up popular grievances; people resorting to agitation on their own was out of question.

Consequently, even the common people, and not merely intellectuals and political workers, began to live in an atmosphere of fear and insecurity. The poor discovered that they too required civil liberties and freedom and, therefore, missed having them.

Not only were people's expectations of better administration belied, in one respect administration became much worse. Having emasculated the Congress party and having no other organization to rely upon, Mrs Gandhi and the Central and state governments depended almost entirely on the bureacracy and the police both for routine administration and implementation of the 20-Point and family planning programmes. Inevitably, the bureaucracy and the police had a free hand and were answerable to none except the highest authorities which were easily kept in the dark and ignored. Their enhanced powers now were unchecked by the judiciary, members of legislature, political parties, popular organizations and movements and by criticism and exposure in the Press. Some had thought that the Emergency would at least improve institutions of governance; instead it led to a worsening of the character and functioning of the police and bureaucracy, while simultaneously undermining the authority of the Parliament and the cabinet, besides tying the hands of the judiciary.

With the silencing of all forms of protest, the police and bureaucracy set out to abuse their newly-acquired power in various forms, forced vasectomy being only its extreme and visible manifestation. They also used their authority to settle personal scores and carry out personal vendettas. The result was that the few gains of the Emergency were negated. Mrs Gandhi was to admit this later to her biographer in July 1978, that the Emergency 'did get a little bit out of hand because people started misusing power at different levels.'[60]

The fact is that such misuse of power was built into the Emergency itself. An inherent defect of an authoritarian regime is its inability to control arbitrary behaviour of its instruments, especially at the lower levels. Indian police and bureaucracy were in any case not known for their display of probity and sympathetic approach towards the common people even in normal times and as a rule treated them in a high-handed manner. This tendency was now generalized and given free rein. The rule of law virtually disappeared and the Emergency rule became in time a bureaucracy-cum-police raj. If the Emergency regime did not fortunately degenerate into military rule, this was in part because Mrs Gandhi did not involve the armed forces in the Emergency in any form and at any stage.

Bureaucratic police power had a wide range and extended across many areas of people's lives and touched all sections of society, but, inevitably, the poor and the weaker sections were the most affected—they were its main victims. Their oppression by the police, the petty bureaucrats, the urban *dadas* (organized bullies) and the rural rich was enhanced and intensified. They lost the little protection provided to them under the right to protest, and by the local peasant and political leaders and public exposure through the Press and other means. This was particularly true of North India.

At the same time, the choking off of all channels of protest and honest information led to the government being uninformed about the goings-on in the country and the impact of its policies or Emergency measures on the people. Mrs Gandhi and others, who might have been serious about implementing the new ameliorative and developmental measures, were now completely cut off from public sentiment or reliable information as all lines of communication except those of intelligence agencies and sycophants got blocked. Moreover, knowledgeable officials tended to report only what they thought the powers that be would like to hear. They hushed up anything that could create a bad impression. Also, whenever a loyal but brave person dared tell Mrs Gandhi the truth, he or she was disbelieved and treated or seen as a potential dissident, as all bearers of bad news are by autocrats. Therefore, even her senior ministers and chief ministers or senior Congress leaders did not stick their necks out. As one of Mrs Gandhi's biographers was to note, 'she never seems to have heard the real truth about the state of the country from anyone.'[61] And another of her biographers was to point out, 'As Indira herself admitted later, she lost touch with her basic constituency—the poor and deprived masses . . . For the first and only time in her life, the Emergency clipped her political antennae.'[62]

This explains why she continued to be unaware of the public disquiet and even anger that her rule gradually aroused, especially the prolongation of the Emergency, despite her initial promise of its being temporary, her serious tampering with the Constitution, police and bureaucratic authoritarianism, and the compulsory sterilization campaign which was in full swing in North India after May 1976. She also remained insensitive to the change in the mood of the intellectuals and other politicized Indians. The government policies were now framed and implemented in an information vacuum. Mrs Gandhi, thus, became a victim of the forces she had herself unleashed, for, as pointed out above, the abuse of power for which the Emergency was to become notorious was built into the very structure of the regime; likewise was the absence of any corrective mechanism for this abuse, for those who could have rectified the situation remained ignorant about it.

Mrs Gandhi's total domination over the party and the government had one other consequence. It not only eroded the power of her cabinet colleagues, chief ministers, party president and other senior party leaders, but left no institutional or personal breakwaters for sharing the blame for failures in policies or administration. The blame, when it came, fell entirely on her and her younger son's shoulders.

The government also began to lose credibility among the people almost from the beginning. This was the paradoxical result of the Press censorship. Because the people knew that what appeared in the Press or on the radio was heavily censored, they no longer had faith in it. Every government source or statement became suspect and people increasingly disbelieved anything given out by the government. Rumours and gossip were circulated freely and became major sources of information. In reply to the official mythology a counter-mythology of rumours became widespread.

Initially, wild rumours regarding the government's capacity to spy on people, to ferret out subversive ideas, or identify suspect persons, helped the government instil fear in the minds of the people and thus to silence them. But, later, rumours led to the plummeting of the government's popularity as the people tended to believe any story, however irrational or groundless, regarding its actions or intentions. For example, there were the rumours that JP and Morarji Desai were on hunger-strike and were being forcefully fed, or even that JP had passed away, or that the deterioration in his health—he was released in November on health grounds—was the result of the neglect by the government or was perhaps even deliberately caused by it. One of the most widely circulated stories, which first made the cocktail circuit of New Delhi and was even reproduced in the *Washington Post*, related to Sanjay Gandhi slapping his mother, Mrs Gandhi, six times at a dinner party, in the presence of guests. Rumours regarding the sterilization drive circulated all over North India in cities, *mohallas* and villages. According to a story, as a result of police firings over 1,000 persons had died in UP. Many rumours of powerful resistance developing against the Emergency all over the country and of large-scale strikes by industrial workers were also floating around.

The denial of civil liberties gradually began to pinch common people as it started to impact their daily lives by way of harassment and corruption by petty officials and police. An example was the ban on the broadcast of popular singer Kishore Kumar's songs on the radio because he had refused to perform without his usual fee in a programme organized by the Youth Congress in praise of the 20-Point Programme. People could understand the arrest of political opponents and agitators but why this mindless attack upon a politically harmless film actor and singer, they wondered.[63]

There was disquiet among the people regarding the character of the Emergency and an apprehension of authoritarianism, as they gradually became aware of its oppressive features: Centralization and personalization of executive power, subordination of the President, emasculation of the cabinet, stifling of the Parliament, inordinate power of the prime minister's secretariat (and later of the prime minister's house), total control by the prime minister of her political party which also led to its becoming dysfunctional, crippling of the judiciary, censorship of the Press and total government control of the media, subordination of a pliant and callous bureaucracy, wide reach of the police, subversion of the rule of law, widespread corruption, and, in the end, emergence of extra-constitutional centres of power responsible to none but themselves. These features were antithetical to the political ethos built up during the freedom struggle, the Nehru era and, in fact, the earlier period of Mrs Gandhi's own rule. People also began to realize that authoritarianism and its perversions, including all the inadequacies of administration, were inherent in the very proclamation of the Emergency.

As elections due in February 1976 were postponed twice, first in January 1976 and then in November 1976, and the Constitution was repeatedly amended, apprehension was aroused in the popular mind that the Emergency might not remain a temporary phenomenon and that the authoritarian structure of Mrs Gandhi's rule might be made permanent or might last a long time. As indicated earlier, people had accepted the Emergency without much resistance because they had seen it as a short-term expedient to meet a specific situation and not as an alternative form of government or a substitute for democracy. Consequently, Mrs Gandhi's repeated assurances and promises, readily believed earlier, of the temporary character of the Emergency and of the restoration of full democratic functioning, including full freedom of expression, when conditions returned to normal, began to sound hollow and hypocritical.[64] And, as the political consciousness of the people and their perception of the Emergency began to undergo a change, it began to lose legitimacy and arouse alarm and hostility instead. There were murmurs of dissent within Congress and simmering protests among the people. The opposition parties began to find listeners on a growing scale. Moreover, not only the common people and the intelligentsia but even many of those entrusted with the enforcement of the Emergency began to see it as illegitimate and to drag their feet. This, combined with the mild character of the Emergency during the early months and the low level of repression due to which the people had tolerated it, also permitted dissent and opposition to develop. Once it became clear to the people that the government was not yet taking very severe steps to suppress dissent, that it was not liquidating its opponents or putting in jail a large number of persons or even depriving them of their livelihood, they were willing to oppose it before the threshold of repression was crossed and the Emergency regime became a ruthless dictatorship.

This seemed a possibility with the rise to power of Sanjay Gandhi and his coterie, their assumption of extra-constitutional authority, and further concentration, subversion and misuse of power, together with the increasing eclipse of institutions and the accompanying 'excesses'. I will turn next to this last aspect.

8   *The Emergency: The Later Phase*

A major reason for the growing unpopularity of the Emergency regime was the predictable development of a parallel apparatus of governance at the Centre. This was bound to happen once checks on the executive's exercise of powers diminished; the regime began to act more and more outside the constitutional, administrative framework and the law. This process reached its zenith with the emergence of an extra-constitutional centre of power associated with the rise to political and administrative power of Mrs Gandhi's younger son, Sanjay Gandhi, who held no office in the government or the party.

I

Born on 14 December 1946, Sanjay had hardly any political or administrative experience, or academic or any other achievement to his credit, except his sudden emergence in 1970 as the head of Maruti, the company he set up to manufacture the first wholly Indian car—a project which had been grounded from the beginning. As the political crisis facing Mrs Gandhi deepened after the Allahabad judgement, Sanjay Gandhi emerged as her close confidant and adviser and became a major influence over her. According to many persons in the know, it was on his firm advice that Mrs Gandhi was finally persuaded not to resign.

Sanjay Gandhi assumed importance from the outset of the Emergency, even though he occupied the centre stage only later. His political and administrative power grew over time, and by April 1976, he had emerged as a parallel authority who wielded a great deal of power, equalling perhaps even that of Mrs Gandhi. Despite not having any official position in the government or the party, he interfered at will in the working of the government and administration, had access to cabinet papers and other government files, and often participated in decision-making in the name of his mother. He also intervened in decisions regarding appointments and postings of high officials in the government, public sector undertakings and even the armed forces. As he regularly toured the country, he would issue verbal orders which were invariably obeyed. In particular, he exercised control over the home and health ministries and the Delhi administration. His was the dominant voice in the Prime Minister's House.

Regarded as the second most important person in the country, Sanjay was courted, praised, fawned upon, kowtowed to, consulted and obeyed by cabinet ministers, Congress party leaders, chief ministers, chief secretaries and other senior and junior civil servants, and business magnates. Chief ministers came to receive him at the airports. His visits to the states were elaborately organized and, with garland-laden welcome arches, loud bands and red carpets, resembled those of the prime minister. Large rallies were organized for him. Sycophancy of Congress leaders sometimes crossed all bounds of decency.[1]

Very soon, the personality cult built around Mrs Gandhi began to be rivalled by that of the son. Radio, television, the Films Division and newspapers gave him enormous coverage and publicity, fostering his personality cult. Newspapers, weeklies and other magazines vied with each other in displaying his photographs, publishing interviews with him and reporting prominently and at length his speeches and statements and his visits to and activities in different parts of the country.

Sanjay wielded this immense extra-constitutional power, both in the government and the party, through a coterie that soon came up around him. A prized instrument of this—and with whom he had a special bond—was Bansi Lal, the chief minister of Haryana, who was inducted into the cabinet as defence minister on 23 December 1975. In addition, Sanjay Gandhi had his own men in the council of ministers, who were willing to act as his rubber stamp. These men were often junior ministers in key ministries who came to exercise operational control over their ministries. An outstanding example of this phenomenon was Om Mehta, the minister of state for home affairs, who ran the ministry with the help of a pliant home secretary, with Brahmananda Reddy, the cabinet minister for home affairs, being reduced to a hapless, non-performing position. Similarly, the control of the crucial departments of banking, income-tax and customs was taken away from C. Subramaniam, the finance minister, and put under the charge of his junior minister of state, Pranab Kumar Mukherjee, who was much more 'flexible'. Similar was the position of the minister of state for industries, A.P. Sharma, vis-à-vis his senior minister T.A. Pai. When I.K. Gujral lost his portfolio as minister of information and broadcasting on 27 June because he would not let Sanjay Gandhi decide how the All-India Radio was to deal with news, he was replaced by V.C. Shukla, a puppet of Sanjay. It was through him that Sanjay managed to exercise influence over the Press and the All-India Radio. Sanjay also reduced Dr Karan Singh, the health minister, to nought. D.P. Chattopadhyaya, the commerce minister, too readily did Sanjay's bidding. In many cases, power came to be wielded by special assistants and private secretaries in the name of, or on behalf of, the ministers or senior bureaucrats. The most notorious example was that of Kishan Chand, the hapless and spineless lieutenant-governor of Delhi, who readily became just a figurehead, while the actual reins were in the hands of his special assistant, Navin Chawla, who acted at Sanjay's behest. Because of this, the Emergency measures were implemented with a vengeance in Delhi.

Mrs Gandhi had no worthwhile political organization to implement the Emergency and its programmes—the Congress party was neither equipped to perform the task nor did she and Sanjay Gandhi trust the average Congressman who remained a mere spectator. Instead, she relied almost entirely on the bureaucracy. But even here, Mrs Gandhi did not use the well-ordered, well-coordinated bureaucratic machine at her disposal. Instead, increasingly, as Sanjay Gandhi took control of the Emergency, especially in North India, there was dependence on a select group of bureaucrats and policemen who were willing to act as his henchmen. Inevitably, Sanjay's pet ministers and bureaucrats and their lower-level deputies used their power to serve personal interests and settle political or personal scores. Sanjay Gandhi was himself to initiate the process by harassing P.N. Haksar's old uncle, proprietor of the shop Pandit Brothers, for alleged violation of new rules relating to display of product-prices. Haksar had earlier, in 1973, advised Mrs Gandhi not to support Sanjay's Maruti enterprise.

Inevitably, extra-constitutional power centres and the system of political satraps, caucuses and coteries and their bureaucratic agents tended to be replicated in the states, especially in North India.

The development of extra-constitutional power at the Centre was also manifested in the growth of the non-official institution of Prime Minister's House (PMH), which comprised of a small caucus consisting of Sanjay Gandhi, Bansi Lal and R.K. Dhawan, aided by a small, carefully chosen secretariat. Dhawan's official position was that of additional private secretary to the prime minister. He enjoyed the favour and trust of Mrs Gandhi and worked in close collaboration with Sanjay Gandhi, to emerge as the most influential bureaucrat at the time.

PMH was Sanjay Gandhi's power base. It was through PMH that he operated and interfered in the administration and policy-making at the Centre and in the states.[2] Even the list of those to be arrested on 26 June was carefully prepared in the PMH, with the full participation of Sanjay Gandhi. The non-official PMH was not only a rival of the official and powerful Prime Minister's Secretariat (PMS or PMO), but in many respects replaced it. For example, P.N. Dhar, principal secretary to the prime minister and head of PMO, was not privy to a great deal of what happened politically or administratively. PMH even gave orders to PMO and, according to P.N. Dhar, its members even tried to get rid of him.[3] According to B.N. Tandon, who was joint secretary in the PMO, already by 9 July 1975, all Emergency related work was 'decided upon in the PM's house and the decisions are conveyed to Om Mehta'.[4] The worst aspect of Sanjay Gandhi's rise to power was the damage done to institutions of governance. In B.K. Nehru's words, this 'so damaged all the institutions of democratic government and civilized progress . . . so as to make it almost impossible to restore them. The independence of the civil services, of Parliament and the state legislatures, the judiciary, the Chief Ministers of the states, the cabinet ministers of the Union government and of the Press were all destroyed during this period . . . The rule of law was totally destroyed.'[5]

Domination of politics and administration by a caucus was also possible because of most avenues of information and redressal were blocked, so far as the higher echelons of the government were concerned. The caucus could manipulate even Mrs Gandhi by regulating access to her; it was Dhawan, for instance, who in general decided whom she would see. Very often she was kept ignorant of the orders issued from her house in her name or of what was happening in the country and in the administration. It must, however, be said that Mrs Gandhi cooperated in this respect, for she did not permit people to talk to her about the activities of her son or his coterie.

Seen in a wider perspective, the emergence of extra-constitutional centres of power was inherent in the Emergency as was the possibility of temporary authoritarianism being transformed into a long-term dictatorship by a handful. After all, as we have seen earlier in Chapter 7, the coterie around Sanjay Gandhi did try, with partial success, to perpetuate the Emergency by getting elections postponed twice, to subvert the Constitution and modify its basic structure and also to gain control of the state apparatuses.

II

Within Congress, Sanjay Gandhi emerged as the leader of its youth wing, the Youth Congress. Even in that body he had no official position, at least not until December 1975 when he was made a member of its Executive Committee with a great deal of fanfare at the Chandigarh session of the Congress. He soon emerged as the *de facto* head of the Youth Congress, which became his main political vehicle and was to provide him an independent political power base with a following, cadres and organization, which were personally loyal to him and under his direct control.

Gradually, the Youth Congress began to be built up as a rival centre of political power vis-à-vis Congress. Echoing JP, Sanjay Gandhi gave a call for youth power and started mobilizing urban petty bourgeois youth, many of whom would have earlier joined the JP movement. During 1976, the Youth Congress claimed to have recruited five million members. By the end of 1976, it rivalled the parent body in political weight. Many considered it as even more important than the main Congress, with Sanjay Gandhi eclipsing the latter's older leaders, including its president. By mid-1976, the Sanjay cult had been successfully promoted with the help of government and private media. At the Guwahati session of Congress at the end of November 1976, leader after leader praised Sanjay from the podium. Mrs Gandhi endorsed this sentiment and declared that the Youth Congress had 'stolen our thunder'. She also declared that the future of India was safe in the hands of youth.[6]

A result of the rise of Youth Congress and the emergence of the extra-constitutional centres of power was the devaluation of Congress as an organization and the demoralization of its leaders and cadres, who were suppressed and silenced and felt unhappy with the sycophancy they were forced to display towards Sanjay Gandhi and his lieutenants. Whatever the faults of Congress bosses, overthrown by Mrs Gandhi in 1969, they were at least partymen who had a long history in politics. The new men and women who came to the fore in the Congress and the Youth Congress during 1975-76 were unknown persons, who were suddenly catapulted into prominence, and were seen by Congress workers as undesirable upstarts. This was true of Sanjay Gandhi himself.

The Youth Congress also represented the lumpenization of Indian politics. In the absence of any ideology, its largely non-political membership had its quota of unemployed youth, young hoodlums and ruffians who had all the making of stormtroopers, ready to do Sanjay Gandhi's bidding, and who could make up for his lack of a proper party apparatus to be used to physically suppress his opponents, in or outside the Congress. Along with the emergence of extra-constitutional centres of power, it was in the Youth Congress that lay the fascist potential of the Emergency or at least its orientation towards dictatorship. The Congress party was not geared to play that role. It could not even act as an instrument of mass mobilization. Congressmen could at the most act as cheer leaders of those in power. On the other hand, the members and cadres of the Youth Congress could play the role of Mussolini's fascist bands, Hitler's Brown Shirts or Chiang Kai-shek's Blue Shirts, especially as Sanjay Gandhi was right-wing, anti-communist and authoritarian in his outlook. He told a West German newspaper in an interview that he liked dictatorship but 'not of the Hitler type'.[7] P.N. Dhar writes that he had reports that one of the few books Sanjay Gandhi admired was Filipino dictator, Ferndinand Marcos', *The Democratic Revolution in the Philippines*, and 'that had fired Sanjay's imagination and made him look upon Marcos as his role model.'[8]

In August 1975, Sanjay created quite a public sensation by giving a long interview to Uma Vasudev in which he aired his right-wing views, criticized the government's earlier economic policies and the public sector, praised private enterprise and advocated giving it a freer hand, expressed aversion to nationalization of economic enterprises, and spoke against Indian communists. We may quote him in regard to the last aspect: 'The communists may have a small cadre that actually works but if you take all the people in the Communist Party, the big wigs—even the not-so-big wigs—I don't think you'd find a richer or more corrupt people anywhere.'[9]

Thoroughly embarassed and upset by the interview, Mrs Gandhi attempted damage control by getting it withdrawn from the newspapers. But by then many newspapers, both in India and abroad, had already published it. She also persuaded Sanjay Gandhi to partially retract the part which was anti-communist.[10] The significance of the interview lay in its giving a peep into the ideological make up of Sanjay. It is also interesting that, according to P.N. Dhar, in his interview with Sugata Dasgupta in late September and early October, JP 'liked' Sanjay's interview and was 'pleasantly surprised at the views expressed by the young man.'[11]

Sanjay Gandhi continued throughout to attack communists and former communists who were in the Congress or government. For example, the *Indian Express* published the following news item on 10

January 1977: 'Mr Gandhi said certain parties and forces, which could be termed as traitors as they had acted as agents of the British regime during the freedom struggle, were trying to disrupt unity and solidarity of the Congress and the Youth Congress. He said they had also infiltrated into the Congress organization.'[12] According to P.N. Dhar, Sanjay also tried to establish contacts with US and other foreign embassies.

III

According to some observers, a stage was reached by the end of 1976 when Sanjay Gandhi not only operated an imperium within the imperio and as an alternate power centre, but his authority and orders carried more weight than even Mrs Gandhi's. While this may not have been so, I tend to agree with Balraj Puri, who in his highly perceptive analysis of the JP movement and the Emergency, has observed that Sanjay Gandhi 'more than anybody else shaped the eventual form and content of the Emergency.'[13] A little differently, Sanjay's young widow, Maneka Gandhi, was to comment later: 'Sanjay was the face of the Emergency. Even if a leaf dropped, people said Sanjay must have done it.'[14]

Undoubtedly, during the Emergency Mrs Gandhi relied upon Sanjay a great deal and let him operate freely in the party and the government. Despite wide divergence between their views, she promoted him and publicly endorsed his political initiatives. She encouraged him to take up the leadership of the Youth Congress and did not object even when it began to overshadow the parent Congress party. She declared his 5-Points, which I will discuss later, to be part of the national agenda along with her own 20-Points Programme.[15]

Sanjay Gandhi was Mrs Gandhi's blind spot; he could do no wrong. She would not listen to a word against him or to any complaint against his or his coterie's functioning. This was despite her promise in the first few months of the Emergency to entertain all complaints and her seeking free and frank reports from officials of the impact of the Emergency measures on different aspects of the public's life, as also the doings of the police and bureaucracy.[16] Even her elder son, Rajiv Gandhi, or other persons close to her, did not dare broach the subject of Sanjay's activities with her. What B.K. Nehru, a cousin of Mrs Gandhi, senior bureaucrat and high commissioner of India in Britain, who had valiantly defended the imposition of the Emergency and had full access to her during that period, has written in this respect is significant enough to be quoted at length.[17]

I told Baboo (PN Haksar) . . . that I was going to talk to Indira about what Sanjay was doing. He said to me that it would be the greatest mistake for me to say anything critical in the slightest degree about Sanjay. She was absolutely blind as far as that boy was concerned; she regarded him as perfect, he could do no wrong. The slightest expression of doubt about Sanjay was resented . . . He said that I had unlimited right of access . . . If I ever said anything which implied any criticism of Sanjay, the immediate effect would be that access would be denied. I would never be able to meet her again . . . I followed Baboobhai's advice . . .

B.K. Nehru added:

Virtually all the politicians and even quite a large number of civil servants were taking orders from Sanjay Gandhi. Remembering Babhoobhai's prohibition on mentioning her son to the Prime Minister I did not do so. But I did discuss Sanjay's doings with Rajiv. He was as discontented, disgusted and depressed with what was happening as was everybody . . . I asked Rajiv why his mother allowed all this to happen; he said that the fact was that she had abdicated in favour of her son.

Similarly, N.K. Seshan, Mrs Gandhi's private secretary, was to say later that whenever he brought certain wrong actions to her attention, 'she would brush me aside or would behave as if she had not heard me.'[18] One reason why Mrs Gandhi would not pay attention to the complaints regarding forcible vasectomies was her belief that these were an aspect of anti-Sanjay propaganda. But more on this later.

Mrs Gandhi even expressed unhappiness with the CPI, her only political ally, for its lack of support to Sanjay's 5-Points even while being enthusiastic about her 20-Points.[19] She warned the CPI and others that she viewed any attack upon Sanjay as a personal one.[20] Yet, it is interesting that while deciding in January 1977 to hold general elections, she tried to keep Sanjay in the dark and then rejected his advice not to hold them. Earlier, she had kept him out of the discussions on constitutional reform and had rejected recommendations sponsored by him favouring a presidential form of government or for transformation of the existing Parliament into a constituent assembly.[21]

The relationship of Mrs Gandhi and Sanjay is shrouded in mystery and has been a subject of speculation, particularly for Mrs Gandhi's biographers. Why she relied upon him so heavily during the Emergency, allowed him to function as he did, and defended him so vehemently then, and later on, are questions that have puzzled them. A clear picture will be gained perhaps once Mrs Gandhi's private papers become available—and perhaps not even then, for Mrs Gandhi was a very private person and quite isolated.

One view, which is hard to swallow, has been that she did not know what her son and people around him were doing—and nobody dared tell her. The latter is not true. Many did, and starting with P.N. Haksar paid a price for doing so.

According to another, more credible, view Mrs Gandhi was angry with fellow Congress leaders for not defending her adequately from the Opposition's 'calumnies'; she also felt it was difficult to distinguish between those who could be trusted and others. She felt the one person she could trust fully was Sanjay Gandhi, who had firmly stood by her after 12 June.[22]

Some have argued that Mrs Gandhi was a doting mother with dynastic ambitions—she was grooming Sanjay as her eventual successor. This could be the explanation as to why she was promoting him, but not why she exercised little control over him, or why she was unmindful of any criticism of his doings. Consequently, a large number of commentators have fallen back on psychological explanations. After discussing Mrs Gandhi's handling of Sanjay's anti-communist interview, P.N. Dhar, who was personally involved in the episode, wrote: 'Mrs Gandhi was, in some ways, afraid of her son, at least to the extent of fearing his displeasure.'[23] Dhar also refers to Mrs Gandhi's 'obsessive love for Sanjay'.[24] And concludes: 'All one can say is that Mrs Gandhi's problem with Sanjay was psychologically complex and far from being a simple case of a widowed mother's difficulties with an impetuous son.'[25] Some others have argued that she had a guilty feeling of having neglected her children because of her preoccupation with looking after her father.

Mrs Gandhi's friend and biographer, Pupul Jayakar, also had a psychological explanation to offer. According to her, after the June events, Mrs Gandhi's 'capacity to listen and observe, to enter into situations, was at its lowest ebb. She turned to her favourite son, Sanjay, and drew energy from the youth. She saw him . . . a son she could trust, who stood by her side and took over her burdens.[26] Jayakar then quotes R.N. Kao, the RAW chief: 'She wrapped Sanjay around herself like a blanket to keep out the cold. It was as if she had the shivers.'[27]

Zareer Masani[28] and her latest biographer, Katherine Frank[29], have argued in the same vein. It is, however, interesting that none of the four writers cited above, or many others who think like them, are trained psychoanalysts. Psychological analysis of the actions of historical characters is in any case of doubtful validity. But to have any credibility it must be based on adequate personal data, such as private diaries, and be made by trained psychoanalysts. Even Erik Erikson who was successful in making a psychological analysis of young Luther was a failure when he tried to do so in the case of Mahatma Gandhi, in part because of the absence of adequate source material.

IV

One result of Sanjay Gandhi's rise to power and eminence was that the 5-Points he put forward in July 1976 gradually rivalled and then became more important than the official 20-Points. His 5-Points were: Abolish the dowry system and refuse dowry at the time of marriage; practise family planning and birth control and limit families to only two children; plant trees; promote literacy—each literate person to teach an illiterate one; end caste distinction and give up belief in the caste system. Sanjay Gandhi was also determined to clean up and beautify the cities and relieve the intense congestion by clearing slums and demolishing encroachments and unauthorized structures that were impediments on roads, bazaars, parks, monuments, etc.

In themselves the 5-Points were quite sound and socially relevant, though far less radical and egalitarian than the 20-Points. Still, because they dealt with some of India's important problems, these steps, if even partially implemented, would have helped transform Indian society in a significant manner. However, family planning and to a certain extent slum clearance and city beautification were sought to be implemented as crash programmes, in an illegitimate, hamhanded, authoritarian and coercive manner, especially in North India where Sanjay Gandhi and his coterie could operate with impunity. This led to some of the worst excesses of the Emergency and contributed significantly to the unpopularity of the regime. His other four points remained on paper. Uma Vasudev has depicted the paradoxical situation: 'Everything that Sanjay said was right. Everything that he did turned out to be wrong.'[30]

There is no doubt that the birth rate needed to be brought down, especially as the death rate had come down sharply from 47.2 to 17.4 per thousand since 1921 and the growth of population had recorded the all-time high rate of 24.8 per thousand in the 1971 census. All efforts of the last twenty years to control population having proved inadequate, the government rightly decided to promote family planning more vigorously and to reduce the annual birth rate from about 35 to 25 per thousand by 1984. A new population policy based on more stringent measures was therefore adopted in April 1976. In addition to stronger incentives and disincentives for not having more than three children, the new policy mainly aimed at persuading people to limit their families by undergoing voluntary sterilization, vasectomy in the case of men and tubectomy in the case of women, with greater emphasis on the former. The minimum age of marriage was also raised to eighteen for girls and twenty-one for boys.

Two negative factors intervened at this stage. First, the quota system or the system of setting high targets for sterilization was put in place for every state and district. In April 1976, a national target of 4.3 million sterilizations was announced for the next twelve months. This was more than twice the figure achieved in the same duration the previous year. Corresponding quotas were fixed for every state and district. Compulsion was thus built into the target-oriented approach itself. Moreover, even in normal times, the quota system compelled the bureaucracy to become overzealous, overstep the voluntary nature of the programme, cross the bounds of law and take to forcible sterilization to fulfil the quotas.

Second, very soon Sanjay Gandhi took over the programme and made it his own. Under his guidance and direction the voluntary nature of the programme, including relying on incentives and disincentives, education, propaganda and persuasion, was replaced, especially after July 1976, by compulsion and coercion, usually by cruel methods. The state governments and municipal authorities now competed with each other to raise and fulfil targets. This was especially the case with Punjab, Delhi and Haryana and to some extent with UP and Bihar, which were Sanjay's special turf and whose governments were known to be keen to placate him and obey his commands.

Family planning was now sought to be aggressively promoted, above all through compulsory sterilization, with few daring to oppose the new approach. According to a report in the *Times of India* of 1 November 1976, 'Mr Sanjay Gandhi today warned the "so-called leaders" within and outside the Congress opposing the family planning programme that they would have no place in national life. "Such persons will have no place in the country nor in the Congress and sooner they are driven out the better" he added.'

Government servants, village officials and municipal employees, school teachers, doctors and family planning and other health workers and even government contractors were assigned arbitrarily fixed quotas of the number of persons they had to 'motivate' to undergo sterilization and 'deliver' to the sterilization centres. They were themselves to be motivated by a system of threats and rewards. Failure to meet the individual target led to official reprimand and in some cases to denial of promotions and increments, withholding of salaries, and even loss of jobs. On the other hand, those who fulfilled their quota could be rewarded handsomely through promotions and increments, and shown other official favours. The hapless employees went around searching for 'volunteers', willing to pay them out of their own pockets or reward them in other ways. The search was particularly unedifying and harrowing for women employees. The government servants and others, when eligible for sterilization, were themselves threatened in all sorts of ways, including with loss of their jobs, unless they produced a certificate that they or their wives had undergone sterilization. Similarly, heads of institutions such as schools, hospitals, municipal committees, traders' bodies, business enterprises, cinema halls were assigned targets and were expected to meet them by 'motivating' their employees. Inevitably, sterilization soon became business. Middlemen or *dalals* now came in to provide the beleagured employee with a case, i.e., a poor, needy person whom they had lured or trapped in all sorts of ways to accept sterilization, for a monetary consideration. In return for cash, some needy persons themselves volunteered to be sterilized.

The administration and police added their might to the enforcement of sterilization targets. According to D. Banerji, of the Centre of Social Medicine and Community Health, JNU, whose researchers carried out fieldwork in villages between October 1976 and January 1977:[31]

> The issue of license for guns, shops, sugarcane crushers and vehicles, issue of (government) loans of various kinds, registration of land; issue of ration cards; exemption from payment of school fees or land revenue; supply of irrigation canal water; submission of applications for any job; any form of registration; obtaining of bail and facilitation of court cases; all these were linked up with the procurement of cases for sterilization.

The police was widely used to harass, coerce and intimidate people to make up the prescribed quotas. Quite often in the cities, the police would pick up persons from their homes or waylay the homeless and the vagrants on streets and drag them to sterilization clinics and camps where vasectomies were performed on them despite their protest. In rural areas, squads of sterilization teams in vans accompanied by armed police roamed and 'raided' villages. Very often, the victims, both in cities and villages, were picked up, irrespective of their age or marital status—old men, young boys, newly married and unmarried. One of the worst-affected states in this respect was Haryana, where sometimes an entire village would be surrounded and men forced to undergo vasectomies. Delhi and parts of UP also faced extreme stringency in the implementation of the family planning programme. Nor were school and college teachers spared.

Vasectomies were not always carried out in hospitals. More often than not they were performed in camps, set up in tents or school buildings, without even rudimentary facilities. Nor was there any after-care of patients. There were several deaths following sterilization, the number of such cases brought before the Shah Commission being over 1,770. Moreover, thousands suffered from post-operation infections and immense psychological damage.

Forcible sterilization created and spread such a fear psychosis among the people that many ran away and hid when they saw even an ordinary van. *Nasbandi* (vasectomy) became a dreaded word and its terror spread like wild fire all over North India. An additional reason for the terror was people's ignorance regarding sterilization or vasectomy. In the absence of adequate education and information, the widespread belief was that vasectomy would lead to impotence and 'demanning' or loss of virility and interest in sex. In fact, many people thought it was another name for castration. After all, the only sterilization that ordinary people were familiar with was the castration of bulls. Moreover, apart from physical injury, forced sterilization hurt people's self-esteem; it created in them a sense of helplessness and humiliation, of being treated as animals. No effort was made to redress their concern. Many Muslims were against vasectomy on religious grounds, but little heed was paid to their feelings.[32]

At no stage did Mrs Gandhi campaign in favour of family planning as she had done on other issues during 1969-72 or would do later in 1977-79. And Sanjay Gandhi, who was virtually incharge of family planning programme, believed not in convincing people but in getting things done by instilling fear among them.[33]

The target officially set in April 1976 for the next twelve months was 4.3 million sterilization. This target was soon surpassed as state governments and bureaucrats competed with one another to continually and indiscriminately enhance their targets and achievements. This wholesale raising of targets to win favour with Sanjay Gandhi was undoubtedly a major cause of sterilization excesses. In June 1976, before Sanjay Gandhi took full charge, about 330 vasectomy operations were performed per day in the country. This figure shot up to 5,644 per day in August. In Delhi alone, the number of sterilizations per day rose by thirteen times in less than two years. However, Datia, a small district in Madhya Pradesh, beat even this record. It surpassed the whole year's target of 2,000 vasectomy operations in just fourteen days, between 1 September and 14 September 1976. For the country as a whole, the number of sterilizations was 1.354 million in 1974-75 and 2.669 million in 1975-76; in 1976-77 this figure shot up to 8.261 million.

A significant aspect of the sterilization programme was that those worst affected were the rural and urban poor and low-level government employees and school teachers, though sometimes middle-class men were also victims. The poor protested in all sorts of everyday ways, including recourse to flight, hiding, demonstrations and slogan-shouting. Sometimes entire families of a village would hide in the fields or neighbouring jungles, even in cold winter nights, to avoid being 'caught' by family planning squads. Sometimes when their patience was exhausted, or a heinous act of forced vasectomy came to light, the people's resentment exploded and in place of passive resistance, they took to rioting and violent protest. This happened several times in UP and Haryana.

In one, widely-publicized instance, for example, nearly forty persons were killed and scores injured in police firing in the town of Muzaffarnagar in western UP in October 1976, when a large crowd resisted the efforts by the police to seize persons and take them to a sterilization centre. Earlier thirteen persons had been killed in a similar instance on 27 August in village Rankidhi in Sultanpur district, UP. Another notorious case was that of a village in Pipli in Haryana. In December, Hawa Singh, a twenty-five-year-old childless widower was forcibly taken off a bus at the block headquarters and sterilized. The surgical incision failed to heal, and Hawa Singh died. The resentment in the neighbouring area led to more than 100,000 villagers gathering and thwarting several efforts of the police to raid Hawa Singh's village to pick up young men. Similar cases, though of lesser intensity, occurred all over North India in the winter months of 1976.

Moreover, as was inevitable in view of press censorship and total ban on any criticism of the family planning programme—any criticism or opposition to forcible sterilization made a person liable to be arrested under DIR—stories, true or false, of forcible vasectomy operations, of police brutality and violent resistance by the people, of the large number of deaths as a result of vasectomy operations or police firing on protesting crowds, started circulating by word of mouth and were believed. These stories, like all rumours, were grossly exaggerated. Still, undeniably, there was a strong element of truth in them.

The family planning programme during the Emergency was an example of a vital national issue being handled in an insensitive, heartless and inhuman manner. It not only did immense immediate harm and created a strong anti-government and anti-Emergency feeling but brought the concept of family planning itself into disrepute. Years of effort to popularize birth control and the small-family norm were wasted; the family-planning programme was set back by a decade. For example, the number of sterilizations fell from 1,354,000 in 1974-75 and 8,261,000 in 1976-77 to 949,000 in 1977-78. The family planning programme was to take years to recover from the prejudice generated against it during the Emergency.

Far less significant, but equally controversial, was the Sanjay Gandhi-led programme of slum clearance, demolition of unauthorized structures and removal of congestion in bazaars and around historical monuments and, in general, of the beautification of cities. Renovation and beautification of cities was not a part of Sanjay Gandhi's 5-Points and was largely confined to Delhi, though it did to some extent extend to a few other cities and towns such as Bombay, Jaipur, Varanasi, Agra and Lucknow, but with far less severity. The slum clearance campaign in Delhi has been dealt with and criticized at length by a large number of authors who wrote immediately after the Emergency. Their view has been controverted at length by Jagmohan who, as vice-chairman of the Delhi Development Authority, implemented the slum clearance and resettlement scheme. Perhaps far more research is needed to make a proper evaluation of the scheme and its implementation. A beginning has, however, been made by Emma Tarlo's study of one resettlement colony, 'Welcome' or Seelumpur Phases III and IV, published in 1995.[34]

The elements of Delhi's slum clearance-cum-resettlement programme had been worked out much earlier—in case of some of its parts as early as 1958. It could not, however, be fully or properly implemented as slum-dwellers would either refuse to shift to new resettlement colonies or would do so and then come back having sold off their plot or house, or the mere claim thereof, or gifted it to a family member. New migrants to the rapidly growing city would rebuild the old slums or build new ones on empty spaces designated for parks, new housing, etc. Sanjay Gandhi and DDA authorities saw the Emergency as providing an opportunity to make Delhi a modern, non-congested city, above all, free of slums.

Starting in July 1975, virtually at the onset of the Emergency and by the end of 1976, nearly 120,000 *jhuggi-jhopris* and other structures in the slum areas of Delhi were demolished with the help of bulldozers. Their nearly 700,000 inhabitants were carted in government trucks to new resettlement colonies on the outskirts of the city. The resettlement colonies were ill-prepared, unhealthy and disease-ridden and lacking in all amenities, including drinking water. The long-term plans for the colonies had included modern housing, schools, hospitals, playgrounds, parks, water supply, and electrification. But these plans were still on paper. All that a settler got in the new colonies was twenty-five square yards of land, free of cost, on which he could construct his own house. Invariably, the resettlement colonies were far away from places of work of the new residents, most of whom were hawkers, *kabadis* (ragmen), construction workers, rickshaw pullers, domestic workers and workers in small factories. With no jobs available in the new colonies, they had to travel several kilometres by bus or cycle to their old places of work. Moreover, because of the Emergency, no protest by the slum dwellers or on their behalf was tolerated.[35]

The poor were the main victims but not the only victims of the drive to beautify and de-congest Delhi. Many shopkepers, businessmen and middle and upper class persons also suffered when their illegal encroachments were demolished or their shops and houses came in the way of de-congestion of roads and markets. Many truck owners suffered as they were forced to park their vehicles outside residential and market areas. The old Sabzi Mandi (vegetable market) in Old Delhi was demolished and the merchants forced to move to Azadpur Mandi. Similarly, in April 1976, nearly a thousand illegally-constructed cabins of lawyers in the compound of Tis Hazari courts in Delhi court premises were demolished.[36]

The most notorious case of slum clearance, which has found prominent place in every account of the Emergency, was that of the Muslim-majority Turkman Gate area. People resisted the demolition drive but their resistance was ruthlessly suppressed. Turkman Gate is at the end of several streets which emanate from the historic Jama Masjid. Over the years, the entire area of about seven acres had become one huge slum, dingy, full of stench and filth and cluttered with structures within each house, with each house hosting multiple families.

Sunlight never peeped into most of the houses. Sanjay Gandhi and the DDA authorities were keen to remove the slums and restore the old glory of the Jama Masjid and at the same time promote sterilization in this congested area.

A great deal of resentment had already been caused among the people of the area, especially among the local shopkeepers, when decades old unauthorized shops and stalls around the outer walls of the Jama Masjid had been demolished. Popular anger was also aroused by the sterilization campaign which, as usual, was also carried out in a heavyhanded and brazen manner, with the socialite Rukhsana Sultana, one of Sanjay's favourite family planning campaigners, going around the area accompanied by armed police.

The trouble in Turkman Gate area started on 13 April 1976, with the large-scale demolition of the overcrowded structures just outside the Gate. People had lived in this transit camp for over ten years and were now sent across Jamuna. Fearing further demolitions in the area, a large crowd of men, women and children gathered on 19 April to prevent the entry of bulldozers. However, anticipating popular resistance, nearly twenty companies of Delhi armed police and CRPF had been deployed. When the bulldozers resumed their demolition operation, the people blocked their passage. By the afternoon tempers ran high on both sides and the people opposed the police and demolition teams by throwing stones and bottles at them. The magistrate accompanying the police ordered a lathi-charge and arrested over 100 persons. The people retaliated and forced the police to release them. Firing ensued as a result of which six persons died, according to the police. Independent observers, however, put the number of dead at twenty. Several hundred were arrested. The police beat up men, women and children, ransacked houses and in some cases even molested women. A curfew lasting forty-five days was imposed on the area surrounding Turkman Gate. Those whose houses were demolished were forcibly sent to an underdeveloped and inhospitable tract of land, Khichripur, across the Jamuna.

As news of the Turkman Gate events spread all over North India, rumours were rife; the figure of persons killed in police firing got inflated to 150 or even 300. Apart from its inhumanity, the episode assumed an anti-Muslim colour, resulting in the alienation of a large number of Muslims from the Congress.

Jagmohan's account[37] of the slum-clearance programme as well as of the Turkman Gate affair is, however, very different. He has put up a strong defence of both. It is not possible to take up have his well-argued and well-documented, though not necessarily correct, account. Accusing his critics of passing over the ugly picture of the slums, where people lived under subhuman conditions, he says that in the resettled colonies the erstwhile slum-dwellers were given developed land worth Rs. 200 crore on secure tenure, free of cost, and provided cheap loans to construct houses and 'infrastructural facilities of high order'. He argues, this was why the Congress, which lost everywhere else in Delhi in the municipal elections of June 1977, won in the resettled colonies.

So far as the Turkman Gate affair is concerned, he points out that the slum-clearance scheme was conceived in 1938, compensation for the 120 houses to be demolished was paid in 1940. The scheme was revived several times in the forties and fifties and later in 1969-70. The Emergency gave this plan a fillip. Moreover, as against 120 houses demolished, alternative allotments of 200 flats, 600 residential plots and 200 industrial and commercial plots were made. Jagmohan also asserts that the events of 19 April had little to do with slum clearance which was proceeding smoothly. The riot and firing on that day, he says, were because of the strong emotional reaction to the family planning programme and incitement by the Shahi Imam and other vested interests. He also accuses his critics of giving the incident a communal colour.

What is surprising, and to an extent inexplicable, is why someone as sensitive, imaginative and politically-shrewd as Mrs Gandhi failed to perceive the gravity of the situation and didn't provide a healing touch, especially when the poor, her major political power base, were being alienated. One major radio address explaining the rationale of the sterilization and slum-clearance programmes and promising their humane implementation would have acted as a balm to people's hurt feelings. Why did she not do so? It has been suggested that Mrs Gandhi was uninformed or rather was deliberately kept ignorant of the grave excesses of the two programmes by those controlling her access to people and information. According to P.N. Bahl, Joint Secretary in the PMO, 'when the incipient reports came about the atrocities being perpetrated by the lower staff in the interior, the information fed to the capital was that it was nothing but a propaganda gimmick of the Opposition.'[38] Ignorance is, in any case, a handmaiden of an authoritarian regime. In this case, ignorance was also enhanced by the Sanjay factor.

Even so, a very large number of her political followers and colleagues and personal friends and admirers did seek to keep her informed of happenings on the ground. Her CPI allies regularly complained to her of the excesses. Her party MPs and MLAs begged her to stop vasectomy atrocities and police *zulum* (oppression) in UP. Moreover, she had a wide network of intelligence agencies to keep her informed—not all of them could have been remiss in their task. But she refused to believe them, and even turned against those who brought the bad news. She even criticized her ally, the CPI, in early October 1976, for its 'opposition to our family planning programme'.[39] And because Sanjay was so deeply involved in the two programmes she went on defending them, and denying that force was being used in their implementation or that the poor were suffering as a result. Instead, she construed all complaints regarding these programmes as propaganda to defame Sanjay or her government or as highly exaggerated, isolated instances.[40]

Finally, when she did come to realize the enormity of the misuse of the family planning programme, she tried during November and December 1976 to stall the campaign, dissociate herself from it and blame its excesses on overzealous bureaucrats. She stopped the enactment of the bill on compulsory national sterilization for those having two or more children and asked the state governments to abjure coercive methods during the family planning campaign and to take remedial measures in cases where excesses had already occurred. But these correctives came rather late in the day.

In any case, the already existing climate of fear and repression, corruption and abuse of authority had been further worsened by the family planning excesses. In the people's minds, these excesses came to be regarded as the central feature of the Emergency and Sanjay Gandhi as its chief villain. Undoubtedly, a major reason for the change in people's mood towards the Emergency was the emergence of Sanjay Gandhi as an extra-constitutional centre of power. As we have seen earlier, people's initial acceptance was partly because the Emergency was within legal and constitutional bounds. All this changed when Mrs Gandhi and particularly her son seemed to act against the constitutional framework and outside the law and to subvert democracy. Many still had faith in her political and democratic credentials, but none in Sanjay's.

It is now widely accepted that the backlash against compulsory sterilization and the daily acts of highhandedness, oppression and corruption by the petty officials and the police and people's detestation of Sanjay Gandhi were responsible for antagonizing all sections of society and bringing down Indira Gandhi's government in March 1977. This is borne out by the fact that Congress losses in the elections were confined mainly to North India where most of the excesses had occurred. In contrast, Congress did quite well in South India which had been largely out of Sanjay Gandhi's reach, and where the Emergency had been less severe, and the 20-Point Programme better implemented. The people in the South, therefore, continued to believe that the Emergency was a temporary phenomenon designed to deal with a specific situation, which had arisen mainly in the North.

V

What was the approach of the major political parties, social classes and groups to the Emergency and what was their role during its period?

The Congress party fully supported the Emergency and Indira Gandhi. The party, even otherwise gradually weakened since 1947, more or less ceased to function during the period of the Emergency. Moreover, at the very outset, action was taken against Mrs Gandhi's critics within the party, some of them being put in prison, while others were marginalized. Already before 1975, regional and other party leaders had been losing clout. This process went further during the Emergency. The party's Working Committee, Parliamentary Board, for example, seldom met and were rarely consulted. Gradually, the independent among the party leaders and cadres, especially those critical of Sanjay Gandhi or not willing to be his cheer-leaders, lost influence. These included earlier stalwarts, such as Jagjivan Ram, Y.B. Chavan, Brahmananda Reddy and Siddhartha Shankar Ray. As pointed out earlier, the independent-minded H.N. Bahuguna and Nandini Satpathy, Congress chief ministers of UP and Orissa respectively, lost their posts. Many others, afraid of Sanjay Gandhi, kept quiet. Others cringed before him and his coterie. Still others echoed the official line, but unenthusiastically, and were on the way to being upstaged or replaced by the members and cadre of the Youth Congress. The ex-communists among the Congress leaders and those suspected of being sympathetic to CPI—and this included the President of the party, D.K. Barooah—were kept away from positions of influence within the party or the government during the period of Sanjay Gandhi's dominance. In any case, even those who remained loyal and devoted to Mrs Gandhi were cut off from her—she had no time to meet them or the coterie surrounding her did not let them meet her. They become politically irrelevant. They could also not act as her eyes and ears.

The Jan Sangh, Congress (O), BLD, Socialists, Akalis and RSS were, of course, on the receiving end of the Emergency because of their being part of JP movement. Though not banned (except for RSS) their top leaders were arrested at the beginning of the Emergency. These parties were not able to forge a movement or organize even any popular protest against the Emergency on a significant scale[41], except for the Akalis, who for quite some time, offered group *satyagraha* in Punjab.

George Fernandes, the trade union leader and chairman of the Socialist party, could not activize either his trade union or party base, but unwilling to remain passive, decided to enthuse the people by organizing acts of sabotage, primarily disruption of communications by blowing up bridges with the help of a few followers. The plan was, as Sachchidanand Sinha has pointed out, 'Childishly naïve. It was neither full-fledged terrorism which could overawe the government nor a plan of action whose message could be made to reach the people.'[42] Fernandes and his co-conspirators failed to dynamite a single bridge or train-track, and were soon arrested and were being tried when the Emergency ended.

Several months into the Emergency, most of the opposition leaders saw with despair its acceptance by the people and the failure of their own parties in organizing resistance. They were also disillusioned and demoralized when they found a large number of their colleagues at the lower levels, mainly from the Jan Sangh, Congress (O) and to some extent from the BLD, join the ruling party.

An example of this demoralization was the recipe of veteran nationalist and opposition leader, J.B. Kripalani, for bringing about political normalcy. He wrote on 25 September 1975 in a letter to the Press: 'I have not suggested here the withdrawal of the Emergency or of censorship of the Press. These things the Government may do when they think it proper. I have only pleaded for the release of the leaders, under altered circumstances.'[43] Another indication of the state of mind of some of the opposition leaders was Biju Patnaik's letter to his party chairman, Charan Singh, in March 1976, praising the gains of the Emergency, expressing his elation over 'Young Sanjay's exhortation to his Party workers' and stressing the need 'to stop political quibblings for some time to get on with the task of nation-building at the grass-roots level.'[44]

Consequently, from the beginning of 1976, some of the opposition leaders sought a negotiated compromise with the government as a way out. They were ready to withdraw the Opposition-led movement announced on 23 June 1975 if *status quo ante*-26 June was restored. Some early overtures to the government were made by opposition leaders who had not been arrested. These efforts were accelerated from

March 1976 when a large number of the top opposition leaders, including Charan Singh, chairman of BLD, and Asoka Mehta, president of Congress (O), were released on 7 March. Atal Behari Vajpayee had already been released on health grounds soon after his arrest. N.G. Goray of Socialist party had not been arrested. Almost all these leaders were keen for a rapprochement with Mrs Gandhi. On 20 March, Charan Singh, who was never enthusiastic about a mass movement, met JP in Bombay and asked him to suspend the struggle proposed on 25 June 1975 in order to facilitate a dialogue with the government. He repeated this suggestion in May and was supported by Hare Krushna Mahtab and Vajpayee.[45] The general terms on which a settlement with the government could be arrived at were laid down by Charan Singh in a letter to Mrs Gandhi on 26 June, appealing to her to release political prisoners, lift censorship of the Press, restore fundamental rights and announce firm dates for elections to Lok Sabha and state assemblies.[46]

In October-November 1976, Asoka Mehta undertook another initiative and wrote twice to Mrs Gandhi advocating direct discussion between her and opposition leaders. By the end of 1976, many of the opposition leaders wanted to settle with Mrs Gandhi on 'almost any terms', i.e., they were willing to surrender before her. In mid-December K. Karunanidhi, the DMK leader and the deposed chief minister of Tamil Nadu, who had in an article in *Murasali* daily welcomed the 'letter and spirit' of Mrs Gandhi's 'appeal' for cooperation by the Opposition,[47] convened a meeting of opposition leaders to initiate talks with Mrs Gandhi without laying down any prior conditions with a view to normalize the political situation. The opposition leaders declared their faith in parliamentary democracy, peaceful and non-violent action and secularism, their opposition to communalism and regional chauvinism and their willingness to accept 'reasonable restraints' on forms of political action and a code of conduct, provided they were binding on both the ruling party and the Opposition.[48]

But these attempts at the opening of a dialogue with Mrs Gandhi could not go far, for there were two snags. One was the need to get JP's approval, for these efforts could not bear fruit without his nod: JP was still the unquestioned generalissimo of the Opposition. The second obstacle was Mrs Gandhi's agreement. But JP would not give his approval to the proposals as framed by the opposition conclave, and, in the absence of his assent, Mrs Gandhi would not pay much heed to the toothless opposition leaders' pleas.

Initially, JP was in two minds. His reaction to the proclamation of the Emergency was of disbelief, shock, despair and disillusionment with the lack of popular opposition to the proclamation.[49] He was also, in the beginning, in a compromising mood. In a letter to Mrs Gandhi on 21 July 1975, after berating her for imposing the Emergency, he wrote at the end: 'But let me assure you that if you do the right things, for instance, your 20-points, tackling corruption at Ministerial levels, electoral reforms, etc., take the Opposition into confidence, heed its advice, you will receive the willing cooperation of every one of us.'[50] Later, his altitude stiffened, but it was still basically defensive. He was willing to withdraw his movement if the situation prior to 26 June was restored and the postponed general elections were held. However, he no longer demanded Mrs Gandhi's resignation as prime minister. For example, in a statement made on 30 October 1976, he gave the assurance: 'I can say that no question of any demonstration, mass movement, or civil disobedience, or any kind of trouble will arise if the decision for elections is announced.'[51]

At the same time, JP would not agree to the unilateral withdrawal of the movement. In a self-critical mood, he said, in an interview on 12 February 1976, that if he had known what would be the result of a movement he would have taken to a political path in place of 'direct action'.[52] But when it came to the opposition leaders' efforts to open negotiations with Mrs Gandhi, he would agree to join or approve of their efforts only after political prisoners had been released and civil liberties and freedom of the Press restored. What is more significant, JP wanted that negotiations with Mrs Gandhi should be confined to the question of holding elections.[53] JP's position made it difficult for opposition leaders to continue their attempts to make a deal with Mrs Gandhi.

Perhaps another reason for this failure was the strong opposition by a section of the socialists headed by George Fernandes and Madhu Limaye, an important ideologue of the party, to any dialogue with 'a woman who will never surrender power'. They described the Karunanidhi-led efforts of December as a 'sell-out' to Mrs Gandhi, which would 'succeed only in giving some legitimacy and hence credibility and respectability to Mrs Gandhi's dictatorship.'[54]

On her part, knowing the political stature of JP and his unchallengeable position in opposition politics, Mrs Gandhi made several overtures to him, using P.N. Dhar as an intermediary.[55] These moves, however, failed as from the heterogenous Opposition she wanted complete surrender.

At the Guwahati Congress session in November 1976, she said a dialogue with the Opposition could begin if it agreed to behave 'in a responsible manner' and for the 'good of the country'.[56] In her reply of 29 December 1976 to Asoka Mehta's letters of 12 October and 23 November, she demanded from the Opposition a 'clear disavowal of communal and separatist violence', repudiation of 'extra-constitutional action', and a recognition and 'genuine acceptance' of 'the changes that have taken place' in the last few months. Similarly, on 4 January 1977 she told the Press that a fruitful dialogue could start only if the Opposition promised that it would not attempt to subvert democratically elected governments.[57] As Kuldip Nayar has put it, Mrs Gandhi's conditions were like asking 'when did you stop beating your wife?'[58] Mrs Gandhi probably felt that if, and when, she had to withdraw the Emergency, restore normal democratic conditions and declare elections, she would rather do so unilaterally, as a gift to the people, and not as a bargain with the opposition leaders.

Simultaneously with their efforts to bring the Emergency to an end through negotiations with Mrs Gandhi, the opposition leaders tried repeatedly to merge into one party so as to strengthen their position, both in the parleys with Mrs Gandhi and in the general elections, whenever they might be held.[59]

Strong pressure in this direction came from JP who had, immediately after his release, expressed a strong desire to promote the unification of the opposition parties. On 12 February 1976, in his interview to *Swaraj*, he had argued: 'History has shown that they have a responsibility to create a national political alternative. If they fail to do so, the opposition groups will be held responsible, by history, in India, of bringing fascism to India.'[60]

During January-February 1976, the opposition leaders in different jails began to moot the idea of their coming together to form a single party. These efforts received a fillip with the release of some leaders in March. The first major step in this direction was taken later that month when some of the opposition leaders met in Bombay on JP's invitation. On 26 March, four major parties—the Congress (O), BLD, Jan Sangh and Socialist party—announced a plan for their merger under JP's 'advice and guidance', and formed a steering committee for the purpose.

But nothing concrete emerged for months, for each party jockeyed for better influence over the new party. There were differences over the new party's name, flag, election symbol and president. Personal, party and power equations among the leaders were also not easy to work out. Another bone of contention, which was to break up the Janata Party later in 1979, was that of the role of RSS and the links of the members of the new party with it, i.e., the question of 'dual loyalty'.[61] Moreover, while BLD and some of the socialists were keen on formation of a united party, Congress (O), Jan Sangh, and other socialists resisted the move and dragged their feet.

The leaders of the four parties met again in May under JP's stewardship and asked him to lead a new party. JP announced his willingness to do so; he also declared that the new party would see the light of the day at a conference of opposition leaders to be held in June. But the announcement proved to be premature as a unified party could not be formed because the mutual trust between the leaders that this needed was yet to be built.[62] However, following a fresh initiative, on 17 December the four-party leaders announced the formation of a single party to be known as Bharatiya Janata Congress, which would have a common symbol. The question of who would lead the party was, however, left undecided, the final approval of the Congress (O) was pending until its meeting in February 1977.

The RSS[63] was one of the organizations that were banned on 4 July 1975 under the Defence of India Rules. By 5 August over 2,000 RSS members had been arrested. However, a large number of RSS leaders and cadre succeeded in evading arrest and going underground. But they remained politically passive and the leadership disbanded the RSS as an organization. Though the RSS was expected to be the spearhead of the civil disobedience projected in June 1975, its leadership decided not only to adopt a passive stance towards the government but tried to buy peace with it and get the ban on RSS removed.

Bala Sahib Deoras, head of the RSS, who was detained in Yervada jail, Pune, made a major overture to Mrs Gandhi in a letter on 22 August 1975. Praising the speech that she had made on the Independence Day as appropriate and well-balanced, he asked her to utilize the 'power of the Sangh for the upliftment of our country.' In another letter to Mrs Gandhi on 10 November 1975, Deoras congratulated her on the successful election appeal before the Supreme Court, asserted that the RSS had no connection with JP movement, refuted other charges against his organization, repeated, as in 1948-49, the assurance of its non-involvement in politics, and appealed to her to lift the ban on the RSS and release its workers. He also suggested that she use RSS's strength to implement government's programmes. Later, in January and February 1976, he wrote at length to Vinoba Bhave detailing the positive features of RSS and asking him to intercede on its behalf with Mrs Gandhi so that it could contribute to the country's progress under her leadership. RSS's Hindi organ, *Panchajanya*, also welcomed in December 1975 the emergence of Sanjay Gandhi as a youth leader.

Deoras letters were, in my view, not so much the result of cowardice or fear, but of political tactics, what the RSS calls *Krishna niti*, i.e., deception for a good cause, to avoid government repression and protect the RSS organization in a period of authoritarian regime that was expected to last long. Perhaps, following the same tactics a very large number, perhaps as high as 70 per cent, of RSS detenus sent letters of apology to the state governments to secure their release. Many RSS-Jan Sangh members who were not arrested resigned from their organizations, in some cases even denounced them and made statements supporting the Emergency. Cowardice or tactics, these actions of RSS and its members were not appreciated by those in jail. Nor did the government relent. It neither released the apologizing prisoners nor lifted the ban on the RSS. It, too, judged their and Deoras's actions as 'tactics' for which the RSS was well-known.

The CPM's relationship with the JP movement had been complex. It had refused to join the movement because of the large presence of right-wing and communal parties. At the same time it had given the movement support because of its objective of bringing down the Congress regime.

The CPM, too, was unprepared politically for the promulgation of the Emergency. It denounced the Emergency as a total war on democracy, an offensive against the working class, and a step towards establishing an authoritarian one-party rule. In its view, the Emergency proved that the bourgeoisie of an ex-colonial country was incapable of ruling in a democratic manner. Consequently, there would be no return to democracy. It also argued that the Emergency was designed to ensure the unbridled exploitation of the people by the big capitalists and landlords; it would facilitate the designs of the imperialists and multi-national corporations, increase India's dependence on foreign aid, which mortgaged the country's economy to the imperialist world, and undermine its national freedom.

The party condemned the 20-Point Programme as a cruel hoax designed to mislead the people. It was critical of the Soviet Union for supporting the Emergency. It condemned the Swaran Singh Committee report on amendment of the Constitution, and declared that the forty-second constitutional amendment was totally unacceptable.

The CPM opposed the Emergency but did not actively work against it. Though politically paralyzed, it remained more or less intact. Nor did the government launch an attack on it. A few of its leaders and some of its cadres were arrested but were soon released. This was deliberate as the government wanted to keep up its image of battling against only the right.

The leadership of the CPM was bewildered by the proclamation of the Emergency and could make sense of it only by seeing it as marking the dawn of a long-term dictatorship.[64] It was convinced that the Emergency regime would go all-out in repressing the party and its front organizations, and that a tough, long-term and protracted struggle lay ahead of it. But the party had neglected underground work and was not prepared organizationally for an immediate struggle against the government. The immediate task, therefore, was to avoid premature confrontation with the regime, to preserve its forces for the time being, and to avoid large-scale arrests of its cadres. The party, therefore, decided to keep a low profile for the time being and not to organize any protest movements against the imposition of the Emergency, or later, against its excesses. In the meanwhile, the party was to concentrate on building up its underground apparatus and prepare for the long-drawn out revolutionary struggle against the dictatorship. The time for action would come when the inevitable popular discontent would bubble to the surface. The party also hoped that contradictions within the block of the ruling classes would deepen further, accentuating the political crisis and weakening the state's capacity to suppress popular movements.

A reason for the paralysis of the party was the continuous—almost one-year-long—internal division on the question of joint political work with the Jan Sangh and other rightist parties in the struggle against the Congress and the Emergency. This led, in the end, to the resignation by P. Sundarayya from the post of general secretary, because he was opposed to such cooperation.[65] Nor did the latter materialize.

As mentioned before, the CPM did organize a few token protests and some of its leaders and cadres were arrested but were invariably released very soon. The Centre for Indian Trade Unions (CITU), the party's trade union wing, did, however, face repression and large-scale arrests of its cadres, as the government stifled all opposition to its policy of maintaining industrial peace.

The various banned Naxalite groups called for the restoration of civil liberties and real implementation of Mrs Gandhi's 20-Point Programme. In the meanwhile, they prepared to wage the inevitable, prolonged armed struggle against what they regarded as a fascist regime.

The CPI had been highly critical of the JP movement and had actively supported the Congress and mobilized the people against the

JPM. Consequently, it extended active support to the Emergency as a necessary and justified step against right reaction and counter-revolutionary forces aided by the imperialists. It argued that counter-revolution could not have been defeated only by political mobilization and the power of the state had to be used for the purpose.[66]

The CPI was also enthusiastic about the 20-Point Programme and tried to mobilize popular support for its effective implementation. The party also hoped that just as, at the mass level, it had been the chief force in mobilization against JPM in Bihar during 1974-75, it would now be able to play a similar role nation-wide in the implementation of the 20-Point Programme at the mass level, especially as the Congress had no organizational capacity to do so. It would thus be able to influence government policies, strengthen the progressive forces in the Congress as also the CPI itself and its mass organizations. It was heartened by the fact that throughout the period of the Emergency, C. Achutha Menon remained the chief minister of Kerala, heading a Communist-Congress coalition, and was able to follow jointly-evolved radical policies.

But these tactical aspirations of the CPI did not fructify. The regional Congress leaders as also Mrs Gandhi had no intention of either organizing joint political actions with the CPI or letting it go down among the people and gain from the political harvest to be reaped from the implementation of the 20-Point Programme. Thus, for instance, the communists were given a very small role—and sometimes none—in the people's committees set up at local level, though on a miniscule scale, to oversee the programme.

As the Congress began to shift to the right, especially after Sanjay Gandhi gained power, the CPI gradually started moving away from unqualified support to the Emergency measures and increasingly became critical of the negative features of government policy, such as attack on the trade unions. It complained of the inadequate and tardy implementation of the pro-rural poor aspects of the 20-Point Programme and of the active role of landlords and other rural elite in this regard. It complained of Sanjay Gandhi's 5-Point Programme having replaced the 20-Point Programme. It continuously made muted criticism of the abuses and excesses of the Emergency and tried to seek Mrs Gandhi's and other ministers' intervention. It objected to large-scale concessions being given to the private sector, especially in the 1976 budget. It organized a one-day country-wide strike against the ordinance issued in September 1975, reducing and eventually stopping the minimum guaranteed bonus to industrial workers. In January 1976, it advised the government to lift the Emergency by early 1976 and to hold general elections on the due date. It later criticized the second postponement of general elections in November 1976, as a grave misuse of the Emergency. It opposed the demand for the convening of a constituent assembly being orchestrated by Sanjay Gandhi and Bansi Lal. While supporting the Forty-second Constitution Amendment Bill, it objected to several of its draconian clauses. It also bemoaned, and to a limited extent opposed, the extra-constitutional authority of Sanjay Gandhi and his coterie and their activities. By the end of 1976, the CPI's discomfort had considerably increased and it was talking of the growing powers of a 'reactionary caucus' within the Congress. Its General Secretary, C. Rajeshwar Rao, went to the extent of writing that 'the main thrust of reaction is now coming from inside the Congress'.[67] Even so, the CPI continued to support the government and the Emergency.

The ambivalence of the CPI and its critical attitude towards Sanjay Gandhi led the latter and many of the Congress leaders to openly attack the party[68] and even get some of its activists arrested. Even Mrs Gandhi started distancing herself from CPI. On 4 October 1976, in a letter to C. Rajeshwar Rao, she complained against 'the manner in which your party is working against us' and said: 'Last time also I specifically told you about the CPI's opposition to our family planning programme. This is now reaching limits which cannot coexist with cooperation with us.'[69] Accusing the communists of having collaborated with the British against the Congress and those fighting in the Quit India movement, she also complained that the CPI was interfering in the Congress party's internal affairs and had launched a full-scale attack on Sanjay and added she saw this as really an attack on her.[70] Subsequently, she did try to soften the blow by saying that the CPI had not gone against the concept of independence and was not nation's enemy, and the CPI, too, made attempts to mend fences by saying that the party would support the 5-Point Programme and that unity with the Congress was essential.[71] By January 1977, however, the bonhomie between the two had come under severe strain and the rift between them had widened into a chasm, at least so far as Congress leaders were concerned.

Vinoba Bhave was an institution by himself and a barometer of a major strand of political opinion. Despite his differences with JP, he remained a guide and philosopher with regard to Gandhian opinion, which no Gandhian or Sarvodayite could easily ignore. Even the two groups of Sarvodayites that emerged during the JP movement (see Chapter 3), and were at loggerheads, continued to respect Vinoba and tried to win him over to their side. At the beginning, Vinoba seemed to be supporting the Emergency when he declared the period to be *Anushashanparva* or 'an era of discipline', though he did not clearly say that discipline was to be imposed by the government. This statement, widely reported in the Press, was used by the government and reproduced on huge posters and even on postage stamps. Also, soon after, Indira Gandhi visited Vinoba Bhave at his ashram at Paunar, near Nagpur, on 7 September and promised to take up prohibition, one of his pet projects, for implementation.

Vinoba's expressed concern over JP's health probably influenced the government's decision to release him. On his release, Vinoba sent him a message indirectly suggesting that he should cease to concern himself with worldly affairs. All the same, Vinoba was keen to bring together the ruling and opposition parties in the interests of healthy national development. He, therefore, asked Shriman Narayan to organize a conference of *acharyas* or learned men to objectively take stock of the situation in the country and suggest ways and means of improving it. Their unanimous recommendations would then be put before Mrs Gandhi. The *acharyas*—prominent vice-chancellors, professors, writers, jurists (including Justice Shah who later headed the Shah Inquiry Commission to investigate the Emergency) and social workers, none of whom were involved in active politics or had party affiliation—met from 16 to 18 January 1976 under Vinoba Bhave's guidance. They issued a carefully worded, balanced and unanimous statement, parts of which read as follows:[72]

> Without seeking to apportion blame for past events, the Sammelan (conference) considers that it is now imperative to initiate a process of normalizing the situation and creating a climate of unity and cooperation within the country so that, in the words of the Prime Minister, 'democracy could be put back on the rails'.

The Sammelan appreciated a number of constructive developments in recent months, following the declaration of the Emergency, notably, greater concern for the needs of the poorer sections of the population, calm in educational institutions, improved industrial relations, containment of inflation, effective action against smuggling, hoarding and black money, absence of communal, regional and linguistic tensions, improved economic management and administration. At the same time, the Sammelan felt that the detention of large numbers of social and political workers who fully believed in *ahimsa* and *sarvadharma sambhava* (equal respect for all faiths), curtailment of civil liberties, and press censorship, including the coverage of parliamentary proceedings, were not good for the health of the nation, if continued indefinitely. . . .

> . . . in the overall national interest, the time has come to reverse some of the recent trends. A fresh start is essential so that the Emergency could be ended and, at the same time, the gains made could be maintained and consolidated. . . . It is desirable to bring about normalcy through a series of steps to create necessary conditions for holding the next General Election as early as feasible.

The *acharyas* had tried to tread the middle ground but seemed to suggest that the Emergency had outlived its use. They had, for example, also said: 'Time is of the essence and undue delay may worsen the situation leading to untoward developments.'[73]

Finding that the government was not receptive to the acharyas' advice, Vinoba decided to convene a larger conference of them sometime in June, with one acharya coming from each district. But the proposal did not fructify; on 16 April 1976, he suddenly announced his decision to take up the issue of a complete ban on cow slaughter. He also declared on 31 May that from 11 September he would go on an indefinite fast over this issue. Two diverse explanations for Vinoba's change of front have been offered. One, that he did not persist with the course indicated by the acharyas and took up an otherwise irrelevant and inconsequential issue because 'that would have involved open confrontation with Indiraji and open association with the movement of resistance led by Jayaprakashji'; he was, thus, indulging in diversionary tactics;[74] the other that his fresh action represented a veiled criticism of the continuation of the Emergency and that he 'was contemplating a test of the sincerity of the Prime Minister's claims.'[75]

Vinoba Bhave's announcement regarding his fast was published in the Ashram's Hindi monthly, *Maitri*, but was censored in the main newspapers. Moreover, the police raided the ashram and confiscated over 4,000 copies of *Maitri*. Simultaneously, Mrs Gandhi decided to placate Vinoba and announced the government's intention to pass legislation in consultation with states, banning cow slaughter in most of them. This satisfied Vinoba who decided to give up the proposed fast and declared in a message on 8 September: 'The problem of ban on cow slaughter in India is, by and large, solved. The credit goes to 1. the God; 2. Mother Rukmini (his mother); 3. Gandhiji; 4. Indiraji. The first three are in heaven. Indiraji is on earth. Thanks to Indiraji! Ram Hari.'[76]

Vinoba called another conference of the Sarvodayites from all over India at Paunar from 23 to 25 December 1976. Here he renounced all public activity for the rest of his life. He also advised the delegates to 'give up petty things of politics' and to concentrate their energies on 'enhancing friendship and love' and 'on the 20-Point programme and other items of constructive work enunciated by Gandhiji'.[77]

VI

We may now turn to the response of social classes and groups. As brought out in Chapter 2, the Indian capitalists had felt constrained by Indira Gandhi's economic policies during 1969-73 and were suspicious of her government. While they had, by and large, supported the 'Grand Alliance' of the right-wing opposition parties in 1971, they had been cautious in their approach to the government during 1973-75. As a matter of fact, many of the large capitalists had gone on 'investment strike' against the government's anti-big business policies. Mrs Gandhi too, having seen the negative political and economic consequences of antagonizing the capitalist class during 1973-75 as a result of some of her radical measures—designed to control the growth of big business—and her radical rhetoric, decided to return to the pre-1971 economic policies, of relying upon the cooperation of the capitalists in economic development. She realized that imposition of the Emergency was not enough and that the government must overcome the economic crisis which had fuelled the JP movement and the popular unrest of the years after 1972.

She now decided to follow economic policies which above all favoured acceleration of economic growth and, in particular, faster expansion of industrial production and exports. Inevitably, this required greater scope for growth of the private sector, and therefore a business-friendly environment, even while maintaining the active role of the public sector and the basic contours of a mixed economy. The new policies marked the beginnings of what later came to be known as liberalization. Simultaneously, the Emergency witnessed a reduction in the level of radical rhetoric.

Aware of the hostility of the capitalists, Mrs Gandhi tried to win them over. At the very outset of the Emergency, in her broadcast of 27 June, she declared that the government had no plans for further nationalization of industries or of imposing drastic fresh controls on the private sector. In her next broadcast, on 1 July, she promised simplification of licencing procedures and raising of the investment limit in some industries.[78]

A spate of concessions and incentives to the corporate industrial sector followed. Emphasis was placed on improvement in industrial relations, labour discipline and efficiency in production. Strikes were virtually banned. While lock-outs and closures were also prohibited, in practice, they were overlooked. By an ordinance in September 1975, the minimum annual bonus guaranteed to workers was cut by half, from 8.33 per cent of the annual wage to 4 per cent. Later, it was decreed that it was not necessary for firms not making profit to pay any bonus. Moreover, bonus was to be linked to productivity. There was also a gradual easing of restrictions on the growth and functioning of the large business houses. They were now permitted to enter some of the industrial areas which had been prohibited to them earlier. Licencing restrictions in some areas were relaxed. Procedures for regularization of unauthorized capacity installed by certain big capitalist houses and foreign companies were also liberalized. Financial incentives were provided to exporters, and restrictions on imports of spare parts, components and machinery and raw materials were eased to some extent.

As part of the effort to curb inflation, a ceiling of 12 per cent had been laid down in 1974 on payment of dividends and curbs placed on issue of bonus shares by companies, besides restrictions on workers' wages, dearness allowance and bonus. While the latter restrictions continued, the ceiling on payment of dividends and the curbs on the issue of bonus shares were later relaxed in order to boost the share market.

The budget for 1976-77, presented on 15 March 1976, aimed at increasing industrial production and gave several concessions to the capitalists. Among these were: reduction in the maximum marginal rate of income tax from 77 per cent to 66 per cent for incomes of over Rs. 1 lakh, and in the rates of wealth tax; revival of development rebate in the form of investment allowance to certain priority, especially export-oriented, industries; certain tax reliefs to them and such as reduction in the tax on royalties earned by them and in tax burden on dividends received by them; also reduction in excise duty on televisions, cars and their accessories, such as tyres, tubes and batteries, water coolers, refrigerators and several other consumer products. In March 1976, Foreign Exchange Regulation Act (FERA) was amended so as to provide slightly greater scope for foreign capital.

The industrialists, in particular, were on the whole satisfied with the Emergency regime and supported it. They were primarily interested in faster economic development, albeit on capitalist lines, and the maintenance of the existing social order. The Emergency regime did not challenge the latter and was fully committed to the former. The industrialists were also much more interested in social discipline in general and in labour discipline in particular and a favourable political, administrative and economic climate. All of this was now at hand. They were also not opposed to, or unhappy with, the disciplining of the unruly elements of the capitalist class, such as tax evaders, hoarders, speculators, blackmarketeers and smugglers. The growing dominance of Sanjay Gandhi with his anti-communist views and pro-free enterprise pronouncements further allayed their fears.

But the commercial, speculative and rentier elements of the capitalist class were unhappy with the record of the government during the Emergency. Also, to a certain extent, Sanjay Gandhi's urban beautification campaign hurt traders and shopkeepers and not only hawkers, and others such.

While some big industrialists such as K.K. Birla and J.R.D. Tata were enthusiastic about the concessions given to the corporate sector and about the budget of 1976-77, the capitalists as a whole, while welcoming them, reacted cautiously. After all, no capitalist group or big capitalist had demanded before 26 June the imposition of the Emergency or an Emergency-type authoritarian regime. A large number of them, even while supporting the Emergency regime, did not fully trust Mrs Gandhi and retained their pre-1975 suspicion of her. She had not only allied with the CPI but had made too many anti-big business pronouncements since 1969, and even during the Emergency. Happy with the Emergency as long as it lasted, the capitalists would have preferred in her place a conservative political leader like Morarji Desai. This was borne out when many of them turned against her during the 1977 elections and backed the Janata Party.

The working class was 'disciplined' during the Emergency and was on the whole politically passive as well as in the work place. As indicated earlier, strikes were virtually banned; and protest meetings and demonstrations against the management not permitted. Consequently, there was a drastic reduction in the number of work-days lost due to strikes in industry. From 40.3 million in 1974, their number came down to 21.9 million in 1975 and 12.8 million in 1976. Lock outs, lay-offs and retrenchment, though prohibited, occurred on a large scale since employers freely took recourse to them and workers were unable to protest and the administration turned a blind eye. During the first year of the Emergency over 800,000 workers were thrown out of employment, primarily in the unorganized manufacturing sector. Also as we have already seen, the minimum guaranteed bonus of the workers was first cut and then abolished; bonus was tied instead to productivity and profit. On the other hand, the impounding of half of their Dearness Allowance under the Compulsory Deposit Scheme continued.

Still, despite all these steps, there was not much discontent among workers or protest by them during this period. This was partly because the authoritarian character of the Emergency made protest difficult. The penalty for any protest was quite high and could range from arrest to loss of the job. Some of the trade union leaders and militant workers who tried to organize protests were arrested and often detained under MISA and DIR. Some of the trade union offices in different parts of the country were sealed. Also, three of the five major trade-union organizations, namely, the All India Trade Union Congress (AITUC), Indian National Trade Union Congress (INTUC) and Hind Mazdoor Sabha (HMS), were supporting the Emergency, even if they were unhappy with certain of the government's labour policies and the employers' anti-worker measures.

Moreover, because of economistic orientation, workers and trade unions, with the exception of CPI-led AITUC, had not intervened in the political crisis of 1974-75 and had remained utterly inactive. Their activity had been reduced to militancy on economic issues. The suppression of the railway strike in early 1974 had also demoralized workers. In any case large segments of the working class were unorganized and fragmented as they were employed in small industrial units and, therefore, were outside the purview of the government's labour legislation, and its regulations regarding bonuses and strikes.

Also responsible for the workers' inactivity was the fact that their existing living standards had not been affected, except in the case of bonus, but that concerned only those working in loss-making industrial units. On the contrary, because of fall in prices, real wages of workers, both in the organized and unorganized sectors, had increased by over 13 per cent in 1975-76 after having fallen constantly from 1972-73 to 1974-75.

Moreover, certain measures taken during the initial period of the Emergency, such as pushing down of prices, greater social discipline, especially in schools, colleges and government offices, and less corruption in government offices, did benefit the workers as citizens. On the other hand, excesses of the family planning programme and slum clearance did not much affect the organized working class since they were not targetted in these programmes. Even so, the workers—and their leaders—too started becoming restive during the latter part of the Emergency, with strikes occurring in different parts of the country. As pointed out earlier, even in 1976, during the heyday of the Emergency, twelve million work-days were lost because of strikes. Even earlier, all-India trade unions had together organized a one-day strike against the bonus ordinance.

The rich peasants, especially in North India, were antagonized by the Emergency. Their opposition was to find reflection in the March elections to the Lok Sabha. They were the main beneficiaries of land reforms as well as of the policies of agricultural development since the fifties, including, in particular, the Green Revolution. Yet, most of them, carrying the middle peasants with them because of caste ties and common aspirations and outlook, had been already deserting the Congress in the Hindi-speaking states, Punjab and Gujarat since the sixties. These peasant strata had been over time 'acquiring' their 'own' lower-middle class as also intelligentsia and been represented by parties such as the BKD (later BLD), Akali Dal and Lohia socialists. They also controlled the votes of many marginal farmers and agricultural labourers dependent on them. Next to the urban petty bourgeoisie, rich peasants and their progenies had formed the backbone of the JP movement.

The rich peasants were the primary surplus farmers in the countryside. Since 1974, and during the Emergency, they were denied increased procurement prices for their agricultural produce and were told to enhance their income through higher production. This affected them adversely. They were further antagonized by the rural segment of the 20-Point Programme, aimed at poor peasants and agricultural labourers. Even though it was implemented to a very limited extent, the possibilities were frightening. The possibility of land ceiling laws being implemented, the payment of enhanced minimum wages to agricultural labourers, the release of bonded labourers and remission of rural debt, held mainly by them, would hurt them badly, as would dehoarding of agricultural produce in the long run.

In the North, alienation of the rich peasants from the Congress and Mrs Gandhi for class reasons, starting in the sixties, was more or less completed during 1975-77. But the process had just begun in the South and got aggravated only in the eighties.

However, even in the North, the rich peasants still controlled the rural administration including the panchayats; they could command the old as well as the new emergency powers wielded by the police and the village and taluka level officials. The local Congress leaders, too, tended to conciliate them and represent their interests at the state level. The rich peasants remained the base of the government's strategy of agricultural development, and it could not ignore their interests for that reason also. It had, in fact, to cater to them.

I may point out, parenthetically, that the attempt, however half-hearted, to implement land ceiling laws and thus virtually destroy the rich peasantry was basically foolhardy.[79]

The relative non-implementation of the 20-Point Programme and the absence of any mobilization of the marginal farmers and the rural landless kept the rural poor, which formed the main political base of Congress and Mrs Gandhi, politically inactive, except in Kerala; to a large extent they continued to be subject to the vote-bank politics of the rich peasants and other large landowners.

The rural poor would also not favour authoritarian rule which enhanced their oppression by police, lower bureaucracy and the rural rich. Along with the urban poor, they were also the main victims of the sterilization drive excesses in North India. Many suffered and many more believed the widely-circulated rumours of what was happening to their kind in the villages. Large segments of the rural poor turned sullen and became indifferent. Others turned hostile. In March 1977, they hit back.

The urban middle classes, the main social base of the JPM, politically the most volatile and most affected by inflation and scarcity of goods, in the initial stages of the Emergency welcomed the fall in prices, the anti-corruption measures and social and administrative discipline, especially of others. Mrs Gandhi also tried to placate them through concessions. Shortly following declaration of the Emergency, on 1 July, she declared that the minimum exemption limit for income tax would be raised from Rs. 6,000 to Rs. 8,000. Several concessions in the 1976 budget, for example, reduction of excise duties on the sale of the lower end of refrigerators and TV sets, supply of books and stationery to students at controlled prices and the new apprenticeship scheme, were aimed at the middle classes. But over time, large sections of this stratum were alienated from Mrs Gandhi because of the denial of civil liberties, especially freedom of the Press, and of democracy in general. After all, they had been deeply influenced by the emphasis on democracy by the national movement and by political parties and the educational system after 1947. Also, the meagre concessions given to the government employees did not compensate for the oppression they felt because of the discipline imposed on them. Several sections of the salaried middle classes—school teachers, municipal employees, and the like—were also severely harassed during the vasectomy campaign and became disgruntled.

VII

The role of the intellectuals during the Emergency was complex. They were quite divided in their reaction to and attitude towards the Emergency regime except near its end. In general, they did not speak up against the Emergency or resign their jobs in protest: teachers continued to teach, journalists to produce dailies and weeklies, poets and writers to publish, actors to perform, bureaucrats to obey orders, judges to pass judgements and lawyers to practise law. But to see in this behaviour cowardice, as some commentators did during 1977-78, would be, in my view, simplistic and erroneous. For example, Arun Shourie wrote in 1977 that intellectuals 'lacked even the most elementary courage . . . collapsed without struggle in the face of the mildest possible dictatorship . . . were almost totally ineffective.'[80] Kuldip Nayar's indictment was equally severe: 'Here were the best of intellectuals—educationists, jurists, civil servants, doctors, lawyers and so on—but most of them preferred to keep quiet.'[81]

Conformism and cowardice of the intellectuals is to be decried whether it occurs under normal democratic conditions or an abnormal authoritarian situation. But this kind of indictment of the Indian intellectuals' behaviour during the Emergency is not entirely warranted. The reality was much more complex and nuanced; perhaps, it was even very different from what the critics have alleged.

It is true that there was no large-scale protest against the imposition of the Emergency or its unfolding dark record. At the same time, it has to be noted that hardly a handful of intellectuals of any substance or influence gave public support to it. Moreover, a small section of the intelligentsia willingly supported or was sympathetic to it on political-ideological grounds as, along with or under the influence of the Congress and the CPI, they believed that the Emergency was necessary to meet the threat of fascism, communalism and foreign penetration. This stand was not necessarily an outcome of expediency, taken because of actual, or expectation of, material gain or the desire to kow-tow before the authorities, though as in normal times an element of that was also present.

Many intellectuals sat on the fence. They were very much influenced by the same factors which affected the ordinary citizens, as brought out above in sections IV and V of Chapter 7. However, they were unwilling to support the Emergency despite government's efforts to persuade them to give it public support. According to Inder Malhotra, 'As there was an outburst of shock over, and criticism of, the suspension of democracy by Indira the world over, her emissaries tried hard to get a statement signed by Satyajit Ray, the famous film director, and other eminent authors, professors and scientists to the effect that the Emergency was necessary. . . . No one with a reputation to lose was prepared to sign it.'[82] That there was large-scale shouting of slogans in favour of Indira Gandhi by intellectuals or gleeful, enthusiastic support for her, is, to our knowledge, not borne out by evidence. Many among them kept quiet and waited believing that the Emergency would not last long. Many made a difference between the authoritarianism of the Emergency and the dictatorship which they had read about in fascist Germany, Italy or Japan. Many were not willing to believe that Mrs Gandhi was becoming, or could become, a dictator or fascist. Moreover, many even among those unhappy with the Emergency and critical of Mrs Gandhi were not her opponents; they were willing to wait and give Mrs Gandhi a chance to prove her democratic credentials. However, with the second postponement of elections and the introduction of the forty-second constitutional amendment the patience of many of them was exhausted.

Undoubtedly, fear and anxiety about personal security affected a large section of the intelligentsia—more middle class than intelligentsia. But it was fear of the unknown, fear produced by lack of comprehension of what was happening and of the character of the Emergency and its implication for them, fear of what arrest under Emergency would mean. Up to now, for most protesting teachers, students, journalists, professionals courting arrest meant detention during the day and being let off in the evening or next morning, without any charges being framed against them. But now people were being arrested without possibility of trial, under MISA or DIR. This was a new situation and it would take time for people to get used to it. At the same time, fear did not make many ordinary teachers or journalists or professionals or judges vocal supporters of the Emergency. Nor is it true that there was, as suggested by JP, a large-scale shift of intellectual opinion away from the the JP movement. This was for the simple reason that very few intellectuals had supported JPM at any stage.

Moreover, many of the fence-sitters turned against Mrs Gandhi as time passed and the ugly face of the Emergency regime began to surface. They were to play an important role in the defeat of Congress in the elections of March 1977.

In any case, a large number of intellectuals were opposed to the Emergency from the beginning. But they were also critical of the alternative, the Janata Morcha of JP and the opposition parties. This attitude of many of them, of 'curse on both houses', was put very well by Rajni Kothari, one of India's leading intellectuals and a strong critic of the Emergency, in an article in the *Seminar* of January 1976:[83]

> Together, the actions of the opposition and the government signalled a breakdown of the basic consensus that had informed more than twenty-five years of democratic functioning ... There were some who thought that neither the opposition nor the government really cared for the people and that it was all a game of power within a narrow elite which had lost all contact with the people ... This feeling ... increased sharply during 1975 as the show of power on both sides transcended the bounds of propriety and decency and as the political process came to be dominated by new cliques of self-styled leaders who indulged in raw and naked means of demonstrating their power ... In point of fact, however, the situation was somewhat improving just at the time when the opposition decided to adopt an aggressive posture and the government over-reacted to it ... (after the Allahabad judgement) the opposition went for Mrs Gandhi's blood and the government responded by virtually suspending the Constitution ... a climate of confrontation was being built up—and continuously aggravated—over a much longer time ... Two inter-related aspects of this were a basic transformation of the power structure within the Congress ... and a highly frustrated opposition incapable of making itself felt through the parliamentary system and taking recourse to the politics of the street for bringing down duly constituted governments and elected legislatures. While radicals in the Congress (backed by the CPI and its fellow travellers) succeeded in manipulating State politics and backing corrupt politicians in Congress governments and ad hoc PCCs in the States, the opposition looked for shortcuts to bringing down elected governments and legislatures, often supporting violent and strong arm tactics of youthful rebels who knew not what they were doing.

Kothari also made a critique of long-term trends and distortions in the Indian political and administrative system that contributed to the crisis of 1975, the decline of institutions, the rise of arbitrary power, the Opposition's consuming passion to remove Mrs Gandhi from power and the steady erosion of confidence in the system. On the basis of his analysis, he concluded that the Emergency or its prolongation or the postponement of elections or 'the atmosphere of fear and repression that has been unleashed by the new bearers of power' were 'no answer to the crisis that we face' and the need was for the 'basic restructuring' of the system. He also condemned the contemporary efforts by Bansi Lal and others of 'turning upside down the present constitution and the noble principles on which it is based.'

The critics of the Emergency regime, however, did not know how to oppose it, or how to on their own offer effective resistance against it. Historically, except for a rare individual, intellectuals have stood up to an authoritarian regime only as participants in a movement of protest or resistance. But there was no such movement in sight in 1975 or 1976. As pointed out earlier, none of the opposition parties, from the Jan Sangh and the BLD to the CPM and the Naxalites, were yet ready to launch a movement against the government or its excesses; they all waited for the trend of events to become clear. And so did most of the intellectuals. Moreover, many agreed with the assessment of the CPM and others that democracy had been set aside for some time to come, a long era of totalitarianism had dawned, the struggle for restoration of democracy was going to be a long one, and the opponents of the regime must, therefore, conserve and harness their energy and resources to strike at the right moment and not act in haste. Meanwhile, the intellectuals were expected not to collaborate with the authoritarian regime and its dark deeds, for example helping implement censorship of the Press, informing on colleagues and extending assistance to the vasectomy drive. And, to their credit, very few intellectuals collaborated. As in the case of India's national liberation struggle, the intellectuals could have initiated and led a movement against the Emergency. But that would have taken years, if not decades, and the Emergency ended in ninteen months! Meanwhile, they could at best issue statements. But Press censorship took care of that.

Most of the Emergency's critics then often expressed their anger and resentment in private and waited for the right moment to voice it in public. A result of this resentment was that the Congress lost face and support among the intelligentsia. This was to have long-term political consequences, for after all the intelligentsia had been the leader of India's anti-imperialist national liberation struggle and had provided a major thrust to post-independence India's economic and social developmental effort.

Thus, though very few intellectuals openly defied or critiqued the Emergency regime, their opposition took the form of not joining the ranks of its supporters, keeping their distance from it and foregoing any material or professional gains that would accrue with support. This was noted at the time by the *Marxist Review*, edited by Ajit Roy: 'Even our not very heroic intelligentsia, including academics, lawyers, and other intellectuals, with a few inglorious exceptions, have refused to succumb to either intimidations or temptations but have maintained a healthy distance from the bandwagon of the ruling coterie.'[84] Many would also agree with the cartoonist Abu Abraham's statement: 'To the question: "What did you do in the Great Emergency?" my simple answer is I remained myself.'[85]

Another form of resistance that many adopted was that of opposing specific actions of the regime at their work place or at the individual level or in their organizations. We may give a few examples. The Indian History Congress passed a resolution at its annual session in December 1975 protesting against the arrest of one of its members, L.B. Kenny, who was scheduled to read a paper in the session. The Indian Political Science Association followed suit. The Executive Committee of the Bombay University Teachers' Union passed a resolution protesting against the arrest of two of its office-bearers. The Maharashtra Bar Association and several other state Bar Associations passed resolutions condemning repressive laws. In Delhi, the Congress candidate for presidentship of the High Court Bar Association was defeated and P.N. Lekhi, at that time a prisoner in Tihar Jail, was elected. Similarly, the Delhi District Bar Association elected another anti-Congress lawyer, Kunwar Lal Sharma, as its president. The Supreme Court Bar Association passed a resolution arguing against any constitutional amendment during the Emergency. The famous Marathi writer Durga Bhagwat was arrested for denouncing Press censorship when presiding over the Marathi Sahitya Sammelan in September 1976. Uma Shankar Joshi, one of India's leading writers, opposed the Emergency in the Rajya Sabha, of which he was a nominated member. In Jawaharlal Nehru University (JNU), several departments successfully opposed the Vice-Chancellor's attempt to interfere with the admission process. Subsequently, in November 1975, when the students went on a three-day strike and the Vice-Chancellor asked for the names of absentee students, the teachers unanimously refused to oblige. The Academic Council of the University also refused to endorse the UGC-sponsored code of conduct for the teachers.

However, it needs to be said that the mettle of the university and college teachers was not really tested because the government made no attempt at thought control or to interfere with courses, teaching or research. Nor did teachers usually protest unless the authorities took overt action in their institutions. Still, the charge of cowardice might stick in cases where non-cooperation or resistance was possible but was not undertaken. Limited discussion with teachers of several universities would indicate that such cooperation with the authorities was rare, partly because the latter did not demand it.

So far as journalists were concerned, a large number took a heroic stand at the outset. A hundred of them met at the Press Club in Delhi on 29 June and passed a resolution deploring 'the imposition of censorship', urging the government 'to remove it immediately' and demanding 'the release of journalists already detained.'[86] But, as in the case of teachers, fear gripped them when Kuldip Nayar, who had organized the gathering at the Press Club and sponsored the resolution, was arrested (he was released only after fifty-seven days) and the government took harsh measures against dissident newspapers. Thereafter, most journalists mellowed and dutifully accepted the government-sponsored code of ethics, which did not include the phrase 'freedom of the Press'. Later on not even half-a-dozen of the journalists who had passed the resolution on 29 June at the Press Club agreed to repeat it. Forty-seven editors—most of them inconsequential—belonging to the All India Newspapers Editors' Conference, Sikh Press Association, Urdu Editors Conference, All India Industrial Editors Council and All India Small and Medium Newspapers Association, met Mrs Gandhi on 9 July 1975 and assured her of their support. But then, like many other intellectuals, there were journalists such as N.J. Nanporia, editor of the *Statesman*, or Girilal Jain of the *Times of India* who supported the Emergency because they were convinced of its necessity in view of the political situation preceding it. However, no respected journalist agreed to sign a statement in favour of the Emergency. Some journalists did of course 'crawl' and went out of their way to curry favour with the authorities. Editors of a few weeklies glorified the Emergency and gave undue publicity to it, or showered praise in extravagant language on Sanjay Gandhi. But most others felt that they could not defy the law of the land and had no choice but to work within the limits of censorship laws. Accordingly, most journalists carried on their day-to-day activities, but did so sullenly and in guarded language, treading warily even when censorship was relaxed in the second half of the Emergency.

A few brave journalists carried on as long as they could within the constraints of censorship rules, though often clashing with the censors and receiving repeated warnings, and then rebelling when pressed too hard. For example, the satirist 'Cho' Ramaswamy, editor of the fortnightly *Tughlak*, suspended its publication when served a pre-censorship order on 25 July 1975 requiring submission of the manuscripts to the censor's approval before publication. Romesh Thapar carried on with the monthly *Seminar* till July 1976, obeying the censorship rules. But when he was asked to submit to pre-censorship he preferred to close down the journal. The weekly *Mainstream*, edited by Nikhil Chakravartty, often clashed with the censor for its carefully crafted comments; it also received pre-censorship orders on 10 December 1976 and its printing press was given a warning. It, too, decided to stop publication from 1 January 1977. E. Narayanan, managing director of the *Patriot*, was a supporter of the Emergency, but he refused to print news about Sanjay Gandhi, as he had no political standing. The *Patriot* was thereafter denied government and private advertisements but Narayanan did not budge. The fortnightly *Opinion*, edited by A.D. Gorwala, repeatedly had trouble with the authorities and was harassed until in May 1976 they ordered its closure on the ground that it was a danger to public safety, public order and internal security. Several other English and Indian language weeklies also came to harm because of censorship. The reputed *Economic and Political Weekly* and the monthly *Marxist Review* continued to be published throughout 1975-77, but though they did not directly criticize or condemn the Emergency, they did not compromise with their independence either.

The judiciary and the legal profession had quite a praiseworthy record during the Emergency. Though many judges fell in line, a significant number of High Court judges heroically resisted government pressure and stood up for citizens' civil rights, however truncated, especially the freedom of the Press. They upheld the right of judicial review in the cases that came before them. Though constrained by ordinances and constitutional amendments, which reduced space to manoeuvre, they tried to maintain that a citizen could be deprived of his civil liberties only on the basis of reasonable evidence. The government often retaliated by transferring the recalcitrant judges—sixteen of them were transferred—and sometimes reverting them as session judges, but because of long-established tradition, it could not dismiss them. But independent judgements would not have been possible without the large number of independent and equally courageous lawyers who took up civil rights cases. The latter had the advantage of their profession being an independent one whereby their livelihood did not depend on the government. I may point out that it is for this reason that lawyers had, unlike academics, played such an important role in India's freedom struggle. The academics could have done so only by resigning their job; the lawyers could do so while continuing practice.

Among the judges who stood up to the authorities were Justice Sesha Rangarajan and R.N. Agarwal of the Delhi High Court, who accepted Kuldip Nayar's appeal in September 1975. For this, the former was transferred and the latter reverted as sessions judge. In his judgment R.N. Agarwal had held that 'the executive has no absolute power to deprive a person of personal liberties' and that 'an order of detention under MISA would be beyond challenge only if is passed under the law.'[87] Rangarajan had stated that the courts retained the right to review detention cases even under the Emergency and that 'the rule of law will not permit arbitrary executive action.'[88]

More instances of the courageous stand taken by some judges can be cited. Justice J.R. Vimaldalal and Krishna Gawde of the Bombay High Court stood up for the rights of the detenus to a decent treatment in jail. Acting Chief Justice V.D. Tulzapurkar upheld the right of lawyers to hold a private meeting to discuss civil liberties and the rule of law under the Constitution.[89] The Bombay High Court struck down the censor's order banning two articles by Y.D. Lokurkar titled 'Pre-censorship: Nature and Scope' and 'Emergency situation and courts'. Justices V.D. Tulzapurkar and N.C. Gadgil of Bombay High Court quashed the order closing down the Sadhna Printing Press of Poona for publishing the *Sadhna* Weekly. According to their judgment, 'As a citizen the writer is entitled to criticize the policies and measures adopted by the Government during the Emergency and also say that these are suggestive of fascist trends' unless the article tended 'to create disorder or disturbance of law and order'.[90]

Minoo Masani, as editor of the monthly *Freedom First*, had filed a case against the actions of the censor in deleting eleven items from the copy of his journal submitted for pre-censorship. In his judgement, Justice D.P. Madan of Bombay High Court held that it was not for the censor 'to exercise his statutory powers to force public opinion in a single mould or to turn the Press into an instrument of brainwashing the public. Under the censorship order the censor is appointed as the nursemaid of democracy and not its gravedigger.'[91] Earlier, in the case of the censorship and forfeiture order passed on the publisher of the Sarvodayite periodical *Bhumiputra* of Baroda in November 1975, Justices J.B. Mehta and S.H. Sheth of the High Court had struck down the order and maintained: 'Whereas the Government owes a duty to the nation to curb the violent and marauding activities of its opponents, the Opposition must be vigilant to see that in the name of curbing such activities, the ruling party does not destroy the foundations of democracy and assume a dictatorial or authoritarian form.' Condemning the chief censor's guidelines, the judgement stated: 'There cannot be a more draconian assault on people in a democracy than one which is disclosed by the guidelines.'[92] Justice Sheth was immediately transferred to Hyderabad.

The higher bureaucracy, both civil and military, also, like the higher judiciary, form part of the intelligentsia. Some observers have severely condemned their role during the Emergency. T.N. Seshan, himself a bureaucrat who later became India's Chief Election Commissioner, has, for example, written: 'The bureaucracy, for the most part, utterly caved in. It carried out illegal orders, accepted transfers of upright officers without a murmur of protest, collaborated in the massive detentions of opposition leaders, the temporary destruction of civil liberties and assisted, almost gleefully, in the gagging of the press.'[93]

This should not be accepted at face value. Invariably, with the exception of many of the orders emanating from the Prime Minister's House (PMH) and Sanjay Gandhi, the instructions the bureaucracy obeyed and the policies it carried out without resistance or opposition during the Emergency were legal according to the Constitution, whatever their deficiencies from the point of view of democracy. The approach of the bureaucracy, built into its structure, training and tradition, hinged on the dual principle that responsibility for making policies lay with the elected representatives of the people or the duly and constitutionally constituted executive authority, while the onus and duty for the implementation of these policies, under the supervision of the political executive, was that of the bureaucracy, though within the ambit of the legal and bureaucratic procedures laid down by the Constitution and the administrative manual. The position of the bureaucracy in this respect was not very different from that of the judiciary, as the independent judges, too, did not denounce the Emergency as such but decided on constitutional grounds that certain acts of the government were illegal even within the confines of the Emergency and Emergency legislation.

The real question, therefore, is how many persons belonging to the higher bureaucracy went beyond the call of duty and bureaucratic rules and ethos to implement orders from above during the Emergency, especially when illegally transmitted, in order to win favour of the higher authorities. In other words, what was the extent of moral corruption among them?

Considered in this perspective, the majority of civil servants did resist the pressure they were subjected to, to function outside the call of duty, and executed orders carefully following the bureaucratic norms.[94] Some of them had to pay a price for standing by the rules and were promptly transferred or harassed—in some cases their homes were raided by income-tax authorities. It is, however, true that most of the bureaucrats did not 'stick their necks out'. The fear that prevailed among the people pervaded the bureaucrats to even a greater extent, especially as nearly 26,000 public servants and public sector employees were prematurely retired on reaching the age of fifty, nearly 4,500 were dismissed and over 8,000 were superseded on grounds of being corrupt or inefficient or belonging secretly to the banned organizations.

However, a small minority among the bureaucrats, especially in the North, did actively collaborate and act as willing tools of the ruling coteries at the Centre and in the states. They functioned outside rules and often broke them to placate ministers and others in power. Most despicable was their habit of obeying oral orders both of the legitimate authorities as well as of those exercising extra-constitutional power. This phenomenon was to become endemic in later years. Some bureaucrats even agreed to act as the hatchetmen of the Emergency authorities. This was in particular true of several junior officers who agreed to oversee and even lord over their more upright seniors.

Just as before the Emergency, the armed forces remained out of politics. There was no involvement of the armed forces in the Emergency nor was the officer corps affected in any manner by it, except for the supercession of a few high-ranking officers who were suspected of being secret members of the banned organizations. Still, the behaviour and outlook of the military officers continued to be the same as before.

Gradually, over time, large number of intellectuals began to get disillusioned with Indira Gandhi and started turning against the Emergency. Many of even those who had earlier supported it 'got sick of it'.[95] They found demeaning the loss of civil liberties, the vasectomy and slum-clearance excesses, the dynastic overtones, and above all the extra-constitutional power wielded by Sanjay Gandhi and his cronies and the manner in which senior Congress political leaders toadied to him. An increasing number of intellectuals, young and old, found it difficult to support or remain apathetic towards the regime after May 1976 with Sanjay Gandhi's naked exercise of power, and the beginning of the vasectomy drive. This situation was reflected in the comments of the young, twenty-year-old intellectual, Vir Sanghvi, who would later become a leading journalist.[96]

> By 1974, things had begun to go badly wrong: inflation, lawlessness, corruption—these were all on the rise. Still, I retained a sneaking admiration for her (Mrs Gandhi) until 1975, when she declared the Emergency and suspended the Constitution and jailed thousands of her political opponents. Even then, I was prepared to buy her story: that the Opposition through its unruly, disruptive agitations, had left her with no choice. By late 1976, though, when her younger son Sanjay rose to be heir-apparent, it was impossible to defend Indira Gandhi.

Moreover, with the passage of time, Press censorship and loss of civil liberties were seen to be getting institutionalized, and the temporary loss of freedom turning permanent. As B.K. Nehru put it, 'All the institutions of democratic government and civilized progress' which Nehru had 'built up with such infinite care' were being weakened and damaged so as 'to make it almost impossible to restore them.'[97] Many intellectuals started feeling that the slide of the Indian polity towards fascism had begun. A psychological and emotional factor strengthened the growing antagonism of the Indian intellectuals towards the Emergency regime. Despite her abysmal poverty and illiteracy they had taken pride in India being a democracy and considered themselves superior to their counterparts in the Third World on that account. They now experienced a deep sense of loss of this 'one mark of superiority'. Giving vent to this feeling as early as January 1976, Rajni Kothari wrote: India 'is one country that has maintained a democratic structure and ethos over a long period and has strongly believed in its efficacy while most other Third World countries have given in to authoritarian trends. There is no reason why it should follow their example instead of setting an example to them as it did for so long.'[98] Shashi Tharoor also expressed similar feelings as a young student in the US at the time: 'For me, living and studying in America, the discovery that my country, which had so proudly described itself as the world's largest democracy, was now descending into becoming the world's second largest banana republic was more than I could bear.'[99] This sense of shame was to strongly affect those journalists, academics and writers who often came into contact with foreign intellectuals in the course of their work.

The disillusionment and anger of the intelligentsia burst forth as the forty-second constitutional amendment was mooted. The bulk of intellectuals had regarded earlier constitutional amendments and control of the Press as undesirable but temporary aberrations motivated by Mrs Gandhi's desire to meet the threat to herself and the polity. But this amendment, on the other hand, was perceived as one that would permanently dent and alter democratic institutions and the constitutional structure and in time turn India into a totalitarian state and society.

Resistence to this soon gained force. At the end of October 1976, as pointed out earlier, more than 300 of India's leading intellectuals issued, published and circulated in pamphlet form a statement opposing the Forty-second Amendment to the Constitution Bill on the grounds that the existing Lok Sabha having outlived its term had no political or moral authority to enact such fundamental changes in the Constitution. Many of the signatories did not belong to a political party, or had remained 'detached from party politics' and had been sympathetic to Mrs Gandhi earlier because of her efforts at radical transformation of the country and her handling of the Bangladesh crisis.

Interestingly, the vigorous effort of the Congress party and the government to have a counter-mobilization of intellectuals failed miserably. The statement supporting the amendment, issued a few days later, had only sixty signatories, and not even half a dozen were intellectuals of any eminence.

In the end, the widening ranks of the anti-Emergency intellectuals came to include many who were earlier opposed to the JP movement, and were votaries of a strong state which would expedite economic development and who would have been, in normal conditions, enthusiastic about the 20-Point Programme, especially its agrarian component. These were left-wingers and Nehruvians, as also many who had supported the JP movement and had been opposed to Mrs Gandhi since 1969 because of her left-wing measures and pronouncements, or had suspected her sincerity as a champion of the poor and of social change. The common factor was their perception that the Emergency was an assault on democracy and, in particular, on the freedom they had enjoyed earlier to freely and publicly express their opinions. They also came to believe that the attack on democracy would not only have immediate but also long-term negative consequences.

The strong opposition by leading intellectuals to the forty-second amendment and the continuation of the Emergency probably played a role in Indira Gandhi's decision to announce elections on 18 January

1977. She was, during the Emergency, seemingly indifferent to the intelligentsia and, echoing JP, accused it of being unconcerned about Indian conditions and more attentive to what foreigners thought.[100] The fact was she had always been keen to have their support and good opinion.[101] Though not publicly responding to their criticism, she was worried over the silent but growing opposition of the best of India's intellectuals. It was an important reason why she did not permit even Sanjay Gandhi and his coterie to take punitive action against any of the prominent Indian intellectuals, even when they publicly criticized the Emergency measures.

VIII

The imposition of the Emergency had a mixed reaction abroad. The non-aligned states and their leaders, such as Josip Broz Tito continued their existing fraternal relations with India and expressed full understanding of the situation and of the reasons advanced by the Government of India as to why it had come about. Mrs Gandhi played a leading role in the conference of the heads of states of the non-aligned countries, held in Colombo, Sri Lanka, in August 1976.

The Soviet Union and the Socialist bloc of Eastern Europe welcomed the Emergency as representing a defeat of the forces of reaction and destabilization in India. The Soviet and East European press lauded Mrs Gandhi and the 20-Point Programme and condemned the 'rightists' in India, and the 'imperialists' for attempting to upset the Indian government's progressive policies and to destabilize India. North Vietnam and the communist parties the world over adopted a similar approach. The Socialist bloc sent delegates to the World Anti-Fascist Conference held in India on 11 September 1975. Indo-Soviet relations remained close despite Sanjay Gandhi's anti-communist pronouncements. Mrs Gandhi was given a warm welcome when she visited Soviet Union in June 1976.

A major development of the Emergency period was the normalization of India's official relations with China and exchange of ambassadors between the two countries, even though the Chinese press had earlier denounced the imposition of the Emergency in strong language.

Western countries as a whole were critical of the Emergency. Caught totally unawares by the turn of events in June 1975, the initial official approach of the United States and Western European countries was formal—cold and proper—and that of watching and waiting to see what would happen. Moreover, the US government was heavily influenced by Cold War calculations. In any case, since the fifties, India had been seen by US officials and most of India experts as a soft state that had come under Soviet influence and was lost to the Western camp. The Emergency was, therefore, a cause of worry lest India move further left, both in internal and foreign policy. In September 1975, President Ford called off his forthcoming visit to India as a mark of disapproval, pointing out to the Press that 'it was very sad that 600 million people have lost what they had since mid-1940s as I recall.'[102]

There was, however, a difference between the official and non-official liberal political and intellectual opinion in the West on the issue of the Emergency. In contrast to their governments' formal attitude and the policy of wait and see, the liberal democratic press and intelligentsia reacted very strongly and adversely, especially because of the strident control of the Press, detention of thousands without trial and expulsion of foreign correspondents. Unlike their governments, liberal intellectuals and the liberal press had been for years friendly to India and admirers of its democracy in the midst of dictatorships all over the Third World. After the imposition of the Emergency, they became highly critical of Mrs Gandhi, especially as they believed that she had subverted the democratic system just to keep herself in power.

The anger felt by the liberals and the main reasons for it were exemplified by the reaction of Dorothy Norman, biographer of Jawaharlal Nehru and friend of Mrs Gandhi since 1950. Shocked and dismayed, she, along with Sidney Hertzberg, former US correspondent of the *Hindustan Times*, and New York-based Indian writer Ved Mehta, drafted a joint appeal, which was signed by eighty prominent US intellectuals, including Noam Chomsky, Linus Pauling and Allen Ginsberg, and released to the Press, radio and television. The appeal read in part:[103]

> We are distressed by the loss of fundamental human rights in India following the proclamation of a national emergency there on June 25, 1975. We deplore these events, especially in India, because there democracy was established after a long struggle for freedom led by some of the greatest contemporary exponents of human rights, and also because the respect of democratic India for these human rights was for so many years a beacon light for all newly independent and developing countries.

These sentiments were echoed by socialist and labour leaders and liberal newspapers all over Europe and the United States, from Austria to California. There were only a few exceptions. For example, the two well-known Labour Party leaders from Britain, Michael Foot and Jennie Lee, visited India on Mrs Gandhi's invitation and issued statements defending and praising Mrs Gandhi. So did the Conservative leader and the future prime minister of Britain, Margaret Thatcher, after a visit to India.

While many Western liberals were genuinely critical of the Emergency measures and concerned about the emerging authoritarianism in India, others adopted a self-righteous and patronizing attitude of 'we told you so', implying it was inevitable that democracy would fail in India for it was not suited to the genius of a non-Western people. Still others adopted the 'rice bowl theory', that is, a poor, developing country could not afford the luxury of democracy, and that economic well-being was more important to a poor people than civil liberties. The Emergency should, therefore, be judged by its success or failure in the economic field.

With the passage of time, the US government, however, veered round to a more neutral, even friendly, attitude, as it became clear that Indian government had no intention of moving farther left and that there was no change in India's independent foreign policy, despite friendly relations with the Soviet Union. Sanjay Gandhi's emergence as a major force in the government was another reassuring feature. The Government of India too reciprocated for, as V.P. Dutt has pointed out, 'a hostile relationship with the United States was no part of India's foreign policy'.[104] Consequently, there was some improvement in the relationship between the two countries.

The first meeting of the Indo-American Joint Commission, with the two delegations headed by India's foreign minister and the US Secretary of State, took place in Washington in early October 1975. An agreement on cooperation between the two countries on 'education and culture', 'science and technology', and 'trade and investment' was signed. Similarly, India's relations with the major West European powers also showed an improvement.

In time, the banking and financial circles in the West came to appreciate the economic performance and policies of India during the Emergency, as also the new business investment climate prevailing there. In March 1976, the World Bank's annual report on India recommended increased aid to India because conditions in India 'are once again ripe for an upturn in the growth rate of the economy'.[105] It also praised the import and labour policies of the Indian government and its efforts to encourage private investors and control inflation. The changed attitude of the Western financial circles was reflected in the increased quantum of consortium aid, from Rs. 1,069 crores in 1973-74 to Rs. 1,418 crores in 1974-75 and to Rs. 1,565 crores in 1975-76.

Despite her apparent indifference to Western liberal opinion, Mrs Gandhi was quite sensitive to it; their criticism hurt her. However upset she was with them, she wanted their approval; and made every effort to secure it. With this in view, despite her heavy work schedule, she gave long interviews to a large number of western journalists in the very early months of the Emergency.[106]

At the same time, she was quite piqued at the implied criticism by US and other western governments that she was a dictator. She accused them of hypocrisy and practising double standards. She chided them for 'shedding tears for Indian democracy' and criticizing the Emergency, which was of a temporary character, but for years having given moral and material support, by way of money and arms, to brutal military dictatorship throughout Africa, Asia and Latin America.[107] She also referred in this context to the US support to the autocratic Pakistani regime in 1965, as well as at the time of the Bangladesh crisis in 1971.[108] Mrs Gandhi also took note of the fact that just after President Ford's visit to India was cancelled, his visit to China, ruled at the time by the murderous 'Gang of Four', was announced with great fanfare. Whatever the other achievements of China, she said, neither 'the Chinese themselves or anybody have really said they have a democratic system as it is understood in the West. But that is acceptable. But what is happening in India is not acceptable. Now is this intellectual or any other kind of honesty?'[109]

It is interesting that this stand of Mrs Gandhi found resonance among many Indians who were otherwise opposed to her politically. Many Indians also reacted adversely to the patronizing tone of many of the Western critics of the Emergency.[110]

Another factor that prevented close relations between India and the United States was Mrs Gandhi's feeling that because of India's non-alignment and independent foreign policy and her growing strength, Western powers were against India and had always been so. Mrs Gandhi repeatedly charged that foreign intelligence agencies—meaning CIA—were interfering in India's internal affairs and that 'foreign forces'—meaning the USA—were out to disrupt and destabilize India as they had done in the case of Chile with the killing of Allende and, more recently, Bangladesh with the assassination of Mujibur Rahman.

9 *The Emergency Revoked*

In as sudden and dramatic a manner as she had declared the Emergency, Mrs Gandhi, sprung another surprise and announced on 18 January 1977 that the existing Lok Sabha stood dissolved and fresh general elections would be held in March.

Rumours had been circulating in political circles during December 1976 and January 1977 that Mrs Gandhi had been consulting selected Congress leaders in this regard and that elections were around the corner. But few believed these rumours,[1] especially as she had, on 5 November, just got Parliament's approval to postpone general elections for another year. Moreover, it was known that Sanjay Gandhi opposed fresh elections and Bansi Lal had announced as late as 7 January 1977 that the Emergency would continue for some time and elections were not going to held anytime soon.[2]

In her speech announcing the elections, Mrs Gandhi indicated that she had done so because 'our system rests on the belief that Governments derive their power from the people and that the people give expression to their sovereign will every few years, freely and without hindrance, by choosing the Government they want and by indicating their preferences for policies.' She had also declared that it was 'because of this unshakeable faith in the power of the people' that she had advised 'the President to dissolve the present Lok Sabha and order fresh elections.'[3]

The government simultaneously released political prisoners, lifted press censorship and removed other restrictions on political activity such as holding of public meetings. The opposition parties could now function normally and freely undertake electioneering. The Emergency was not lifted but that was a mere formality for the steps taken to relax it amounted to that; in reality, the Emergency had ended.

I

Prodded by JP and faced with a situation where their survival was at stake, the opposition leaders sank their personal and ideological differences and lost no time in forming a single party. The Janata Party was born on 20 January 1977 when the Congress (O), BLD, Jan Sangh, and Socialist party decided to merge and form a party and fight the coming elections with a common election symbol and with Morarji Desai as their head.

Another dramatic development took place when, on 2 February 1977, the senior Congress leader, Jagjivan Ram, resigned from the cabinet and the party, condemned the Emergency, and along with H.N. Bahuguna, ex-chief minister of UP, Nandini Satpathy, ex-chief minister of Orissa, and several other Congress leaders announced the formation of a new party named Congress for Democracy (CFD). The defection of Jagjivan Ram and other Congressmen was a big blow to the Congress and gave a huge boost to the morale of the Opposition. It also helped common people shed their fear. Another immediate fallout was that a large number of Sanjay Gandhi's nominees were dropped from the list of Congress candidates and replaced by older MPs and Congress leaders.

Very soon an electoral pact was signed between the CFD and the Janata Party to share seats and to fight on a common election symbol. In fact, the entire Opposition closed its ranks when the new combination entered into seat adjustment with the CPM, Akali Dal and DMK, in order to give a straight fight to the Congress and its allies, the CPI and AIDMK. People felt that a credible alternative to Congress had emerged. Despite his ill-health, JP campaigned vigorously for opposition candidates, putting all his heart and energy into the campaign, telling people that the survival of democracy was at stake. In his last appeal to the voters on 13 March, he said: 'This is the last chance. If you falter the nineteen months of tyranny will become nineteen years of terror.'[4]

Mrs Gandhi, too, carried on a whirlwind campaign around the country, claiming credit for having put an end to violence, indiscipline and political disturbances, saving the country from political disaster, improving the economic situation, and setting the country on the path of progress. The Opposition concentrated on authoritarianism, deprivation of democracy and loss of civil liberties, especially freedom of the Press, and the excesses of the sterilization and slum-clearance campaigns. Both sides asked the people to judge the record of the Emergency, treating elections as a referendum on it.

There was a great deal of scepticism, both in India and abroad, whether Mrs Gandhi would permit free and fair elections to be held. It was widely believed that the announcement regarding elections was designed to divide and disarm her opponents and to mislead world opinion. This view was expressed in an extreme form by George Fernandes, who advised his party, the Socialist party, and the Opposition to boycott the 'bogus' and 'sham' elections and not to 'take part in Mrs Gandhi's gigantic fraud on the Indian people.' 'Fighting elections under the existing conditions means giving respectability, credibility and legality to the existing electoral system,' he added. The Opposition, he said, should 'deny Mrs Gandhi the legitimacy she is trying to secure through illegitimate means,' fight elections only if 'conditions for their being free and fair are assured and they are held only nine months to a year after "normalcy" is restored.'[5] In any case, Fernandes and others believed that Mrs Gandhi would never voluntarily surrender power. She would rig elections the way dictators did all over the Third World.[6] Or she would nullify them if the electoral verdict was adverse. During the election campaign rumours spread regularly that Mrs Gandhi was going to get the President to cancel elections because she realized which way the wind was blowing. From the very outset, a Janata wave swept the whole of North India, and massive crowds greeted with cheers the opposition leaders wherever they went.

However, when elections were held between 16 and 20 March, like the election campaign, they proved to be quite free. In any case, rigging was not possible without the cooperation of the polling officials, invariably lower-level government servants and school teachers, and they had been thoroughly antagonized by sterilization and other Emergency policies. If anything, these officials quite often helped the opposition candidates.

When the results came in, it became clear that Congress had suffered a comprehensive defeat. The Janata Party, along with the CFD, swept North India, winning 43.2 per cent of the total all-India votes and 298 out of 542 seats. Of its allies, the CPM won 21 seats, Akali Dal 8 and DMK 1. The Congress trailed far behind with 34.5 per cent of the votes and 153 seats. Of its allies, the CPI got 7 seats and AIDMK 19. The Congress was virtually wiped out in North India. It won only 2 out of 234 seats in the eight states of Punjab, Himachal Pradesh, Haryana, Delhi, Rajasthan, UP, Madhya Pradesh and Bihar. Both Indira Gandhi and Sanjay Gandhi were defeated by large margins. The Congress's worst defeat was in Bansi Lal's Haryana where only 18 per cent of the votes were cast in its favour and many of its candidates lost their security deposits. In UP and Delhi its vote percentage was only 25 and 30 respectively, and in terms of seats it drew a blank in both.[7]

The electoral verdict was mixed in the western states of Maharashtra and Gujarat where Congress won 30 of the 74 seats, with the Janata winning 33 and the CPM 3. In the four southern states of Tamil Nadu, Kerala, Karnataka and Andhra, the result was the exact opposite of that in North India. In these states, the Emergency had been less vigorous, the vasectomy and slum-clearance drives rather mild, the pro-poor measures of the 20-Point Programme better implemented, and in Tamil Nadu, President's rule had proved to be better than the corrupt Karunanidhi administration. In these states, the Congress improved its tally from 71 out of 122 seats in 1971 to 92 seats. Its allies, the CPI and AIDMK, won 26 seats. The Janata Party got only 6 seats in these four states.

As soon as the election results were out, once again many asked: Will Mrs Gandhi accept the verdict and step down from office? Rumours circulated that she had a contingency plan to hold on to power, that she had asked army generals to help her to do so, or to take over power themselves and impose martial law in the country so that there would be no retribution against her. Another rumour was that she was planning to flee the country to avoid being tried for the happenings during the Emergency.

But Mrs Gandhi again surprised the sceptics. She promptly resigned, asked the President to formally end the Emergency, and issued a dignified statement accepting the verdict of the people 'unreservedly and in a spirit of humility' and offering her 'good wishes' as well as 'constructive cooperation' to the new government.[8] She wrote her party president a letter owning up 'full responsibility for this defeat.'[9]

II

A very important historical question is, why did Mrs Gandhi suddenly abandon the Emergency and decide to hold elections? Few accept the explanation she offered in her 18 January speech that her decision was the result of her resolve to 'reaffirm the power of the people' and to provide them an opportunity to 'give expression to their sovereign will.'[10] And why did she hold open and free elections and not rig them? What were her motives in doing all this? What were her tactical considerations? She had persuaded Parliament in early November to postpone general elections by another year. Then what made her change her mind? Was the November decision a ploy to placate Sanjay and lull him to sleep?

It is noteworthy that at this time there was also little overt opposition in the country to the Emergency. People seemed to have reconciled themselves to it. Nor did the divided and despondent Opposition pose any political threat to Mrs Gandhi's regime. It seemed that she could have continued as she was or even taken more authoritarian measures as her counterparts were doing elsewhere in South Korea, Philippines, Taiwan, Malaysia, Indonesia, Singapore. Moreover, Sanjay Gandhi was consistently opposed to any recourse to elections. He was behind the postponement of elections in January as well as early November 1976. Though he declared that elections should be held only when 'the country's economy was stabilized',[11] he actually needed time to consolidate his power and marshall his political resources; after all his Youth Congress brigade was just establishing itself. In January 1977, when consulted, he had advised Mrs Gandhi against her contemplated step and said: 'You are committing a most horrible mistake.' But, according to Maneka Gandhi, 'for the first time he found her immovable.'[12] Why?

So far there is no satisfactory answer to this basic question. Contemporaries were puzzled and could only speculate. The answers will remain shrouded in mystery until government archives and the private papers of Mrs Gandhi are thrown open to the public. And, perhaps, not even then will the picture be entirely clear since Mrs Gandhi was a very private person. On the other hand, there can be, and have been, a great many educated guesses and deductions. Perhaps, there is no single answer and we have to look for multiple causes. The reasons suggested so far, overlapping sometimes, can be grouped under three broad categories.

III

The unfriendly point of view put forward by many of Mrs Gandhi's critics is that she completely misread the popular temper in North India and that her decision to go in for elections was a case of her calculations going wrong. But how did she make such a gross error? Because, it has been said, she was misinformed by sycophants, who told her what they thought she liked to hear. Or because her intelligence agencies, out to please her and afraid of bringing unpleasant tidings, deliberately withheld their true findings from her. Or, as is the case with all authoritarian regimes, because of the atmosphere of conformity, silencing of all criticism, censorship of the Press, political passivity generated by fear, and control of access to her by Sanjay Gandhi and his coterie, she was unaware of the true extent to which her government and, therefore, the Congress and she had become unpopular. She had no idea of the simmering anger against the excesses of family planning, or of the silent opposition that was building up against her, or of the strength of the democratic feelings among the people. Perhaps she wrongly assumed that if economic conditions improved, then democracy mattered little to them.

Some people have maintained that Mrs Gandhi calculated that at the moment the economy was in good shape, both industrial and agricultural production had gone up in 1975-76—in fact national income had grown at 9 per cent, the highest rate of growth in several years—and prices had been brought under control. But the good times might not last; in fact they were perhaps already coming to an end. There could be greater difficulties ahead and then elections might have to be held in more adverse circumstances. The monsoons were always a gamble. Inflationary pressures were building up and prices were beginning to rise—it was later found that in 1976-77 the wholesale price index had moved up by nearly 2 per cent, foodgrains production had declined by 5 per cent and national income growth had come down to less than 2 per cent. Also nearly all the increase in industrial production had occurred in the public sector; the private sector had continued to stagnate. Clearly, as Francine Frankel has put it, 'the structural obstacles to achieving sustained economic growth had still not been removed.'[13] Tougher economic measures were needed to initiate a consistent upward economic spiral. It was necessary to get breathing space for these stronger measures. But the Emergency regime could not last for years; she had to go to the polls within a year or two. Better now when things were better than later when they might be worse.

There was another political consideration. The disparate Opposition was in disarray and resourceless but, given time, they could unite and with the charismatic JP at their head become a formidable force. At the moment they were starved of funds and political workers, their organizations having been made dysfunctional by arrests, suppression and political inactivity. Immediate elections would catch them unawares. Nor would they be able to organize and they wouldn't be able to organize and mobilize for elections and mount a campaign. Trapped, the parties couldn't refuse to participate in elections nor would they be adequately prepared to do so. Within the Congress, too, dissidence was under control, the pre-1975 dissidents having been arrested or expelled. From the Congress's point of view, then, a number of economic and political factors favoured an early election.

A few have argued against some of the assumptions behind this reasoning. Pupul Jayakar writes, on the basis of Maneka Gandhi's authority, that Mrs Gandhi 'had asked the Intelligence Bureau (IB) to assess the results of an early election. The IB reported back that Indira's Congress would lose.' Similarly, on the basis of her interview with R.N. Kao, head of the RAW, Jayakar writes: 'R.N. Kao came back to the Prime Minister with an assessment that there was some danger in immediate elections. He advised her to release the Opposition, allow for a cooling off period and call elections in six months.'[14] P.N. Dhar, Mrs Gandhi's principal secretary, says about the role of sycophancy: 'To be sure, there was much sycophancy, but Indira Gandhi was too mistrustful a person to have swallowed the flatterer's opinion entirely.' About false reports by intelligence agencies, P.N. Dhar, who must have had access to many of these reports, says: 'Their reports did tone down the negative parts here and there, but it is not true that they did not reflect the current and crosscurrents of public opinion.' And he adds: 'Actually, Indira Gandhi knew more about the situation in the country during the Emergency than she was prepared to admit.'[15] Pupul Jayakar also says that when Mrs Gandhi took the decision to hold elections, 'she had considered the possibility of defeat; she realized that the future was unknown, the possibility of great travail lay in the months ahead.'[16] Indira Gandhi herself told a journalist later: 'I was by no means sure that I would win. I was sure that we would not get a big majority. I thought that we would just get through perhaps. I did not really give a thought to our winning or not.'[17]

IV

The second view is that Mrs Gandhi felt that she had to add to her legitimacy and strengthen the moral basis of her rule, both in her own eyes and that of the people. The imposition of the Emergency had been legitimized at the outset by a constitutional provision. But this legitimacy could not last long, especially in view of the deep-seated, over a century old, democratic traditions of the Indian people. The longer the Emergency lasted and began to lose its temporary character the more was this legitimacy eroded. The two postponements of the general elections and the forty-second constitutional amendment further undermined it. In fact, the very success of the Emergency regime in suppressing the opposition movement deprived it of the reason for its continuance.

Consequently, the Emergency and the policies under it had to be legitimized further in a credible constitutional manner, and Mrs Gandhi knew that under Indian conditions, elections alone were 'an indispensable test of legitimacy.'[18] The choice was elections now or next year. A dictatorship or authority that was not legitimate had little chance of gaining allegiance or even acquiescence of the people.

Furthermore, there were clear signs of restlessness and discontent among the people, not only against the excesses but also against the loss of liberties and the emergence of the extra-constitutional centres of power and their coteries. Moreover, in the absence of authentic news in the Press and on the radio, people were willing to believe the wildest of rumours regarding government and its intentions. Even the CPI was beginning to express its displeasure; it had opposed the postponement of elections in November and was putting pressure for the ending of the Emergency and the holding of polls. Contradictions were beginning to emerge within the Congress too; many partymen and MPs were becoming restive. Many veteran Congressmen resented the power of Sanjay Gandhi and the caucus around him and the growing political and organizational clout of the upstart Youth Congress. Some of them urged Mrs Gandhi to end the Emergency. There was even talk of a split in the Congress parliamentary party.

Thus, though there was no overt opposition to her in sight, Mrs Gandhi, who had shown that she had sharp political antennae, was likely to have realized that the Emergency regime was getting discredited and that the status quo could not last long.

Increasingly, Mrs Gandhi was faced with two choices: either to go further on the road to dictatorship or make a retreat; either, following the logic of the system put in motion with the Emergency, to strengthen and deepen the authoritarian content of the regime and take recourse to increasing ruthlessness and brutality in suppressing dissent and, as Sanjay Gandhi, Bansi Lal and their like desired, to give India given a more totalitarian direction; or to acquire greater legitimacy and political authority by switching back to a democratic system through free and fair elections. It has been argued that Mrs Gandhi realized that the former option would not work in a country of India's size, diversity and democratic traditions;[19] that India could not be ruled that way. Besides, it would go completely against the political culture that the Indian people had imbibed during the freedom struggle and the years since 1947. The people of India would not accept the level of repression that this involved. The totalitarian alternative was not a feasible choice for the country or an answer to her dilemma. Elections were, therefore, the only way out.

Some critics have also suggestd that by holding elections Mrs Gandhi hoped to reshape and streamline the Congress party, acquire greater control over party's MPs and contain the incipient rebellion among them. During elections, those MPs whose commitment to her was doubtful could be replaced with those more loyal and trustworthy.

Moreover, the legitimacy argument holds good on another count. According to some critics, Mrs Gandhi wanted enhanced legitimacy not only for herself but also for her son. By holding and winning fresh elections, she not only hoped to vindicate, strengthen and perpetuate the policies followed during the Emergency, she also planned to clear the way for Sanjay Gandhi to succeed her through a due constitutional process. She knew that he could not wield extra-constitutional power for too long. Elections, with many of his men and women elected to Parliament, would stamp Sanjay's power with the people's approval.

Critics in India and abroad have put forth two other explanations, the first more credible than the second. First, that by ordering fair elections Mrs Gandhi hoped to appease liberal democratic opinion in the West, to which she was very sensitive and which had by and large turned against her.[20] Some have extended this argument to India and held that despite her anger against liberal Indian intellectuals she wanted to remain in their good books and not be treated by them as a pariah and an unworthy successor to Jawaharlal Nehru.[21] Second, that the need to defer to world opinion and hold elections was felt even more strongly by Mrs Gandhi when Zulfiqar Ali Bhutto ordered elections to be held in March in Pakistan. How could India be shamed as less democratic by Pakistan, and Indira Gandhi by Bhutto?

V

There is also a view that builds upon the second one, but is more favourable to Mrs Gandhi, though sometimes held by her vehement critics. According to this view, Mrs Gandhi's decision to hold elections was an expression of her underlying commitment to liberal democracy and democratic values, particularly as it is noteworthy that throughout 1975-76 she had never wavered from the commitment to hold elections.

Mohit Sen sees her decision of 18 January as 'a testimony to her faith in democracy', though he adds that 'it was an ill-prepared decision'.[22] Similarly, S.S. Gill, one of her critics, has written: 'Freedom, democracy, elections, public opinion were the concepts she had grown up with. Her own political instinct was still sound enough to tell her that the Emergency was wrong.'[23] The socialist leader, Madhu Limaye, who spent the entire period of the Emergency in jail, has commented as follows on her speech of 18 January: 'The false reasoning, self-justification, is all there, but above all, there is the saving grace of her ultimate faith in the supremacy of popular democracy—though not liberal democracy—and her deep craving for legitimacy. After all said and done Indira Gandhi could never forget that she was the daughter of Jawaharlal Nehru and, like us, the child of the Freedom Movement led by Mahatma Gandhi.'[24]

It has also been said that, like her father, she was very conscious of her place in history. She did not want to be remembered as a dictator or a destroyer of democracy that was nurtured by the freedom struggle and by her father after independence.[25] Perhaps she remembered the words JP had written to her from jail on 21 July 1975: 'Please do not destroy the foundations that the Fathers of the Nation, including your noble father, had laid down ... You inherited a great tradition, noble values and a working democracy. Do not leave behind a miserable wreck of all that.'[26] According to Inder Malhotra, Mrs Gandhi 'wanted to regain her credentials as a democratic leader which she had lost ... She was prepared to lose the poll and power, if necessary, to bring democracy back—a claim she was emphatically to repeat in August 1984, just over two months before her death.'[27] Similarly, Mary C. Carras, another of Mrs Gandhi's biographers, writes that Mrs Gandhi's training had 'fostered a democratic temperament and personal style' and argues:[28]

> Throughout her life her self-image had been that of a democrat; indeed her self-respect derives in good part from this self-image ... She was compelled to prove to the world and, above all, to herself, that she is and always has been a democrat. Since childhood the democratic ideal had been very closely related to her sense of personal worth and, equally importantly, to her sense of India's greatness.

Mrs Gandhi's most recent biographer, Katherine Frank, in her rather superficial assessment, seems to give qualified approval to this view.[29] Surprisingly, Nayantara Sahgal, the bitterest of Mrs Gandhi's biographer-critics, also accepts, though in a hostile manner, elements of this analysis. She writes: 'She was not a democrat by belief or instinct ... Democracy was not Mrs Gandhi's style, but it remained an insistent craving ... The modern Indian imagination could not easily set democracy aside. It was a spectre that haunted Mrs Gandhi. She longed for a democratic image ... It was an image an election could only strengthen and brighten and a continuing Emergency could only tarnish.'[30]

A more sophisticated version of the above perception has been suggested by several writers who had prolonged personal contact with Mrs Gandhi. Of course, none of these authors have put forward a connected, coherent or organized narrative or argument in this regard. I have pieced it together from bits of their writings, or in the case of Mohit Sen, from his oral account.

In essence, the explanation put forward is that Mrs Gandhi was deeply worried by the political situation as it was developing and the wrong direction in which the Emergency was going. By the end of 1976, it is said, she had become aware of the Emergency excesses and, what is more important, realized that the political and administrative situation was getting out of control (nearly all the authors quoted below use this or a similar phrase) and she was being isolated, politically, by the coterie around Sanjay Gandhi. She was also repelled by the type of people Sanjay had gathered around himself. The list of these undesirable people seemed to include his wife, Maneka. In addition to what was actually happening, she was even more worried about the direction in which the situation was moving, or the fact that Sanjay and his coterie were working towards fascist-style political control. She also felt uneasy about the openness of Sanjay and many in her own secretariat to the influence of the US. The type of situation developing was similar to the one she had wanted to avoid by imposing the Emergency.

Contrary to her disclaimers, Mrs Gandhi had certainly encouraged and fully supported Sanjay in assuming political and administrative importance, but she had hoped that he would gradually mellow down, get 'trained' in democratic politics and perhaps in time replace her.[31] But she had not bargained for his becoming a Marcos or a Mussolini or a tin-pot dictator. And now there wasn't time left to mould him in the desired direction.

She now wanted to somehow get out of the trap of the Emergency and end her political isolation and recover her political control. But she was too close emotionally to Sanjay to be able or even want to disown him publicly and confront him. The only way she could stop him from acquiring full control was to go in for a poll and lift the Emergency, even if it meant losing power. And she did so ignoring Sanjay's strong advice to the contrary.[32] Of course, she still hoped that with a democratic environment and the passage of time he would mature, his rough edges would smoothen, and he would become a major national leader, if not her successor, in due course.

We may first take up the view of Mrs Gandhi's friend and confidante, Pupul Jayakar, that Mrs Gandhi was uncomfortable with the position she had landed in and was desperate to get out of it:[33]

For a long period Mrs Gandhi was isolated from persons and events as 'all flow of news was controlled' and 'the darkness of the Emergency hemmed her in.' But towards the autumn of 1976, she began to learn about the family planning and police excesses and their aftermath in popular anger. She tried to stem the rot, but the orders she issued to the state governments to withdraw the coercive measures were ignored or perhaps never issued. 'A feeling grew in her that the situation was out of control.' But she would not passively accept this situation. 'The miasma that clouded her started to dissolve. Her superb instincts came alive, intimations arose within her that all was not well in the country . . . She started to listen and to doubt her advisers.' Near the end of October 1976, she met the sage-philosopher, J. Krishnamurti who told her, 'Madam you are very disturbed,' and she replied, 'Yes. The situation has become very dangerous. What shall I do?' She met Krishnamurti again on 28 October and told him, 'I am riding on the back of a tiger. I do not mind the tiger killing me, but I do not know how to get off its back.' Krishnamurti told her that she would herself know what to do, if she thought deeply enough. It was on that day, says Jayakar, that Mrs Gandhi decided to end the Emergency 'whatever the consequences'.

P.N. Dhar, who was Mrs Gandhi's principal secretary during the period of the Emergency, in his autobiographical *Indira Gandhi, the 'Emergency', and Indian Democracy* is quite guarded but still does make his point:[34]

Mrs Gandhi had gradually begun to feel uneasy about the 'human and political implications' of the family planning programme and the way in which it was being implemented. In early October, he 'got several indications from Mrs Gandhi that she was very concerned at the situation as it had developed. She felt that things were getting out of control and that something had to be done.' She was also 'becoming apprehensive of the arbitrary power wielded by some of Sanjay's supporters, such as Bansi Lal, whom she seemed unwilling to curb lest she annoy Sanjay.' She also complained to the home minister about police excesses and said something should be done about them. She was quite 'uncomfortable' about the second postponement of elections in November. She thought it 'gave out the wrong signal—that she was afraid to face the people. It hurt her self-respect and her pride in her own leadership.'

At this stage of his narrative, Dhar becomes quite cautious and does not commit himself. But, on the basis of his interaction with Mrs Gandhi during the last months of 1976, he asks: 'Was Sanjay proving too wild even for her?' and 'Was she herself becoming afraid of him?' He also tells us that Mrs Gandhi had 'kept Sanjay out of all discussions on constitutional reforms' and later out of the exercise regarding the holding of elections. Dhar also writes of Sanjay 'trying to establish contact with foreign missions' and of 'one of his cronies' reported to be meeting 'a US embassy official in a very suspicious manner.' Dhar, however, does not say anything about Mrs Gandhi's knowledge or comments on this; but we may draw our own inference. And Dhar concludes his chapter on the Emergency with the comment, 'Was her decision to hold elections a calculated risk—or was it something else? There may never be a conclusive answer, but I believe she was not comfortable with the Emergency, and she wanted to get out of it, somehow, anyhow.'[35]

Mohit Sen, who regularly interacted with Mrs Gandhi during 1977-84, is quite specific: 'Smt. Gandhi sensed that the Emergency had defeated counter-revolution but was in danger of itself being used to subvert our democratic system. She lifted the Emergency and called for elections.'[36] Also: 'She knew she could lose but she also knew that this was the only step which could result in the victory of our democracy.'[37] Sen has elaborated this view further in his interview to Mridula Mukherjee for the Archives on Contemporary History, JNU. According to Sen's account, Mrs Gandhi came to realize that the Emergency was becoming the opposite of what she had intended. Well-read as she was, she could see the authoritarian potential in the rise to power of Sanjay Gandhi and his coterie. Simultaneously, she felt that not only was US influence over Sanjay growing, but the Americans had penetrated the apparatus, both personal and official, around her. The threat of internal fascism and foreign influence which she had perceived in the JP movement in 1975 she could now apprehend in the Youth Congress and its leadership. She was also worried about Sanjay's strong anti-communist views. The answer, she felt, was to roll back the Emergency and once again appeal to the people.

P.N. Bahl, who was joint secretary in prime minister's secretariat during the Emergency and who, as part of Sanjay Gandhi-R.K. Dhawan's loyalist team, observed the prime minister as well as the ruling caucus from close quarters, has made similar comments and a long extract from his book may be in order:[38]

> The above report on lady prisoners, the excesses in respect of family planning programme, the misuse of MISA especially when one of the amendments did away with the requirement for furnishing of grounds of detention to the detainee as also the abrogation of fundamental right to life etc., were more than sufficient to convince the PM that something seriously had gone wrong somewhere. In meetings and during briefing sessions with advisors of different disciplines, a perceptible change was more than apparent in the attitude of the PM. The majority of the members of the Council of Ministers appeared to be of the same impression. The PM was coming round to a definite view that remedial measures had to be taken straightway. . . . Time and again, the state governments were told that excesses of any kind whatsoever should be avoided at all cost and the dignity of the citizens living in every nook and corner of the country ought to be protected. But nothing changed. The reports which came from the states were as pathetic as ever. Thus, the PM was more or less convinced totally that any further prolongation of the New Situation was bound to boomerang irretrievably sowing seeds of threatening the very existence of the Indian polity and its constitutional framework. . . . She (Mrs Gandhi) had fully realized that despite the advice to the contrary, things had started slipping out of (her) hands. . . . PM further realised that the entire Nation was feeling suffocated.

Several other authors and contemporaries also support elements of the hypothesis presented in this section. Later, in 1977, Mrs Gandhi's finance minister and a long-time cabinet colleague, C. Subramaniam, told Uma Vasudev: 'All sorts of undesirable persons got into positions of real or assumed authority. I think one of the reasons she went in for the elections was because she felt this might be the last opportunity to get out of their clutches.'[39] Similarly, Vasant Sathe told Vasudev that Mrs Gandhi consulted him about elections in December 1976 and 'she said she was a bit afraid about UP and the northern states. She knew what she was going in for. I think she was so entrapped by a succession of events that this was the only way to break out of it and bolster the democratic forces.'[40]

Granville Austin writes that 'a senior official in the Prime Minister's office recalls that she had become anxious about the direction being taken by Bansi Lal and son Sanjay.'[41] Mary C. Carras has stated: 'She may have realized that control of the decision-making machinery was slipping out of her hands and that she was no longer master of the political situation—and soon might not be master of herself.'[42] Inder Malhotra also feels 'in retrospect at least' that 'far from laying a trap for her opponents . . . Indira was trying frantically to get out of one she had landed herself in.'[43] Max Jean Zins, in his pioneering study of the Emergency, expresses the same view as a counter-question: 'Did the Prime Minister realize that she was caught in a trap of her own making and did she then decide to stop the logic of the newly emerging system in time by calling for elections?'[44]

Why did Mrs Gandhi decide to hold elections may perhaps be explained by a combination of all the four reasons discussed above, with each analyst placing greater weight on one or the other reason. I am inclined to regard the last one as being the more important reason.

VI

In the end, it is of some interest to take note of the reasons Mrs Gandhi herself gave later for her decision. One was that the Emergency was imposed with a specific objective in view, namely, to put an end to the JPM's unconstitutional bid for power and also to the conditions which had led to JPM; the objective having been achieved the Emergency was ended and the normal political processes resumed.[45] In conversations with Mohit Sen she pointed out that she declared the Emergency to prevent a forcible seizure of power by a small but well-organized group and imposition of a dictatorial regime. But she had no ideological objection to being defeated in elections by a democratic party even if she disliked the party, for the resulting regime would still be a democratic one. To Dom Moraes she emphasized that fear of foreign penetration was a major factor in her 18 January decision. The following extract from Dom Moraes' *Mrs Gandhi* is illuminating: 'She had this feeling when she decided to suspend the Emergency and declare elections: something awful would happen unless she did. "To you, ma'am?", I inquired. "No", she said. "Not to me. To the country. I had this sense that more and more foreign influences were seeking for excuses to disrupt, perhaps even to destroy, this country".'[46] On the other hand she denied that the declaration of elections in Pakistan or Sri Lanka or the need to project to the world the image of a leader supported by her people influenced her decision.[47]

10 Conclusions

There are several conclusions to be drawn and lessons learnt from the JP movement and the Emergency. The defence of Indian democracy seems to have been the main justification of both the JPM and the Emergency regime. As seen before, in the narratives devoted to them, both JP and Indira Gandhi accused each other of creating a threat for democracy and of being dictatorial or fascist. Both appealed to democracy as a justification for their actions and gave calls for fighting against 'the rising menace of dictatorship and fascism'. In my view, while there was some truth in what both said, neither was free of blame. Both were responsible for the situation arising on 26 June, with neither of them showing a willingness to take the democratic way out. Nevertheless, it cannot be said that either was really in favour of dictatorship or fascism or worked for it, though their actions were full of contradictions and contained contrary possibilities. My assumption, expressed and implicit, has been that there was danger to democracy from both. Both had in their actions the potential of dictatorship or fascism. JP made an attempt, however well-intentioned, to change the government through an extra-parliamentary and extra-constitutional movement. Mrs Gandhi, faced with the Hobson's choice of total surrender or fight to the finish, responded with an authoritarian regime. The JPM could have brought communal fascists to power, and Mrs Gandhi's Emergency regime, which by its very nature was authoritarian, could in time have 'graduated' to full dictatorship or fascism. India, however, escaped both outcomes, though the JPM and the Emergency did scar our polity. However, Indian democracy proved resilient enough to survive both. But both were a strong warning to the Indian people and the democratic system.

I have already examined the JPM and the Emergency at great length, the former in Chapters 3, 4 and 6 and the latter in Chapters 7 and 8. Here I will analyse the potential of the two for dictatorship and fascism, taking up first the direct threat of dictatorship posed by the Emergency regime.

I

How is the Emergency regime to be characterized? Politically, it was, by definition virtually authoritarian. It tampered with governmental structures and weakened all government and civil institutions. Parliament and the Cabinet were made ineffectual and their powers and functions concentrated in a few hands. The Congress party's role was circumscribed; it was disciplined, but beset by a paralysis. The Opposition was denied any political role. The Constitution was repeatedly amended and, in the end, significantly so by the onerous forty-second amendment. The federal structure was damaged and general elections postponed twice.

Civil liberties guaranteed by the Constitution, including freedoms of expression and association and the right of *habeas corpus*, that is, the right to appeal to the courts against arbitrary arrest, were suspended. Unprecedented and draconian censorship was imposed on the Press. The radio and TV were used exclusively to propagate the government's viewpoint. 'By this means the government converted a hitherto "transparent" society into an opaque one.' All political dissent and free expression of opinion were suppressed. Major opposition leaders were arrested and over 100,000 persons were put behind bars without trial for varying periods during the nineteen months that the Emergency lasted. The judiciary was subverted and emasculated.

Inevitably, the Emergency, in both its repressive and developmental aspects, was implemented almost entirely through the agency of the bureaucracy. On the one hand, the latter lost its autonomy and, on the other, it acquired arbitrary powers without being accountable except to a small number of persons, who controlled the levers of political power. The police and bureaucracy became even more oppressive towards the ordinary citizen. A parallel apparatus of administration and policy-making and extra-constitutional power developed. Even the prime minister operated less through the Prime Minister's Secretariat and more, unofficially, through the Prime Minister's House.

Thus the Emergency amounted to the concentration of power in the hands of a few persons, some of whom had no constitutionally-designated position, gagging of the Press, suppression of civil liberties and rule exclusively through the bureaucracy. It appeared as if the very character of the state was being changed, ignoring all the traditions of the freedom struggle and of the Congress's own rule since 1947. Yet, in the end, that was not how things turned out.

In spite of all these authoritarian features, the Emergency regime was not yet a full-blooded dictatorship nor totalitarian or fascist in character. Nor was it perhaps designed to be so. Here a word of caution is in order. The presence of fascism cannot be deduced from isolated 'fascist' traits. A minimum of these is necessary for such an inference. Besides a distinction needs to be made between fascism and mere suppression.[1] Totalitarian regimes seek a monopoly of power throughout society, covering all aspects of civil society, including the family, business, educational institutions, political organizations, trade unions, and the ideological realm. Also, they do not permit any conceivable rival source of social, economic or political power.

The Emergency had many paradoxical characteristics. Despite its many tyrannical aspects, it was not all-pervasive or utterly ruthless. The actual degree of repression or brutality practised did not amount to fascism. In the words of Granville Austin, 'ugly as the Emergency was, New Delhi in 1976 was not Berlin under Hitler.'[2] The repressive measures were, moreover, being relaxed towards the end of the Emergency, except for the sterilization campaign. Of the 100,000 or so persons arrested, most were released after a few weeks or months. Very few political opponents were liquidated. Though there were cases of political prisoners being tortured, this was an exception and not the rule.[3] Besides, despite a great deal of tinkering with it, the rule of law still prevailed. In fact, significant opposition to the Emergency began to emerge, especially among the intellectuals, because after the early arrests which struck fear in the hearts of the people, it became clear over time that the government would not imprison or kill a large number of people, or even deprive them of their jobs.

Except for preventing strikes and some political intimidation of teachers and students, schools, colleges and universities were left to themselves and continued to function as usual. Little or no effort was made to control fresh faculty appointments or the content and syllabi of class-room teaching and academic publications. Student unions, teachers' associations, and universities employees' unions were rendered inactive, but no effort was made to establish alternative government or Congress party-controlled unions or associations. The Press was subject to stringent censorship rules but was not forced to publish what it did not want to. It was not able to criticize the regime or publish news unfavourable to it, but apart from this the Press was left alone. The government had complete monopoly of news and sources of information, but newspapers were still privately owned, subject only to censorship.

Kuldip Nayar was arrested and kept in jail for two months. But, then, after his release he rejoined his paper, the *Indian Express*, and wrote regularly for it throughout the Emergency, though within the limits of censorship.

Views critical of the regime could not be published or widely publicly disseminated, but could still be discussed privately. The government created no machinery for monitoring private discussions or exchange of views. Consequently, as Sachchidanand Sinha points out: 'So after the initial hush, criticism began to be voiced against the government though confined to close circles of friends or family . . . Jokes about the Prime Minister and her family and the stupidity of the police could be heard everywhere.'[4] Hardly any dissident intellectual of any stature was arrested. On the whole, people's consciousness or ideas were not actively manipulated, nor were efforts made to change them. There was no thought control or machinery for the purpose. To quote Granville Austin again: 'The Emergency had its limits. Considerable individual and political freedom existed within it, ideological purity was not demanded, opponents were not shot.'[5]

Trade unions were stifled. In particular, going on strike was made difficult, though some strikes did occur. Work-days lost due to strikes in 1976 declined from forty million to thirteen million. But this number of work-days were still lost. Trade unions, however, were not controlled or run by the state or monopolized by the Congress party. Some trade-union leaders were arrested. But no attempt was made to substitute men from the ruling party in their place. Existing trade unions were neither annihilated nor replaced with new ones. Private business was not interfered with. Instead, existing government controls were relaxed. Business organizations continued to function outside government or party control. Professional associations of say lawyers, doctors, scientists, journalists, economists, historians, political scientists carried on their normal activities. The government also made no move to interfere with religious or social or non-government organizations. In other words, there was little effort to 'corporatize' or bring under government purview major organs of civil society. Nor were non-government organizations, such as trade unions, business organizations, student unions, teachers' and other professional associations utilized to popularize the Emergency regime or its measures. Some of them did so, but then they were acting as front organizations of the Congress or other political parties on a voluntary basis even before the Emergency.

Missing was a mass fascist party. There was no Nazification of the Congress, nor was it replaced by a fascist party. Congress was not used as a vehicle for thought control or for regulating civil society as a whole or its voluntary organizations, or as the main agent for implementing the Emergency policies—the bureaucracy and the police were assigned this role. Already, before 1975, the Congress as a political party was decaying; during the Emergency it became even more dysfunctional, with its organizational leaders the subject of popular contempt. Mrs Gandhi could also not rely upon any fascist or dictatorial mass base created earlier; if she had, she would have fought the JP movement in the streets and not through the Emergency. The Emergency was purely a creature of the moment without any design or ideological or organizational preparation. Whatever extra-parliamentary agitations occurred before June 1975 were by the Opposition and not by the Congress. Mrs Gandhi also did not make efforts to take over the JPM's mass base. Besides, there were no stormtroopers. In totalitarian dictatorships power is most often exercised by the party or its leadership in close cooperation with stormtroopers, who are in turn the creations of a mass movement or are created after the fascist regime comes into existence. Though they generally have a subordinate political role in the ruling order, in the beginning they are used to attack the cadres of the opposition parties and to 'discipline' or 'keep in line' the people. This was not the case in India before or during the Emergency.

One of the first acts of all totalitarian regimes, whether in Germany, Italy, Spain and Japan or in the erstwhile Socialist bloc, was the annihilation of traditional parliamentary parties. Though the functioning of the opposition parties, especially with regard to organizing popular protest, was restricted during the Emergency, they were not stamped out. Only some communal or extremist organizations, such as the RSS, Jamaat-i-Islami, Anand Marg and Naxalite groups were banned. However, all the mainstream parliamentary parties, including the Jan Sangh and CPM, remained legal, with most of their cadres and leaders (except of the Jan Sangh's) remaining outside jail. Moreover, most of the top opposition leaders were released during March-June 1976 and were free to meet and plan the merger, alliances and the like of their parties. Interestingly, Mrs Gandhi not only released her main political opponent, namely JP, within five months, throughout she carried on political negotiations with him and several other major opposition leaders.

Another important component of fascism is that it not only restricts the spread of liberal democratic ideas but actively attacks them. Mrs Gandhi did restrict propagation of democratic ideas in the Press but did not herself or through the state agencies attack them. She did not try to discredit parliamentary politics and the parliamentary form of government. She also made no effort to construct and offer to the people a new ideological framework around the Emergency for winning their allegiance. On the contrary, she appealed to the liberal democratic ideology generated during the freedom struggle and nurtured during the Nehru era, repeatedly asserted her faith in it and, as shown in Chapter 4, justified the imposition of the Emergency as a step in defence of democracy. It is also important that while she wielded political and administrative power, she did not try to exercise intellectual hegemony over the people. In fact, she had no machinery for the purpose and had few intellectuals to help her do so. Not surprisingly, one of the long-term consequences of the Emergency was her alienation from intellectuals even when she had won back popular support.

Very significantly, the Emergency did not lead to alteration of the basic structure of the Indian polity. Hardly any attempt was made to institutionalize it. No abiding authoritarian institutions were established. The government continued to function within the constitutional framework. Parliament functioned and all ordinances, laws and constitutional amendments were passed by it, though some of its members were arrested and its proceedings could not be freely reported in the Press. Despite draconian laws curbing civil liberties and constitutional amendments reducing jurisdiction of the courts, the judicial system remained intact and lawyers and courts performed their tasks. The judiciary retained a large degree of independence. The bolder judges continued to give judgements against the government in cases involving civil liberties. What is also significant is that elections were postponed twice but were not abandoned or rigged and, in the end, they were held in a free and fair manner within a year of their being due. Also, despite the spate of constitutional amendments, the basic structure of the Constitution was not changed and all proposals for switching over to the presidential form of government or for the conversion of the existing Parliament into a constituent assembly with a view to drastically transform the constitutional structure were in the end rejected. It is worth quoting Granville Austin at some length on this aspect:[6]

> And the Forty-second Amendment, with all the evils here described, did not abolish the Supreme Court, left the judiciary with considerable powers, did not end the elections and legislatures of representative government; and did not abolish the Fundamental Rights. Even under the amendment, there

would have existed genuine potential for its electoral overturn. All sense of democratic restraint had not deserted its drafters, although it may have deserted Sanjay Gandhi and his coterie.

Jean Max Zins also advances an interesting argument for the non-subversion of the constitutional structure. 'Confronted by a crisis of hegemony and of the political system,' the Congress leadership, with its back to the wall, he writes, 'declared Emergency not to establish something new, but basically to maintain the previous *status quo*.'[7]

In fact, we may take Mrs Gandhi at her word that with the imposition of the Emergency she did not intend to abandon democracy for ever or to change the political system. She did try to stretch the constitutional framework to its limit but lifted the Emergency and held free elections when she found that she had to go beyond constitutional limits to keep the Emergency going.[8] We may agree with the interesting comment that Mrs Gandhi failed to maintain the Emergency regime because, besides the people, even she had no faith in it, nor had she an alternative system to offer.

There has hardly been any dictatorship which has not had to negotiate power with the armed forces and get their support and approval. Yet, the Indian armed forces were not involved in the Emergency in any form or at any stage, from its promulgation and its enforcement to its withdrawal. Mrs Gandhi scrupulously kept the armed forces out of politics. In fact, as we have argued in Chapter 4, probably a major reason why she declared the Emergency was that she might have been forced to use the army for suppressing the huge crowds projected to gherao her house as part of the Opposition's civil disobedience movement.

Unlike other totalitarian regimes, the Emergency regime also did not acquire a secure social base for itself. Though workers were not protesting, they were unhappy with the Emergency; the intellectuals were hostile; the poor were passive because they saw little in their lives about which to be enthusiastic. In the later part of the Emergency the poor, in fact, turned hostile to the government because of the vasectomy excesses. Also, the government had alienated the petty bourgeoisie and the rich peasantry who have, in other countries and other situations, served as the social base for totalitarian, regimes of the Right.

Another important reason why the Emergency regime avoided becoming totalitarian or a long-term dictatorship was because the roots of the crisis leading to it were entirely political. It was not, as argued by some, the result of a systemic crisis or the failure or disequilibrium of the political system.[9] Both the JPM and the Emergency were entirely contingent upon the specific political situation and not the result of long-term structural problems of the social system or of the working of economic and political processes since 1947. They were not inevitable. As we shall see later in this chapter, the only systemic failure was the inability of political parties and groups to evolve suitable methods of popular agitation within the realm of the parliamentary democracy and of the ruling authorities to evolve a proper response to them, again within the existing constitutional framework.

Further, the Emergency was not an effort to bolster a failing system threatened by a movement which was opposed to the existing social or political system. The JP movement had no such design or content despite the talk of Total Revolution. Nor was the system under threat from the left. Whatever challenge existed from that quarter—there wasn't much at any stage since 1947—had already been overcome with the suppression of the railway strike.

The Emergency was also not part of a long-term political strategy of Indira Gandhi or the ruling classes to evolve and enforce a repressive regime because there was no demand or support from the dominant classes for a change in the form of government and the structure of the state before or during the Emergency. The view that the indigenous or foreign capital or the semi-feudal landlords needed a different political order because they were threatened by a challenge from below, by a revolutionary working class and/or peasantry has no real basis. There was also no sign that Indian capital had reached a stage where profits could not be made without the aid of an authoritarian regime. No major capitalist or capitalist group had at any stage since 1947 or before June 1975 called for a dictatorship or an authoritarian regime. The only capitalist group to intervene politically before June 1975 had asked for the formation of a national government, jointly by the Congress, the opposition parties and prominent non-party persons.[10] The capitalists did, of course, want a strong government to enforce social discipline in general and labour discipline in particular. But this was a demand within the existing political system and very different from a demand for dictatorship. A few in the middle classes had clamoured for dictatorship, but they had done so in opposition to the Congress government and Indira Gandhi and not to the JP movement. Thus, in my view, the Emergency was not an expression of the wishes or interests of the capitalist class or the middle classes for a dictatorial regime. In fact, one reason why the Emergency did not last long was because, as pointed out earlier, it had no strong social base or class support. In other words, the Emergency had no class 'motivation', or a distinct and new class base. Whatever were the previous class alignments, or the nature and content of class domination before the Emergency, continued through that period, without any departure or break being made from them.

The Emergency can also not be characterized as Bonapartism because it did not meet the most elementary criterion for the title as laid down by Karl Marx, who coined the term. The Emergency had not been brought into existence because 'it was the only form of government possible at a time when the bourgeoisie had already lost, and the working class had not yet acquired, the faculty of ruling the nation.'[11] No such stalemate or disequilibrium existed between classes in India of the seventies or, in fact, of any period after 1947.

As pointed out in Chapter 2 above, the JP movement was also the result of certain administrative defaults and economic difficulties that had arisen during 1972-1974 and of the failure of the ruling authorities to deal with them in a manner that satisfied the people. But the resulting political turmoil had subsided by December 1974 even in Bihar, because both the government and JP had agreed to abide by the rules of parliamentary democracy and to test the veracity of their claims to represent the people at the polls in early 1976. Both sides then carried on normal political campaigns to win popular support to back up their claims. Elections in Gujarat were held, in more or less normal circumstances, in early June 1975 as a result of political bargaining between the government and the Opposition.

In this situation an unexpected and conjunctural development intervened. The judgement of Justice Sinha disqualifying Mrs Gandhi as an MP created a political crisis which the vacation judge of the Supreme Court failed to resolve decisively. JP and the opposition parties were now bent upon forcing Mrs Gandhi to resign, even through extra-parliamentary means. Mrs Gandhi was equally determined not to give up power and, perceiving a civil coup d'etat by right-wing opposition forces, though led by a radical, imposed the Emergency. The Emergency was thus purely political in origin and character and was imposed to meet a specific short-term political situation. This is so even if we accept that it was promulgated to save Mrs Gandhi from losing power. In fact, in historiographic terms, the Emergency was a very good example of the relative autonomy of the political.

In summary, I would argue that India during the Emergency was not fascist or totalitarian; it was just flirting with totalitarianism, though it was an authoritarian state with some highly undesirable features. Even as such, the Emergency was not a pre-planned move, though it was undeniably a derailment of democracy. Consequently, it can be argued that it was because of the conjunctural and short-term character of the Emergency that democracy could be put back on the rails with such ease, without any upheaval or even a significant mass movement. I may also point out in this context that JP, the opposition parties, the CPM, the Naxalite groups and the Lok Sangharsh Samiti, formed by JP and the opposition parties on 25 June 1975, had the opposite understanding, that the Emergency was a long-term dictatorship. That is why they felt so despondent and failed to organize a popular movement against it.

I would also like to stress at this point that I have not brought out the non-fascist, though authoritarian, character of the Emergency as also the negative character of the JP movement with a view to absolve Mrs Gandhi of blame. The character of the Emergency was determined by her. She has much to answer for having established an anti-democratic regime, especially when, as brought out in Chapter 5, there was an alternative available to both surrender and the Emergency. She was also responsible for the Emergency's severe character, the excesses and violations of human rights under it and its prolongation even after calm had been restored in the country. Her complicity in the development of an extra-constitutional power centre and the downgrading of her senior cabinet colleagues and her party president and other party functionaries is also not to be ignored. But, in fairness to her, the fact of her having unilaterally lifted the Emergency before it could inflict long-term damage to the political and administrative institutions and morale of the people has also to be noted.

My main purpose in this study has been to understand the character of the Emergency regime. But, to a certain, though subsidiary, extent it has also been to point to the danger Indian society faces today from RSS, an organization and movement which is at present in a position to strongly influence and guide the government. As brought out in the next section, the RSS has many of the attributes which the Congress under Mrs Gandhi's leadership lacked, to successfully establish a fascist or totalitarian dictatorship.

To come back to the main theme of this section, the totalitarian risk was, however, always present in the Emergency. Authoritarianism can, and has historically been in several cases, a prelude to a fascist or totalitarian state. It is in the very nature of autocratic power to so degenerate over time, even if initially it is not so designed. Hence, a situation in which a choice has to be made between the two—authoritarianism and totalitarianism—should not be permitted to arise.

In case of the Emergency, the incipient trend towards totalitarianism was certainly present. In the absence of checks and balances provided by a democratic political structure, the emergence of an extra-constitutional centre of power was not accidental. The likelihood always existed of persons constituting this centre making an attempt to seize power and establish a totalitarian regime with the help of the police and bureaucracy, which had, after all, become the chief instruments of administrative and political control during the Emergency.

Already, by the middle of 1976, if not earlier, Sanjay Gandhi and his coterie had started taking charge, though without any legal sanction, of the administration at the Centre and in Delhi and most of the northern states. The manner in which the sterilization drive was conducted could have been a foretaste of what would come.

Sanjay Gandhi was also creating a mass base for himself and the Emergency regime. In fact, he was trying to take over the mass base of the JP movement. He laid great stress on 'youth power'. Through the Youth Congress, he was trying to create an organized force of largely unemployed, petty-bourgeois youth, including the lumpen elements, and thus to set in motion the process of making up the dual deficiency of stormtroopers and a mass fascist party. Moreover, the cadres and members of the Youth Congress were personally loyal to him. He also tried building up a personality cult around himself with the aid of the media, state governments and Youth Congress members. Attempting to supersede the Congress by the Youth Congress, he was also bringing the Congress organization under his control and attempting to replace its old leaders with new ones, who were more obedient to his wishes. He got H.N. Bahuguna and Nandini Satpathy dismissed as chief ministers and replaced with more pliant ones. He would have done the same to Siddhartha Shankar Ray in West Bengal if elections had not intervened. He was also making efforts to acquire a political base among the capitalists and get the support of the United States.

Sanjay Gandhi denigrated all 'isms' and ideological commitment, asserting that it was not ideology but character and purpose which mattered. He was strongly anti-communist. Unlike his mother, he had little commitment to democracy or the traditions of democratic functioning. His respect for the democratic and egalitarian ideas Nehru, his grandfather, had stood for was scant.

Sanjay Gandhi and his coterie made strenuous efforts to radically amend the Constitution with a view to reduce the powers of the

Parliament and to free the prime minister from the Parliament's control and judicial supervision. The objective of the various schemes for Presidential form of government they put forward was to concentrate power in the hands of the executive. Their effort to get the existing Parliament transformed into a new constituent assembly was directed at modifying the basic structure of the Constitution. They also made persistent attempts to prolong the Emergency so that they could consolidate their power over the administration and make it permanent.

It is also significant that the threat of the subversion of the regime by fascist forces was at this time coming more from within the prime minister's camp than from the Opposition. Possibly, the forces of subversion could have even overthrown Mrs Gandhi if at some stage she had come in their way.

II

The perception whether the JP movement posed an authoritarian or fascist threat depends on one's understanding of its strengths and weaknesses, its strategic perspective or lack of it, its leader's capacities, and the character of the RSS and its role in the movement, as also of the political situation in June 1975.

I do not agree with the view that JPM was authoritarian or fascist in character to begin with or became so in practice at any stage. Nor was there any indication that JP wanted to or intended to move in an authoritarian direction. One has, however, to keep in mind the difference between a movement giving voice to popular discontent and the purpose to which this discontent is harnessed and the actual consequences of the movement. And the JPM as it was developing, particularly with the formation and programme of the Lok Sangharsh Samiti in June 1975, I believe had the potential of bringing about a coup d'etat that could lead to an authoritarian, possibly a fascist socio-political order. The authoritarian or fascist potential of the JPM rested basically on four factors: the character of the constituent political parties and forces, the role of the RSS in it, its social base, and JP's personal frailties.

The political parties united under the JPM banner and on the basis of whose support and participation JP hoped to make Total Revolution were, with the exception of the socialists, entirely right-wing; their only political objective was to unseat Mrs Gandhi and to take her place. Thus, the coalition JP headed had no radical, not to speak of revolutionary, potential. The challenge it posed to the existing political regime was basically right-wing in character.

The major reason why it is legitimate to question the character of the anti-Indira Gandhi forces and the JPM and their fascist potential by the end of June 1975 lies in the organizational position of RSS in their organization. As I have pointed out in Chapters 4 and 6, the JPM's organizational muscle was provided by the cadres of the RSS and those of the Jan Sangh and its student wing, the ABVP, and to a certain extent by the activists of the rich-peasant based BLD in UP and the communal Akali Dal in Punjab. On the other hand, JP had no grassroots organization of his own to organize the movement, or a political party he could rely on. He realized that students, however enthusiastic, were not up to the task. Besides, he had hardly any control over them. As matters stood, he had to harness the cadres of the RSS-Jan Sangh, especially if the programme chalked out on 24-25 June 1975 was to be implemented. Consequently, while JP remained the movement's chief mobilizer and public face, organizationally it came to be increasingly dominated by the RSS-Jan Sangh.

As is well known, the RSS was a well-disciplined cadre-based organization and, in fact, a movement in itself. It was ideologically and organizationally close to Italian Fascists and German Nazis, believing in the virulent fascist version of communalism.[12] It was organized on the Fuhrer principle, its head, *Sar Sangh Chalak*, exalted above everyone else, being selected by his predecessor and serving as such for life. Believing in the doctrine of absolute and undefined discipline and complete obedience to its higher authorities, the RSS glorified militarism and violence. It preached the cult of strong men and trawled through Indian history to find and glorify such figures. It propagated the cult of youth power, and so-called Hindu pride and male chauvinism. 'Positively hostile to' parliamentary democracy, it was ignorant or contemptuous of the heritage of India's freedom struggle, as it had been towards the actual struggle and had failed to imbibe its political culture. The RSS preached to its members that politics was inherently amoral and that what mattered was its objectives. With little respect for the spirit of the Indian Constitution, it found no place for the country's cultural diversity and secularism in the India it wanted to build. It flaunted its communalism, and propagated it through means heavily influenced by fascist methods of propaganda such as the 'big lie' and rumours. Muslims and Christians were hated, and excluded from its membership; even Jains and Buddhists were looked down upon. Its founding cadres and members, who, held commanding positions in the organization by 1975, were taught till 1943-44 to admire Nazism and Nazi Germany.[13] The organization's social base lay in the petty-bourgeoisie, the rich peasants and remnants of the semi-feudal strata, upper castes, shopkeepers and small businessmen.

The social base of a movement is quite important in determining its potential or actual character. True, the JPM was a popular people's movement, but who were its 'people', its participants. The social base of the JPM, formed primarily of the petty-bourgeoisie (the lower-middle classes) was the classic base of potential fascism. Petty bourgeois insecurity and discontent, fuelled by price rise and unemployment, and rich peasant dissatisfaction, arising from frustration of their freshly-born aspirations, however genuine, were not an expression of the need or desire for fundamental social transformation or revolution of any type. Significantly, urban workers, poor peasants, agricultural labourers, tribals and most of the intelligentsia kept away throughout from the JPM even in Bihar.

The activists of the JPM or its mobilized segments comprised mainly students and youth coming from the traditional middle classes and newly emerging rich and middle peasants. JP declared that he chose the youth as the chief vehicle for Total Revolution because they were idealistic and disinterested in personal gain. Undoubtedly, the movement had an aura of idealism around it and attracted many youth. In the Nehru era, the best of the young, dissatisfied with the existing structure of society and the prevailing system of values, had been silently inspired by Nehru and the communist and socialist movements; during the second half of the sixties they were drawn to the the Naxalite movement, but by 1972 this pull was a thing of the past. Thereafter, the youth in several parts of the country, especially in Bihar, turned to JP and his movement. Unfortunately, many of these youth, though idealistic and disinterested, were basically non-political. They wanted change of some kind, but had little idea of the changes they wanted or how to bring about them. Most of them hardly had any ideological moorings or leanings and lacked in organizational discipline. Many of them soon became lumpens. They were totally unlike the young members of the Congress Seva Dal of the pre-1947 era who were trained in specially organized camps, imbued with the contemporary liberal democratic nationalist ideology and committed to non-violence. Moreover, the youthful followers of JP felt 'strong' in a period of administrative decline, weakening of state authority and state inaction against them, but 'quietened down' when faced with the Emergency regime willing to take strong steps against them. It was JP's failure to understand the character of his chief instruments of revolution that made him lament on the morrow of his arrest: 'My world lies in a shambles all round me ... Where have my calculations gone wrong?'[14] Moreover, in politics it is not enough to be idealistic and disinterested; an ideological grasp of politics is needed. Otherwise, one is likely to be used by forces contrary to one's convictions, and which would be opposed if properly understood. This was the danger the youthful followers of JP faced; that is, of being used by the RSS-Jan Sangh.

JP's inadequacy as its leader constituted a major shortcoming of the movement. We have earlier spoken of his positive qualities and good intentions. He was honest and sincere and all his political life he struggled for a just, humane, democratic and egalitarian social order. However, as brought out at length in Chapter 6, he was unable to translate his good intentions into practice. Moreover, his competence as the leader of a mass movement under democratic conditions and his understanding of revolution and revolution-making left much to be desired. In particular, he had a shallow and subjective understanding of the political and economic situation of the country and of the role that leadership, organization and cadres play in a movement. He had also hardly any talent or time for organization or for rearing cadres, nor did he have others around him who could perform the task except the RSS *pracharaks* (organizer-cum-propagandist). Revolutionary rhetoric without ideology, organization and cadres could have been a recipe for disaster, opening the door to something even worse than what actually happened, for others not him were in command of the forces that had been unleashed.

The threat to democracy did not, however, come from JP himself. He was not the stuff of which dictators are made. He was no Mussolini or Hitler—nor had he a strong social, class or mass base or organizational structure of his own. But he could have been a Victor Emmanuel or Marshal Hindenburg.[15] Because of his innocence of the risks involved in the effort to overthrow a democratically elected government through a mass movement, which was under the organizational influence of the RSS, JP could have paved the way for communal fascism. Nor would that have been a historical oddity. As Max Zins has pointed out, 'many a time, the world over, history has witnessed such movements which, anchored in social discontent, have united a large spectrum of national sensibilities going from the left to the right, and have led to the establishment of dictatorial or very authoritarian systems of government: fascism, bonapartism, populism ...'[16] We may also, in this respect, further develop an interesting metaphor used by Balraj Puri. Puri criticizes JP for cornering Indira Gandhi and not leaving any space for her to retreat; he adds that a cat that is cornered must be left a way out, otherwise it will bare its claws, turn a killer and attack its keeper.[17] But there is another possibility: what about the wolf hiding behind the keeper and pretending to be a mouse? The wolf could devour both the cat and the keeper and everybody else around!

It has been argued with hindsight that since democracy was not endangered or weakened when the Janata Party, consisting basically of parties and groups which had coalesced in the JP movement, came to power in 1977, it follows that JPM did not and could not have threatened democracy in 1975 or have had a fascist potential. However, the circumstances—the context—of Mrs Gandhi's electoral defeat and these parties coming to power in March 1977 were very different from those of June 1975. There is a vast difference between a party or a movement coming to power through duly-held democratic elections and it doing so, riding the wave of a mass movement and through extra-constitutional means.

In June 1975, the JPM and the multi-party coalition were threatening to overthrow an elected government and force the prime minister having a majority in the Parliament to resign through the extra-constitutional pressure of a mass movement which JP did not control, though he thought he did, and which was increasingly coming under the organizational control of RSS-Jan Sangh. JP was relying on the mass base of Jan Sangh in Delhi and the surrounding areas to succeed. On the other hand, in 1977, the Janata coalition came to power through the entirely different process of parliamentary democracy and duly-held elections resulting in a parliamentary majority. Moreover, it had asked the people for a mandate not to bring about Total Revolution but to restore the pre-26th June political and administrative structure and the original form of the Constitution. It defeated a regime which had outlived its term and imposed authoritarian rule. It came to power under conditions of heightened democratic consciousness among the people. It was a parliamentary coalition in which traditional democratic leaders such as Morarji Desai, Charan Singh, Jagjivan Ram, and Chandra Shekhar and other Young Turk Congressmen played an important role. Being primarily an electoral, parliamentary party, and not a mass movement, it did not depend primarily on the RSS cadres and was, therefore, not under its control. Moreover, the Jan Sangh component of the Janata had been obliged to abandon communalism, its ideology of Hindu nation based on so-called Hindu culture and its ideological moorings in the RSS, to break all organizational ties with the RSS, as also to give up its own separate organization and been made to merge with members of other parties and form a new party.

The former Jan Sangh was now part of a secular democratic party. In fact, later on the socialists and some others broke up the Janata party and the Janata government in 1979 when the Jan Sanghis refused to break all links with the RSS and insisted on retaining 'dual' membership.

I may go further and say that, even after the break-up of the Janata government, failure of the Janata party to survive, and the formation of the Bharatiya Janata Party (BJP) by the ex-Jan Sanghis and RSS, the Emergency and Janata party experiences forced the extreme right-wing communal forces to take their political fight to the terrain of parliamentary democracy, secularism, and India's cultural and linguistic diversity. Moreover, the RSS, which had more or less directly and openly jumped into the JP movement, was unable to make a bid for power for nearly a quarter century; it was forced to go back to its non-political posture, to once again wear the mask of a socio-cultural outfit and to operate politically through BJP and its other front organizations, at least till 1998, when BJP for the first time came to power at the Centre.

As brought out in Chapter 6 above, for years, and throughout the period of the JP movement, JP had been skeptical of parliamentary democracy, party system and elections as held in India. He had maintained that the existing parliamentary system and processes had become so corrupt that they did not represent people's will or their interests. He, too, now endorsed both parliamentary democracy and processes and the party system. Despite bad health, he led a vigorous electoral campaign for their restoration. After his release from jail in November 1975 he devoted himself to unifying the multiple opposition parties into a single parliamentary party and to put pressure on Mrs Gandhi to revoke the Emergency and hold elections to Lok Sabha. This change in JP did not occur only because of the need to end the Emergency. Rather, he also did not put into practice any of his previous favourite ideas such as non-party candidates in the June assembly elections.

III

It is still difficult to be definitive about the character of the JP movement or the Emergency regime. Even over a quarter of a century later, the answers have to be tentative and open to questioning. There is, however, no doubt that Mrs Gandhi's decision to virtually revoke the Emergency and to hold free and fair elections, her defeat and the opposition's victory that followed, and her acceptance of that defeat and easy surrender of power were a remarkable achievement, 'a veritable triumph', of Indian democracy. The years 1975-77 have been described as the years of 'the test of democracy'; there is no doubt that the Indian people passed the test with distinction if not a perfect ten. The resilience of democracy in India stood proven.

During 1975-77, many Indians and India's friends abroad started having doubts about the future of the democratic system in India. They had the sinking feeling that India had finally joined the ranks of other post-colonial societies as an authoritarian state, though they hoped that it would somehow survive its crisis. The less sympathetic of the foreign observers felt that democracy in India was 'finally and permanently in eclipse', that India had undergone a permanent systemic change, and that whatever Mrs Gandhi's intentions, the logic of the Emergency led straight to never-ending authoritarian rule.[18] Even such a perceptive and friendly observer as Henry C. Hart thought that the Emergency would last five to ten years.[19]

Many others were of the view that the basic changes initiated by the Emergency and the essential features of the new regime would persist even if the Emergency was ended and the parliamentary system restored—there would be no going back to the pre-Emergency open society; the Indian political system would never be the same again. 'It is quite evident now,' wrote Ram M. Roy, Professor of Political Science in California, in 1975, 'that the era of a free-wheeling press, impassioned parliamentary debates and brilliant oratory by the opposition is over. It would be unrealistic to expect a willy-nilly return to the pre-Emergency openness and freedom.'[20] Some commentators went further and argued that the shift towards authoritarianism had been going on since 1950.[21] Some others argued that the democratic constitutional system established in India in 1950 was not suited to the genius of the Indian people, who, like other people of the Third World, craved authority or were concerned only with their basic physical needs. They saw the Emergency 'as in many respects a natural development.' For example, Robert A. Huttenback, an American academic, wrote in 1975 that it was possible that the period of democracy 'was but an historical anomaly in a country where autocracy has been the traditional mode of governance.'[22]

A very popular view, especially in the West, was that if the economic conditions improved, democracy would not matter. Many said that democracy was an anomaly in a poor country where people needed a bowl of rice to fill their stomachs and not democracy, which was of little use to a hungry person. *Newsweek*, for example, wrote at the time: 'In India, it is more important to be fed than to be free.'[23]

More surprisingly, Ved Mehta too wrote: 'With some justification, critics denounced the Indian democracy from its inception . . . Since most of India's people were so poor . . . they had to be concerned primarily about having food in their stomachs rather than about enjoying their civil liberties; as a "bourgeois democracy", whose main beneficiaries were the well-to-do, as an "alien institution" . . .'[24] Another version of the anomaly theory was that since high economic development was a pre-requisite for the successful working of democracy, India's efforts to make democracy work were not likely to succeed. Many argued that India's democratic political structure was not compatible with its developmental goals as these required a certain degree of coercion if not dictatorship to be achieved. India's effort to combine economic development with democracy was, therefore, bound to fail. This view was quite popular in many authoritarian Third World countries which saw the Emergency as 'further proof that democratic development models are inappropriate for the so-called emerging nations.'[25]

Many radicals also argued that, in any case, liberal democracy in India was only a sham, a façade, hiding the underlying brutal reality of class domination and the suppression of people's struggles. The Emergency had only removed the façade, exposed the sham, and made the reality more visible. It had only accentuated the process of authoritarianism being followed earlier.[26]

To some commentators, the case with which the Emergency could be imposed and people cowed down virtually without any resistance pointed to the fragile nature of the democratic system and its shallow roots in India. Many who were in any case sceptics from the beginning of the democratic process now felt vindicated.

There were, of course, many in India and a few abroad who believed in the strength of the democratic feeling among the Indian people and a large part of the Indian political leadership. They were, therefore, convinced that the Emergency was a temporary departure from the normal trajectory of Indian political development and that democracy would be restored sooner than later in the country. As pointed out earlier in Chapter 8, many Indian intellectuals did not publicly protest against the Emergency because they believed Mrs Gandhi when she said that it was a temporary or short-term expedient.[27] Two major political scientists working on India, W.H. Morris-Jones and Norman D. Palmer, came very close to grasping this aspect of the reality at the height of the Emergency, despite their apprehensions regarding Mrs Gandhi's plans and motives. W.H. Morris-Jones wrote in March 1976: 'The elements of paradox, incoherence and indeed uncertainty in Mrs Gandhi's authoritarian regime are substantially a testimonial to the depth and quality of India's espousal and experience of liberal democracy.'[28] And N.D. Palmer observed in November 1975: 'Indian democracy functioned quite successfully for more than 25 years and has thus far shown a remarkable flexibility and capacity to overcome threats to its operation ... (the political system) has shown a remarkable capacity for adaptation without losing its essential character ... the democratic system may overcome the present crisis and emerge with its essential foundation still unimpaired. This is, I suggest, the most probable scenario of all.'[29]

However, the optimistic view regarding the fate of democracy was held by very few and seldom found expression in print in India. That is why Mrs Gandhi's ending of the Emergency after a short duration of nineteen months and calling for and holding free and fair elections and graceful acceptance of defeat came as a surprise to a large number of epople. Tariq Ali was to write later, 'All those who had talked of a permanent dictatorship in India began to look rather foolish.'[30] Some, of course, remained sceptics for some more time. According to them, the end of the Emergency, Congress defeat in the elections and the formation of Janata government did not mean that democracy had won a big victory: democracy would remain highly unstable even if it survived because the crisis of the system which had brought about the JPM and the Emergency was still unresolved and, therefore, the same old political and economic factors which operated in 1975 would lead to another Emergency.[31]

In reality, however, the democratic system in India not only survived the JP movement and the Emergency, it emerged stronger, even though, in the words of JP, it had been damaged 'greviously' though not 'fatally'.[32] Paradoxically, even the Emergency experience strengthened democracy. It inoculated Indian people not only against another bout of authoritarianism but also against an irresponsible movement like the JPM. In the words of Granville Austin:[33]

> In retrospect, the ugly experience (of the Emergency) may have been the saving of democracy in ways not thought of by the Prime Minister ... It taught Indians about the dangers to democracy that lurk anywhere: of demagoguery, of leaders uncaring of liberty, of hero-worship and placing power in the hands of a few, of the dangers from citizen abdication of responsibility. Like the 'McCarthy period' in the United States,

it taught that vigilance would be the price of its not happening again.

Both the common people and the intelligentsia learnt to value democracy and civil liberties more. The relative failure of the Emergency regime to implement the 20-Point Programme or to improve the administration in the long-run showed that India's problems could not be solved without respect for the civil and political rights of the people. Democracy, freedom and parliamentary form of government were further entrenched. The Indian people's recent experience 'pushed down the roots of democracy in that country (India) more deeply than in many other places,'[34] making it hard for future rulers to impose an authoritarian regime. Since 1977, there has been little talk of the need to scrap or change the existing political system and replace it by military rule or dictatorship or some sort of non-party democracy in order to have faster economic development or to end corruption, even though corruption has vastly increased since 1974-75. No major intellectual or political leader has expounded such views for several years now. Nobody anymore says what B.K. Nehru did in March 1976 that 'civil liberties are a luxury we can no longer afford.'[35] Interestingly, there is no echo of this statement even in B.K. Nehru's later writing; no doubt because he came to see first-hand what absence of civil liberties does to administration and society.

The only believers in an authoritarian structure of polity left in the country are the hard-core leaders and cadres of the RSS. That democratic political structure had acquired a certain stability was shown by the fact that, in late eighties, Rajiv Gandhi, with a massive majority in the Parliament, never thought of imposing an Emergency under some pretext or the other, even when he could see power slipping out of his hands. Nor was there any speculation in the Press or by the opposition parties that he might do so.

Thus, the lifting of the Emergency and the announcement and holding of elections were to a certain extent a defining moment in the history of modern India—perhaps as significant as 15 August 1947 or 26 January 1930 when *Poorna Swaraj* or complete independence was proclaimed. These two developments revealed the Indian people's underlying attachment and commitment to the right to vote, the right to information and other democratic values. These values, in turn, were the product of the democratic political culture the Indian people had imbibed during the freedom struggle and the democratic functioning, including repeated, basically free, elections, in independent India since 1947.

A short detour may be in order here since it is widely held that one reason the Emergency could be so easily imposed was that democracy was an exotic, foreign plant brought to Indian soil by colonial authorities.[36] But, in fact, it was the national movement which provided the soil and the climate in which democracy could strike deep roots. It is true that democracy or the doctrine of popular sovereignty was not part of the ancient or medieval Indian tradition. However, democracy and civil liberties were not a part of the colonial rulers' political culture or thinking in India either. Having initially introduced elements of freedom of speech, the Press and association in the first half of the ninteenth century in India, the colonial rulers soon turned against them to weaken the rising national movement. They began to develop the political theory that because of India's culture, religious and social structure and historical traditions, democracy was not suited to it and that it must be ruled in an authoritarian and despotic manner. Increasingly, over the years, they tampered with and curbed the freedoms of speech and the Press through draconian laws. They also denied Indians representative institutions and, when they had to do so under popular pressure in India and Britain, they retained the real levers of power.

In the meanwhile, democratic and civil libertarian ideas were imbibed by Indian intellectuals when they came in contact with the ideas of English, French and American Revolutions and the nineteenth century radical movements. Consequently, a polity based on representative democracy and civil liberties from the outset became an important part of the nationalist political vision. The Indian National Congress, the main leader of the anti-imperialist struggle, was organized on a democratic basis and in the form of a parliament. The national movement was from the beginning zealous in defence of civil liberties and made the struggle for the freedoms of the Press and speech an integral part of the freedom struggle. The nationalists also struggled for the introduction of a representative form of government on the basis of popular elections and from the beginning of the twentieth century demanded that elections be based on adult franchise.

Thus, it was the national movement and not the colonial state that internalized, indigenized, popularized and rooted parliamentary democracy and civil liberties in India. Over the years, the nationalist movement also created, as an alternative to the colonial and pre-colonial political culture based on authoritarianism, bureaucracy and obedience and paternalism, a political culture based on respect for dissent, freedom of expression, the majority principle and the right of minority opinions and trends to exist and grow. It was this political culture of the national movement which found reflection in the Constitution and the adoption of a democratic political system by independent India. The Constitution was an act of faith in the Indian people by the leaders of the freedom struggle and the founders of the Republic that despite poverty and illiteracy they were capable of sustaining a democratic and civil libertarian state.

The working of the democratic Constitution since 1950 further heightened the democratic political consciousness of the people and made democracy the only form of government possible in India. Both the JP movement and the Emergency, therefore, proved to be mere passing interludes in the long march of Indian democracy. A large number of observers were to note after March 1977 that no social group in India was committed to authoritarianism and that, above all, it had been proved that the Indian poor wanted both bread and freedom. J.B. Kripalani, for example, wrote in an article titled 'Food and Freedom': 'Those who said that freedom is required only by intellectuals and the cultured few, have been proved wrong. It was required by the many, the poor and the despised in India.'[37] That despite the fact that 'the Emergency did provide some relief to the poor people', they voted against the Emergency regime, wrote Sachchidanand Sinha; 'belies that contemptuous theory that poor people need only bread, and free institutions are not for them.'[38] Inder Malhotra, covering the election campaign in UP, reported that the manner in which 'village audiences in the remote countryside react to sophisticated arguments about civil liberties, fundamental rights and independence of the judiciary is truly remarkable.'[39]

The Emergency experience also made it difficult for those not enjoying legitimacy to occupy office. It is important to remember that it was not only the excesses and the lack of civil liberties during the Emergency that hurt people. The strenuous efforts to boost Sanjay Gandhi's personality and power, when he held no position in the government or Congress party, and the authority he wielded, while being outside the constitutional-administrative framework, generated unease and even a feeling of disgust among a large number of people. After all, they had accepted the Emergency and its various measures in the beginning precisely because they were in accord with the Constitution and constitutional procedures. Many people said sarcastically during 1976: 'If Mrs Gandhi wants Sanjay to rule why does she not make him a Deputy Prime Minister.'

In the end, I may sum up my discussion on the democratic impact of the Emergency experience by quoting W.H. Morris-Jones who wrote in 1977:[40]

> I have taken strong lines against prophets of doom who have foreseen cataclysmic collapse of the political fabric. But, more generally, my optimism ... consists in my belief that India has to her credit remarkable political achievements since independence and that the greatest of these is the creation of the foundations for a system of accountable government. It lost its way in the years preceding 1977 but retraced its steps before it was too late ... It remains a system capable of response and change, capable therefore of its own improvement.

IV

The Indian people stood well the test of fire presented by the JP movement and the Emergency. The strength and resilience of Indian democracy and its constitutional system were proved beyond doubt. Nevertheless, the two-sided experience also sounded a warning. If something similar to the JPM or the Emergency happened again in the future, the country might not be that lucky; there was no guarantee that things would turn out as well, especially because the administrative downslide and weakening of many of the political institutions continued after 1977. The JPM and the Emergency revealed major chinks in India's political system and raised several important issued which need to be addressed if the country is not to again undergo similar experiences.

Perhaps the most important of these questions relates to the role of protest movements and mass agitations in a parliamentary democracy, the methods to be employed in their conduct, and the necessary limits of both. While it is true that in a democracy people must have an opportunity for genuine and effective participation in the political process, it is equally a maxim of democracy that political forces and formations have to wage their battles in the arena prescribed by the Constitution. The disadvantaged in society are also no longer willing to accept their social deprivation and inequality and believe that it can be changed through the assertion of their political rights. They have become aware of the power and value of their right to vote at various levels from the panchayat to Parliament. Elections at all levels have repeatedly shown that people have little hesitation in voting against those in power.[41] However, to bring about social changes, to cleanse the social system of its inequities and to make democracy more meaningful, clearly voting every five years is not enough, as repeatedly argued by JP. Voting in periodic elections cannot be regarded as the only avenue for the effective expression and assertion of people's will or their participation in the political process. People cannot be expected to remain politically passive and to wait for the redressal of their grievances till the next elections. Their discontents and their political will have also to find expression in between elections.

Furthermore, as JP rightly pointed out, those elected must be accountable to the voters. But how is that accountability to be enforced? How are the voters to exercise some control over their parliamentary representatives? Clearly, the people have to apply pressure from below to force legislators, legislatures, governments and administrators to respond to their demands. Invariably, the most important form in which the people can do so is through popular protest movements. For the poor, in fact, this is the only means of making those in authority listen to them. Consequently, the politics of protest have rightly burgeoned as the more disadvantaged and oppressed classes and groups have come on to the political stage. In fact, the right to agitate, along with the right to vote, has over time become a basic ingredient and a normal part of democratic politics. But some of the major problems for the theorists of democracy and advocates of the active role of the common people in politics are: how is this right to be exercised and for what purposes and objectives? What are to be the types of issues around which protest movements are to be organized; what form are the movements to take; what methods are they to employ; to what extent are they to go in a representative democracy? For, though protest movements have to cover a vast ground, taken beyond a point, they may also endanger the democratic system itself. Unfortunately, these issues were not dealt with effectively, or the underlying questions even posed during the period of the JPM and the Emergency. One result was that the JP movement, which did not recognize the limits of agitation, put forward unattainable objectives and adopted unacceptable forms of protest and agitation. It has, therefore, to share some part of the responsibility for the imposition of the Emergency.[42]

Let me start with the first question. In my view, it is not possible, or even desirable, to organize protest agitations and mass movements against a democratically-elected government on wide-ranging or very broad and comprehensive issues and goals. They should be organized around specific problems or attainable or negotiable demands or reforms or concrete and precise changes in government policies, or particular aspects or features of society, economy or polity, or for removal of specific social, economic, or political evils. Also, the representative democratic structure, suffering from many ills, is to be reformed and renovated and not dismantled or replaced, or given a death blow.

There is another reason for advancing this proposition. In a democracy, there is need for continuous dialogue and consultation between those in power and those contesting this power, between the government and the protest movements. There is constant endeavour to reach concensus on contentious issues. Democratic politics is based on creating room for compromises. However, the politics of consensus can develop only around concrete issues. There can be negotiations with movements putting forth specific demands and acceptance of, or compromise around, or even appeasement of such demands. The authorities can even respond with changes in policies. On the other hand, very widespread or comprehensive demands leave the authorities with no choice except to surrender or fight to the end. They tend to leave the adversary little or no space for retreat. For example, Mrs Gandhi was faced with the concrete demands first for the dismissal of Gujarat government, thereafter for the dissolution of the Gujarat assembly, and lastly for the immediate holding of elections to the Gujarat assembly. She first resisted but then yielded to each of them. But when she smelled a design for her own overthrow by the Bihar movement and was faced with an actual demand for her resignation in June 1975, which amounted to a general demand for change of government, she struck back. As I have suggested in Chapter 5, if JP and the opposition parties had been willing to wait for next general elections due in nine months or had asked for preponement of the elections to settle the issue of the legitimacy of Mrs Gandhi's government after the Allahabad judgement, a compromise might have been possible. Instead, threatening to organize a massive movement to back the demand for her immediate resignation, they put before her the choice of surrendering or hitting back with the Emergency. And there is no question that in the parliamentary form of government, for the Opposition to call for a change in the leader of the ruling party is tantamount to asking for a change of government and has a different connotation and consequence from the demand for the holding of fresh elections.

I can advance some examples in support of my proposition. The largest and the most destructive in terms of loss of life and property were agitations around the demand for linguistic states. These movements were successful in forcing the Nehru government to revise its firm decision not to take up the issue of linguistic division of the states' boundaries for several years more, not only because they were backed by massive public opinion but also because they were organized around a specific issue. The government could, therefore, yield without endangering the parliamentary framework or unity of the country. Similarly, a settlement with the Naga and Mizo rebels could be arrived at only when they gave up their general demand for independence and consented to negotiate concrete terms for greater autonomy and, giving up the path of violence, agreed to abide by the rules of parliamentary democracy. I may also point out that it was because the JP movement ignored these rules and went in for Total Revolution and the demand for Mrs Gandhi's ouster that it was not only defeated but left behind no abiding legacy, or even popular memory—its impact was ephemeral.

A few more examples of what can be and what cannot be the issues or objectives of popular agitations and movements may be considered. Protest movements cannot be for removal of political corruption in general but only for investigation of particular acts of corruption and punishment of the persons involved. The outstanding example was the Mundhra affair leading to the resignation of T.T. Krishnamachari as finance minister. Likewise, in 1958, was Pratap Singh Kairon's ouster as chief minister in Punjab. It may be suggested that instead of a general anti-corruption campaign which made little impact and bore no fruit during the JPM years or Janata government's tenure or in the long run, if there had been a movement for investigation of the Maruti affair, Mrs Gandhi might have found it difficult to survive politically and would certainly not have been able to, or perhaps even wanted to, impose an Emergency.

To continue with my examples. In a representative democracy, there can be a movement for specific changes in the electoral system, but not for its general cleansing, for specific changes in the working of the political system, not for its overhauling: for specific constitutional changes, not for constitutional reform in general; for changes in specific government policies or administrative measures or even in the administrative structure, or for the dropping from the Cabinet of a particular, undesirable minister, but not for change of government as a whole; for specific steps to alleviate poverty or generate employment, not for the removal of poverty or increase in employment in general; for specific steps for women's employment or for specific rights for women, not for women's empowerment as such; for specific reforms in the educational system as suggested by various educational commissions but not for the 'overhauling' of the educational system. The general issues can only become the subject of wide-ranging ideological or political campaigns, or intellectual debates, or part of revolutionary projects. It would be futile and even counter-productive to make them electoral issues. One reason why Mrs Gandhi had to face serious erosion of her political influence within two years of her massive electoral victory and the glory of the Bangladesh war was the non-specific promise of *garibi hatao* she had made in 1971 elections.

An aspect of the political tragedy of the seventies was the failure of JP to see the difference between these two types of agitational demands. In fact, he recognized the distinction in November 1974 when he opted for elections to settle the fate of the issues he had raised in the Bihar movement. He seemed to have decided to follow the same course after 12 June 1975, when he went to Bihar to carry on political work there. It is unfortunate that he let the opposition leaders persuade him to change course after 22 June and make a bid for the removal of the government without following parliamentary procedures or without recourse to elections. He again went back to a politically-more-correct position when he wrote in his *Prison Diary* on 22 August 1975 regarding the terms of a political compromise with Mrs Gandhi at that stage, that there was 'no possibility of the Opposition mounting a campaign' to make her resign and that it would 'gird its loins to prepare for the next elections, which Mrs Gandhi promises at some future date convenient to her.'[43]

In an extreme situation, as JP suggested, the people have a right to demand resignation of the government but they should then either work for a majority against the government in the legislature or demand fresh elections. Certainly, the seizure of power cannot be the objective of a protest or mass movement in a representative democracy; it can only be a project of those forces which reject the liberal democratic system.

JP himself did not fully understand the import of his raising general demands which would be difficult for any democratic government to accept, but Vinoba Bhave did have an inkling. He told JP at the outset that nothing would come of the Bihar movement, and advised him to in any case confine the movement to Bihar and not make it an all-India one. Bhave later observed, in 1976, that Total Revolution had only led to 'total disillusionment'.[44] He would not let the Sarvodaya movement become a part of the JP movement, and, when he found that a majority of the Sarvodayites were determined to do so, he split the movement.[45] This did not save the movement, which became virtually defunct, partly as a result of the participation of the majority of Sarvodayites in the JPM. The deaths of Vinoba Bhave and

JP delivered it the final blow.

There is a different, more valid and wider general question which I may mention, though not discuss here: can basic structural changes in the social system be brought about through liberal representative democracy or is social upheaval necessary for the purpose? My own view is that nationalization of banks and several industries, radical land reforms in Kerala and West Bengal, 30 per cent reservation of seats for women in panchayats, successful and unopposed working of the system of reservations for the Scheduled Castes and Tribes have shown that political democracy as such is not an obstacle to more equitable social transformation and socio-economic reforms. In any case there is little doubt that in case a society opts for the latter, the road to structural changes does not lie through protest movements but through wide and large-scale mobilization of public opinion, getting the requisite majority in legislatures and bringing about the needed legal, administrative and constitutional changes.

There is one another aspect of the issue-based protest movements that needs to be raised in the context of a study of the JPM. Even protest movements around specific demands and issues are not to be carried on continuously to the end, i.e., till they are won or lost. One reason lies in the fact that people tire after a time and cannot carry on a movement for too long. It is then the function of a leadership to determine when a movement's participants are reaching the point of exhaustion and to try to call off the movement before then. But the other more important reason is that often the authorities against whom the movement is directed can, with their accumulated political capital and the official machinery at their command, refuse to bend. In such a case, and at that stage, what should the movement do becomes paramount. JP raised this question in May 1974 in the article 'Role of People's Movement': 'But what are the people to do when constitutional methods and the established democratic institutions fail to respond to their will or to solve the problems under which they have been groaning?'[46] His own solution, put forth in February 1975, was that 'the right of the masses to engage repeatedly in non-violent direct action' must be clearly accepted and that 'continuous mass action is a necessity.'[47]

The real answer to JP's question, however, lies in part in the deeper purpose of a protest movement itself. In a democracy, the aim of a protest movement is not only to win a demand, it is also to increase the political cost of its rejection to those in authority. In fact, the main political purpose has to be to weaken or undermine 'the intellectual and political leadership' or hegemony or long-term influence of the ruling or dominant groups, even if the movement fails to win its demands substantially. Irrespective of whether it wins or loses, the real failure of a movement is if, as its result, the hegemony or the political influence of the ruling authority is not reduced or is even enhanced. The crucial issue of significant political movements and agitations is that of hegemony over society, or as Gramsci put it, the social revolutionary task in democratic societies is to wage a war of position and not a war of manoeuvre against the ruling classes, the terrain of war being hegemonic influence. Victory or defeat of a particular movement is, then, seen in terms of the relative growth or lessening of the movement's or the government's influence in the minds of the people. This was also the framework of the strategy that Gandhiji and the national leadership followed in the struggle for independence.[48]

JP also vaguely realized this, though, unfortunately, it did not find reflection is his theoretical perspective. After November 1974, he set out to carry on an all-India political campaign with the objective of reducing Mrs Gandhi in the eyes of the people. When he left Delhi after 12 June 1975 to work among the people in Bihar his aim was to further undermine Mrs Gandhi's popularity among the people by partly using the Allahabad judgement to discredit her.

JP also showed an understanding of this deeper strategic aspect of political work and protest movements when he wrote in jail on 22 August 1975:[49]

> As I look at it, the primary role of an Opposition in a parliamentary democracy is to endeavour to replace the ruling party through the electoral process. Between elections the Oppositon works as an Opposition to the Government in parliament and through propaganda, constructive work, peaceful demonstrations and other usual democratic means of winning public support, on the one hand; and by putting public pressure on the Government, on the other, the Opposition tries to enlarge its sphere of influence over the electorate as well as bring relief to sections of the public who may have been adversely affected by administrative or legislative action.

In fact, the only situation in which an all-out continuous mass action is warranted would be that of the threat of dictatorship or fascist takeover or against an authoritarian regime which leaves no space for popular political mobilization. But it is precisely in this type of situation that it is difficult to organize a continuous mass movement, as the history of the twentieth century shows. Such a mass movement would, however, have been justified if the Emergency had lasted longer.

I have argued that protest movements and direct mass action are perfectly legitimate political instruments for voicing people's concerns especially when authorities are unwilling to listen to organized public opinion and the opposition parties fail to perform the task of protecting the people's interests. But the JPM, as also other post-1947 protest movements, give rise to one further question. What are the type of agitational methods—proper forms and norms of protest—suited to a representative democracy, and what are the limits within which they are to be used?

Unfortunately, a convincing solution still eludes us, despite efforts since 1947, and JP's proved to be no exception. As Bhola Chatterji has pointed out, 'the ideas and approaches, methods and manoeuvres he (JP) banked upon were unequal to the task he had set himself.' [50] Since 1947, popular protest movements by political parties, students, workers, farmers, government employees and common citizens have most often taken the form of demonstrations, hunger strikes, hartals, strikes in educational institutions, *dharnas*, *bandhs*, *gheraos*, *rasta roko*, satyagraha, disobedience of laws leading to mass arrests, rioting, and burning of private and public propery such as buses, cars, trains, college buildings and so on. The JP movement took recourse to all these and added to them the picketing of government officers, legislatures and the houses of the legislators. While some of these forms of protest are inherently coercive, others more often than not culminate in violence and breakdown of law and order and wanton violation of laws duly enacted by elected legislatures or rules laid down by those authorized to do so. In many cases the protestors coerce into joining their actions the very people they are supposed to represent—this is how most *bandhs* are made a success. However, just as the effort to prevent or suppress peaceful protest is undemocratic, violent or coercive protest, too, poses a threat to the functioning of democracy and curtails the democratic rights of others.

Protestors have often tried to acquire legitimacy for their approach and methods by drawing on Gandhian satyagraha. There are two problems with seeking such justification which may be discussed very briefly. First, it is problematic whether even satyagraha or non-violent disobeying of laws, which was used by Gandhiji against a foreign authoritarian non-representative regime, is legitimate in a democratic system. If so, under what conditions or circumstances and limits is it acceptable must be clarified. Should satyagraha be confined to specific demands and objectives or can it be used for overthrowing a duly elected government? Instead of imitating Gandhiji, should not there be a great deal of innovation of civil disobedience and other Gandhian forms of protest to suit the conditions of a self-governing democratic and civil libertarian India? That this can be done is shown by the Civil Rights Movement in USA and the Anti-Nuclear Peace Movement in Britain.

There is, however, a second question: to what extent were the methods used by the JP movement or projected by the Lok Sangharsh Samiti on 25 June 1975 really Gandhian? Or, in other words, to what extent was JP an heir to Gandhi in regard to his forms of protest? Even against the British, Gandhiji insisted on satyagraha and civil disobedience being completely non-violent in word and deed. In any case, they were to be 'the weapons of last resort', where gross injustice or immoral action by the government or the authorities was involved and all other methods of redressal had been tried and failed. The forms of protest tried out in independent India—including those by JPM—have been, in fact, more akin to what Gandhiji described as *duragraha*. We may give a long quotation from the *Conquest of Violence* by the Gandhian scholar, Joan V. Bondurant, to make clear the difference between satyagraha and *duragraha* as Gandhiji perceived it:[51]

> In the refinement of language for describing techniques of social action, duragraha serves to distinguish those techniques in which the use of harassment obscures or precludes supportive acts aimed at winning over the opponent. . . . In those instances where democratic procedures have been damaged through default or design, and where the legal machinery has been turned towards a travesty of justice, civil disobedience may be called into play. . . . But if civil disobedience is carried out in the style of duragraha, and not within the framework of satyagraha, it may well lead to widespread indifference to legality and lend itself to those who would use illegal tactics to undermine faith in democratic processes.

I would hazard to say that while Gandhiji would never have advised giving up of the right to protest, which was to him the breath of the life of a citizen, he would also not have followed the route which JP, some of the Gandhians and most of the non-Gandhians have adopted since his death.

The protest movements alone are not, however, to be blamed for the faulty approach adopted by them. The situation is often worsened by the absence of a positive response to protest and by the authorities putting it down by police violence. This often leads to a vicious circle. This was often the case with the JP movement in Bihar. One reason why many protestors take to violence is that those in power turn a deaf ear to peaceful protests and respond only to violent agitations. In other words, not only the organizers of popular agitation must not try to coerce the authorities and should instead, to use a Gandhian phrase, try to change their hearts, the authorities too must be willing to respond positively to normal political agitation and mobilization. There is need for authorities at various levels to have a dialogue with protestors, and, when their demands are not accepted, to carefully and assiduously explain why they are not, instead of adopting a high and mighty attitude, which they often do. At the parliamentary level, this would require greater civility among political parties, a civility which was missing during 1974-75 and was in part responsible for exacerbating the political atmosphere of the period.

There remains another set of important questions regarding popular agitations and opposition movements. How is a democratic state to deal with anti-democratic movements enjoying a degree of popular support and capable of creating a mass upheaval? How is the liberal democratic system to be protected against those who set aside democratic and constitutional norms and challenge the very basic character of the system and aim at overthrowing it?

Such opposition movements can be countered in several ways. Efforts may be made to redress their grievances through dialogue and concessions. But if demands are such as cannot be satisfied or the democratic government does not regard it as expedient to do so, what then? The government may then try to wear down the opposition movement and, in the end, go in for a mid-term poll.

Another way would be to meet the movement with counter-mass mobilization. This solution is, however, problematic on several grounds. First, parliamentary parties are, by their very nature, not equipped for the task. There is hardy any example in the history of modern democracies where a ruling party, however popular, and enjoying mass support, has tried to do so. Second, there is the danger that such an effort would result in street fighting and a virtual civil war with the advantage lying in favour of cadre-based, non-democratic parties. And, in any case, organs of the state would then have to move in to check or control the ensuing violence.

Consequently, there is no escaping the fact that state power has to be used to firmly meet the challenge of undemocratic movements and parties. Not doing so was the gross mistake that the liberal democratic governments of Italy and Germany made in 1922 and 1931-33 when faced with fascist parties. As Arun Shourie, in his previous radical *avatar*, pointed out in 1976, 'It is the misfortune of democracies that they cannot be defended against fascist assault by democratic means.'[52] And he quotes Hitler as saying that 'only one thing could have broken our movement—if the adversary had understood its principle and from the first day had smashed, with utmost brutality, the nucleus of our mass movement . . .'[53]

In conclusion, with hindsight, it can be said that the JP movement, with its undefined goal, inadequate forms of struggle, gross ideological confusion, absence of an autonomous organization and dependence on the RSS cadres for mass mobilization, was not the answer to the problems that the Indian people were facing during 1974-75. Far from saving democracy, the movement was responsible for actually putting it in danger without leading to any long-term political gains: the political system was no less corrupt nor more efficient, democratic and people-friendly after March 1977 than it was before February 1974 when the JPM began. The Emergency, too, was out of step with the Indian people's interests and traditions. Not only were people subjected to all the inequities of an authoritarian and irresponsible regime, the Emergency brought the country to the verge of long-term dictatorship. But these two developments did have a positive outcome. The people and the intelligentsia became chary of unthinking mass movements and authoritarian measures by those in power. Neither has been witnessed in the last twenty-five years. The legitimacy of the Indian political system has been further enhanced. India's 'political miracle' has continued. [54]

Appendix

The March on Rome[1]

The immediate, post-World War I years were in Italy, as in most other countries of the world, years of social disquiet and political turmoil. There was immense economic turbulence and virtual economic collapse from the beginning of 1920. Industries were in a slump and the railway system in crisis. The 1920 harvest failed. Prices rose nearly six-fold while wages and salaries lagged behind. There was shortage of food-stuffs and other consumer goods and large-scale unemployment. There were food riots and looting of shops and granaries. All over Italy, peasants occupied surplus and uncultivated land, while agricultural labourers forced the landowners to yield better wages and terms of employment. Angry workers closed factories. Prolonged strikes took place all over Italy as also a nation-wide general strike, followed by postal, railway, dock-yard and tramway strikes and strikes in cotton mills. Strikers often clashed with the police, armed forces and fascist and right-wing gangs. Even many among government servants and school teachers went on strike. The state appeared helpless before strikes, civil turbulence and 'armed illegality'.

The political situation was no better and the economic crisis coincided with a political crisis. People felt let down by the post-war settlement at Versailles when some of Italy's territorial claims and colonial ambitions in Africa were denied. The demobilized soldiers were discontented with the utterly inadequate/gratuities and other compensations. Nor were they given the psychological satisfaction of being welcomed home as heroes at the end of the war.

The prevailing parliamentary political system also was enveloped in utter confusion and crisis and nearing a breakdown, with the parliament being divided and ineffective. A succession of pitifully weak, short-lived coalition governments, with the constituent parties distrusting and disliking each other even while making uneasy compromises, had ruled the country after the war. The governments had enjoyed little active support in the parliament or the country. People were unhappy with the incompetent parliament and its corrupt liberal leaders, who seemed to be interested only in holding office. They were increasingly estranged from the state and the political process. There was administrative chaos and collapse of public order with the state helpless before the rapidly multiplying armed bands. Of all the state institutions, the army alone was untouched by the prevailing corruption and skepticism.

In this atmosphere, taking advantage of popular discontent, Mussolini-led fascist movement, founded in March 1919 and taking recourse to militant political actions and worse, began to grow rapidly.[2] Fascist bands, especially the blackshirts acting as shock troops, often led by retired army officers, began to browbeat city and other local governments, often occupying their offices. In particular, the fascists adopted a policy of violence towards the socialists. They attacked socialist-led trade unions and cooperatives and socialist newspapers and printing presses and forcibly broke up strikes.

Local police, judges and other officials and military authorities often sided and collaborated with the fascist bands or, at least, adopted a passive tolerant or neutral attitude towards their marauding, criminal activities. Overtly or covertly, they disobeyed the orders of the constitutional local and central government authorities to enforce the law. The fascists claimed to be the creators of a new, revolutionary social order though as part of the Italian revolutionary tradition, the harbingers of a 'continuing revolution' that would change men's ideas and spirit and awaken their sense of morality and centuries-old Italian culture.[3] However, the fascist notion of revolution remained a myth. The fascists did not define the nature of the new order, except that their revolution would destroy ' the old Italy of decadent liberalism and democracy' and overthrow the system of parliament, political parties and elections. Fascism, claimed Mussolini, was not a party but a movement for power. It was, he said, anti-party and above party. Though, sometimes, for tactical reasons, he promised to abide by the constitution, he increasingly and openly pleaded for the monopoly of power for the fascists and for dictatorship as providing the answer to Italy's social, economic and political problems.[4]

Initially, in 1919, the fascists had proclaimed a radical programme, but soon abandoned it, declaring that being revolutionary was enough, that, in any case, it was not a programme but power that mattered, and that they were a party not of programmes but of action.[5] Apart from that, they proclaimed that their mission was also to save Italy from Bolshevism and, instead of diagnosing the more fundamental political and social ills from which society and politics were suffering, they emphasized the corruption of parliamentary parties and politicians and promised an honest and efficient administration. Consequently, they glorified force, violence, war and a strong state, and their organization was military in structure and mental outlook and based on iron-discipline.

Though the fascists did take part in parliament and elections, they saw electoral participation as just another step in their march towards unbridled power. They emphasized extra-parliamentary struggle and non-parliamentary seizure of power. Consequently, the blackshirts, organized on military lines, formed the core—the shock troops—of the fascist organization.

The fascists promoted, during 1920-22, political disorder and administrative chaos so that they could come before the people as the nation's autocratic saviours who were capable of imposing the needed discipline and law and order. Claiming all truth and morality for themselves, they used propaganda, based on lies and rumours, to defame their opponents.[6]

The active membership of the fascist movement and squadrons consisted of the idealistic students and other youth, demobilized soldiers and officers, disillusioned socialists, right-wing extremist nationalists, adventurers of all sorts, and declassed lumpens and criminal elements.

The social base of the movement was provided by several social classes and strata: (a) Rich peasants and landlords who felt threatened by peasant and agricultural labour unions, agitating for land distribution and higher wages, and by rapidly multiplying cooperative and credit societies. (b) Small and big capitalists who felt that not only the socialists and trade unions were working against them but that the liberal governments too were, under parliamentary pressure from the socialists and the Catholic left, harming their interests through social legislation, such as eight-hour day and old-age, health and unemployment insurance, higher income and property taxes and stricter tax enforcement. They also felt endangered by the gains workers had made during 1920-21, thereby putting pressure on their profits, the continuous strikes, growing powers of factory councils, and the movement for factory occupation by workers in 1920, even though it had failed. (c) The middle classes as a whole, who formed the backbone of the movement, were antagonized by the erosion of their incomes and salaries by inflation, frightened by the rising tide of socialism and the growing disorder and the breakdown of law and order, and unhappy with the incompetent and corrupt parliament and politicians. The shopkeepers, in particular, were opposed to the official efforts at price control, the taxation and regulatory powers of the socialist-controlled local authorities, and the growing cooperative societies, and furious at the looting of their shops and the looters going unpunished. (d) The non-ideological students and unemployed youth were often moved by undefined patriotism and 'romanticized' by fascist squadrons. (e) Many of the poor, unemployed or underpaid, joined the movement in its last stages for some of the reasons which had attracted the middle classes and youth to it. (f) Many Catholics and the Church sensed a danger in the atheism and anti-Church outlook of the socialists and communists. The financial support to the fascists came in the main from the big capitalists and the large landowners.

As against a determined fascist movement, with its belief in the efficacy of violence and 'the will to victory and power', the socialists, the Catholic left, the communists and the liberals lacked the will to resist it; they were too preoccupied with their own politics.

The left as a whole was totally ineffective against the fascist onslaught. Buoyed up by the rapid growth of their party and trade union membership, the socialists did not bother about the collapse of the parliamentary system— rather, most of them hoped to uproot it themselves. Alternatively, they hoped to acquire a parliamentary majority on their own. Hence, they refused to collaborate with the bourgeois parties to stop the fascist march to power. Instead, they used their large numbers in parliament to overthrow one government after another or to force the governments to grant concessions in the form of social legislation. The socialists were also prone to internal dissension and soon got divided into left and right-revolutionary and reformist-factions which were primarily interested in pulling down each other. They also detested the liberal and conservative democrats more than they feared the fascists. Moreover, they assumed that the fascist movement would soon disintegrate as its more radical and boisterous elements would leave it. Consequently, the socialists were totally ineffective in opposing the fascist *putsch* when it came, even though they had the strength to crush the fascists.[7]

The Catholic left, represented by the Popolari party, was equally sectarian. Hostile to the socialists and Marxism, it was willing to join hands with the fascists. The communists and the left socialists believed that 'the crisis of the bourgeois state was no affair of theirs' and that they could not surrender their revolutionary principles at any cost by joining hands with the liberals. They were happy to indulge in purely verbal extremism. The communists saw fascism as the last stand of the ruling classes and believed that suppression by the fascists would destroy the 'democratic illusions' of the masses and thus create conditions for the eventual success of the communists in making Bolshevik-type revolution. The task now was not to preserve parliamentary (bourgeois) democracy but to initiate the process of permanent revolution.

The liberals were confused and preoccupied primarily in rivalry with each other and the socialists. Unaware of the fascist threat to democracy and liberalism, they hoped to assimilate the fascists into the political system and make them harmless. Many of them thought that they could use the fascists to put down the socialists and then easily brush them aside and themselves remain in control. All the liberal leaders were willing to give the fascists a share in the government, since, in any case, they themselves would form the majority in any government. As early as May 1921, the most influential, strong and able liberal leader, Giolitti included the fascists in his electoral list or national bloc, hoping thus to temper their extremism, but, in fact, conferring respectability on them and their leader Mussolini. The right wing, of course, wanted a 'strong' government with fascists having a due share in it. In September-October 1922, just before the fascist take-over, most of the liberal and right-wing political leaders adopted positions which would enable the fascists to occupy some posts in the new government.

Thus none of the political parties or liberal and left intellectuals took the danger from Mussolini and the fascist movement seriously till it was too late.[8] On the other hand, the liberal press, at first of its own volition and later under pressure from the fascist bands, adopted a highly critical position towards the weak liberal governments, thus further undermining public confidence in the parliamentary democratic governments and political order.

By the middle of 1922 the fascists had become impatient as the economic situation had started becoming better and there was a growing revulsion in the country against their violence and killings. The conditions for a coup d'etat had begun to disappear. The fascist party and its auxiliaries, therefore, decided to go into action and move towards a seizure of power. From the summer of 1922 the blackshirts and other armed fascist squads went on a rampage all over northern and central Italy. They disbanded regional and local governments, forced socialist mayors, councillors and prefects to resign, occupied local offices of the socialist party and trade unions, overpowered socialist strongholds. The government led by Facta, however, took no action; the state stood-by helpless, its writ no longer running in most parts of the country. The police, army and guards at the disposal of the government were not used. The few steps taken by it were weak, half-hearted and ineffective. The higher bureaucracy displayed neutrality if not support. The liberal leaders, lacking the will to act, did not even have the courage to brand the fascist activities as illegal. The inactivity of the government strengthened the fascists day by day. In a situation that needed determined, firm and vigorous action, the divided left stood totally paralysed and helpless. The fascist success was, however, not inevitable. Strong action by the state and a nation-wide mobilization of all anti-fascist forces could have succeeded in stopping the fascists. Neither took place.

In this situation of chaos where the fascists had acquired virtual control of administration in large parts of Italy, on 24 October 1922 Mussolini, aping Mazzini and Garibaldi, called for a March on Rome (the Capital) by three armed columns to seize the levers of central state power. The March started on 26 October and was to complete its mission by the 28th.

The Facta-led cabinet resigned on the 27th, thus further weakening the state. But Victor Emmanuel, the King, did not accept the resignation. As news of the fascist plans of the March and of the fascist occupation of cities all over Italy reached Rome, the left and the liberals woke up to the situation and asked for strong state action against the fascists. Faced with a choice between fascism and authoritarianism, the liberal government picked up courage and at 6 o'clock on the morning of the 28th prepared a decree to proclaim Martial Law from noon of that day. It asked the army to remain ready to disperse the rebel columns. But when Facta went to the King at 9 o'clock for the royal ratification of the decree, he refused to sign it.[9] The fascist take over of the state became inevitable. As D. Mack Smith points out, 'for the constitutional impropriety of his final act, he (Emmanuel) must bear full responsibility.'[10]

Though the outcome of state action against the fascists could not have been certain, most historians agree that it was not inevitable that the March on Rome would succeed. The commanders of the armed forces in the capital were loyal to the government, had sufficient forces at their command, and were willing, confident and strong enough to have suppressed the small number of ill-armed fascists columns.[11] In fact, the March on Rome would most likely have turned into fascism's funeral march. One thing that Mussolini also feared was army's intervention. Even otherwise fascist victory was not inevitable. Up to the very end, vigorous and firm joint action by the socialists, Catholics, communists, liberals and the state could have saved the situation.

Instead of taking action against the rebel columns, the King invited Mussolini to come to Rome and form the government. Mussolini did so on 30th morning. By this act, the King had delivered Italy into the hands of Mussolini and the fascists. The King and the parliament immediately accorded Mussolini the extraordinary power to rule through decree for twelve months. (This power had been denied to Giolitti earlier). A large number of people, including most of the socialists, communists and Catholic radicals, did not realize the gravity of the situation even now. Many others heaved a sigh of relief. They welcomed the king's step, hoping that Mussolini would put an end to the confusion, uncertainty, disorder and violence and bring back normalcy in the country. Many liberals and Catholics, including a democrat like Salvemini, preferred Mussolini to the liberal democrat Giolitti, the other option, 'because of the latter's reputation for the corruption of public life.'

Italy's experience also showed that it is necessary for the government of the day or a significant section of it and the institutions of civil society to stand up to a fascist threat. Any weakness on the part of the state in this regard or its penetration by the fascists is bound to lead to disaster.

Notes

1. Introduction

1. The story of JP's political and intellectual journey from Marxism in the 1930s to *Bhoodan*, Sarvodaya and Total Revolution in the latter part of his life has been the subject of several works, prominent among them being those of Bimal Prasad, Brahmanand, Ajit Bhattacharjea, Bhola Chatterji, Lakshmi Narayan Lal, and Vasant Nargolkar. See bibliography for full references.

2. For Indira Gandhi's biographies, see Krishan Bhatia, Inder Malhotra, Zareer Masani, Dom Moraes, Mary C. Carras, Pupul Jayakar and Katherine Frank. For a brief discussion of Indira Gandhi's prime ministerial tenures, see Bipan Chandra, Mridula Mukherjee and Aditya Mukherjee, *India After Independence*, 1999. See bibliography for full references.

3. Quoted by Inder Malhotra, *Indira Gandhi*, 1989, p.165. For his detailed criticism of Indira Gandhi, see Chapters 4 and 6 below.

4. Indira Gandhi, *Democracy and Discipline*, 1975, pp.1-2. For her detailed criticism of the JPM, see Chapter 4 below.

5. Eric Hobsbawm, *On History*, 1997, p.258.

6. For example, there is no satisfactory class analysis of the Cultural Revolution in Chin or the student movement of the late 1960s, or of the de-Stalinization of the 1950s and the Gorbachev phenomenon of the 1980s in the Soviet Union.

7. Emma Tarlo, 'From Victim to Agent: Memories of Emergency from a Resettlement Colony in Delhi,' *Economic and Political Weekly*, 18 November 1995.

8. Balraj Puri, 'A Fuller View of the Emergency,' *Economic and Political Weekly*, 15 July 1995, p.1736. Also see his, 'Counter-Total Revolution,' in Balraj Puri, ed., *Revolution Counter-Revolution*, 1978, p.100.

2. The Years of Disillusionment

1. Quoted in Zareer Masani, *Indira Gandhi—A Biography*, 1975, 1977 reprint, p.241.

2. Quoted in Tariq Ali, *The Nehrus and the Gandhis*, 1985, p.177.

3. Inder Malhotra, *Indira Gandhi*, 1989, p.147.

4. Francine R. Frankel, *India's Political Economy, 1947-1977*, 1978, pp.521-2.

5. P.C. Joshi, 'Congress Base,' *Seminar*, 185, January 1975, pp.62-3.

6. Comment to the author.

7. Howard L. Erdman, 'The Industrialists,' in Henry C. Hart, ed., *Indira Gandhi's India*, 1976, p.135.

8. Antonio Gramsci, *Selections from the Prison Notebooks*, edited and translated by Quintin Hoare and Geoffrey Nowell Smith, 1971, p.210.

9. Iqbal Narain, 'Ideology and Political Development: Battle for Issues in Indian Politics,' *Asian Survey*, Vol.XI, No.2, February 1971, p.196.

10. See, for example, Inder Malhotra, n.3, pp.146-7.

11. Dom Moraes, *Indira Gandhi*, 1980, p.215.

3. Popular Movements and Political Crisis

1. I have relied a great deal on Ghanshyam Shah's study of the Gujarat and Bihar movements, *Protest Movements in Two Indian States*, 1977.

2. Quoted in Bhola Chatterji, *Conflict in JP's Politics*, 1984, p.258.

3. Jayaprakash Narayan, *Towards Total Revolution*, Vol.IV; *Total Revolution*, 1978 (hereafter referred to as TR), pp.98-9. JP was to write in August 1975 in his *Prison Diary*, '... the Gujarat movement was a path-finder in India's march towards democracy ... (it) established for the first time in India the primacy of the people, going over the heads of organized parties and asserting their will ... India and Indian democracy will never be the same after the Gujarat movement.' Jayaprakash Narayan, *Prison Diary 1975* (hereafter referred to as *PD*), 1977, p.46.

4. Ghanshyam Shah, n.1, p.48. Rajni Kothari was to write later: 'respectable leaders of society (including leading academicians and highly respected Gandhians) ... failed to curb the use of fascist tactics to force elected members to resign. In the atmosphere of terror and hatred that was thus

generated, local Congressmen were not allowed to face the public and even national Congress leaders (other than Mrs Gandhi) were assaulted when they came to address election meetings.' 'End of an Era,' *Seminar*, 197, January 1976, p.23.

5. Ghanshyam Shah, n1, pp.47-8.

6. *Ibid.*, pp.58-9.

7. Francine R. Frankel, *India's Political Economy, 1947-1977*, 1978, p.527.

8. Ghanshyam Shah, n.1, p.91.

9. David Selbourne, 'A Political Morality Re-examined,' in David Selbourne, ed., *In Theory and Practice: Essays on the Politics of Jayaprakash Narayan*, 1985, p.186.

10. Bhola Chatterji, n.2, p.212.

11. Quoted in *ibid.*, p.216.

12. Quoted in *ibid.*, p.223.

13. Minoo Masani, *Is J.P. The Answer?*, 1975, p.42.

14. Quoted in Lakshmi Narain Lal, *Jayaprakash—Rebel Extraordinary*, 1975, p.164.

15. Jayaprakash Narayan, *TR*, n.3, pp.44-5.

16. *Everyman's*, 12 January 1974, pp.6-7.

17. *Times of India*, 24 June 1974.

18. *Everyman's*, 23 February 1974, p.1.

19. Jayaprakash Narayan, *TR*, n.3, p.97.

20. *Ibid.*, p.111.

21. Ajit Bhattacharjea, *Jayaprakash Narayan—A Political Biography*, 1975, p.23.

22. *Everyman's*, 22 June 1974, p.1.

23. *Ibid.*

24. Jayaprakash Narayan, *TR*, n.3, p.57.

25. Quoted in Lakhsmi Narain Lal, n.14, p.172 and in Allen and Wendy Scarfe, *J.P. His Biography*, 1977 reprint, p.422.

26. *Everyman's*, 22 June 1974, p.1.

27. Quoted in Nayantara Sahgal, *Indira Gandhi: Her Road to Power*, 1982, pp.117, 118.

28. Vasant Nargolkar, *JP's Crusade for Revolution*, 1975, p.141.

29. *Everyman's*, 21 September 1974, p.2.

30. Quoted in Minoo Masani, n.13, p.77.

31. Ghanshyam Shah, n.1, p.99.

32. Bhola Chatterji, n.2, p.312.

33. Ghanshyam Shah, n.1, p.133.

34. *Ibid.*, pp.133-4.

35. *Ibid.*, pp.134 and 98-9.

36. Reproduced in R.K. Karanjia, *Indira-JP Confrontation: The Great Debate*, 1975, p.43.

37. Bhola Chatterji, n.2, pp.274, 275.

38. Reproduced in Karanjia, n.36, pp.47ff.

39. *Everyman's*, 21 September 1974, p.2.

40. For example, he told L.K. Advani in December 1984: 'Each party says it is against corruption vitiating the election scene. But it is not enough. They should all sit with Indira Gandhi and together find ways and means to end corruption.' Quoted in Geoffrey Ostergaard, *Nonviolent Revolution in India*, 1985, p.127.

41. Jayaprakash Narayan, *PD*, n.3, p.7. Also see *ibid.*, p.21; Geoffrey Ostergaard, n.40, pp.84-5.

42. Quoted in Geoffrey Ostergaard, n.40, p.85.

43. Quoted in Vasant Nargolkar, n.28, p.87.

44. *Economic and Political Weekly*, 14 December 1974, p.2049.

45. Ghanshyam Shah, n.1, p.122.

46. *Ibid.*, p.116.

47. Minoo Masani, n.13, p.93.

48. Ghanshyam Shah, n.1, p.129. Also see Narendra Panjwani, 'Bihar: Politicisation of Middle Class Youth,' *Economic and Political Weekly*, 21 September 1974, pp.1605-06.

49. Indradeep Sinha, *Red Face of JP's 'Total Revolution'*, Communist Party Publication No.16, November 1974, pp.4, 25.

50. Statement by CPI, *Mainstream*, 13 April 1975, pp.28ff. Also see *New Age*, 13 April 1975, p.3.

51. Jyoti Basu, et. al., editors, *Documents of the Communist Movement in India*, Vol.XVI (1973-74), 1998, p.464. The signatories also agreed: 'In

this background we felt that the demand for the dissolution of the unrepresentative Bihar Assembly and Ministry and emergence of a truly democratic alternative on the basis of free and fair elections must receive priority,' p.462.

52. Minoo Masani, n.13, pp.131-3.

53. Quoted in Bhola Chatterji, n.2, p.3. For details of Chandra Shekhar's views as publicly expressed in 1974 and later narrated to Bhola Chatterji, see *ibid*., pp.283-5 and 303-4.

54. Pupul Jayakar, *Indira Gandhi—A Biography*, 1988, 1992 reprint, pp.285-6.

55. Indira Gandhi, *Selected Speeches and Writings of Indira Gandhi*, Vol.III (September 1972-March 1977), 1984, p.248.

56. Quoted in Pupul Jayakar, n.54, p.286.

57. Quoted in *ibid*., p.391. B.N. Tandon, joint secretary in the prime minister's secretariat, recorded in his diary on 5 November 1974 that Mrs Gandhi 'believed that JP is a frustrated man and he wants power now'. B.N. Tandon, *PMO Diary-I*, 2003, p.7.

58. Quoted in Pupul Jayakar, n.54, p.227.

59. Quoted in *ibid*., p.246.

60. Quoted in *ibid*., p.227.

61. Quoted in P.N. Dhar, *Indira Gandhi, the 'Emergency', and Indian Democracy*, 2000, p.255.

62. *Ibid*.

63. Minoo Masani, n.13, p.133.

64. Quoted in Pupul Jayakar, n.54, pp.246-7. Similarly, B.N. Tandon records in his diary that, on 17 February 1975, she told the officials in her secretariat that 'JP was not able to think things through properly and that he never bothered about the results of what he was doing or saying.' N.57, p.202.

65. Minoo Masani in an interview with the author.

66. Unrecorded part of the interview with the author. Also see, Pupul Jayakar, n.54, pp.259-60.

67. JP's personal conversation with Bimal Prasad in January 1975. Bimal Prasad, *Gandhi, Nehru and J.P.—Studies in Leadership*, 1985, p.240. Also see, for a slightly different version, Jayaprakash Narayan, *PD*, n.3, p.122.

68. Interview with *Blitz* in December 1974. R.K. Karanjia, n.36, p.38.

69. Quoted in Minoo Masani, n.13, p.91 and *Everyman's*, 23 November 1974, p.10. Even earlier, in an 8 November statement he had declared: 'Our struggle will continue and finally it will be settled at the next election.' *Indian Recorder and Digest*, December 1974, p.22.

70. Quoted in Vasant Nargolkar, n.28, p.170.

71. Reproduced in R.K. Karanjia, n.36, pp.63-4.

72. *Ibid.*, p.71. Also see Jayaprakash Narayan, *TR*, n.3, p.164.

73. Quoted in Vasant Nargolkar, n.28, p.172.

74. Jayaprakash Narayan, *TR*, n.3, p.147. (Article in *Everyman's*, 20 April 1975).

75. *Ibid.*, p.146.

76. For example, justifying his appeal to such leaders, he said in April: 'If I help the Congress to restore its internal democracy and to stop infiltration into it by those whose loyalties are elsewhere (i.e., communists, BC), I consider it something worth doing. With all their faults, these two Congress leaders mentioned by me can play a part in this process.' Jayaprakash Narayan, *TR*, n.3, p.149. It is another matter that JP's appeal made these leaders show even greater zeal in their loyalty to Mrs Gandhi and their party by attacking him and the JPM. Thus, Jagjivan Ram said on 7 March: 'JP's movement is a new menace. His march on Parliament yesterday is an insult to the Constitution.' And Y.B. Chavan on 9 March: 'JP's "revolution" aims at total chaos. Total revolution cannot be brought about by self-seekers and opportunists.' Quoted in Arun Shourie, 'JP: Misappropriation', *Mainstream*, 20 October, 1979, p.13.

77. *Times of India*, 2 and 3 March 1975.

78. *Times of India*, 3 March 1975.

4. The Emergency Imposed

1. Kuldip Nayar, *The Judgement—Inside Story of the Emergency in India*, 1977, p.4. Earlier, in June itself, James Cameron had commented in a similar vein in the *Guardian*: 'It is as though a head of government should go to the block for a parking ticket.' Quoted in the *Statesman*, 18 June 1975.

2. Quoted in Pupul Jayakar, *Indira Gandhi*, 1988, 1992 reprint, p.371.

3. Nikhil Chakravartty, who was to later become a major critic of the Emergency, wrote in the *Mainstream* of 14 June 1975: 'A nation does

not lose its identity nor its greatness just by the verdict of a court of law. The Rule of Law, claimed to be the basis of parliamentary democracy, does not mean that political process of a country can be stifled or distorted by one stroke of the pen, however eminent the person wielding the pen may be.' P.4.

4. P.N. Dhar, *Indira Gandhi, the 'Emergency', and Indian Democracy*, 2000, pp.259, 260.

5. Quoted in Dom Moraes, *Indira Gandhi*, 1980, p.220.

6. Quoted in Mary C. Carras, Indira Gandhi—*In the Crucible of Leadership*, 1979, p.232.

7. Kuldip Nayar, n.1, p.10.

8. *Ibid.*, p.34.

9. Rajni Kothari, 'End of an Era,' *Seminar*, 197, January 1976, pp.24-5.

10. Kuldip Nayar, n.1, pp.31-2.

11. *Times of India* (Bombay), 26 June 1975; *Hindustan Times*, 26 June 1975; R.K. Karanjia, *Indira—JP Confrontation*, 1975, pp.108-09; D.R. Mankekar and Kamla Mankekar, *Decline and Fall of Indira Gandhi*, 1977, p.12; and in Oriana Fallaci, 'Mrs Gandhi's Opposition—Morarji Desai,' *New Republic*, 2 and 9 August, 1975, pp.17-8.

12. Quoted in Oriana Fallaci, n.11, pp.13, 14, 17-8. Later, in his letter to the prime minister from jail on 21 July 1975, JP denied that there was any 'plan to paralyze the government'. Such a plan, he wrote, 'is a figment of your imagination thought up to justify your totalitarian measures ... If there was any plan, it was a simple, innocent and short-time plan to continue until the Supreme Court decided your appeal ... The programme was for a selected number of persons to offer Satyagraha before or near your residence in support of the demand that you should step down until the Supreme Court's judgement on your appeal.' Jayaprakash Narayan, *Prison Diary 1975*, edited with an introducton by A.B. Shah, 1977 (hereafter referred to as *PD*), p.104.

13. Oriana Fallaci, n.11, p.18.

14. Jayaprakash Narayan, *PD*, n.12, p.21.

15. Jayaprakash Narayan, *Towards Total Revolution*, vol.IV, *Total Revolution*, edited and with an Introduction by Brahmanand, 1978, p.57 (hereafter referred to as *TR*).

16. *Everyman*'s, 22 June 1974, p.8.

17. Jayaprakash Narayan, *Total Revolution*, second edition, 1992 (first edition, 1975), p.23. Also see *TR*, n.15, pp.21, 22, 86, 87, 110, 111.

18. Jayaprakash Narayan, *PD*, n.12, p.104. Also see *ibid.*, pp.41, 126.

19. Jayaprakash Narayan, *TR*, n.15, pp.67-8. Also see *ibid.*, p.135.

20. Jayaprakash Narayan, 'Youth for Democracy', *TR*, n.15, pp.43-4. For similar views expressed earlier in 1972, see *ibid.*, pp.2-5; and Vasant Nargolkar, *JP Vindicated*, 1977, p.17.

21. Jayaprakash Narayan, *TR* n.15, pp.119, 124, 133-5; *Everyman's*, 23 November 1974, p.10; quoted in Geoffrey Ostergaard, *Nonviolent Revolution in India*, 1985, p.168; quoted in Inder Malhotra, *Indira Gandhi*, 1989, p.165; quoted in Nayantara Sahgal, *Indira Gandhi: Her Road to Power*, 1982, p.143; Jayaprakash Narayan, *PD*, n.12, p.3.

22. Jayaprakash Narayan, *PD*, n.12, p.104.

23. *Ibid.*, pp.28, 92.

24. *Ibid.*, pp.42, 67.

25. *Ibid.*, pp.72-3, 8, 6, 3-4. Also see *ibid.*, p.114.

26. Official summary of the White Paper, in Balraj Puri, *Revolution Counter-Revolution*, 1978, Appendix I, pp.130-1, 136. Also see Indira Gandhi, *Selected Speeches and Writings of Indira Gandhi*, Vol.III, September 1972-March 1977, 1984 (hereafter referred to as *SSW*), p.245.

27. Indira Gandhi, *Democracy and Discipline, Speeches of Shrimati Indira Gandhi*, 1976 (hereafter referred to as *DD*), p.61. Also see R.K. Karanjia, n.11, p.116.

28. Indira Gandhi, *DD*, n.27, p.31. Also see *ibid.*, pp.61, 125.

29. Quoted by Arun Shourie, 'JP: Misappropriation,' *Mainstream*, 20 October 1979, p.13.

30. *Times of India*, 17 July 1974. Also see report of JP's speech in *Times of India*, 2 March 1974.

31. Indira Gandhi, *DD*, n.27, p.1. Also see *ibid.*, pp.3, 10, 13, 15, 17, 18, 125, 140, 160, 172, 174; and *SSW*, n.26, pp.290, 245, 255.

32. Indira Gandhi, *DD*, n27, pp.31-2, 33.

33. *Ibid.*, pp.22, 18, 17, 178-9. Also see *ibid.*, pp.16, 62, 141, 173; *SSW*, n.26, p.244.

34. Indira Gandhi, *DD*, n.27, pp.79, 117; *SSW*, n.26, pp.240, 242, 263, 284. Also see *DD*, n.27, pp.41, 63, 169. Also see official summary of the White Paper, in Balraj Puri, n.26, p.132. For a critique of the Bihar movement in the *White Paper*, see *ibid.*, pp.132-4.

35. Indira Gandhi, *DD*, n.27, pp.85, 105, 162, 168; *SSW*, n.26, pp.244, 263.

36. Indira Gandhi, *SSW*, n.26, p.241. Also see *DD*, n.27, p.174.

37. Indira Gandhi, *DD*, n.27, p.11. Also see *ibid.*, pp.19, 32, 40, 79-80, 173, 174, 175.

38. *Ibid.*, pp.27-8.

39. *Ibid.*, p.161.

40. *Ibid.*, p.78. Also see *ibid.*, p.175.

41. Indira Gandhi, *SSW*, n.26, p.262.

42. Indira Gandhi, *DD*, n.27, p.63.

43. *Ibid.*, pp.1, 3, 5, 10, 11, 15, 17, 18, 19, 37, 38, 44, 50, 57, 77, 85, 86, 105, 116, 117, 120, 125, 167, 168, 173, 179.

44. *Ibid.*, pp.1, 2, 4, 15, 18, 61, 115, 173; *SSW*, n.26, pp.228, 258.

45. Indira Gandhi, *DD*, n.27, p.144. Also *ibid.*, p.173.

46. Indira Gandhi, *SSW*, n.26, p.296.

47. Indira Gandhi, *DD*, n.27, p.2. Also see *ibid.*, pp.3, 69.

48. *Ibid.*, pp.1, 94, 145; *SSW*, n.26, pp.289, 299.

49. Indira Gandhi, *DD*, n.27, pp.10, 1. Also see *ibid.*, pp.3, 22.

50. *Ibid.*, pp.1, 123.

51. *Ibid.*, p.98. Also see *ibid.*, pp.4, 5, 51, 57, 87, 88, 90, 132.

52. *Ibid.*, pp.1, 58, 147; *SSW*, n.26, 244.

53. Indira Gandhi, *SSW*, n.26, p.245.

54. Quoted in Pupul Jayakar, n.2, p.273.

55. Quoted in Dom Moraes, n.5, p.215.

56. Indira Gandhi, *DD*, n.27, pp.17, 25-6, 52, 53, 62, 95, 124, 142, 144, 176; *SSW*, n.26, pp.226, 227.

57. Quoted by Henry C. Hart, 'Introduction', in Henry C. Hart, ed., *Indira Gandhi's India*, 1976, p.29. Also see P.N. Dhar, n.4, p.254; and Katherine Frank, *Indira—The Life of Indira Nehru Gandhi*, 2001, pp.374-5. According to Mohit Sen, the Soviet Union, Fidel Castro and Yasser Arafat warned Mrs Gandhi that there was a conspiracy to murder her and her family on the pattern of the killing of Allende. *New Thinking Communist*, 15 July 2000, p.2.

58. Henry C. Hart, n.57, p.29. Also P.N. Dhar, n.4, p.254.

59. Mary C. Carras, n.6, pp.253 and 249. Also see *ibid.*, p.248.

60. Indira Gandhi, *DD*, n.27, pp.18, 22-3, 116.

61. *Ibid.*, p.10. Also see *ibid.*, p.123; *SSW*, n.26, p.241. For her criticism of the Press, see Indira Gandhi, *DD*, n.27, pp.3-4, 10, 11, 16, 20, 24, 38, 48, 64, 112, 113, 167, 168; *SSW*, n.26, pp.241, 251, 252, 300.

62. Francine Frankel, *India's Political Economy, 1947-1977*, 1978, p.527.

63. Sudipta Kaviraj, 'Indira Gandhi and Indian Politics,' *Economic and Political Weekly*, September 20-27, 1986, p.1703.

5. The Democratic Option

1. Rajni Kothari, 'End of an Era,' *Seminar*, no.197, January 1976, p.23.

2. Balraj Madhok, *Stormy Decade—Indian Politics 1970-1980*, 1980, p.88.

3. Oriana Fallaci, 'Mrs Gandhi's Opposition—Morarji Desai,' *New Republic*, 2 and 9 August 1975, p.17.

4. JP, for example, wrote in his *Prison Diary* on 21 July: 'Where have my calculations gone wrong? I went wrong in assuming that a Prime Minister in a democracy would use all the normal and abnormal laws to defeat a peaceful democratic movement, but would not *destroy* democracy itself and substitute for it a totalitarian system.' *Prison Diary*: 1975, 1977, p.1.

5. Mrs Gandhi too sensed this. She was to tell Mary Carras in 1978: 'I felt—and some chief ministers also said—that if the opposition sensed a victory over me, they will not allow any other Congress person to remain.' Mary C. Carras, *Indira Gandhi: In the Crucible of Leadership*, 1979, p.232.

6. *Ibid.*, p.214.

7. Nikhil Chakravartty, a major critic of the Emergency, had been urging Mrs Gandhi to take strong pre-emptive measures against the 'fascist' threat for many months. For example, he wrote in the *Mainstream* of 8 February 1975: 'Despair on the part of the Right leads it inexorably to fascism unless prompt counter-action smashes its base and defeats it before it raises its head.' (p.4) Or even earlier in the *Mainstream* of 30 March 1974: 'The Government has to be forced to take pre-emptive action against all these forces of dark Reaction. If five thousand militant youth could be kept behind bars in West Bengal for years for the crime of having dabbled in Naxalism, why can't the RSS storm troopers be kept in detention in UP, Bihar and Madhya Pradesh?' (p.6)

8. P.N. Dhar, *Indira Gandhi, the 'Emergency', and Indian Democracy*, 2000, p.309.

9. Jayaprakash Narayan, n.4, p.89. Also see his note of 22 August 1975 in his *Prison Diary*, pp.30-1.

10. *Ibid.*, p.119. In his earlier letter of 21 July to Mrs Gandhi, he had maintained that there was no plan to paralyze the government, that he was going to wait till the Supreme Court decision on her appeal, and that the entire attention of the Opposition was turned towards the coming elections. *Ibid.*, pp.101 ff.

11. Quoted in Geoffrey Ostergaard, *Nonviolent Revolution in India*, 1985, p.272. Also see *ibid.*, pp.232, 265, 360.

12. Indira Gandhi, *Democracy and Discipline—Speeches of Shrimati Indira Gandhi*, 1975, p.117.

13. *Ibid.*, p.153. Also see *ibid.*, p.179.

14. Indira Gandhi, *Selected Speeches and Writings of Indira Gandhi*, Vol.III, September 1972-March 1977, 1984, p.244. Also see *ibid.*, p.241.

15. *Ibid.*, pp.304, 302.

6. JP as a Leader and Thinker

1. Vasant Nargolkar, *JP's Crusade for Revolution*, 1975, p.213.

2. Ajit Bhattacharjea, *Jayaprakash Narayan—A Political Biography*, 1975, p.vii.

3. As he put it in his article 'First Things First': 'the masses have a sixth sense and their perception is largely true. Besides, they have enough direct experience of the pervading corruption to generalize from. They find that they can hardly transact any business in a government, quasi-government, or even a branch bank office without greasing somebody's palm.' Jayaprakash Narayan, *Towards Total Revolution*, 4 volumes, edited with an introduction by Brahmanand, *Total Revolution*, vol.IV, 1978 (hereafter referred to as *TR*) , pp.14-5.

4. *Ibid.*, p.13.

5. See, for example, *ibid.*, pp.16, 21-2, 44, 67-8, 98, 135.

6. Jayaprakash Narayan, *Prison Diary*, edited with an introduction by A.B. Shah, 1977 (hereafter referred to as *PD*) , p.1.

7. *Ibid.* and Jayaprakash Narayan, *TR*, n.3, p.67.

8. Jayaprakash Narayan, *TR*, n.3, p.168; Jayaprakash Narayan, *PD*, n.6, p.1.

9. Jayaprakash Narayan, *TR*, n.3, p.188.

10. Jayaprakash Narayan, *PD*, n.6, p.34. Also Jayaprakash Narayan, *TR*, n.3, pp.66-70, 168.

11. Jayaprakash Narayan, *PD*, n.6, pp.102-03.

12. Jayaprakash Narayan, *TR*, n.3, p.55.

13. *Ibid*.

14. *Ibid*., p.133.

15. *Ibid*., p.11.

16. *Ibid*., pp.31, 110.

17. *Ibid*., pp.126-7.

18. See, for example, *ibid*., pp.155, 157, 173, 177 ff.; Jayaprakash Narayan, *PD*, n.6, p.127; Minoo Masani, *Is J.P. The Answer?*, 1975, p.54. Also see Ghanshyam Shah, *Protest Movements in Two Indian States*, 1977, pp.104-05; Francine R. Frankel, *India's Political Economy, 1947-1977*, 1978, p.533.

19. C.N. Chitta Ranjan, 'Gandhi and "Gandhian" JP', *Mainstream*, 5 October, 1977, pp.10, 27.

20. Analyst, 'J.P. Some Reflections,' *Mainstream*, 13 October 1979, p.4.

21. Jayaprakash Narayan, *TR*, n.3, pp.10-1.

22. *Ibid*., p.27.

23. He wrote on 28 September 1973 that so far as opposition parties were concerned 'from the past experience of non-Congress coalition Governments, and from the apparent unconcern of these parties about this terrible disease (corruption), except as a whip to flog the Congress with, there seems to be little hope from them.' (*Ibid*., p.34) And again at the end of December 1973: 'the difference between the performance, as distinct from the manifestoes, of the various parties, in or out of government, has not been more than between Tweedledum and Tweedledee.' (*Everyman's*, 12 January 1974, p.7). At the beginning of the Bihar movement, he again said: 'I do not know if there is a single party in this country that is free from the evils of corruption and nepotism. . . . Is there a party that can lay its hands on its breast and assert that it harbours no corruption, does not engage in malpractices at elections or does not receive blackmoney? Only it may be coming in larger quantities to the party in power and in lesser amounts to the others.' Jayaprakash Narayan, *Total Revolution* (Varanasi), second edition, 1992 (first edition 1975), p.44. This work is different from *TR*, n.3.

24. *Everyman's*, 20 April 1974, p.6.

25. *Ibid.*, 22 June 1974, p.8.

26. Minoo Masani, n.18, p.125.

27. *Ibid.*, p.48.

28. Jayaprakash Narayan, *TR*, n.3, pp.132 and 125. Also in R.K. Karanjia, *Indira-JP Confrontation, The Great Debate*, 1975, pp.71 and 64.

29. Jayaprakash Narayan, *TR*, n.3, p.59.

30. *Ibid.*, pp.66-7.

31. *Ibid.*, pp.93-4.

32. *Ibid.*, p.150.

33. *Everyman's*, 16 November 1974, p.2.

34. Jayaprakash Narayan, *PD*, n.6, pp.57-8. And he had also written a few days earlier that all these parties were, in fact, 'being radicalized in the process of struggle'. *Ibid.*, p.42. Also see *ibid.*, p.26.

35. Jayaprakash Narayan, *TR*, n.3, p.143. Also see *ibid.*, p.125; Jayaprakash Narayan, *PD*, n.6, pp.26-7.

36. JP did not anticipate this possibility. In his *Prison Diary*, he was convinced that once these parties had committed to social change, they would work for it after the elections. *PD*, n.6, pp.27, 34, 42, 44. For an even earlier expression of this view, see Vasant Nargolkar, n.1, p.183.

37. As Ajit Bhattacharjea, his biographer, admirer and confidant, put it in 1975: 'Time and momentum had become a crucial consideration, leading him not only to accept as an ally anyone willing to go along with him, but occasionally to sanction tactics without working out all the implications. At 72, and with a heart condition, his hurry was understandable.' N.2, p.23.

38. Jayaprakash Narayan, *PD*, n.6, p.56. JP records in the *Prison Diary* certain other instances which many would see as opportunistic. *Ibid.*, pp.26-7, 42. Also his invitation to CPM and CPI(ML) groups to join the movement despite his strong anti-communism smacks of opportunism.

39. W.H. Morris-Jones, 'Whose emergency—India's or Indira's,' *The World Today*, November 1975, p.455.

40. Jayaprakash Narayan, *TR*, n.3, p.57.

40a. Minoo Masani, n.18, p.44.

41. *Ibid.*, p.33.

42. *Ibid.*, p.60.

43. These remarks are strewn in his writings and speeches of the period. See, for example, Jayaprakash Narayan, *TR*, n.3, pp.75, 123; *PD*, n.6, p.126;

Everyman's, 12 January, 1974, pp.6-7; David Sellbourne, in 'A Political Morality Re-examined,' in David Selbourne, ed., *In Theory and In Practice: Essays in the Politics of Jayaprakash Narayan*, 1985, p.206.

44. Jayaprakash Narayan, 'Inaugural Address to All-India Radical Humanist Association Conference,' Calcutta, 29-30 December 1973, *Everyman's*, 12 January 1974, p.7. For greater details based on his earlier, pre-1973 writings, see Bimal Prasad, *Gandhi, Nehru and Jayaprakash Narayan*, 1985, chapter 3.

45. An MLA who had resigned his seat at the behest of Jayaprakash Narayan would be given preference, for by doing so he would have qualified as the best people's candidate! Vasant Nargolkar, n.1, p.127.

46. Jayaprakash Narayan, *TR*, n.3, pp.89-91.

47. *Ibid.*

48. *Ibid.*

49. Jayaprakash Narayan, *PD*, n.6, p.125. He qualified this by adding that a minority could not exercise this right.

50. *Ibid.*, pp.125-6.

51. And he added: 'This, I hope, will make a permanent contribution to the effectiveness of our democracy.' Jayaprakash Narayan, *TR*, n.3, pp.91-2.

52. *Ibid.*, p.78. Also see *ibid.*, p.62.

53. See Jayaprakash Narayan's Foreword to J.D. Sethi, *Gandhi Today*, 1978, and Radhakanta Barik, *Politics of the JP Movement*, 1977, p.59 (the reference given by Barik is wrong but what he writes has to be based on *Everyman*'s for it does reflect Jayaprakash Narayan's thinking.

54. Jayaprakash Narayan, *TR*, n.3, p.103. What would, then, take the place of a degree, he asked and then answered: 'Just a certificate stating the number of years a student has been at a college, the number of hours he has attended classes and worked in shops, factories, offices and fields etc., and the studies he has been interested in.' *Ibid.*, p.104.

55. *Ibid.*, p.62.

56. Jayaprakash Narayan, *TR*, n.3, p.113.

57. Jayaprakash Narayan, *PD*, n.6, p.126. He added: 'Here we might follow the example of China in which all the schools and colleges were closed down and the students were sent out to the villages and slums of the towns to impart the rudiments of education to every citizen, young or old.' *Ibid.*, pp.127-8.

58. Jayaprakash Narayan, *TR*, n.3, p.186. Also see, *ibid.*, pp.204, 208.

59. *Ibid.*, p.132. Also see *ibid.*, p.139.

60. Quoted in Vasant Nargolkar, n.1, p.3.

61. Jayaprakash Narayan, *TR*, n.3, p.142. Seeing himself as a revolutionary leader, Jayaprakash Narayan repeatedly compared himself with or claimed to be following in the footsteps of Lenin, Gandhi and Mao Ze-dong.

62. *Ibid.*, p.111.

63. The movement, he said, was not 'against any *individual*, but against *a system*.' *Ibid.*, p.124.

64. *Ibid.*, p.82. And again: 'The arena we have entered is not that of elections but of the ongoing revolutionary struggle whose aim is not merely a change of government but a total social change.' *Ibid.*, p.132. From the movement for Total Revolution 'a completely new society will emerge.' *Ibid.*, p.77. Also see *ibid.*, p.115.

65. *Ibid.*, p.110. He also said: 'We want the entire system changed; we do not want the ruling party to be simply replaced by the Jan Sangh or the BLD.' Quoted in Minoo Masani, n.18, p.50.

66. Quoted in Minoo Masani, n.18, p.123.

67. Raj Krishna and Jayaprakash Narayan in David Sellbourne, n.43, p.127.

68. Jayaprakash Narayan, *TR*, n.3, p.88. He repeated this in August and December 1974, *ibid.*, pp.93 and 110-11. Also see Minoo Masani, n.18, p.50.

69. Jayaprakash Narayan, *TR*, n.3, p.116; Also see *ibid.*, pp.93, 126; Jayaprakash Narayan, *PD*, n.6, p.25.

70. *Everyman's*, 22 December 1974, p.8; Jayaprakash Narayan, *TR*, n.3, p.115; Ajit Bhattacharjea, n.2, pp.14, 21.

71. Jayaprakash Narayan, *TR*, n.3, p.93. Also *ibid.*, p.116.

72. Jayaprakash Narayan, *PD*, n.6, pp.21-2. Also *ibid.*, pp.25, 33.

73. *Ibid.*, p.87. Also see *ibid.*, pp.88, 197, 200.

74. Jayaprakash Narayan, *TR*, n.3, p.200. Also see *ibid.*, p.203.

75. Jayaprakash Narayan, 'A Long Battle,' *A Revolutionary's Quest— Selected Writings of Jayaprakash Narayan*, ed., Bimal Prasad, 1980, p.369.

76. Jayaprakash Narayan, *PD*, n.6, p.21.

77. See, for example, Jayaprakash Narayan, *TR*, n.3, pp.68-9, 76, 170; *Everyman's*, 29 June 1974, pp.1, 3, and 8 December 1974, p.7; Minoo Masani, n.18, p.50; Francine R. Frankel, n.18, p.532.

78. Jayaprakash Narayan, *TR*, n.3, p.166. Also *ibid.*, p.93.

79. Jayaprakash Narayan, *TR*, n.3, pp.77, 95, 119, 130, 155-7, 169, 173-4.

80. *Ibid.*, pp.77, 113, 166; *Everyman's*, 8 December 1974; Vasant Nargolkar, n.1, p.215.

81. Jayaprakash Narayan, *TR*, n.3, p.169.

82. 'A Long Battle' in n.75, pp.370 and 369.

83. Jayaprakash Narayan, *TR*, n.3, p.202. Also see *ibid.*, p.203; Jayaprakash Narayan, *PD*, n.6, p.127.

84. See *Statesman*, 12 January 1975, quoted in P.N. Dhar, *Indira Gandhi, the 'Emergency', and Indian Democracy*, 2000, p.251.

85. Jayaprakash Narayan, *TR*, n.3, pp.67-8.

86. Quoted in Minoo Masani, n.18, p.116. Also see Vasant Nargolkar, n.1, p.166; Jayaprakash Narayan, *PD*, n.6, p.33. However, he seems to have had some doubts on this score, perhaps because of the lack of adequate response from students and the youth to the imposition of the Emergency. In an interview in July 1976, he told his private secretary: 'Change might be either revolutionary or reactionary. The motive force for changes of the former kind naturally comes from the deprived and unprivileged sections of society.' *TR*, n.3, p.188. Also see Jayaprakash Narayan, *PD*, n.6, p.48.

87. Jayaprakash Narayan, *TR*, n.3, pp.110, 111, 113, 131. Also see Vasant Nargolkar, n.1, p.169.

88. Quoted in Minoo Masani, n.18, p.117.

89. Vasant Nargolkar, n.1, p.166; Jayaprakash Narayan, *PD*, n.6, p.34.

90. Jayaprakash Narayan, *TR*, n.3, p.93.

91. See, for example, *ibid.*, pp.76-7, 80, 88-90, 155-7, 162, 168-70, 199.

92. *Ibid.*, pp.92-3.

93. *Ibid.*, p.116. Also see *ibid.*, p.55.

94. David Sellbourne, 'A Political Morality Re-examined,' n.43, p.189. Also *ibid.*, pp.189-90.

95. Jayaprakash Narayan, *TR*, n.3, p.197.

96. Jayaprakash Narayan, n.53, p.viii; *Everyman's*, 8 May 1974; Bimal Prasad, Jayaprakash Narayan, *Quest and Legacy*, 1992, pp.138 ff. Also see Jayaprakash Narayan, *PD*, n.6, pp.62 ff. And *TR*, n.3, pp.195 ff.

97. Zareer Masani, *Indira Gandhi—A Biography*, 1977 Indian edition, p.309.

98. Minoo Masani, n.18, p.126.

99. S.K. Ghose, 'Total Revolution: What Jayaprakash Narayan Meant,' *Mainstream*, 20 October 1979, p.12.

100. R.K. Karanjia, n.28, pp.47 ff.

101. Jayaprakash Narayan, *TR*, n.3, p.113.

102. *Ibid.*, p.141. Similarly, Ajit Bhattacharjea, JP's co-worker, biographer and editor of *Everyman's*, wrote in 1975: 'He (Jayaprakash Narayan) quoted Gandhi's maxim that to know the next step was enough to counter the tendency of politicians and intellectuals to sit back and pick holes in any programme put before them. He also believed that if the right conditions were created through militancy and stress on values, the rest could be left to work out itself.' N.2, p.22.

103. *Everyman's*, 'Jayaprakash Narayan's Manifesto For a New Bihar,' 11 May 1975, p.7. It may, however, be noted that Gandhiji at the time claimed to be leading not a total revolution for the total reconstruction of society, but only a struggle for independence from British rule. Moreover, Gandhiji had the Congress Working Committee and the AICC to draft programmes and policies (which they did at Karachi in 1931 and also afterwards). JP, as the sole leader of the movement, had to rely on himself. A defence of JP's position has been put up by A.B. Shah, though on similar lines, in *Jayaprakash Narayan Abhinandan Granth*, edited by K.L. Sharma, 1978, p.34.

104. Jayaprakash Narayan, *TR*, n.3, pp.165-6.

105. *Ibid.*, p.113.

106. *Ibid.*, pp.113, 116; Jayaprakash Narayan, *PD*, n.6, pp.121-2.

107. Jayaprakash Narayan, *TR*, n.3, pp.93-4.

108. *Ibid.*, pp.126, 129-30. Also in R.K. Karanjia, n.28, pp.65, 68.

109. Jayaprakash Narayan, *TR*, n.3, pp.167-8.

110. *Ibid.*, p.158.

111. *Ibid.*, p.136. Also Vasant Nargolkar, n.1, pp.197-8.

112. Jayaprakash Narayan, n.53, p.xi.

113. Jayaprakash Narayan, *TR*, n.3, p.130.

114. *Ibid.*, p.113.

115. Jayaprakash Narayan, n.53, p.xi.

116. Jayaprakash Narayan, *TR*, n.3, p.165.

117. *Ibid.*, p.55.

118. *Times of India*, 7 March 1975, and *Hindustan Times*, 7 March 1975. Also Radhakanta Barik, n.53, p.83.

119. Ajit Bhattacharjea, n.2, p.22.

120. Apart from other reforms discussed above, JP asked the Students and People's Struggle Committees to secure the fulfilment of he following demands as part of the second phase of JPM: (1) formation and deployment of a Students' Vigilance Squad to check hoarding and profiteering with the co-operation of the people; (2) posting of volunteers at ration shops to check irregularities; (3) recruitment of volunteers who would check bribery among officials; (4) peaceful protest in front of wine shops; (5) mobilization of volunteers' to ensure speedier implementation of land ceilings; (6) utilization of medical students for mass vaccination; (7) utilization of agricultural graduates for improvement of production; (8) formulation of active study circles to propagate the message of a total revolution; and (9) establishment of an open university so that students who had boycotted classes might continue their study. Radhakanta Barik, n.53, pp.82-3.

121. JP told Karanjia in December 1964: 'But, in spite of all that Mrs Gandhi has done, the Bihar movement has not reduced itself to just an "Indira Hatao" affair, because it is not against any individual, but against a system'. He did, however, warn: 'If Mrs Gandhi does not take any steps to change radically the system and persists in standing in the path of revolutionary struggle she cannot complain if, in its onward march, the movement pushes her aside with so much else.' *TR*, n.3, p.124. Also in R.K. Karanjia, n.28, pp.63-4.

122. JP sometimes showed an awareness of this. See Minoo Masani, n.18, p.102.

123. Jayaprakash Narayan, *TR*, n.3, pp.141-2.

124. *Everyman's*, 9 November 1974, p.1.

125. *Times of India*, 28 November 1974.

126. Jayaprakash Narayan, *PD*, n.6, p.33.

127. Jayaprakash Narayan in R.K. Karanjia, n.28, pp.36-7.

128. Jayaprakash Narayan, *PD*, n.6, p.104.

129. Quoted in Allan and Wendy Scarfe, *J.P. His Biography*, 1977 reprint (originally published in 1975), p.422.

130. Jayaprakash Narayan, *TR*, n.3, pp.21-2.

131. Jayaprakash Narayan, n.23, p.23.

132. Jayaprakash Narayan, *TR*, n.3, p.127.

133. *Ibid.*, p.22.

134. *Ibid.*

135. Jayaprakash Narayan, *PD*, n.6, p.41.

136. Jayaprakash Narayan, *TR*, n.3, p.22.

137. Mrs Gandhi's letter to Jayaprakash Narayan, dated 29 June 1974, reproduced as Appendix-A7 in Bhola Chatterji, *Conflict in Jayaprakash Narayan's Politics*, 1984, p.383.

138. Jayaprakash Narayan, *TR*, n.3, p.127. Also in R.K. Karanjia, n.28, p.66.

139. Jayaprakash Narayan, *TR*, n.3, p.87.

140. Jayaprakash Narayan, *TR*, n.3, p.62.

141. Jayaprakash Narayan, 'From Socialism to Sarvodaya,' in Jayaprakash Narayan, n.75, p.197. Already in the early 1950s after joining *Bhoodan Movement*, Jayaprakash Narayan defined Bhoodan as politics of a different kind—'not the politics of parties, elections, parliaments and governments, but politics of the people. No *Rajniti*, but *Lokniti* as Vinoba says.' Quoted in Bimal Prasad, n.44, p.199.

142. Quoted in Ajit Bhattacharjea, n.2, p.127.

143. In Jayaprakash Narayan, n.75, pp.223-6.

144. Quoted in Balraj Puri, *Revolution Counter-Revolution*, 1978, p.102.

145. *Everyman's*, 12 January 1974, pp.6-7. Later he wrote in the *Prison Diary* that changes in the social structure could not be brought about through the ordinary democratic process.' *PD*, n.6, p.33.

146. See a very perceptive analysis of this aspect in Bimal Prasad, n.44, p.240.

147. Jayaprakash Narayan, *TR*, n.3, p.110; *Everyman's*, 8 December 1974, p.7, and 12 January, 1974, p.7.

148. He told the members of the Parliament in 1958: 'I personally believe and fully believe that it is possible to develop a partyless democracy. But I am not asking you here and now to abolish the party system. Nobody would be prepared for it and it would be foolish to do that today because there is nothing to take its place.' Quoted in Ajit Bhattacharjea, n.2, p.128.

149. *Times of India*, 9 December 1974. Vajpayee however said that he would send his resignation to the speaker after his party president, L.K. Advani cleared it. The move was ultimately dropped as Advani said that the

party could not spare Vajpayee from parliamentary work, Minoo Masani, n.13, pp.103-4.

150. Minoo Masani, n.18, p.110.

151. Quoted in Ajit Roy, *Political Power in India*, second edition, 1981, p.36.

152. Kuldip Nayar, the perceptive journalist, reported on 'the widespread belief that the present system of parliamentary democracy cannot deliver the goods. People openly talk in terms of military dictatorship or Communist revolution.' *Statesman*, 24 April 1974. Quoted in *ibid.*, p.36. Similarly, the *Statesman* of 23 May 1975 reported Minoo Masani as saying on 22 May that 'he saw in the army and Mr Jayaprakash Narayan two *hopeful* and *stable* factors in the country'. Quoted in *ibid.*, p.35.

153. Earlier, in 1967, too, he had suggested that military might take over in case of political instability. See Bhola Chatterji, n.137, pp.215-6; and Mary C. Carras, *Indira Gandhi*, 1980, p.184.

154. See, for example, Jayaprakash Narayan, *TR*, n.3, p.70. Also see David Sellbourne, n.43, p.205. In this respect, Jayaprakash Narayan not only echoed the obscurantist elements but had a pernicious effect on the more forward-looking socialist intellectuals. For example, writing at the height of the JP movement, the socialist leader and thinker and active participant in the JPM, Madhu Limaye echoed Jayaprakash Narayan by describing nationalism, industrialism and parliamentary democracy as 'three unique institutions of modern western culture' and as 'three western secular shrines'. He critiqued the Indian Constitution for being based on the liberal ideology which 'has remained a hot house plant in India'. According to Limaye, the reason why the three ideologies—the liberal, the social democratic and the communist—which had reigned supreme in India had failed to remove the poverty of the masses or to transform Indian society lay in the fact that they were 'imported' and not 'revolutionary ideologies arising from the soil of India and taking sustenance from it.' Instead, Limaye called for the emergence of a 'distinctive Indian ideology'. Praising JP and the JPM, he wrote: 'The search for an Indian ideology has received an impetus as a result of the non-violent mass action.' *Seminar*, 185, January 1975, pp.64-6 and 69.

155. *Statesman*, 18 September 1974, quoted in Balraj Puri, n.144, p.102.

156. Jayaprakash Narayan's, n.53, p.x.

157. *Ibid.*, p.viii.

158. *Times of India*, 23 June 1974. Earlier, *Times of India* of 5 May 1974

reported that, speaking at Vijaywada on 4 May 1974, 'after a fiery speech, he exhorted the people to remove the government "even by using force if it came in the way of such a (total) revolution." '

159. *Pioneer*, 25 June 1974, quoted in Mary C. Carras, n.153, p.182.

160. Minoo Masani, n.18, p.1. Earlier in 1969, Jayaprakash Narayan told a Sarvodayite audience observing the Gandhi Centenary: 'I say with a due sense of responsibility that if convinced that there is no deliverance for the people except through violence, Jayaprakash Narayan will also take to violence. If the problems of the people cannot be solved democratically I will also take to violence.' Jayaprakash Narayan, n.75, p.285.

161. Jayaprakash Narayan, *TR*, n.3, p.67.

162. *Times of India*, 29 July 1974.

163. Jayaprakash Narayan, *TR*, n.3, p.101.

164. According to Minoo Masani he also told the government employees that those who did not leave seats of power after the majority of people had demanded, as in Bihar, should be treated as 'traitors'. He asked the government servants to refuse to obey such orders as were 'immoral' or 'wrong'. Minoo Masani, n.18, p.121.

165. Jayaprakash Narayan, *TR*, n.3, pp.145-7. His life-long friend Minoo Masani wrote in 1977 that he had pleaded with JP 'to desist from references to the army and the police not obeying illegal orders.' Minoo Masani, *Jayaprakash Narayan—Mission Partly Accomplished*, 1977, p.128.

166. Jayaprakash Narayan, *PD*, n.6, pp.101, 104, 106.

167. *Ibid.*, p.102.

168. See, for example, Raj Krishna and Jayaprakash Narayan, in David Sellbourne, n.43, pp.127-8.

169. Jayaprakash Narayan, *TR*, n.3, p.101; *Everyman's*, 23 February 1974, p.1; *PD*, n.6, p.108.

170. Jayaprakash Narayan, *TR*, n.3, pp.188, 186, 179, and 188.

171. Jayaprakash Narayan, *PD*, n.6, pp.29-30.

172. Jayaprakash Narayan, *TR*, n.3, pp.207-8.

173. After March 1977 he did not intervene in the government and administration because of ill-health, but, in fact, this was mainly because of his basic approach to political and administrative office. He had already told his colleague Sugata Dasgupta in early October 1975, before he fell seriously ill, that 'if elections are announced and I am

freed, I will try to support the opposition. Of course, I would not take part in the elections or have anything to do with with them after they are over.' Quoted in P.N. Dhar, n.84, p.311.

174. This was also the view of his friendly critic, Bhola Chatterji. N.137, p.282.

175. Ajit Roy, n.151, p.35.

176. Jayaprakash Narayan, n.53, pp.vii-viii. For an example of personal antipathy to Nehru, see Jayaprakash Narayan, *PD*, n.6, p.85.

177. Jayaprakash Narayan, *Towards Total Revolution*, 4 vols, edited by Brahmanand, 1978, *Politics in India*, Vol.II, p.115.

178. Jayaprakash Narayan, *TR*, n.3, pp.144, 149.

179. *Ibid.*, p.5; Jayaprakash Narayan, *PD*, n.6, p.71.

180. During the freedom struggle, Jawaharlal Nehru too suffered from this weakness, though he was a major inspiration to the youth. But, then, Gandhiji, Sardar Patel and others were there to fill in the gap. Jayaprakash Narayan had neither a Gandhi to lean on, nor a Patel to provide the organizational muscle; nor had he created and trained, as Gandhiji had done, any lieutenants.

181. *Motherland*, 17 April 1974, quoted in Barik, n.53, p.65.

182. Quoted in Vasant Nargolkar, n.1, p.177.

183. *Times of India*, 9 December 1974.

184. Quoted in P.N. Dhar, n.84, p.247.

185. In the same article, Patwardhan also criticized JP for his repeated 'wooing' of Jagjivan Ram and Y.B. Chavan, neither of whom 'have been particularly known for honesty or moral courage', and asked: 'Are Ram and Chavan revolutionary material? Are Charan Singh and Piloo Modi revolutionary material? The list is a long one.'

186. That RSS organizers and cadre were trained in fascist ideology and looked up to Mussolini and Hitler was fully acknowledged, or rather proclaimed, in the RSS *shakhas* till 1943.

187. M.S. Golwalkar, *We, Or Our Nationhood Defined*, 1947 edition, pp.39-40, 43.

188. *Ibid.*, chapters II and III.

189. *Ibid.*, p.19.

190. *Ibid.*, pp.55-6.

191. *Ibid.*, pp.20, 52, 68, 70-3, and M.S. Golwalkar, *Bunch of Thoughts*, 1966 edition, pp.149ff., and 1996 edition, pp.139 ff.

192. M.S. Golwalkar, n.191, p.152 (1966 edition) and p.145 (1996 edition).

193. *Ibid.*, p.151 (1966 edition) and p.144 (1996 edition)

194. Similarly, the editorial in the Jan Sangh weekly, the *Organizer* of 4 January 1975 stated: 'We dare say that but for the exit of Gandhi—and the political exploitation of his murder—the Nehrus would never have been able to dominate the Indian scene ... We accuse the Nehrus of having had a vested interest in the murder of the Mahatma ... It is significant that Gandhiji had visited RSS shakhas and addressed an RSS rally before he was mysteriously bumped off. And Gandhi's murder itself was preceded and followed by the liquidation of top leaders opposed to the Nehru dynasty. The mysterious disappearance of Netaji Subhas Chandra Bose, who could have easily become the first Prime Minister of India, has never been explained. The mysterious death of Dr Shyama Prasad Mookerji in Nehru's jail was never even inquired into. Lal Bahadur died very conveniently—and suspiciously—to make room for Indiraji. And Jana Sangh President Deendayal Upadhyay was brutally murdered just when that party was emerging as a serious rival to the Congress in 1967 ... Such is the murderous history of the Nehru dynasty in India ... She (Mrs Gandhi) was never expected, to come into power ... But there she is, thankful to the physical and political genocide of bigger leaders.'

195. Jayaprakash Narayan, 'A Grave Disease,' in Jayaprakash Narayan, *Nation-Building in India*, ed., Brahmanand, n.d., pp.132-3.

196. *Statesman*, 30 October 1969, reproduced in *Gandhi Sangrahalaya*, January-February 1992, pp.7-9.

197. Balraj Madhok, *Stormy Decade, 1970-1980*, 1980, pp.76-7.

198. *Times of India*, 6 March 1975; *Indian Express*, 6 March 1976; *Everyman's*, 16 March 1976, p.5; *Organizer*, 15 March 1975, p.3; Geoffrey Ostergaard, *Nonviolent Revolution in India*, 1983, p.163; Nayantara Sahgal, *Indira Gandhi*, 1982, p.131.

199. Jayaprakash Narayan, *TR*, n.3, pp.150-1.

200. *Ibid.*, p.150.

201. P.N. Dhar, n.84, p.316.

202. Jayaprakash Narayan, *TR*, n.3, p.150.

203. Quoted in Nayantara Sahgal, n.198, p.120.

204. In *Illustrated Weekly*, 27 April 1975, quoted in Ghanshyam Shah, n.18, p.136 (n.57).

205. Bhola Chatterji, n.137, p.191.

206. Quoted in *ibid.*, pp.191-2.

207. *Statesman*, 12 January 1975, quoted in P.N. Dhar, n.84, p.251.

208. JP argued in June 1974 that 'there being no "right to recall" in our Constitution and the democratic institutions and processes having been so abused and distorted, the people have no alternative except to demand the resignation of their representatives if and when they forfeit their confidence.' The best method of doing so was 'to go to each constituency and either take a ballot or take signatures or hold large number of public opinion polls whether they have lost confidence in them and want them to resign.' But, he added, 'unfortunately, this programme takes time and energy and the students either of Gujarat or Bihar do not seem to have the patience to follow this course.' Consequently, 'in order to give them a peaceful channel of expression I have approved of peaceful gherao, picketing, dharna, etc.' *TR*, n.3, pp.77, 73-4. Interestingly, in 1977, after Janata Party came to power, Jayaprakash Narayan changed his stance and said (to Minoo Masani): 'As far as influencing Government's behaviour is concerned I rely mostly on the power of the masses. By that I do not mean a rabble shouting slogans at Ministers' residences and Secretariats, but a peaceful, organized expression, in democratic ways, of the will and wish of the people.' Minoo Masani, n.165, p.153. Also see Jayaprakash Narayan, *PD*, n.6, pp.30-1.

209. For example, supporting the Bihar Bandh of 3-5 October, 1974, JP declared: 'From this date there would be no trains running through Bihar, buses would be off the road, work in government offices, including the Secretariat, would be paralysed and shops would remain closed ... A week's paralysis would be enough to end the government in Bihar.' *Statesman*, 9 September 1974, quoted in Mary C. Carras, n.153, p.180. In a statement published in *Everyman's* on 5 October 1974, Jayaprakash Narayan asked the masses 'to squat on the (railway) tracks in groups of a hundred or so' and said that 'if this is done in shifts throughout the day and night, all running trains can be brought to a standstill, blocking all the lines and throwing the entire railway system in the State out of gear.' He did, however, emphasize 'that no other than peaceful means such as squatting on railway tracks' should be employed and that 'there should be no tampering with railway tracks, culverts and bridges and no damage caused to railway property, which after all is the people's property.' *TR*, n.3, pp.106-7.

210. Jayaprakash Narayan, *PD*, n.6, p.67. Statement by Jayaprakash Narayan in October 1974, quoted in *Minoo Masani*, n.18, p.77; Jayaprakash Narayan in a letter to *London Times* in June 1976, quoted in Minoo Masani, n.165, p.147.

211. Oriana Fallaci, 'Mrs Gandhi's Opposition—Morarji Desai,' *New Republic*, 2 and 9 August, 1975, pp.17-8. Also see Minoo Masani, n.165, p.127.

212. *Everyman's*, 1 July 1973.

213. Quoted in Bhola Chatterji, n.137, pp.279-80; *Marxist Review*, May-June 1975, p.344; Radhakanta Barik, n.53, p.57.

214. Jayaprakash Narayan, *TR*, n.3, pp.90-1.

215. *Everyman's*, 23 February 1974, p.1.

216. Quoted by Bhola Chatterji, n.137, p.282. J.D. Sethi also claimed that on the basis of his study of the Soviet, Chinese and Gandhian revolutions he would be able to show that 'what Jayaprakash Narayan has achieved in one year no other movement has achieved before.' Quoted in *Ibid*.

217. *Ibid*., pp.281 and 296. Another friendly biographer of JP and also editor of his speeches and writings has written on similar lines: 'The fundamental issue which requires serious consideration is whether a nation-wide struggle for Total Revolution can be launched without the existence of a well-knit, cadre-based organization and without adequate ideological preparation of the masses, on the basis largely of an upsurge among university students in certain parts of the country, unrelated to the programme of Total Revolution and with the help of political parties and leaders having no genuine interest in such a revolution. Allied to it is the issue whether a movement or struggle for Total Revolution can be successfully carried to its logical conclusion without the existence of a political party fully committed to the cause of Total Revolution and equipped to take over power and implement its programme if and when an opportunity for doing so presents itself.' Bimal Prasad, n.96, pp.142-3.

218. Jayaprakash Narayan, *PD*, n.6, p.23. Also see, JP, quoted in Minoo Masani, n.18, p.41.

219. Zareer Masani, n.97, p.306.

220. Balraj Puri, 'Political System and JP,' *Cross Section*, May-June 1974, p.27, quoted in Balraj Puri, n.144, p.103.

7. *The Emergency: The Initial Years*

1. There already existed a state of External Emergency declared in 1971 at the time of the Bangladesh War and that had not yet been rescinded.

2. The Cabinet was not taken into confidence prior to its declaration as that might have led to the news being leaked before action was taken against the Opposition.

3. Censorship meant that any news or views that were printed had to follow previously-laid down guidelines and the newspaper could be punished for violating them. Pre-censorship meant that the news or opinion had to be submitted to the censoring authority for approval before being printed.

4. Indira Gandhi, *Selected Speeches and Writings of Indira Gandhi*, vol.III, September 1972-March 1977, 1984 (Hereafter referred to as *SSW*), pp.251-2. When Khushwant Singh asked Mrs Gandhi to keep the Emergency but lift the curbs on the Press, Mrs Gandhi told him: 'There can be no Emergency without censorship of the Press.' Khushwant Singh, *Indira Gandhi Returns*, 1979, p.72.

5. DMK had passed a resolution condemning the Emergency and organized protest rallies against it.

6. During the hearing of the habeas corpus appeals, Justice H.R. Khanna asked the Attorney General De regarding suspension of Article 21 of the Constitution: 'Supposing some policemen for reasons of enmity, not of state, kills someone, would there be a remedy?' De replied: 'Consistent with my position, My Lord, not so long as the Emergency lasts.' And he added: 'It shocks my conscience, it may shock yours, but there is no remedy.' Quoted in Granville Austin, *Working A Democratic Constitution—The Indian Experience*, 1999, p.339. Earlier, the following exchange had occurred in the Supreme Court in January 1976, '*Mr Justice Chandrachud*: Supposing a man has nothing to do with politics and he goes morning and evening to a temple but he is detained on some false information. How can he get his right to personal liberty enforced under the rule of law? *Mr V.R. Raman* (Additional Solicitor-General): He has no right to know the grounds or any information or material regarding his detention. His rights are suspended with the suspension of Articles 21 and 22. *Mr Justice Bhagwati*: That means courts even cannot call for the grounds. *Mr Raman*: Yes. Furnishing of grounds to courts means furnishing grounds indirectly to detenus who have been denied this right.' *Hindustan Times*, 10 January 1976.

7. Inder Malhotra, 'June 25, 1975: A Look Back,' *Hindu*, 25 June 2000. n.4.

8. Quoted in Granville Austin, n.6, p.35.

9. The entire document is reproduced as Appendix-I in Max Jean Zins, *Strains on Indian Democracy*, 1988. It was originally published in *Mainstream*, 3.1.1976.

10. The paper is reproduced as Appendix-II in *ibid*.

11. Austin, n.6, p.357.

12. P.N. Dhar, *Indira Gandhi, the 'Emergency', and Indian Democracy*, 2000, p.337.

13. *Times of India*, 22.8.1975, quoted in Max Jean Zins, n.9, p.133.

14. Quoted in Granville Austin, n.6, p.357.

15. Max Jean Zins, n.9, pp.150, 31, and Granville Austin, n.6, p.363, 360.

16. P.N. Dhar, n.12, p.342. Bansi Lal also said to B.K. Nehru, '*Arey Nehru Saheb, yeh sub election phelection ke jhegra khetum kariye. Main to kehta hoon ki Behenji ko President for life banadijiye baaki kucch karne ki jarrorat nahin hai* (Nehru Sahab, get rid of all this election nonsense. If you ask me, just make our sister President for life and there's no need to do anything else).' B.K. Nehru, *Nice Guys Finish Second*, 1997, p.559.

17. The Amendment was introduced as the 44th Amendment Bill and is so referred to by many contemporaries but, because two earlier amendment bills were pending, it was later titled as the 42nd Amendment.

18. The Amendment Bill's 'Statement of Objects and Reasons' said that it was designed to help achieve 'a social-economic revolution which would end poverty and inequality of opportunity'. Granville Austin, n.6, p.308.

19. Indira Gandhi, *SSW*, n.4, pp.283-98.

20. As N.A. Palkhivala, a major champion of free enterprise, put it in October 1976, 'In order to put an end to the perpetual and deliberate distortion of the issue of basic human freedoms by snide references to the right to property, I am wholly in favour of removing the remnants of the right to property from the chapter on fundamental rights.' Quoted in Balraj Puri, *Revolution Counter-Revolution*, 1978, p.20. For the 'National Demand', see *Nation-wide Demand for Postponement of Constitution Amendment Bill*, 1976. Also in *Times of India*, 26 October 1976.

21. Quoted in Norman D. Palmer, 'India in 1976: The Politics of Depoliticization,' *Asian Survey*, February 1977, p.168.

22. As Granville Austin put it, 'The headsman's axe had not fallen definitely on liberty and democracy, but its edge was being honed.' N.6, p.371.

23. Norman D. Palmer, n.21, p.179.

24. As two major critics of the Emergency were to put it in 1977, 'The first impact on the Indian people of the Emergency was favourable ... For

the first six months everything went off swimmingly.' D.R. Mankekar and Kamla Mankekar, *Decline and Fall of Indira Gandhi*, 1977, p.33.

25. Jayaprakash Narayan, *Prison Diary: 1975*, 1977 (hereafter referred to as *PD*), pp.2-3.

26. Sachchidanand Sinha, *Emergency in Perspective*, 1977, p.vii.

27. Sachchidanand Sinha, one of the most perceptive critics of the Emergency, was to point out later in 1977: 'The simple fact was that the leadership of the opposition parties had failed to find their way to the hearts of the people. Their fight, though it occasionally elicited public response when it touched their problems, by and large had appeared a mere struggle for power.' *Ibid.*, p.67.

28. In any case, they were not in sympathy with the JPM whose muscle power, outside Bihar, was largely provided by RSS-Jan Sangh and to a certain extent the rich-peasant-dominated BLD.

29. See, for example, Mrs Gandhi's speech in Lok Sabha on 22 July 1975. Indira Gandhi, *Democracy and Discipline, Speeches of Shrimati Indira Gandhi*, 1975 (hereafter referred to as *DD*), pp.27 ff. Also in Indira Gandhi, *SSW*, n.4, pp.184 ff.

30. B.K. Nehru, who 'wholeheartedly approved' of the Emergency, wrote in his memoirs: 'The Emergency, in the circumstances that had been created, was the only way in which the country could have been saved from chaos.' N.16, pp.557, 568.

31. H.Y. Sharda Prasad, 'Can there be a repeat of the Emergency?' *Asian Age*, 28 June 2000.

32. Mohit Sen, 'Emergency Debate,' *New Thinking Communist*, 15 July 2000, p.5.

33. Mrs Gandhi stressed this point in her address to the nation on 27 June. *DD*, n.29, pp.3-4, or *SSW*, n.4, pp.178-9.

34. See, for example, Indira Gandhi, *DD*, n.29, pp.5, 98, 119, 132.

35. According to Clause I of Article 352, 'If the President is satisfied that a grave emergency exists whereby the security of India or of any part of the territory thereof is threatened whether by war or external aggression or internal disturbance, he may, by Proclamation, make a declaration to that effect.'

36. Indira Gandhi, *DD*, n.29, p.31, Also see *ibid.*, pp.18, 61.

37. *Ibid.*, p.125. Also see *ibid.*, pp.102-04, 138, 148, 152.

38. W.H. Morris-Jones, 'Creeping but Uneasy Authoritarianism: India, 1975-

6,' *Government and Opposition*, Vol.12, no.1, Winter 1977, p.30. S.S. Ray later said that when he advised the imposition of the Emergency in June, he expected that it would be 'for a short period and to be used only for the purpose of bringing back sanity to the country.' Quoted in Uma Vasudev, *Two Faces of Indira Gandhi*, 1977, p.40.

39. See, for example, Indira Gandhi, *DD*, n.29, pp.2, 3, 23, 35, 77, 86, 88, 117-8, 125, 126, 180; and *SSW*, n.4, pp.228, 241.

40. Indira Gandhi, *DD*, n.29, pp.22, 70, 76, 93, 159. Also see *ibid.*, pp.11-2, 53, 102-4, 118-9, 139, 148, 150, 152, 157; and *SSW*, n.4, pp.257-8, 262-4.

41. Also Indira Gandhi, *DD*, n.29, pp.3, 11, 152, 179; and *SSW*, n.4, p.241.

42. Indira Gandhi, *DD*, n.29, pp.101, 103-04, 120.

43. *Ibid.*, pp.21, 62, 93, 125, 166.

44. We have already cited H.Y. Sharda Prasad above (f.n.31) in this respect.

45. Indira Gandhi, *DD*, n.29, p.11. Also see *ibid.*, p.162.

46. Indira Gandhi, *SSW*, n.4, pp.240-1 and 262. Also see *ibid.*, pp.244, 263; *DD*, n.29, p.174; Indira Gandhi, *My Truth*, 1980, pp.161-2.

47. For example, she said in January 1976: 'The country has never been in such grave danger before. Some powers which had tasted success in their destabilization game in Chile nurtured similar designs against India. In Bangladesh they succeeded. Not in India.' Quoted in Henry C. Hart, 'Introduction', in Henry C. Hart, ed., *Indira Gandhi's India*, 1976, p.29.

48. Indira Gandhi, *DD*, n.29, p.69. Also *ibid.*, pp.21, 35, 39; and *SSW*, n.4, pp.239-40, 263.

49. Throughout the Emergency, Mrs Gandhi was to flaunt this support. See, for example, her speech to the Rajya Sabha on 8 January 1976, *SSW*, n.4, p.239.

50. Sachchidanand Sinha, n.26, p.85.

51. Arun Shourie, 'Role of Intellectuals During and After the Emergency,' in Balraj Puri, n.20, p.45.

52. Sachchidanand Sinha, n.26, pp.72-3.

53. The Shah Commission, appointed by the Janata government to investigate misuse of government authority during the Emergency, received a total of 793 complaints of misuse of powers of arrest or detention and maltreatment of detenues and others arrested persons. Of these complaints, the Commission found 109 to be proved and 180 partially proved. *Shah*

Commission of Inquiry, Third and Final Report, 1978, p.224, Table IV(b).

54. See, for example, B.K. Nehru, n.16, pp.561, 564; P.N. Dhar, n.12, pp.312, 313; Abu Abraham, 'Neither Conformism nor Martyrdom,' in Balraj Puri, n.20, p.58; Zareer Masani, *Indira Gandhi—A Biography*, 1977 reprint, p.310-24.

55. *Hindustan Times*, 1 January 1976, quoted in Henry C. Hart, n.47, p.30.

56. Indira Gandhi, *SSW*, n.4, p.264.

57. B.K. Nehru, n.16, p.582.

58. Indira Gandhi, *DD*, n.29, p.64.

59. *Ibid.*, p.106.

60. Mary C. Carras, *Indira Gandhi—In the Crucible of Leadership*, 1979, p.240.

61. Dom Moraes, *Indira Gandhi*, 1980, p.263.

62. Pranay Gupte, *Mother India*, 1980, p.450.

63. Our maid, for example, asked me this question.

64. She also, for example, broke her earlier assurance of tolerating opposition state governments and got rid of them.

8. The Emergency: The Later Phase

1. The Andhra leader and Union Minister Raghuramaiah declared: 'I have served two generations of Nehrus, I'll be happy to serve the third.' Quoted in Uma Vasudev, *Two Faces of Indira Gandhi*, 1977, p.182. Sitaram Kesari, President of Bihar State Congress, declared at a Patna meeting that 'Sanjay Gandhi was the new star on the political firmament and the leadership of the Congress and the country was safe for the next 50 years.' Kuldip Nayar, *The Judgement*, 1977, p.137. In reply to those who said that Sanjay was too young to be an effective national leader, D.K. Barooah, Congress president, said: 'How old was Maharaja Ranjit Singh when he became the King of Punjab? Eighteen! How old was Shankaracharya when he died? How old was Swami Vivekananda when he died? Thirty-nine! How old was Akbar when he conceived the idea of a cosmopolitan empire? He was merely in his teens. In this country lots of things have been done by young people and a lot of mischief has been done by the old.' Quoted in Uma Vasudev, p.183. Similarly, addressing Sanjay and a mass audience, Rajni Patel, President of Bombay Congress said: 'Sanjay is the future of India. His future is very

bright and we are proud to have the grandson of Panditji and the son of Indiraji in our midst. Mr Gandhi, the India of Panditji's and Indiraji's dreams will be realized under your responsibility.' Quoted in S.K. Ghose, *The Crusade and End of Indira Raj*, 1978, p.201.

2. According to P.N. Bahl, joint secretary in the Prime Minister's Secretariat, who also liaisoned with with PMH, and who had been selected for the job by R.K. Dhawan, 'It would be truism to say that the House started exercising formidable power in practically all affairs of the State. Practically, all sections of the Government accepted the new atmosphere. There was no protest from anywhere. Even the State Governments with the exception of a few came largely within its orbit.' He also says that the entire process of the Emergency was 'initiated in a masterly manner and then executed fast the same way.' P.N. Bahl, *Indira Gandhi—The Crucial Years (1973-1984)*, 1994, pp.16-7, 19. According to B.N. Tandon and N.K. Seshan who was Mrs Gandhi's private secretary, already, before June 1975, many administrative decisions were being taken in PMH under the influence of Sanjay Gandhi and his emerging coterie. The latter had also already taken full control of the Delhi administration. B.N Tandon, *PMO Diary I: Prelude to the Emergency*, 2003, pp.xxii, xxiv-xxv, xxxii, 40, 41, 57, 110, 111, 253, 254, 306, 334, 352; and N.K. Seshan, *With Three Prime Ministers*, 1993, pp.113-4.

3. P.N. Dhar, *Indira Gandhi, the 'Emergency', and Indian Democracy*, 2000, pp.320 ff. N.K. Seshan writes that 'Slowly I changed the habit of submitting files directly (to Mrs Gandhi) and started routing [them] through the other centre for power.' N.2, p.123.

4. B.N. Tandon, n.2, p.441. Tandon records in his diary on 29 July 1975: 'Many arrests are made against the PM's wishes. Even the PM is helpless before the palace coterie.' *Ibid.*, p.49. For Tandon's views of the growing strength of the PMH, see *Ibid.*, pp.xvii, xxxiv

5. B.K. Nehru, *Nice Guys Finish Second*, 1997, p.4. The Shah Commission commented, 'What happened during the Emergency was the subversion of a system of Administration.' *Shah Commission of Inquiry, Third and Final Report*, 1978, p.231.

6. *Hindustan Times*, 21 November 1976.

7. Quoted in Kuldip Nayar, n.1, p.24. Nayar does not mention the date of the interview.

8. P.N. Dhar, n.3, p.329.

9. Quoted in Uma Vasudev, n.1, pp.206-07. The entire interview has been reproduced in her book as an appendix.

10. His retraction read: 'I did not mean to make such a sweeping statement about an entire party. Obviously in some parties like the Swatantra, the Jan Sangh and the BLD there are far more wealthy people and there is also more corruption. I felt angry because I have heard that some individuals who call themselves communist Marxists and pose as being superior are in fact rich and also far from honest. I do not agree with the communists but I must admit that their workers are dedicated to their cause and willing to sacrifice for it. They may take advantage of a situation but the CPI has supported and worked wholeheartedly for progressive policies, specially those affecting the poor people ... I should also like to make it clear that about other matters also, anything I said was my personal view.' *Indian Express*, 29 August 1975, quoted in Uma Vasudev, n.1, p.110.

11. P.N. Dhar, n.3, p.312.

12. Reproduced in *Economic and Political Weekly*, 15 January 1977, p.37. According to the *Hindustan Times* of 10 January 1977, he accused the CPJ of having only one-point programme, that of spreading all kinds of lies against the Youth Congress, and added that there was no place for such "liars" and "traitors" in the Youth Congress or the Congress. On 16 January, he accused the Communists of taking recourse to 'falsehood, duplicity and treachery', following an "imported ideology", weakening "national fabric", "telling lies", and forming a 'a party of traitors'. *Times of India*, 17 January 1977. Earlier, on 26 December 1976, he had said at a mammoth public meeting at Bidar, Karnataka, that 'the same people who charged the Congress and the Youth Congress as reactionaries and imperialists were themselves guilty of supporting the imperialist British when the Congress was fighting for the country's independence.' *Hindustan Times*, 27 December 1976. Also 26 December 1976.

13. Balraj Puri, 'Counter-Total Revolution', in Balraj Puri, ed., *Revolution Counter-revolution*, 1978, p.4.

14. Quoted in Pupul Jayakar, *Indira Gandhi—A Biography*, 1992, p.307.

15. Indira Gandhi, *Selected Speeches and Writings of Indira Gandhi*, Vol.III, September 1972-March 1977 (hereafter referred to as *SSW*), p.286.

16. R.K. Karanjia, *Indira-JP Confrontation*, 1975, pp.122, 127; Indira Gandhi, *Democracy and Discipline, Speeches of Shrimati Indira Gandhi*, 1975 (Hereafter referred to as *DD*), pp.128, 129; Indira Gandhi, *SSW*, n.14, pp.249, 270.

17. B.K. Nehru, n.4, pp.560, 564. Pupul Jayakar quotes Rajiv Gandhi as telling her on the day election results were announced in March 1977:

'I will never forgive Sanjay for having brought Mummy to this position. He is responsible. I had spoken to her about Sanjay and what people were saying on several occasions, but she refused to believe.' n.13, p.321.

18. Quoted in Pupul Jayakar, n.13, p.296.

19. Indira Gandhi, *My Truth*, 1980, p.165.

20. *Times of India*, 23 November 1976; 24 December 1976; *Hindustan Times*, 24 December 1976.

21. P.N. Dhar, n.3, pp.337, 348, 349; Uma Vasudev, n.1, p.187; Also see footnotes 11-14 of Chapter 7, and footnotes and 12 of Chapter 9.

22. According to *Times of India* of 24 December, 1976, she said a day earlier that when the judgement of the election petition against her had come, Sanjay 'did feel that I needed help, that I needed protection and also there were not very many sincere people around'. Similarly, she told Dom Moraes in 1978. 'But when I was in difficulties at Allahabad, he was one of the few people who stood by me.' Dom Moraes, *Indira Gandhi*, 1980, p.228. Also see Pupul Jayakar, n.13, p.291.

23. P.N. Dhar, n.3, pp.328-9. He asks a few pages later: 'Was she herself becoming afraid of him?' p.348.

24. *Ibid.*, p.348.

25. *Ibid.*, p.330.

26. Pupul Jayakar, n.13, p.292.

27. *Ibid.*

28. Zareer Masani, *Indira Gandhi, A Biography*, 1975, p.310.13.

29. Katherine Frank, *Indira, The Life of Indira Nehru Gandhi*, 2001, pp.399-400.

30. Uma Vasudev, n.1, p.144. For close resemblance between Sanjay Gandhi's and JP's programme, etc., in 1974-75 see Geoffrey Ostergaard, *Nonviolent Revolution in India*, 1985, p.267. Ostergaard concludes: 'Sanjay's well-staged entry onto the national political stage had all the appearance of a grotesque parody of JP's re-entry into national politics in 1974.' *Ibid.*, pp.267-8.

31. Quoted in Dilip Hiro, *Inside India Today*, 1977, p.291 (note 29). For an intensive, first-hand study of the role of vasectomy drive in a resettlement colony in Delhi, also see Emma Tarlo, 'From Victim to Agent: Memories of Emergency from a Resettlement Colony in Delhi,' *Economic and Political Weekly*, 18 November 1995, pp.2921 ff. (See, in particular,

pp.2922 and 2924). For Shah Commission's version of the family planning excesses, see *Shah Commission of Inquiry—Third and Final Report*, 1978, Chapter XXI.

32. It seems that 'the head Imam of the Jama Masjid had announced the denial of last rites to all Muslims who got sterilized,' thus giving a boost to the view that in Islam 'sterilization was a sin against God.' Emma Tarlo, n.30, p.2926.

33. In the resettlement colony which Emma Tarlo studied intensively after several years, she found that 'of the 30 men interviewed who underwent the operation during Emergency not one of them claims to have wanted it. The same is true of the women who underwent tubectomy. All felt pressured by forces which had nothing to do with family planning: saving jobs; getting children admitted in school, preventing eviction, obtaining plots and so forth. Two decades later some are strongly in favour of family planning, but they resent the way it was forced on them at the time.' N.30, p.2928 (note19).

34. See n.30.

35. Following is the journalist Vinod Mehta's description of some of the resettlement colonies in May 1977: 'A thirty-minute drive from Delhi will take you to the resettlement colonies. I went in May 1977 to places with names like Khichripur, Trilokpuri, Kalyanpuri, and there I saw the full extent of the misery perpetrated by Sanjay on these poor, defenceless people. Most of the so-called houses, even in May 1977, consisted of a few bricks casually cemented together. Usually no roof existed (an intimidating prospect if you have braved one monsoon and were expecting another), mosquitoes abounded, the roads were anything but pucca. I saw no television sets.

Outside their desultory quarters, the uprooted huddled passively motionless in their despair. Miles away from possibilities of employment, they sat resined and despondent.' *The Sanjay Story*, 1978, pp.95-6. For wider discussion of demolitions during the Emergency, see *Shah Commission of Inquiry—Third and Final Report*, 1978, Chapter XXII.

36. Apart from removal of slums, Sanjay Gandhi claimed following achievements for his city-cleansing campaign: '(a) Redevelopment of Jama Masjid complex. (b) Shifting of iron merchants market—Lohar Mandi. (c) Shifting of old motor part dealers/kabadis—Motia Khan. (d) Shifting of Lakkar Mandi. (e) Shifting of cycle market. (f) Shifting of wholesale fruit and vegetable market—Sabzi Mandi'. Also the development of Katwaria Sarai. Vinod Mehta, n.5, p.89.

37. Jagmohan, *Island of Truth*, 1978.

38. P.N. Bahl, n.2, p.46. Also see *Times of India*, 24 December 1971; *Hindustan Times*, 24 December 1976.

39. Quoted in P.N. Dhar, n.3, p.324.

40. Indira Gandhi, *SSW*, n.14, pp.286, 300, 253; B.K. Nehru, n.4, p.564.

41. Occasional acts of individual or group protest, often without any party support, did occur, especially by Sarvodayites, but made hardly any impact on public opinion, especially as they went unreported in the Press because of strident press censorship. A few groups also brought out underground newsletters, usually cyclostyled.

42. Sachchidanand Sinha, *Emergency in Perspective: Reprieve and Challenge*, 1977, p.71.

43. J.B. Kripalani, *The Nightmare and After*, 1980, p.13. Similarly, he wrote in 1977: 'People in those days asked me, as the oldest public man living, as to how and when the reign of terror would end. I always replied: "Humanly speaking, there seems to be no remedy, but God has not become bankrupt".' J.B. Kripalani, 'The Nightmare and After,' in Balraj Puri, n.12, p.13. Also significant was the following item in the *Free Press Journal* of 8 December 1976, reproduced in *Economic and Political Weekly*, 11 December 1976 (p.1912): 'The Shiv Sena has organized an exhibition to propagate the 20-point programme of Prime Minister Indira Gandhi and 5-point programme of Mr Sanjay Gandhi at its new Bhavan at Shivaji Park, Bombay.'

44. Full text of the letter is reproduced in Madhu Limaye, *Janata Party Experiment—An Insider's Account of Opposition Politics: 1975-1977*, Volume One, 1994, pp.120-1.

45. Balraj Madhok, *Storm of Decade (Indian Politics), 1970-1980*, 1980, pp.113-4, 120; Madhu Limaye, n.42, p.181, 200 (note 6); Kuldip Nayar, *In Jail*, 1978, p.97.

46. Balraj Madhok, n.43, pp.121-2. These terms were widely accepted by other opposition leaders. Also Kuldip Nayar, n.43, p.97.

47. Madhu Limaye, n.42, p.200 (note 9).

48. *Ibid.*, p.183.

49. He wrote in his *Prison Diary* on 21 July 1975: 'My world lies in a shambles all round me. I am afraid I shall not see it put together again in my life-time. . . . Where have my calculations gone wrong? I wonder what all those ladies and gentlemen are saying now who used to tell me that I was the only 'hope' for the country.' Jayaprakash Narayan, *Prison*

Diary 1975, 1978 (hereafter referred to as *PD*), pp.1-2. He repeated this disappointment with the lack of popular protest against the Emergency in an interview on 27 June 1976. See Jayaprakash Narayan, *Towards Total Revolution*, 4 vols., *Total Revolution*, vol.IV, 1978 (hereafter referred to as *TR*), p.188.

50. Jayaprakash Narayan, *PD*, n.47, p.109.

51. *India Weekly*, 11 November 1976, quoted in Geoffrey Ostergaard, n.29, p.272. Also see *ibid.*, p.271; JP, *PD*, n.47, p.89; Madhu Limaye, n.42, p.185.

52. Madhu Limaye, n.42, p.27; and Geoffrey Ostergaard, n.29, pp.268-9.

53. Letters to N.G. Goray on 14 December 1976 and Charan Singh on 29 December 1976, in Madhu Limaye, n.42, pp.185 and 187. Also in Sachchidanand Sinha, n.40, p.103. Also see Geoffrey Ostergaard, n.29, p.265.

54. For George Fernandes, see Appendices to Sachchidanand Sinha, n.40, pp.93 ff. For Madhu Limaye, see n.42, pp.181 ff.

55. P.N. Dhar discusses these efforts at length in Chapter 12 of his book. n.3.

56. Kuldip Nayar, n.43, p.97.

57. Madhu Limaye, n.42, pp.186, 198.

58. Kuldip Nayar, n.43, p.97.

59. The Opposition's efforts to unite into a single party are discussed at length in Madhu Limaye, n.42, Chapter VIII and X; Balraj Madhok, n.43, pp.112 ff.; and Geoffrey Ostergaard, n.29, pp.261 ff. The following narrative is based primarily on these three works.

60. *Swaraj*, number 15, quoted in Madhu Limaye, n.42, p.116; and Geoffrey Ostergaard, n.29, p.263.

61. See, for example, Madhu Limaye, n.42, p.158. This issue was, above all, raised by Charan Singh. On the other hand, Jan Sangh made efforts to sideline Charan Singh. The fact was that the main base of both Jan Sangh and Charan Singh was UP, where they were competitors.

62. See, for example, *ibid.*, pp.158 ff.; and Balraj Madhok, n.43, pp.116-7.

63. The following three paragraphs are based on Madhu Limaye, n.42, pp.3-5, 8, 108, 131 ff.; Madhu Limaye, *Socialist Communist Interaction in India*, 1991, p.267; Balraj Madhok, n.43, pp.117-8; Brahm Dutt, *Five Headed Monster—A Factual Narrative of the Genesis of Janata Party*, 1978, Appendix 4, pp.138-48.

64. CPM's Political Bureau's statement on the Emergency had observed that 'a return to pre-Emergency parliamentary democracy seems to be inconceivable. India is now set on the path of one-party authoritarian government. The historical truth that the bourgeoisie of an ex-colonial country cannot continue with parliamentary democracy for long . . . the return to previous rights and freedoms will not be possible. Manipulated elections, truncated Parliament, a truncated democracy functioning within the limits of permanent Emergency such is the prospect that looms before us . . . It means the Party has to function in conditions of illegality, though it should continue to take advantage of all legal possibilities and opportunities.' 'National Emergency and our Task—Decision taken by the Political Bureau of the CPI(M) on 3.9.1975 following imposition of National Emergency with effect from June 26, 1975.' Jyoti Basu, et. al., editors, *Documents of the Communist Movement in India*,, Vol.XVII (1975-77), 1998, p.66.

65. P. Sundarayya, 'Why I resigned from GS and PB,' *Marxism Today* (New Delhi), November 1985, p.7.

66. 'The recent developments inside the country signify that political differentiation and conflict inside the Indian bourgeoisie has reached a new stage, unprecedented since Indian independence. This stage is characterized by the fact that those representing the anti-imperialist democratic sections of the bourgeoisie have been forced into using the repressive organs of state power against those representing the pro-imperialist and most reactionary, pro-monopoly, pro-landlord, anti-communist sections. This situation opens up the most favourable possibilities for strengthening the united front of the working class, peasantry and other toiling sections with the anti-imperialist democratic national bourgeoisie in common struggle against right-reaction, and for moving this section of the bourgeoisie into more radical socioeconomic positions in the very interests of this common struggle. This is the process through which progressive shifts in state power can be brought about in a national-democratic direction.' *National Emergency and Our Tasks*, Resolution adopted by the Central Executive Committee, CPI (1975), 30 June to 2 July 1975.

67. *New Age*, 14 Nov. 1976. To quote him at greater length: 'Since the split in the Congress the main danger to our secular-democratic set up has come from reaction and fascist forces outside the Congress. But now it is coming from the reactionary caucus inside the ruling party, which has taken shape and has grown under the conditions of emergency . . . This is also because sections of reaction and fascism are also infiltrating into the Congress and Youth Congress . . . The reactionary caucus inside the

ruling party conspires to capture power through its activities behind the scene, burroughing in the central government apparatus and capturing the states by putting its stooges in power.

68. See note 11 above.

69. Quoted in P.N. Dhar, n.3, p.324.

70. *Times of India*, 23 November and 24 December 1976; *Hindustan Times*, 24 Decembe 1976. Also see Indira Gandhi, *My Truth*, n.18, pp.164-5.

71. *Times of India*, 28 December 1976 and *Hindustan Times*, 28 December 1976 (for Mrs Gandhi); and *Times of India*, 15 November 1976 and 15 January 1977 (for CPI).

72. Quoted in Geoffrey Ostergaard, n.29, pp.244-5.

73. *Ibid*. Madhu Limaye's interpretation of the *acharya*'s statement is different. He sees it as an indirect justification of the Emergency. N.42, p.103.

74. Vasant Nargolkar, *JP Vindicated!*, 1977, pp.129-30.

75. Geoffrey Ostergaard, n.29, p.247.

76. Quoted in *ibid*., p.253; and Vasant Nargolkar, n.71, pp.133-4.

77. Geoffrey Ostergaard, n.29, p.255. Also Vasant Nargolkar, n.71, pp.149-50.

78. Indira Gandhi, *DD*, n.15, pp.4 and 7.

79. For a wider discussion of this issue, see Bipan Chandra, *Nationalism and Colonialism in Modern India*, 1979, pp.336 ff.

80. Arun Shourie, 'Role of Intellectuals During and After Emergency', in Balraj Puri, n.12, pp.45-6.

81. Kuldip Nayar, n.1, p.65. Sachchidanand Sinha put it even strongly. See n.40, p.53.

82. Inder Malhotra, *Indira Gandhi*, 1989, p.175. Similarly, Rajni Kothari pointed out in January 1976: 'When the government sought to gain legitimacy through strong measures . . . and the twenty-point programme, it failed to have the support of all but a few among the thinking strata.' Rajni Kothari, 'End of an Era,' *Seminar*, 197, January 1976, p.22.

83. Rajni Kothari, n.79, pp.22-6.

84. Editorial, 'On To a Momentous Battle,' *The Marxist Review*, February 1977, p.242.

85. Abu Abraham, 'Neither Conformism Nor Martyrdom,' in Balraj Puri, n.12, p.60.

86. Quoted in Kuldip Nayar, n.43, p.6.

87. Quoted in Sunanda K. Datta-Ray, 'Citadel of Dissent: The Judiciary,' in Balraj Puri, n.12, pp.25, 28.

88. Quoted in Kuldip Nayar, n.43, p.84.

89. For his exact words, see Sunanda K. Datta-Ray, n.84, pp.30-1.

90. Quoted in D.R. Mankekar and Kamla Mankekar, *Decline and Fall of Indira Gandhi*, 1977, p.98.

91. Quoted in *ibid.*, p.111.

92. Quoted in *ibid.*, p.181.

93. T.N. Seshan, *The Degeneration of India*, 1975, p.62; Also see J.B. Kripalani, n.41, p.149.

94. A very good example in this respect is that of B.N. Tandon, joint secretary in the prime minister's secretariat (PMO), who was highly critical of Mrs Gandhi's functioning and the role of Sanjay Gandhi and his coterie. He kept a daily diary of the happenings in the PMO and the government but at the same time followed the rules and loyally and efficiently carried out all her orders, and advised and assisted her 'in every possible way'. B.N. Tandon, n.2, xx, xxi.

95. Abu Abraham, n.82, p.60.

96. Quoted in Pranay Gupte, *Mother India*, 1992, p.86. Similarly, Shashi Tharoor was to write later that, fresh out of college in 1975, he started out 'defending' the Emergency but then came 'to realize why it was indefensible'. Shashi Tharoor, *India: From Midnight to the Millennium*, 1997, p.36.

97. B.K. Nehru, n.4, p.561.

98. Rajni Kothari, n.79, p.28.

99. Shashi Tharoor, n.92, pp.35-6.

100. For example, in her speech in the Rajya Sabha on 8 January 1976, she said: 'Many of our intellectuals are very much enamoured of the written word or speech that comes from other countries, though their whole picture of what India is, how it should grow, is entirely removed from the realities of the situation here.' Indira Gandhi, *SSW*, n.14, p.245. She also publicly decried many of the intellectuals as 'dupes of foreign elements and ideas hostile to us.' Quoted in Inder Malhotra, n.79, p.175.

101. She was responsible for upgrading the salary scales of college and university teachers to those of the IAS.

102. Quoted in V.P. Dutt, *India's Foreign Policy*, 1987 edition, p.115.

103. Dorothy Norman, *Indira Gandhi—Letters to a Friend, 1950-1984*, 1985, pp.148-9.

104. V.P. Dutt, n.98, p.54.

105. Zareer Masani, n.27, p.310.18.

106. For the long list of interviews considered significant enough to be incorporated in the official publication of her speeches and interviews published in October 1975, see Indira Gandhi, *DD*, n.15, items numbered 5, 6, 7, 10, 12, 18, 22 and 23.

107. *Ibid.*, pp.35, 69, 140; Indira Gandhi, *SSW*, n.14, pp.239-40, 263.

108. Indira Gandhi, *DD*, n.15, pp.140-1.

109. *Ibid.*, p.146. Also see *ibid.*, pp.21, 65, 176.

110. Typical, for example, was the comment of Abu Abraham who had worked in Britain as a cartoonist for British newspapers for years: 'I questioned the credentials of some of the Western commentators. When they were not patronizing, they were malicious. We have had long experience of this.' N.82, p.60.

9. The Emergency Revoked

1. P.N. Dhar says that she took the decision to call elections in December and that, not only was he privy to the decision, he had even taken Swaminathan, the Chief Election Commissioner, into confidence. P.N. Dhar, *Indira Gandhi, the 'Emergency', and Indian Democracy*, 2000, p.349. Madhu Limaye has written that by the middle of January 1977, he, Charan Singh and others had heard rumours about Mrs Gandhi announcing elections. Madhu Limaye, *Janata Party Experiment—An Insider's Account of Opposition Politics: 1975-1977*, Volume One, 1994, pp.207-08. Obviously, some of the people she consulted had leaked the news.

2. *Times of India*, 8 January 1977.

3. Indira Gandhi, *Selected Speeches and Writings of Indira Gandhi*, Vol.III, September 1972-March 1977, 1984 (hereafter referred to as *SSW*), pp.303-04.

4. Quoted in Minoo Masani, *JP Mission Partly Accomplished*, 1977, p.150.

5. A note written just before and a letter written just after 18 January 1977, by George Fernandes, reproduced as appendices B and C in Sachchidanand Sinha, *Emergency in Perspective*, 1977, pp.101-12.

6. On the night of 18 January 1977, in a well-known programme of political satire on a US TV channel, the host announced at the beginning of the programme that Indira Gandhi had announced elections. At the end of the half-hour programme, the host announced the 'breaking news' that Indira Gandhi had won the elections with a huge majority!

7. In contrast, in 1971, the Congress had secured 52.6 per cent of the votes in Haryana, 48 per cent in UP and 64.5 per cent in Delhi.

8. Indira Gandhi, *SSW*, n.3, p.304.

9. Quoted in Kuldip Nayar, *The Judgement*, 1977, p.182.

10. Indira Gandhi, *SSW*, n.3, pp.303-04.

11. *Indian Express*, 30 October 1976. Reproduced in *Economic and Political Weekly*, 6 November 1976, p.1744.

12. Maneka Gandhi's interview with Pupul Jayakar. Pupul Jayakar, *Indira Gandhi—A Biography*, 1992, p.313. Vinod Mehta writes that when, after the Congress defeat, Sanjay was asked 'why he sat idly by and watched his mother destroy herself, he said: "I couldn't help it. She was too much influenced by the communists".' Vinod Mehta, *The Sanjay Story*, 1978, p.106.

13. Francine R. Frankel, *India's Political Economy, 1947-1977*, 1978, p.557.

14. Pupul Jayakar, n.12, p.313.

15. P.N. Dhar, n.1, p.35. Mrs Gandhi's former confidante, Dinesh Singh, said later: 'We (in the Congress party) were not in favour of elections at that time. We said that you must first withdraw the Emergency, release the prisoners and give us six months to re-established a rapport with the electorate. I can't imagine any politician having advised her to hold elections at that time.' Quoted in Mark Tully and Zareer Masani, *From Raj to Rajiv*, 1988, p.124.

16. Pupul Jayakar, n.12, p.312.

17. Indira Gandhi, *My Truth*, 1980, p.166. Balraj Puri quotes a chief minister as telling him that while informing them on the evening of 18. January of her decision to go in for polls, Mrs Gandhi prefaced her statement with the humorous remark, which was, feels Puri, a Freudian slip; 'It was a proposal regarding committing suicide that we were discussing.' Balraj Puri, 'Counter-Total Revolution,' in Balraj Puri, ed., *Revolution Counter-Revolution*, 1978, p.90.

18. Henry C. Hart, 'Political Leadership in India: Dimensions and Limits,' in Atul Kohli, ed., *India's Democracy*, 1990, p.49. Also see Madhu Limaye, n.1, p.209.

19. She had repeatedly said so. See Chapter 7 for references.

20. See Section 8, Chapter 8 above.

21. See Section 7, Chapter 8 above. This is also Pupul Jayakar's view: 'It was growing difficult for Indira to face herself or justify continued repressive measures. The title of a benevolent dictator was difficult for her to accept.' N.12, p.309.

22. Mohit Sen, *Glimpses of the History of the Indian Communist Movement*, 1995, p.40.

23. S.S. Gill, *The Dynasty*, 1996, p.288.

24. Madhu Limaye, n.1, pp.211-2. Girilal Jain has also written along similar lines: 'The ghost of Jawaharlal Nehru haunted her. Indira Gandhi sought legitimacy in being seen as not only the daughter but legitimate successor to Nehru, which meant sticking at least to the forms if not the substance, of democracy.' Quoted in Mark Tully and Zareer Masani, n.15, p.123-4.

25. S.S. Gill, n.23, p.288; Inder Malhotra, *Indira Gandhi*, 1989, p.192.

26. Jayaprakash Narayan, *Prison Diary 1975*, 1977, p.108.

27. Inder Malhotra, n.25, p.192.

28. Mary C. Carras, *Indira Gandhi*, 1979, pp.100-01.

29. Katherine Frank, *Indira*, 2001, p.410.

30. Nayantara Sahgal, *Indira Gandhi*, 1982, pp.180-1.

31. When her old friend, the Communist leader Bhupesh Gupta, complained to Mrs Gandhi about Sanjay Gandhi's utterances and behaviour, she told him that as an old friend he should take him in hand and educate him. Similarly, she told an interviewer in 1976 that 'the way to deal with this (i.e., his anti-Communist remarks) is to sit down and explain to him that he is mistaken and so on.' *My Truth*, n.17, p.165.

32. See n.12 above.

33. Pupul Jayakar, n.12, pp.299, 301-02, 309, 310, 312.

34. P.N. Dhar, n.1, pp.341-4.

35. *Ibid.*, pp.348, 349, 329, 351.

36. Mohit Sen, 'Emergency Debate,' *New Thinking Communist*, 15 July 2000, p.5.

37. Mohit Sen, 'Review of P.N. Dhar's *Indira Gandhi, the "Emergency", and Indian Democracy*,' *New Thinking Communist*, 15 May 2000, p.20.

38. P.N. Bahl, *Indira Gandhi—The Crucial Years (1973-1984)*, 1994, pp.48-51. Bahl calls the Emergency 'the New Situation'!

39. Quoted in Uma Vasudev, *Two Faces of Indira Gandhi*, 1977, p.176.

40. Quoted in *ibid.*, p.188.

41. Granville Austin, *Working A Democratic Constitution*, 1999, p.395 (ref. note 6).

42. Mary C. Carras, n.28, p.210.

43. Inder Malhotra, n.25, p.193.

44. Max Jean Zins, *Strains on Indian Democracy*, 1988, p.55.

45. To quote from Mrs Gandhi's interview, given in the summer of 1978 to Mary C. Carras: 'We brought down prices, reduced the rate of growth of unemployment, we built up our foreign reserves, we built up the food reserve . . . Because once we reached stability, there seemed no reason not to have elections. Elections had been postponed for a particular reason. When that reason was no longer there, I announced elections. I did not consider whether I was going to win, or whether I was going to be prime minister.' Quoted in Mary C. Carras, n.28, p.240. Mrs Gandhi reiterated this view in another interview around the same time. Indira Gandhi, *My Truth*, n.17, p.166.

46. Dom Moraes, *Indira Gandhi*, 1980, p.264.

47. *Ibid.*

10. Conclusions

1. It is not the first time that I have put forth this way of looking at an authoritarian regime. In the book *India's Struggle for Independence*, first published in 1987, I have described the colonial state in India as semi-hegemonic or semi-legal authoritarian even though its suppression of the mass movements was far more strident. p.25. Also see Bipan Chandra, *Indian National Movement—The Long Term Dynamics, 1988*, where I have described the colonial state as 'semi-hegemonic, semi-authoritarian in character', (p.18) and pointed out that Gandhiji and other nationalists fully grasped the significance of this character of British rule and based their strategy and tactics of struggle against it on this understanding. See *ibid.*, pp.18 ff. For example, at the height of his struggle against the colonial state in 1942, Gandhiji, on the one hand, referred to the 'powerful elements of Fascism in British rule' and, on the other hand, to the 'fundamental difference between Fascism and even this imperialism which I am fighting.' Gandhiji, *Collected Works*, Volume 76, pp.439 and 400, quoted in *ibid.*, p.21.

2. Granville Austin, *Working a Democratic Constitution*, 1999, p.343. Inder Malhotra's comment is similar: 'But surely New Delhi in 1976 could not be compared to Berlin under Hitler, Moscow under Stalin, Beijing under Mao, Santiago under Pinochet and Islamabad under Zia ul Huq.' 'June 25, 1975: A Look Back,' *Hindu*, 25 June 2000.

3. As Dom Moraes has put it, 'The opponents of those in power disappeared and were not heard from for some time: that they were heard from at all, not quietly butchered in a ditch or cellar, as they might have been in some other countries, says something for the nature of the 1975 emergency.' Dom Moraes, *Indira Gandhi*, 1980, p.222.

4. Sachchidanand Sinha, *Emergency in Perspective*, 1977, p.73.

5. Granville Austin, n.2, p.389.

6. *Ibid.*

7. Max Jean Zins, *Strains on Indian Democracy*, 1988, p.55.

8. We may quote the apt remarks of R.V.R. Chandrasekhara Rao: 'Yet in all fairness she probably did not intend to pervert permanently the political system. This is the major qualitative difference between an authoritarianism brought about by bending constitutional provisions and the imposition of authoritarian or military regimes through coups.' 'India's Constitutional Structures,' in Yogendra K. Malik and D.K. Vajpayee, *India: The Years of Indira Gandhi*, 1988, p.39.

9. Though Sudipta Kaviraj agrees with the structural explanation of the Emergency, he rightly raises the question that if the Emergency was directly the result of structural strains, then were the strains eased by January 1977 so that the Emergency could be revoked. 'Indira Gandhi and Indian Politics,' *Economic and Political Weekly*, 20-27 September 1986, p.1705. Similarly, reporting on a seminar on the Emergency in 1995, the young journalist Ajit Kumar Jha commented: 'The Emergency, we were told by speaker after speaker, was a systemic crisis which can only be understood either as Bonapartism, or as a failure of the Nehruvian model of modernization. If the causes of the Emergency point towards a failure of the system, why then are the conventional explanations for its denouement of a non-systemic nature.' 'Emergency Puzzles', *Times of India*, 1 July 1995.

10. A.K. Roy, 'Emergency at Midnight,' *Statesman*, 24 June 1986.

11. Karl Marx, 'The Civil War in France,' 1871, in Karl Marx and Fredrick Engels, *Collected Works*, Volume 22, 1986, p.330. Also see V.I. Lenin, *Collected Works*, Vol.25, June-September 1917, 1964, p.220.

12. See Bipan Chandra, *Communalism in Modern India*, 1984, pp.331 ff.

13. All this is taught orally in the daily *shakhas* or group meetings. One of the best summaries of the character of fascist forces is provided by Arun Shourie in his article 'Symptoms' reproduced in his *Symptoms of Fascism*, 1978, pp.43-143. Though Shourie sees the Emergency regime as fascist, his description and analysis of the fascist threat fits the RSS and extreme communalism like a glove. In today's context, his article, though written over twenty-five years back, deserves wider circulation.

14. Jayaprakash Narayan, *Prison Diary 1975*, 1977, p.1. However, JP still retained faith in them, though he felt disillusioned with his other followers. *Ibid.*, pp.2-3.

15. Victor Emmanuel was unwittingly responsible for the success of Mussolini's capture of power in Italy in 1922 because he refused to use the army to oppose the fascist occupation of Rome. Marshal Hindenburg was the President of Germany when, in 1932-33, as Chancellor he acquiesced in Hitler's assumption of dictatorial powers.

16. Max Jean Zins, n.7, p.19. He goes on to ask: 'Was this the case in India in 1974-75? Could it be achieved in the political and geographical conditions of India?' *Ibid.*

17. Balraj Puri, 'Counter-Total Revolution', in Balraj Puri, ed., *Revolution Counter-Revolution*, 1978, p.103. He takes the metaphor from remarks made by D.P. Mishra and quoted by Uma Vasudev in *Two Faces of Indira Gandhi*, 1977, pp.1-2.

18. Oriana Fallaci wrote that 'Indian democracy is finished.' 'Mrs Gandhi's Opposition—Morarji Desai,' *New Republic*, 2 and 9 August, 1975, p.12. Hari P. Sharma, a non-resident Indian, wrote near the end of 1975 that the Emergency 'marks the end of an era in the political history of India ... the emergency itself will stay indefinitely'. ' "National Emergency" in India,' *Journal of Contemporary Asia*, Vol.5, no.4, 1975, p.462. Andre Gunder Frank titled his article, written before January 1977 though published in March 1977, 'Emergence of Permanent Emergency in India,' *Economic and Political Weekly*, 12 March 1977, p.463.

19. Henry C. Hart, 'Introduction', in Henry C. Hart, ed., *Indira Gandhi's India*, 1976, p.27.

20. Ram M. Roy, 'The Impact of the Constitutional Emergency on the Indian Democracy in the Near Future,' in Ram M. Roy, ed., *Indian Democracy in Crisis*, 1976, p.79.

21. Ruth Glass, 'Exit Mrs Gandhi,' *Monthly Review*, July-August 1977, p.65; Nirad C. Chaudhuri, 'How and Why Mrs Gandhi Ruled,' in S.L.M. Prachand, ed., *The Great Upheaval*, 1977, p.28. (The article

appeared in 1976 in the *Encounter*); Ajit Roy, *Political Power in India—Nature and Trend*, 2nd edn., 1981, p.157.

22. Robert A. Huttenback, ' "Emergency" in the Context of Modern Indian History,' in Ram M. Roy, n.21, p.32. Nirad C. Chaudhuri was another prominent exponent of this view. N.22, pp.26ff. More recently, discussing the period of the Emergency, Stanley Wolpert has expressed similar views. *A New History of India*, 1977, pp.402-03; Also see P.N. Dhar, *Indira Gandhi, the 'Emergency', and Indian Democracy*, 2000, pp.225-7.

23. Quoted in Shashi Tharoor, *India: From Midnight to the Millennium*, 1997, p.201.

24. Ved Mehta, *The New India*, 1978, pp.53-4. But he also wrote when dealing with the March elections: 'Certainly a poor villager understood the meaning of the choice between dictatorship and democracy, between Emergency measures and democratic procedures . . .'. *Ibid.*, p.163.

25. Leo E. Rose, 'The Emergency and India's External Relations,' in Ram M. Roy, n.20, p.87.

26. Ajit Roy, 'The Indian Events from the Indian Perspective,' in Saral K. Chatterji, ed., *The Meaning of the Indian Experience: The Emergency*, 1978, p.22; Ajit Roy, 'Specificities of Indira Gandhi's Emergency,' *The Marxist Review*, November 2000, p.10; Hari P. Sharma, n.18, p.468; Ruth Glass, n.21, pp.65-6. Ranajit Guha, 'Indian Democracy—Long Dead, Now Buried,' *Journal of Contemporary Asia*, Vol.6, no.1, 1976. This view has been the dominant theme in Naxal literature. As late as 1980, this view was repeated by Harry W. Blair. See his 'Mrs Gandhi's Emergency, the Indian Elections of 1977, Pluralism and Marxism: Problems with Paradigms,' *Modern Asian Studies*, Vol.14, no.2, 1980, pp.255, 259.

27. See, for example, Abu Abraham, 'Neither Conformism nor Martyrdom,' in Balraj Puri, n.17, pp.59-60.

28. W.H. Morris-Jones, 'Creeping but Uneasy Authoritarianism: India, 1975-6,' *Government and Opposition*, Vol.12, no.1, Winter 1977, p.21. The original paper on which the article was based was written in March 1976.

29. Norman D. Palmer, 'The Future of the Indian Political System,' in Ram M. Roy, n.20, pp.10, 11, 16.

30. Tariq Ali, *The Nehrus and the Gandhis*, 1985, p.193.

31. Balraj Mehta, 'Economic Causes and Consequences of Emergency,' in Balraj Puri, n.17, p.75. Pranab Bardhan, 'Authoritarianism and

Democracy: First Anniversary of New Regime,' *Economic and Political Weekly*, 11 March 1978, p.531. This view has been expressed as late as 1983 by Ainslie Embree in 'The Emergency as a Signpost to India's Future,' in P.L. Lyon and J. Manor, eds., *Transfer and Transformation: Political Institutions in the New Commonwealth*, 1983.

32. Jayaprakash Narayan, n.15, p.112.

33. Granville Austin, n.2, p.390. Also see P.N. Dhar, n.22, p.316; and M. Weiner, *The Indian Paradox*, 1984, pp.328-9.

34. W.H. Morris-Jones, *Politics Mainly Indian*, 1978, p.xvii.

35. B.K. Nehru, *The Times*, 11 March 1976, quoted in David Selbourne, *Through the Indian Looking-Glass*, 1982, p.11.

36. See f.n.22 above.

37. J.B. Kripalani, *The Nightmare and After*, 1980, p.73.

38. Sachchidanand Sinha, n.4, pp.82-3. Also JP, quoted in Minoo Masani, *JP Mission Partly Accomplished*, 1977, p.153; Kuldip Nayar, *The Judgement*, 1977, p.179; Tariq Ali, n.30, p.194; W.H. Morris-Jones, 'The Indian Elections and Their Aftermath,' *Asian Affairs*, October 1977, p.289.

39. *Times of India*, 7 March 1977.

40. W.H. Morris-Jones, n.34, p.xviii.

41. JP could not be more wrong than when he said that the electoral malpractices of various sorts have 'robbed the elections of much of their value and eroded the people's faith in them.' Jayaprakash Narayan, *Towards Total Revolution*, 4 volumes, edited with an introduction by Brahmanand, *Total Revolution*, Vol.IV, 1978, p.68.

42. JP also seems to have recognized this later. In an interview given to *Swaraj* (London) in February 1976, he said that if he had foreseen how easily democracy in the country had been converted into dictatorship, he would have tried to lead the people's movement 'with much more thought, given more attention to finding another way. I think I would not have gone as far as non-cooperation, non-payment of land and other taxes—which I advocated, but would have concentrated more on political action rather than direct action. I would not have joined a party myself but I would have paid more attention to elections; in preparing for them; to gather together the opposition parties to see that only one candidate from the opposition parties stood in any constituency . . . I would have paid more attention to this sort of politics; put more emphasis on it rather than on direct action . . . I did not realize that the result of my advocacy

(of direct action) would be that the country would be saddled with a dictatorship.' Quoted in Geoffrey Ostergaard, *Nonviolent Revolution in India*, 1985, pp.268-9. Also see P.N. Dhar, n.22, p.316. Dhar reported JP as telling him in July 1947 that he as well as the opposition groups had learnt their lesson.

43. Jayaprakash Narayan, n.14, p.31. Similarly, according to P.N. Dhar, when JP met him in July 1976 'he made no reference to his demand for the Bihar ministry's resignation. He wanted only electoral and educational reforms and the removal of corruption' and the restoration of democracy. P.N. Dhar, n.22, p.316.

44. Geoffrey Ostergaard, n.42, pp.318, 311.

45. See *ibid.*, Chapters Three and Four.

46. Jayaprakash Narayan, n.41, p.67.

47. Raj Krishna and Jayaprakash Narayan, 'The Socio-Economic Objectives and Programme of the Bihar Movement, 25 February 1975,' in David Selbourne, ed., *In Theory and in Politics*, 1985, pp.127-8.

48. See Bipan Chandra, *Indian National Movement—Long Term Dynamics*, n.1, pp.16 ff. and Bipan Chandra, et. al., *India's Struggle for Independence*, n.1, Chapter 38.

49. Jayaprakash Narayan, n.14, pp.29-30.

50. Bhola Chatterji, *Conflict in JP's Politics*, 1984, p.282.

51. Joan V. Bondurant, *Conquest of Violence: The Gandhian Philosophy of Conflict*, revised edn., 1971, pp.viii-ix. Bondurant has discussed this issue further in her 'Satyagraha versus Duragraha: The Limits of Symbolic Violence,' in G. Ramachandran and T.K. Mahadevan, eds., *Gandhi: His Relevance for Our Times*, 1967; and 'Creative Conflict and the Limits of Symbolic Violence,' in Joan V. Bondurant and Margaret W. Fisher, eds., *Conflict: Violence and Non-Violence*, 1971.

52. Arun Shourie, 'Symptoms', n.13, p.56.

53. Quoted in *ibid.* (The quotation is from Daniel Guerin, *Fascism and Big Business*, New York, 1973, pp.111-2) Shourie also argues that a movement with fascist potential has to be dealt with in its early stages. *Ibid.*, p.44. Similarly, he concludes in another essay in 1978: 'History teaches us three lessons for dealing with a fascist threat. First, it must be crushed; yes, crushed is the right word. Second, it must be crushed in the embryo; crushed, that is, before and not after it has done its evil. Third, to leave the task to palsied governments is to commit suicide.' 'The Janata Years,' in *ibid.*, p.305.

54. W.H. Morris-Jones wrote in 1966: 'The combination of political stability with the establishment of a free, and freely moving, political system is what we are entitled to call India's political miracle.' W.H. Morris-Jones, n.34, p.131.

Appendix

1. This is a narrative not of the origins of fascism in Italy or of its rise to power but only of the surrender of power to the fascists by the democrats and King Victor Emmanuel.

2. In the November 1919 national elections, not a single fascist was elected to the parliament. Mussolini was able to secure less than 5,000 out of 346,000 votes. At this time, there were only 870 fascist members; but by May 1920 their number had gone up to 30,000, and by May 1922 to over 300,000.

3. As Philip V. Cannistraro has pointed out, 'Marinetti's idea that the nation's culture had to be infused with a sense of Italianita—the quality and essence of being Italian—was readily adopted by the fascists.' Philip V. Cannistraro, 'Mussolini's Cultural Revolution: Fascist or Nationalist,' *Journal of Contemporary History*, Vol.7, nos.3-4, 1972.

4. 'The century of democracy is over,' wrote Mussolini in August 1922. 'The ideals of democracy are exploded, beginning with that of "progress" . . . The state of all will end by becoming the state of a few.' Quoted in A. Rossi, *The Rise of Italian Fascism 1918-1922*, 1976 reprint of the 1938 edition, p.237. Earlier, in February, Mussolini had written 'of the constantly growing acute sense of disgust which is being provoked by the existing parliamentary regime, and of the vast and no longer unconfessed aspirations of the people for a government which is capable of governing. I was the first to evoke in open Parliament the possibility of a military dictatorship with the connected consequences.' Quoted in Herman Finer, *Mussolini's Italy*, 1935, p.148.

5. Lacking any definite programme, their propaganda took complex and contradictory forms, so much so that as late as their seizure of power in October 1922, it was difficult for observers to discern their main programmatic design and aims.

6. 'The intellect and character, private and public, of opponents are vilified in terms so unscrupulous and disgusting that the non-political masses come to believe that there must be some truth in what they are told.' A. Rossi, n.4, p.x.

7. 'For a class to be really revolutionary it must, says Marx, "first be aware that it is not a particular class, but the representative of the general needs of society." Italian socialism lacked this leaven, which alone could have raised it to victory ... Instead it shirked its task. It lurked in the background all through the post-war crisis. This desertion is the sole explanation of the fascist success.' *Ibid.*, p.323. Also see *ibid.*, p.52.

8. The famous Italian philosopher Benedetto Groce, who was a member of Giolitti's cabinet, 'explained that fascism was safe because it had no programme, as though this was not precisely one of the very facts which made it so redoubtable.' D. Mack Smith, *Italy—A Modern History*, 1959, p.341.

9. The King did so not because of being sympathetic to the fascists. In all probability, he lost his nerve because he was not sure of the loyalty of the army, because he was afraid that the fascists would depose him in favour of his cousin, Duke of Aosta, and because he was not convinced that the weak liberal leaders would remain firm in their opposition to the fascists.

10. *Ibid.*, p.359.

11. D. Mack Smith, for example, has argued: 'General Badoglio, who had succeeded Diaz as Chief of staff, said in an interview at Rome that at the first shot the whole of fascism would crumble ... His opinion was confirmed by General Pugliese, the military commandant of Rome ... The deficiency was in political sense and in morale, not in physical strength ...' King Emmanuel's refusal to sign the Martial Law decree 'was therefore not only an infraction of constitutional procedure, it also clinched the success of the revolt.' *Ibid.*, p.368. Also see *ibid.*, pp.358, 366. According to A. Rossi, 'up till noon on the 28th the government in Rome could still have saved the situation, for the army was intact and the fascists could not have stood up against a serious attack.' N.4, p.306. Similarly, Adrian Lyttelton writes: 'In reality, the March on Rome, in the strict sense, was a colossal bluff. The city was defended by 12,000 men of the regular army, under the loyal General Pugliese, who would have been able to disperse the Fascist bands without difficulty ... The grandiose "pincer movement" on Rome could never have been carried out with any chance of success'. *The Seizure of Power-Fascism in Italy 1919-1929*, 1973, pp.85-6.

Bibliography

Abbas, Khwaja Ahmad, *India Gandhi: The Last Post*, Bombay, 1985.

Abraham, Abu, 'Neither Conformism nor Martyrdom,' in Balraj Mehta, ed., *Revolution Counter-Revolution*.

Ali, Tariq, *The Nehrus and the Gandhis*, London, 1985.

Analyst, an, 'J.P. Some Reflections,' *Mainstream*, 13 October 1979.

Austin, Granville, *Working a Democratic Constitution—the Indian Experience*, New Delhi, 1999.

Bahl, P.N., *Indira Gandhi—The Crucial Years (1973-1984)*, New Delhi, 1994.

Bardhan, Pranab, 'Authoritarianism and Democracy: First Anniversary of New Regime,' *Economic and Political Weekly*, 11 March 1978.

Barik, Radhakanta, *Politics of the JP Movement*, New Delhi, 1977.

Basu, Jyoti, et. al., editors, *Documents of the Communist Movement in India*, Vol.XVI (1973-74), Vol.XVII (1975-77), Calcutta, 1998.

Bayley, David H., 'The Police and Political Order in India,' *Asian Survey*, Vol.XXIII, no.4, April 1983.

Bhambhri, C.P., *Politics in India, 1947-87*, New Delhi, 1987.

Bhatia, Krishan, *Indira: A Biography of Prime Minister Gandhi*, London, 1974.

Bhattacharayya, Buddhadeva, 'The Gandhism of Jayaprakash Narayan,' *Society and Change*, Vol.IV, no.3, April-June 1985.

Bhattacharjea, Ajit, *Jayaprakash Narayan: A Political Biography*, Delhi, 1975.

Blair, Harry W., 'Mrs Gandhi's Emergency, the Indian Elections of 1977, Pluralism and Marxism: Problems with Paradigms,' *Modern Asian Studies*, Vol.14, no.2, 1980.

Bondurant, Jean V., *Conquest of Violence—The Gandhian Philosophy of Conflict*, Berkeley, Revised edition, 1971.

——'Satyagraha Versus Duragraha: The Limits of Symbolic Violence,' in G. Ramachandran and T.K. Mahadevan, eds., *Gandhi: His Relevance for Our Times*, Bombay, 1967.

——'Creative Conflict and the Limits of Symbolic Violence,' in Joan V. Bondurant and Margaret W. Fisher, *Conflict: Violence and Non-Violence*, Chicago, 1971.

Brass, Paul R., *The Politics of India Since Independence*, New Delhi, 1992.

——'Congress, Lok Dal and the Middle-Peasant Castes: An Analysis of the 1977 and 1980 Parliamentary Elections in Uttar Pradesh,' *Pacific Affairs*, Vol.54, no.1, 1981.

Bright, J.S., *Allahabad High Court to Shah Commission*, New Delhi, 1979.

Budget Speeches of Union Finance Ministers 1947-48 to 1990-91, Ministry of Finance, Department of Economic Affairs, New Delhi, 1990.

Carras, Mary C., *Indira Gandhi: In the Crucible of Leadership*, Bombay, 1979.

Chandra Bipan, *Nationalism and Colonialism in India*, New Delhi, 1979.

——*Communalism in Modern India*, New Delhi, 1984.

——*Indian National Movement: The Long-Term Dynamics*, New Delhi, 1988.

Chandra, Bipan, Mukherjee, Mridula, Mukherjee, Aditya, *India After Independence*, New Delhi, 1999.

Chandra, Bipan, et. al., *India's Struggle for Independence 1857-1947*, New Delhi, 1988.

Chaudhuri, Nirad C., 'How and Why Mrs Gandhi Ruled,' in S.L.M. Prachand, ed., *The Great Upheaval—Some Aspects* (originally published in *Encounter* in 1976).

Chatterji, Bhola, *Conflict in JP's Politics*, New Delhi, 1984.

Chatterji, Saral K., ed., *The Meaning of the Indian Experience: The Emergency*, Madras, 1978.

Chawla, Sudarshan, 'The Opposition and the Crisis of Democracy in India,' in Ram M. Roy, ed., *Indian Democracy in Crisis*.

Chitta Ranjan, C.N., 'Gandhi and "Gandhian JP",' *Mainstream*, 5 October 1977.

Clark, Martin, *Modern Italy 1871-1982*, London, 1984.

Cohen, Stephen P., 'The Military,' in Henry C. Hart, ed., *Indira Gandhi's India*.

Caannistraro, Philip V., 'Mussolini's Cultural Revolution: Fascist or Natioanlist?' *Journal of Contemporary History*, Vol.7, nos.3-4, 1972.

Das Gupta, Jyotindra, 'A Season of Caesars: Emergency Regimes and Development Politics in Asia,' *Asian Survey*, Vol.XVIII, no.4, April 1978.

Datta-Ray, Sunanda K., 'Citadel of Dissent: The Judiciary,' in Balraj Puri, ed., *Revolution Counter-Revolution*.

Dayal, John and Bose, Ajay, *For Reasons of State—Delhi Under Emergency*, Delhi, 1977.

Dhar, P.N., *Indira Gandhi, the 'Emergency', and Indian Democracy*, New Delhi, 2000.

Drieburg, Trevor and Jag Mohan, Sarla, *Emergency in India*, New Delhi, 1975.

Dutt, Brahm, *Five-Headed Monster—A Factual Narrative of the Genesis of Janata Party*, New Delhi, 1978.

Dutt, V.P., *India's Foreign Policy*, New Delhi, 1984, 1987 edition.

——'The Emergency in India: Background and Rationale,' *Asian Survey*, Vol.XVI, no.12, December 1976.

Embree, Ainslie T., 'The Emergency as a Signpost to India's Future,' in P.L. Lyon and J. Manor, eds., *Transfer and Transformation*.

Erdman, Howard L., 'The Industrialists,' in Henry C. Hart, ed., *Indira Gandhi's India*.

Fallaci, Oriana, 'Mrs Gandhi's Opposition—Morarji Desai,' *New Republic*, 2 and 9 August, 1975.

Finer, Herman, *Mussolini's Italy*, London, 1935.

Fox, Richard G., *Gandhian Utopia: Experiments with Culture*, Boston, 1989.

——'Gandhian Socialism, Hindu Identity and the JP Movement: Cultural Domination in the World System,' *The Journal of Commonwealth and Comparative Politics*, Vol.XXV, no.3, November 1987.

Frank, Andre Gunder, 'Emergence of Permanent Emergency in India,' *Economic and Political Weekly*, 12 March 1977.

Frank, Katherine, *Indira—The Life of Indira Nehru Gandhi*, London, 2001.

Frankel, Francine R., *India's Political Economy, 1947-1977*, Delhi, 1978.

Gandhi, Indira, *Democracy and Discipline—Speeches of Shrimati Indira Gandhi*, New Delhi, 1975 (referred to as *DD*).

——*Selected Speeches and Writings of Indira Gandhi*, Vol.III (September 1972-March 1977), New Delhi, 1984 (referred to as *SSW*).

——*My Truth*, New Delhi, 1981.

——*Indira-Gandhi: Letters to a Friend 1950-1984*, compiled and edited by Dorothy Norman, London, 1985.

Gangadharan, Koshy, Radhakrishnan, *The Inquisition: Revelations Before the Shah Commission*, New Delhi, 1978.

Ghose, S.K., *The Crusade and End of Indira Raj*, New Delhi, 1978.

——'Total Revolution: What JP Meant,' *Mainstream*, 20 October 1979.

Gill, S.S., *The Dynasty: A Political Biography of the Premier Ruling Family of Modern India*, New Delhi, 1996.

Glass, Ruth, 'Exit Mrs Gandhi,' *Monthly Review*, July-August 1977.

Godbole, Madhav, *Unfinished Innings—Recollections and Reflections of a Civil Servant*, New Delhi, 1996.

Golwalkar, M.S., *We, or Our Nationhood Defined*, Nagpur, 1939, 4th edn., 1947.

——*Bunch of Thoughts*, Bangalore, 1966 edition and 1996 edition.

Goyal, Des Raj, *Rashtriya Swayamsevak Sangh*, New Delhi, 1979.

Gramsci, Antonio, *Selections from the Prison Notebooks of Antonio Gramsci*, edited and translated by Quintin Hoare and Geoffrey Nowell Smith, London, 1971.

Guha, Ranajit, 'Indian Democracy—Long Dead, Now Buried,' *Journal of Contemporary Asia*, Vol.6, no.1, 1976.

Gupte, Pranay, *Vengeance: India After the Assassination of Indira Gandhi*, New York, 1985.

——*Mother India: A Political Biography of Indira Gandhi*, New York, 1992.

Haksar, P.N., *Premonitions*, Bombay, 1979.

Hart, Henry C., ed., *Indira Gandhi's India: A Political System Reappraised*, Boulder (Colorado), 1976.

——'Introduction' and 'Indira Gandhi: Determined Not to be Hurt,' in Henry C. Hart, ed., *Indira Gandhi's India*.

——'The Indian Constitution: Political Development and Decay,' *Asian Survey*, Vol.XX, no.4, April 1980.

——'Political Leadership in India: Dimensions and Limits,' in Atul Kohli, ed., *India's Democracy*, Princeton, 1990.

Heginbotham, Stanley J., 'The Civil Service and the Emergency,' in Herry C. Hart, ed., *Indira Gandhi's India*.

Hiro, Dilip, *Inside India Today*, New York, 1977.

Hobsbawm, *On History*, New York, 1997.

Huttenback, Robert A., 'Mrs Gandhi's "Emergency" in the Context of Modern Indian History,' in Ram M. Roy, ed., *Indian Democracy in Crisis*.

Jagmohan, *Island of Truth*, New Delhi, 1978.

Jayakar, Pupul, *Indira Gandhi—A Biography*, New Delhi, 1992.

Jha, Ajit Kumar, 'Emergency Puzzles,' *Times of India*, 1 July 1995.

Jones, Dawn E. and Jones, Rodney W., 'Urban Upheaval in India: The 1974 Nav Nirman Riots in Gujarat,' *Asian Survey*, Vol.XVI, no.11, November 1976.

Joshi, P.C., 'Congress Base,' *Seminar*, 185, January 1975.

Joshi, Ram, 'India 1974: Growing Political Crisis,' *Asian Survey*, Vol.XV, no.2, February 1975.

Joshi, Vijay and Little, I.M.D., *India: Macroeconomics and Political Economy 1964-1991*, Delhi, 1994.

Kalhan, Promilla, *Black Wednesday: Power Politics, Emergency and Elections*, New Delhi, 1977.

Karanjia, R.K., *Indira-JP Confrontation: The Great Debate*, New Delhi, 1975.

Kaviraj, Sudipta, 'Indira Gandhi and Indian Politics,' *Economic and Political Weekly*, 20-27 September 1986.

Kiernan, Victor, 'Passages from India,' *Journal of Contemporary India*, Vol.8, no.3, 1978.

Kochanek, Stanley A., 'Mrs Gandhi's Pyramid: The New Congress,' in Henry C. Hart, ed., *Indira Gandhi's India*.

Kohli, Atul, ed., *India's Democracy*, Princeton, 1990.

——*Democracy and Discontent: India's Growing Crisis of Governability*, 1991, New Delhi, 1995 reprint.

Kothari, Rajni, 'End of an Era,' *Seminar*, 197, January 1976.

——'Restoring the Political Process,' *Seminar*, 203, July 1976.

——*State Against Democracy*, Delhi, 1980.

Kripalani, J.B., *The Nightmare and After*, Bombay, 1980.

——'The Nightmare and After,' in Balraj Puri, ed., *Revolution Counter-Revolution*.

Krishna, Raj and Narayan, Jayaprakash, 'The Socio-Economic Objectives and Programme of the Bihar Movement, 25 February 1975,' in David Selbourne, ed., *In Theory and Practice*.

Lal, Lakshmi Narain, *Jayaprakash: Rebel Extraordinary*, New Delhi, 1975.

Limaye, Madhu, *Socialist Communist Interaction in India*, Delhi, 1991.

——*Janata Party Experiment: An Insider's Account of Opposition Politics, 1975-1977*, Vol.One, Delhi, 1994.

——'Ideological Bankruptcy,' *Seminar*, 185, January 1975.

Lyon, P.L. and Manor J., eds., *Transfer and Transformation: Political Institutions in the New Commonwealth*, Leicester, 1983.

Lyttelton, Adrian, *The Seizure of Rome—Fascism in Italy 1919-1929*, London, 1973.

Mack Smith D., *Italy: A Modern History*, Ann Arbor, Michigan, 1959.

Madhok, Balraj, *Stormy Decade (Indian Politics of 1970-1980)*, Delhi, 1980.

Mahajan, V.D., *History of Modern India*, Vol.II, 1974-1980, New Delhi, 1983.

Malhotra, Inder, *Indira Gandhi: A Personal and Political Biography*, London, 1989.

——'June 25, 1975: A Look Back,' *Hindu*, 25 June 2000.

Mankekar, D.R. and Mankekar, Kamla, *Decline and Fall of Indira Gandhi*, New Delhi, 1977.

Manor, James, ed., *Nehru to the Nineties: The Changing Office of Prime Minister in India*, New Delhi, 1994.

Mansingh, Surjit, *India's Search for Power—Indira Gandhi's Foreign Policy 1966-1982*, New Delhi, 1984.

Masani, Minoo, *Is J.P. The Answer?*, Delhi, 1975.

——*JP Mission Partly Accomplished*, Delhi, 1977.

Masani, Zareer, *Indira Gandhi: A Biography*, London, 1975, 1997 edition.

Mayer, Peter B., 'Congress I, Emergency (I): Interpreting Indira Gandhi's India,' in Robin Jeffrey, et. al., eds., *India Rebellion to Republic: Selected Writings, 1857-1990*, New Delhi, 1990.

Mehta, Asoka, *A Decade of Indian Politics 1966-77*, New Delhi, 1979.

Mehta, Ved, *The New India*, New York, 1978.

——*A Family Affair: India under Three Prime Ministers*, New York, 1982.

Mehta, Vinod, *The Sanjay Story*, Bombay, 1978.

Moraes, Dom, *Mrs Gandhi*, New Delhi, 1980.

Morris-Jones, W.H., *Politics Mainly Indian*, Bombay, 1978.

——'Whose Emergency—India's or Indira's,' *The World Today*, Vol.31, no.11, November 1975.

——'Creeping but Uneasy Authoritarianism: India 1975-6,' *Government and Opposition*, Vol.12, no.1, Winter 1977.

——'The Indian Elections and Their Aftermath,' *Asian Affairs*, October 1977.

Mosse, George L., 'Introduction: The Genesis of Fascism,' *Journal of Contemporary History*, Vol.1, no.1, 1966.

Namboodiripad, E.M.S., *Conflict and Crisis—Political India 1974*, Bombay, 1974.

Narain, Iqbal, 'Ideology and Political Development: Battle for Issues in Indian Politics,' *Asian Survey*, Vol.XI, no.2, February 1971.

——'India 1977: From Promise to Disenchantment,' *Asian Survey*, Vol.XVIII, no.2, February 1978.

Narayan, Jayaprakash, *Towards Total Revolution*, 4 volumes, edited and with an Introduction by Brahmanand, Bombay, 1978, (a) *Politics in India*, Vol.II, (b) *Total Revolution*, Vol.IV (referred to as *TR*).

——*A Revolutionary's Quest: Selected Writings of Jayaprakash Narayan*, edited and with an Introduction by Bimal Prasad, Delhi, 1980.

——*Prison Diary 1975*, edited and with an Introduction by A.B. Shah, Bombay, 1977.

——*Total Revolution*, Varanasi, 1975, second edition, 1992.

——'India-Haters Behind Communal Riots,' *Gandhi Sangrahalya*, January-February 1992 (Interview published in the *Statesman*, 20 October 1969).

——Foreword to J.D. Seth, *Gandhi Today*.

——*Nation-Building in India*, ed., Brahmanand, Varanasi, n.d.

Narayan, Jayaprakash Abhinandan Granth, ed., K.L. Sharma, Jaipur, 1978.

Nargolkar, Vasant, *JP's Crusade for Revolution*, New Delhi, 1975.

——*JP Vindicated!*, New Delhi, 1977.

Nation-wide Demand for Postponement of Constitutional Amendment Bill, New Delhi, 1976.

Nayar, Kuldip, *The Judgement—Inside Story of the Emergency in India*, New Delhi, 1977.

——*In Jail*, New Delhi, 1978.

Nehru, B.K., *Nice Guys Finish Second*, New Delhi, 1997.

Norman, Dorothy, *Indira Gandhi*: Letters to a Friend 1950-1984, London, 1985.

Observer, An, 'The Crisis in India,' *Monthly Review*, September 1975.

Ostergaard, Geoffrey, *Nonviolent Revolution in India*, New Delhi, 1985.

Palmer, Norman D., 'India in 1975: Democracy in Eclipse,' *Asian Survey*, Vol.XVI, no.2, February 1976.

——'India in 1976: The Politics of Depoliticization,' *Asian Survey*, Vol.XVII, no.2, February 1977.

——'The Future of Indian Political System,' in Ram N. Roy, ed., *Indian Democracy in Crisis*.

Pandey, S., 'The JP Movement in Retrospect,' *Gandhi Marg*, Vol.17, no.4, January-March 1996.

Pandit, C.S., *End of an Era: The Rise and Fall of Indira Gandhi*, New Delhi, 1977.

Park, Richard L., 'Political Crisis in India, 1975,' *Asian Survey*, Vol.XV, no.11, November 1975.

Poulantzas, Nicos, *Fascism and Dictatorship*, London, 1974.

Prachand, S.L.M., ed., *The Great Upheaval—Some Aspects*, Chandigarh, 1977.

Prasad, Bimal, *Gandhi, Nehru and J.P.*, Delhi, 1985.

——*Jayaprakash Narayan: Quest and Legacy*, New Delhi, 1992.

Procacci, Grovanni, 'Italy: From Intervention to Fascism, 1917-19,' *Journal of Contemporary History*, Vol.2, no.4, 1967.

Puri, Balraj, ed., *Revolution Counter-Revolution*, New Delhi, 1978.

——'Counter-Total Revolution,' in Balraj Puri, ed., *Revolution Counter-Revolution*.

——'Era of Indira Gandhi,' *Economic and Political Weekly*, 26 January 1985.

——'A Fuller View of the Emergency,' *Economic and Political Weekly*, 15 July 1995.

——'Afterthoughts on the Emergency Debate,' *Economic and Political Weekly*, 12 August 2000.

Puri, Rakshat, 'India's Opposition Parties Find a Leader,' *South Asian Review*, Vol.8, no.2, January 1975.

Raghunathan, N., *Memories, Men and Matters*, Mumbai, 1999.

Rao, Balwant, 'Indira Gandhi and Fascism,' *Marxist Review*, April-May 1977 and November 1992.

——'The Concept of Bonapartism,' *Marxist Review*, April-May 1978.

Rao, C. Rajeshwara, *Emergency and the Communist Party*, New Delhi, 1975.

Rao, R.V.R. Chandrashekhara, 'India's Constitutional Structure,' in Yogendra K. Malik and D.K. Vajpayi, eds., *India: The Years of Indira Gandhi*, Leiden, 1988.

Rose, Leo E., 'Emergency and India's External Relations,' in Ram M. Roy, ed., *Indian Democracy in Crisis*.

Rossi, A., *The Rise of Italian Fascism 1918-1922*, New York, 1976.

Roy, Ajit, *Political Power in India*, Calcutta, 1975, 1981 edition.

——'JP's Movement and Indian Democracy,' *Marxist Review*, May-June 1975.

——'Towards Limited Dictatorship,' *Marxist Review*, April 1975.

——'The Indian Perspective,' *Marxist Review*, February 1977 (written in October 1975).

——'Specificities of Indira Gandhi's Emergency,' *Marxist Review*, November 2000.

——(editorial), 'JP's Movement in Perspective,' *Marxist Review*, November-December 1974.

Roy, A.K., 'Emergency at Midnight,' *Statesman*, 24 June 1986.

Roy, Ram M., ed., *Indian Democracy in Crisis*, Northridge, California, 1976.

——'The Impact of the Constitutional Emergency on the Indian Democracy in the Near Future,' in Ram M. Roy, ed., *Indian Democracy in Crisis*.

Roy, Ramashray, 'India 1973: A Year of Discontent,' *Asian Survey*, Vol.XIV, no.2, February 1974.

Rudolph, L.I. and Rudolph, S.H., *In Pursuit of Lakshmi: The Political Economy of the Indian State*, Bombay, 1987.

Sahgal, Nayantara, *Indira Gandhi: Her Road to Power*, New York, 1982.

Scarfe, Allan and Wendy, *J.P. His Biography*, New Delhi, 1975, second edition, 1977.

Schlesinger, L.I., 'The Emergency in an Indian Village,' *Asian Survey*, Vol.XVII, no.7, July 1977.

Selbourne, David, *An Eye to India: The Unmasking of a Tyranny*, Penguin, London, 1977.

——*Through the Indian Looking Glass: Selected Articles on India 1976-1980*, Bombay, 1982.

——ed., *In Theory and In Practice: Essays on the Politics of Jayaprakash Narayan*, Delhi, 1985.

——'Introduction' and 'A Political Mortality Re-examined,' in David Selbourne, ed., *In Theory and Practice*.

Sen, Mohit, *Glimpses of the History of the Indian Communist Movement 1925-1995*, n. place, 1995.

——'Emergency Debate,' *New Thinking Communist*, 15 July 2000.

——' "Review" of P.N. Dhar's Indira Gandhi, the "Emergency", and "Indian Democracy," ' *New Thinking Communist*, 15 May 2002.

——'Interview', Archives on Contemporary History, Jawaharlal Nehru University, New Delhi.

Sen Gupta, Bhabani, 'Communism Further Divided,' in Henry C. Hart, ed., *Indira Gandhi's India*.

Seshan, N.K., *With Three Prime Ministers: Nehru, Indira and Rajiv*, New Delhi, 1993.

Seshan, T.N., *The Degeneration of India*, New Delhi, 1995.

Shah Commission Inquiry—Third and Final Report, 6 August 1978.

Shah, Ghanshyam, *Protest Movements in Two Indian States: A Study of the Gujarat and Bihar Movements*, Delhi, 1977.

——'The 1975 Gujarat Assembly Elections in India,' *Asian Survey*, Vol.XVI, no.3, March 1976.

Sharda Prasad, H.Y., 'Can there be a repeat of the Emergency,' *Asian Age*, 28 June 2000.

Sharma, Dhirendra, *The Janata (People's) Struggle*, New Delhi, 1977.

Sharma, Hari, ' "National Emergency" in India,' *Journal of Contemporary Asia*, Vol.5, no.4, 1975.

Shourie, Arun, *Symptoms of Fascism*, New Delhi, 1978.

——'Role of Intellectuals During and After the Emergency,' in Balraj Puri, ed., *Revolution Counter-Revolution*.

Singh, Khushwant, *Indira Gandhi Returns*, New Delhi, 1979.

Sinha, Indradeep, *Real Face of JP's 'Total Revolution'*, New Delhi, 1974.

Sinha, Sachchidanand, *Emergency in Perspective—Reprieve and Challenge*, New Delhi, 1977.

Sundarayya, P., 'Why I resigned from G.S. and P.B.,' *Marxism Today*, Vol.I, no.2, November 1985.

Tandon, B.N., *PMO Diary-I: Prelude to the Emergency*, Delhi, 2003.

Tarlo, Emma, 'From Victim to Agent: Memories of Emergency from a Resettlement Colony in Delhi,' *Economic and Political Weekly*, 18 November 1995.

Thakur, Ramesh C., 'The Fate of India's Parliamentary Democracy,' *Pacific Affairs*, Vol.42, no.2, 1976.

Thapar, Raj, *All These Years*, New Delhi, 1991.

Thapar, Romesh, 'Election Talk and All That,' *Economic and Political Weekly*, 25 January 1975.

——'The Real Meat of the Emergency,' *Economic and Political Weekly*, 9 April 1977.

Tharoor, Shashi, *India: From Midnight to the Millennium*, New Delhi, 1997.

Timely Steps, Publications Division, Ministry of Information and Broadcasting, August 1975.

Tornquist, Olle, 'What is Wrong with Third World Marxism,' *Akut*, 44, November 1990 (Uppasala, Sweden).

Tully, Marc and Masani, Zareer, *From Raj to Rajiv: 40 Years of Indian Independence*, London, 1988.

Vajda, Mihaly, *Fascism as a Mass Movement*, London, 1976.

Vanaik, Achin, *The Painful Transition—Bourgeois Democracy in India*, London, 1990.

Varkey, Ouseph, 'The CPI-Congress Alliance in India,' *Asian Survey*, Vol.XIX, no.9, September 1979.

Vasudev, Uma, *Two Faces of Indira Gandhi*, New Delhi, 1977.

Vira, Dharam, *Reminiscences*, New Delhi, 1990.

Weiner, Myron, *Indian Paradox—Essays in Indian Politics*, ed. Ashutosh Varshney, New Delhi, 1989.

Wolpert, Stanley, *A New History of India*, New York, 1977.

Wood, John R., 'Extra-Parliamentary Opposition in India: An Analysis of Populist Agitations in Gujarat and Bihar,' *Pacific Affairs*, Vol.48, no.3, 1975.

Why Emergency, Ministry of Home Affairs, White Paper, New Delhi, 1975.

Zins, Max Jean, *Strains on Indian Democracy*, New Delhi, 1988.

Glossary

Akali Dal: Sikh communal party.

Backward Castes: Members of the castes intermediate between the upper castes and the lowest castes.

Bandh: General stoppage of all work, transport and other services, and closure of educational institutions and government offices in a town, city or state.

Bardoli Struggle: Non-violent, no-tax campaign organized under the leadership of Sardar Patel in the Bardoli taluka of Gujarat in 1928.

Bhoodan: Land-gift.

Dalits: 'The oppressed', or the repressed, an appellation preferred by those at the bottom of the caste system, who were earlier known as Untouchables, Harijans (by Gandhiji), or Scheduled Castes (in the Indian Constitution).

Dandi March: Organized by Gandhiji in 1930, initiating the Civil Disobedience Campaign.

Dharna: A sit-down to enforce a demand.

DMK: Dravida Munnetra Kazhagam; a regional party in Tamil Nadu.

Dwijas: Twice-born or the upper castes.

Gherao: Literally meaning to encircle and lay siege; a blockading picket; surrounding a person or office by a crowd so that nobody can get in or come out.

Goonda: thug, bully, gangster, hoodlum.

Hartal: A general strike, a general work stoppage in any institution or place of work or city.

Harijan: A term popularized by Gandhiji for a dalit or untouchable. Literally: Children of God.

Hatao: Remove. For example Indira Hatao (remove Indira from office); *garibi-hatao* (remove poverty).

Jallianwalla (Bagh) Massacre: The unprovoked shooting down of thousands of unarmed people by a unit of the British-Indian army in 1919 in Amritsar, Punjab, thus provoking the massive nationalist upsurge of 1920 in India.

Jhuggi: Make-shift shack or shelter in a slum (by the poor).

Kisan Sabha: Peasant-union.

Lathi-charge: Police attack on a demonstrating crowd using sticks or a bludgeon with the objective of dispersing it.

Loknayak: Leader of the people.

Lokshakti: Power of the people.

March on Rome: See Appendix.

Naxalites: Communist groups who broke away from the Communist Party of India (Marxist) in 1967. They believed in the violent overthrow of the Indian state.

1942 Movement: Same as the Quit India Movement (see below).

Quit India Movement: The movement to end British rule in India initiated in 1942 by Gandhiji and the Indian National Congress.

Rasta Roko: Road-blocking.

Sarvodaya: Welfare of all. Gandhian movement devoted to constructive work.

Satyagraha: Non-violent resistance; holding fast to truth.

Satyagrahi: One who practises satyagraha.

Scheduled Caste: Indian Constitution's term for a *dalit* or *harijan*.

Shudra: A *dalit*.

Untouchable: An earlier, pre-1930 term for a *dalit*.

Index